John George Knight

Narrative of the visit of His Royal Highness the Duke of Edinburgh to the colony of Victoria, Australia

John George Knight

Narrative of the visit of His Royal Highness the Duke of Edinburgh to the colony of Victoria, Australia

ISBN/EAN: 9783337082819

Printed in Europe, USA, Canada, Australia, Japan

Cover: Foto ©ninafisch / pixelio.de

More available books at **www.hansebooks.com**

INTRODUCTION.

So important and auspicious an event as the first visit of a son of Queen Victoria to the Australian Colonies, deserves to be inscribed on the brightest page of our Colonial History. It is not however attempted, in the following narrative, to anticipate the work of the historian, or to weaken the interest in the publication of the travels and experiences of his Royal Highness the Duke of Edinburgh, which will probably be undertaken by some members of the Royal party on their return to England. The object aimed at in the present volume is simple; and although the mode of dealing with the subject may be regarded as hardly commensurate with its importance, it is hoped that the various events herein recorded may prove sufficiently interesting in themselves to excuse any crudeness or lack of skill in the compilation.

The following narrative of the visit of his Royal Highness Prince Alfred to Victoria has been in the main collated from the leading Colonial Newspapers—the *Argus, Age, Herald, Australasian,* and *Leader,* supplying the principal matter; whilst, in describing the visits of his Royal Highness in the Mining and Country Districts, the accounts furnished by the local papers have been generally selected; thus, the *Geelong Advertiser, Ballarat Star, Bendigo Advertiser, Castlemaine Daily News, Hamilton Spectator,* &c., have been laid under contribution, and in referring to events which occurred outside Victoria, the sources of information are also acknowledged. It is believed that those who have the patience to read this volume, will be disposed to agree with the compiler, that the unbroken series of loyal demonstrations and festivities described in the various journals, are most truthfully and accurately written. It may not, perhaps, be found that in all cases the descriptions are as graphic or perspicuous as they might have been; but it must not be forgotten that the tour of his Royal Highness was very rapidly executed—

that a number of important doings would sometimes occur on the same day—that, surrounded by the bewildering elements of an unprecedented excitement, calm writing was difficult, and revision almost impossible; the compiler having seen half-a-dozen gentlemen of the press crowded together in a public room, wildly and almost hopelessly endeavouring to write out copy from their rough notes, under the conscious pressure of a mail about to close. How newspaper men even could write coherently under such conditions, is a matter of wonder; and the general clearness of the various descriptions of the Royal progress is not the least important item of congratulation in connection with the grand reception accorded by the people of Victoria to a son of our most beloved Queen.

It might be urged, that as the reports for the newspapers were prepared with so much haste, and generally under such disadvantages, the duty of the person who might subsequently undertake to describe the visit of the Prince would best be discharged by making himself familiar with the facts, and then writing a fresh and original account. Such a plan would doubtless have been preferable, and might have been adopted had the present writer felt himself strong enough for the task: in the absence of any such assurance, he has taken the safer ground of presenting the facts, opinions, and views of others in preference to his own, contenting himself by stating, that as most of the occurrences herein mentioned took place within his own observation, he can testify to the general accuracy of the various descriptions. Irrespective, however, of the question of ability, the compiler is bound, in justice to himself, to state that the time at his disposal altogether precluded the possibility of writing an original work on the subject of the Prince's visit, the preparation of the volume in its present form being as much as he could accomplish; and as the idea was not suggested to the Publishers until after the departure of his Royal Highness from Victoria, it was at once seen by them, as a point of business, that to secure any interest in such a work, its publication should be hastened as much as possible.

The present volume must, therefore, be taken for what it is worth, and what it pretends to be—not a literary work, either speculative or historical, but merely a collection of reports, revised, adapted, and dovetailed together, so as to form something like a continuous narration; and if this has been effected, all that is sought has been achieved.

It will be observed from a glance at the opening pages, that the narrative commences with the start of the *Galatea* from Plymouth; the visits paid by his Royal Highness on his way to Australia, being briefly noted as they occurred. It must not, however, be supposed that in the small space devoted to the narration of the reception of H.R.H. outside of Victoria, any attempt is therein made to do justice to the loyalty and liberality of those colonies and countries which entertained their distinguished guest. It is left to them to preserve for themselves the record of so auspicious an event, as the object of the compiler of these pages in mentioning anything which took place beyond Victoria, was simply to render the chain of events a little more complete than it otherwise would have been.

Having already stated that the aim of the present publication is restricted to a description of the principal incidents connected with the visit of his Royal Highness to the Colony of Victoria, it may here be remarked, in proof of the desirability of such a work, that, notwithstanding the short time which has elapsed since the *Galatea* departed from our shores, the compiler has found the greatest difficulty in obtaining copies of the newspapers which contained reports of the Royal progress; and it has been a source of considerable trouble and delay to procure even imperfect files. The question, "What becomes of the millions of pins daily made in England?" is no more capable of satisfactory solution than that of "What becomes of all the newspapers?" One thing, however, is well known, that it is always difficult and often impossible to obtain back numbers of any of the colonial journals.

Such being the case, the compiler was led to the conclusion that an event which had evoked more enthusiasm in the breasts of Australians, of all ages and conditions, than any other occurrence in the history of these colonies, was worthy of being put into the form of a permanent record. Many of the details given in the following pages may be pronounced as trifling, uninteresting, or of no importance to the public at large: such doubtless is perfectly true of much that is narrated herein, but the compiler risks the loss of patience by the general reader, rather than do injustice to the loyalty of those whose means, or distant situation from the scenes of the Royal festivities, prevented their taking a prominent part in the public rejoicings.

It would be impossible to adduce stronger evidence of the genuine loyalty of the Australian community to our gracious Queen and the members of her family, than is afforded by the fact that not only where His Royal Highness was enabled to visit, but throughout the whole of Victoria (and the remark applies, it is believed, with equal truth to the adjoining colonies), every little township, even where there were not more than a score or two of inhabitants, set apart a day or two for the special manifestation of its loyalty; and it may with pride be affirmed that there is scarcely a child in the colonies that cannot sing "God save the Queen."

Brief as was the stay of his Royal Highness in many of the towns and places he visited, the demeanour of the thousands of children who everywhere greeted him cannot have failed to have made an agreeable impression on his mind. It is doubted whether in any other part of the Queen's dominions, taking population into account, such a proportion of well-dressed, healthy, and intelligent boys and girls could be brought together of their own free will, and at no inconsiderable expense to their parents.

It may seem to be taking a very hard and prosaic view of such an auspicious event as the visit to Australia of an English Prince of the Blood, to make any reference whatever to the amount of money expended on the festivities incidental to such an occasion. However well in theory a delicate consideration of this kind might appear, no tangible objection is anticipated to be made to the publication of an approximate estimate of the cost of the late rejoicings. The sums thus expended may be very fairly taken as indicative of the state of public opinion; because, under the broadly democratic political institutions of Victoria, no Government would venture to exceed any grant made by the Parliament, unless convinced that the voice of the people would sanction any excess of expenditure; and in the present case, where this excess has been incurred in giving a befitting and generous reception to a distinguished member of the Royal Family, the Government has not hesitated in putting a liberal interpretation on the act of the late Parliament. It thus appears that the grant of £15,000 voted for the reception and entertainment of His Royal Highness (exclusive of the amount required in making additions and alterations to Government House), has been exceeded by somewhere about £20,000; and it is calculated that the amount expended by the Government, the various Corporations and Borough Councils, and the community of Victoria at large, would at least amount to an average of 10s. per head of the population, or a gross sum of £326,872. The expenditure in the adjoining colonies has probably been on a proportionate scale.

Such a money test of the loyalty of the Australians cannot be lightly regarded. Fourteen or fifteen years ago, the "ordeal by gold" would not have been a very safe criterion either of loyalty or intelligence; but now-a-days there is neither the inclination nor margin to squander away wealth. The colony of Victoria is at the present time in a prosperous condition, but the people would be little inclined to go to such an expenditure as is above mentioned, unless their hearts were thoroughly in the cause. That such was the case in the reception of his Royal Highness the Duke of Edinburgh, the events recorded in the following pages prove beyond a doubt; and that his Royal Highness received incontestable evidence of the sterling loyalty and devotion of the people of Victoria to the Throne of Her Majesty the Queen, is conclusively shown by the tenor of the replies to public bodies as made by the Prince himself. After such an impressive and spontaneous display of loyalty on the one side, and so kind an appreciation of it on the other, the incidents appertaining to the course of events are surely worth recording, and the names of those who promoted the success of the Royal Reception deserve also to be gratefully remembered.

Accepting as correct the general conclusion that no Royal personage in any part of the world ever received a more enthusiastic welcome at the hands of the same number of people, it is to be feared that, in testifying our loyalty to a son of our beloved Queen, we were somewhat prone to overtax the physical as well as mental endurance of our illustrious guest, and that the time left at the disposal of his Royal Highness was far too little for his own personal comfort. The motives which caused the time of the Prince to be thus allotted to public bodies and festivities (whether interesting or not) were in themselves highly commendable, and unquestionably had their origin in the most exuberant loyalty to the Queen, and personal regard for her gallant son; but it seemed for a time to be wholly forgotten that a prince of the Royal blood occasionally required sleep, and an hour or two to attend to his own private affairs, and to enjoy a little relaxation. Fortunately, however, for the welfare of his Royal Highness, the discovery that he was mortal was made about a fortnight before his leaving Victoria, and he was then permitted to enjoy uninterruptedly a little liberty and peace.

Throughout his stay, the Duke of Edinburgh underwent the penalties of Royalty with the utmost readiness, courtesy, and grace; all the official ceremonials were duly and willingly performed, and those who were brought most closely in contact with his Royal Highness can testify that no one could be more anxious to oblige everybody, and more ready to sacrifice his own personal comfort and convenience to that end, than he himself.

It is, of course, a matter of conjecture when next the Australian colonies are to be honoured by a visit from a member of the Royal Family, but it may be respectfully suggested that whenever it occurs no Royal guest shall be compelled to devote more than sixteen out of every twenty-four hours to the discharge of official duties, the balance being left for his own enjoyment and rest.

With regard to the beneficial effects which are likely to accrue to the several colonies in consequence of the Royal visit, it is but reasonable that we should look to such a happy event as one of a series of means to render the Australian provinces better known and appreciated in England than they are at present. That the Prince and members of the Royal party have been astonished at the advanced progress of the colonies, is no more than we might have expected to hear; but his Royal Highness has gone much beyond this, and has expressed himself as very gravely impressed with the evidences of general prosperity and of the greatness of Australia. Such assurances as these are highly gratifying, and there can be little doubt that when the Prince returns to England, public attention will be much more directed towards colonial affairs, and it is to be hoped that a more generous tone will be adopted towards these southern portions of the British Empire, after his Royal Highness has enlightened the authorities with regard to their condition and importance.

It would probably be impossible to adduce better evidence in support of the known anxiety of the people of Australia to stand well in the estimation of their kindred at home, than is shown by the way in which the community resents anything like misrepresentation of colonial affairs. It is true that we have grown to submit quietly to such postal superscriptions as "Melbourne, South Australia;" but nothing more offends colonial sensibilities than the glaring mistakes which constantly occur in English literature, in describing scenes and events in the different Australian colonies; and it must be admitted as being rather hard, to find the wealth and prosperity of one place attributed to another, or, what is perhaps worse, the social or political misdeeds of one colony laid to the charge of an innocent neighbour. The strongly-evinced anxiety, which is always unmistakeably shown, to stand high in the esteem of the old country, cannot be otherwise regarded than as a proof of Australian loyalty and devotion to the institutions of the parent state.

Of the external evidence of the appreciation of the honour conferred upon the colonies by the visit of his Royal Highness, the events recorded in the following pages tell their own tale. There are some things, however, not therein mentioned which may be briefly spoken of in this place, as showing the desire of the authorities of Victoria (and it is believed also of South Australia) to give a most generous welcome, not only to the Prince and the friends who accompanied him, but also to the officers and crew of the *Galatea*. During the whole term of the vessel's stay in Hobson's Bay, carriages and horses were placed at the disposal of the officers, and the ship was supplied with fresh provisions daily, a boon which was duly appreciated by the crew. The cost of these indulgences was not inconsiderable, but the feeling which dictated such thoughtful attention is better entitled to be recorded than the mere matter of expense.

That the voyage of the Prince to Australia was something more than a mere excursion for pleasure, or to gratify the colonists with the sight of a favourite member of the Royal Family, there is already ample evidence to prove. From first to last his Royal Highness exhibited an earnest desire to acquire information on all subjects affecting the progress of the several colonies. Books of statistics, files of newspapers, photographs of towns and characteristic scenery, specimens of produce, and such like data, have been placed by request at the service of his Royal Highness for future use and guidance. A notable instance of the practical light in which his Royal Highness regards the industrial resources of the colonies, is afforded by the correspondence which took place with Mr. John B. Hughes, with reference to the increased use of preserved meat. It will probably be remembered that, prior to the Prince's departure from Melbourne, he was waited upon by that gentleman for the purpose of acquainting him with the prospects of the Australian colonies as exporters of large quantities of surplus meat. His Royal Highness evinced considerable interest in the subject, and agreed that Mr. Hughes should place some cases of preserved meat in tins on board the *Galatea*, to be subsequently tested and reported on. The following letter from his Royal Highness is an example of the plain, unaffected, and practical style in which a son of our Queen can deal with such a prosaic matter as that of preserved meat:—

Government House, Launceston, 15th January, 1868.

DEAR MR. HUGHES,—I beg to acknowledge the receipt of your letter of the 8th inst., which I received just as I was starting from Hobart Town to come here. I tried the preserved meat which you placed on board the *Galatea* at Melbourne, and so did my officers and some of my men. A leg of mutton was placed on my table, which I consider was remarkably good, cutting much firmer than any preserved meat I had hitherto tasted. The officers liked what they used, and the men highly approved of the beef which I gave them to try. I consider that so far the trial is very satisfactory, but, of course, it remains to be proved whether the meat will be as good after a longer time of keeping. Should such be the case, always remembering that preserved meat can never be quite equal to fresh, I am certain that many who cannot afford to pay the present very high prices in England, would gladly avail themselves of such good food. The meat preserved in tins which is occasionally given to the ships' companies of Her Majesty's ships, more especially to the sick, during long voyages, as a change from the salt, is inferior in quality to that which you sent on board, and I believe costs the Admiralty eleven pence or a shilling per pound. Should the Admiralty, therefore, approve of your superior article—which I understand you could deliver at sixpence a pound—they would make a great saving, and perhaps would give the men more of it, which would be a great benefit to the Royal Navy. When I receive the other cases which you propose to send me, with the tins painted, so as to withstand corrosion by the atmosphere at sea, I will try them on the homeward voyage, when they have passed through changes of climate, and let you know the result.— Believe me, yours truly, ALFRED.

To John B. Hughes, Esq., Melbourne Club.

The following extract from a letter addressed to his Excellency the Honourable Sir J. H. T. Manners-Sutton by his Royal Highness the Duke of Edinburgh, will probably be regarded as an appropriate conclusion to the introduction to this work:—

" " " " " I will now ask you to express to the members of the Government and of the Legislature, and to the gentlemen of the Reception Commission, my warmest thanks for their unwearied efforts to entertain me to the best of their power, to carry out the wishes of the people that I should visit the most important portions of the colony, and for their evident desire that I should carry away a pleasant recollection of my visit to Victoria. I know that many of these gentlemen had more important matters to occupy their minds, and I am deeply sensible of the manner in which they spared neither time nor trouble in endeavouring to carry out the wishes of the people of Victoria for my reception. I wish to include in these remarks the gentlemen of the Reception Committees of Geelong, Ballarat, Castlemaine, and Sandhurst.

But my chief desire in writing this letter to you is, that you would assure the people of the colony of my grateful appreciation of the manner in which they received me. They may well be proud of the magnificent reception which they gave me; it was a fresh evidence of the true

Introduction.

loyalty they bear to the Queen, my mother. They gladly availed themselves of the opportunity of my coming among them to display their unchanged loyalty to their Sovereign and their affection for England. This was the purport of each of the very numerous addresses which were presented to me; and the answer which I have so often given is, I assure them, no set phrase of words, but most true; I mean that it will give Her Majesty very great pleasure to learn that her Victorian subjects are so loyal and faithful, and that they have not forgotten, but still love, the old country from which they sprang.

I did not need addresses, however, to tell me what the feeling of the people was. The enthusiastic welcome which met me everywhere I went, and on every occasion, manifested the sincerity of their loyalty much more than words could have done.

The people of Victoria are proud, and justly so, of their colony, and are naturally anxious that its present attainments in the pursuit of prosperity, as well as its capabilities of future progress, should be more fully known than they are at present. For the furtherance of this desire I have some hope that my visit may have been of assistance. The people of England will be anxious to hear how the Australian colonies have received the first English Prince who has visited their shores; and I am sure you will agree with me that they will be surprised at the unbounded enthusiasm which my visit called forth, and it is my earnest hope that this will strengthen very considerably the ties of affection which have never ceased to exist between the two countries.

This hope of the good effect which my visit may have in drawing Australia more closely to the mother-country is the only thing which I can look back to with any feeling of self-satisfaction. The duties which I had to perform were, after all, so full of interest to me that there was much more of pleasure than of duty in them; and I really feel myself in the awkward position of having received everything and given nothing in return. I can only assure them, from my heart, of the sincere affection I feel for them, of my gratitude for their reception of me, and of the interest with which I shall ever watch their future progress. My stay in the colony was unfortunately so brief that I was obliged to leave very much unseen that I could have wished to see, but I saw enough to assure me of the future success of the country, and to show me that Victoria is, after all, but in the infancy of her future greatness. * * *

The farewell letter of his Royal Highness to His Excellency Sir Dominic Daly, Governor-in-Chief of South Australia, being mainly of a private nature, was not of course published; but His Excellency, in publicly thanking the Reception Committee, and especially Mr. R. D. Ross, its honorary secretary, as also Messrs. Charnock, Gunn, and Darwent, introduced the following extract from his Royal Highness's communication :—

Will you kindly express my thanks, which I am certain I did not adequately do before leaving, to everyone at large, and the Reception Committee in particular, for all their exertions to make my stay a pleasant one, in which they so thoroughly succeeded.

It must be a subject of regret to the people of Tasmania that during the stay of the Prince the weather should have been so unpropitious. The climate of that colony is so proverbially beautiful that for it to have been otherwise during the royal visit must have been an unexpected and severe disappointment to the guest, as well as to his loyal entertainers. Of his reception his Royal Highness appeared to be as well pleased as heretofore, and wrote thus to His Excellency, Colonel Gore Brown—

> I beg you will also convey my sincere thanks to the members of the Government, and to the colonists generally, for their hearty welcome and kindly efforts to make my stay amongst them a pleasant one, in which they so well succeeded; and assure them that I shall always look back to it with gratitude. ALFRED.

Of New South Wales, the fourth Australian colony on the visiting list of his Royal Highness, the account herein published is necessarily brief, as the tour of the Prince, at the time of our going to press, was a long way from being completed. Enough had, however, transpired to show that, as in the case of the preceding colonies, his Royal Highness's reception had been as hearty as it was loyal, and that his impressions of New South Wales were of the most agreeable and gratifying kind.

In the course of his recent travels and experiences it has probably happened that some of the attentions paid to his Royal Highness have been more or less tiresome; but it has already been claimed, for the loyalty and good feeling of the Australian colonists at large, that any little mistakes in the mode of receiving or treating his Royal Highness were fairly chargeable to the zeal and enthusiasm of the people—that such acts were errors on the right side, and were by no means likely to offend one who represented a profession which, for all time, had been renowned for its love of manliness and truth, and equally for its dislike of shams and hollow pretensions.

It would be inappropriate to introduce statistics in a work of this kind, except for the purpose of illustrating the importance of the colonies visited by his Royal Highness. A few figures will materially assist those who may desire to know something of the progress and prospects of the Australian dependencies of the British Crown.

Quoting from the Official Record of the Intercolonial Exhibition of 1866-7 (prepared by the present writer), the following items are taken with reference to

SOUTH AUSTRALIA.

Its population, according to the census taken in 1866, was 163,452; the population in 1844 numbered only 17,366 persons. The revenue in 1865 was £1,089,189, and expenditure £790,504. The imports in 1865 amounted to £2,927,596, and exports £3,129,846; the chief items of export being wheat (1,001,768 bushels), flour (38,251 tons), copper and ore (21,185 tons), and wool (16,269,890 lbs.). The aggregate number of sheep was 3,779,308, and cattle 158,057.

VICTORIA.

The population of this colony in 1867 was 653,744; thirty-two years ago the number was fourteen! The present population of Melbourne Proper is 47,000, and the suburban municipalities 104,720, making a total of 151,720, or nearly one-fourth of the whole of the people in the colony. There are 21,136 Chinese in Victoria, the greater portion of whom are engaged in mining.

The Commissioner of Trade and Customs kindly furnishes the following returns:—The imports for the year ending 1867 were £11,674,080; and the exports £12,724,427. The latter embrace the undermentioned items:— Wool, 51,314,116 lbs., value £3,824,956; hides (number), 40,897, value £26,775; skins, value £3982; tallow, 938½ tons, value £34,968.

The revenue of the colony for the year 1867 was £3,043,984.

The Editor of *Dicker's Mining Record* has supplied the subjoined information relative to the produce of gold:—

"The total export of Victorian gold from its first discovery to the end of 1867 (sixteen years) has been 35,145,725 ounces, of the approximate value of £140,582,900 sterling. The exportation of Victorian gold in 1867 was 1,392,336 ounces; in addition to 246,220 ounces left in the banks, making a total of 1,638,556 ounces, valued at £6,554,224 sterling. The quantity of gold obtained in 1867 was rather more than in the previous year, notwithstanding that the number of working miners has been steadily diminishing.

"The wealth of the alluvial mines of Ballarat is enormous, and the yield of gold is steadily increasing. The value of gold mined by twenty-four of the Ballarat companies approximates to one million sterling, whilst the capital invested little exceeds £400,000. The dividends paid by, and the market value of these mines, would amount to nearly three millions sterling.

"The monthly dividends of the public mining companies now amount to about £140,000, after payment of working expenses. For the week ending 8th February the amount was £44,270.

"Besides the alluvial mines of Ballarat, the quartz claims at Clunes

Bendigo, Tarrengower, and various parts of Gipps Land, yield large quantities of gold. The value of that produced at the Port Phillip Company's mine at Clunes now verges on one million sterling."

To show the extraordinary progress made by Ballarat, it may be mentioned that in 1851 the only habitation on the site of the present town was a shepherd's hut; and in a circle, having Ballarat as a centre, with a radius of forty miles, the population did not exceed 500 persons. The population of the same area when the census was taken in 1861, was 105,996 persons. The growth of Ballarat from the latter date up to the present time has been proportionately progressive.

The agricultural productions of Victoria are greatly increasing, the yield of wheat in 1866 being 3,514,227 bushels against 1,899,378 bushels in the previous year. The cultivation of the vine has also extended from 280 acres in 1857 to 4111 acres in 1867.

There are ninety-three newspapers and periodicals published in Victoria.

TASMANIA

Has a population of 97,368 persons. The imports in 1866 amounted to £642,107, and exports £834,606, the principal items of the latter being wool, grain, fruit and provisions, timber, and whale oil. Tasmania is rich in coal, iron, building stone, and other minerals. Gold has also been found. The revenue in 1866 was £245,421, and expenditure £242,361.

NEW SOUTH WALES.

In the year 1803 the population was 7097 persons; in 1866 it had grown to 420,000. Sydney and its suburbs now number over 100,000 inhabitants. The chief productions of New South Wales are coal, gold, wool, tallow, wine, and the usual variety of agricultural produce. The revenue for 1866, exclusive of loans, was £2,038,079; and disbursements, £2,100,820. The exports for the same year amounted to £9,913,839; and the imports £9,403,192. The harbour of Port Jackson is considered one of the most commodious as well as one of the most beautiful in the world.

In concluding the above introductory remarks, the compiler desires to acknowledge the valuable assistance he has received in the preparation of the work from his friend, Mr. James Eville, of Emerald Hill.

Contents.

	PAGE
ADDRESSES— Acclimatisation Society	63
Agriculture, Board of	99
Albion Gold Mining Company	128
Amherst, Borough of	69
Ararat, Borough of	70
Assembly, Legislative	49
Ballan, Shire of	74
Ballarat and Ballarat East, Boroughs of	125
Ballarat Children	131
Ballarat Mining Board	158
Baptist Association	69
Beechworth, Borough of	71
Beechworth, Shire of	73
Belfast, Borough of	76
Belfast, Shire of	73
Benevolent Asylum (Bendigo)	147
Bet Bet, Shire of	70
Blues, Society of	77
Brunswick, Borough of	106
Buninyong, Borough of	133
Buninyong, Highland Society of	134
Buninyong, Shire of	133
Campbell's Creek, District of	138
Castlemaine, Borough of	137
Castlemaine Fire Brigade	138
Castlemaine Ministers of the Gospel	139
Chinese Residents, Melbourne and Victoria	67
Chinese Residents, Sandhurst	143
Civil Service, Victoria	65
Congregational Church, Melbourne	62
Council, Legislative	49
Creswick, Borough of	125
Clunes, Borough of	127
Dunolly, Borough of	75
Eaglehawk, Borough of	149
East Collingwood, Borough of	72
East Collingwood, Borough of (second address)	172
Echuca, Borough of	173
Emerald Hill, Borough of	43
England and Ireland, United Church of	60
Fire Brigade, Geelong	116
Fitzroy, Borough of	75
Footscray, Borough of	135
Foresters, A.O. of, Bendigo District	146
Foresters, A.O. of, Castlemaine	139
Foresters, A.O. of, Echuca	147
Foresters, A.O. of, Melbourne	68
Free Gardeners, Victorian Society of	67
Freemasons of Bendigo	143
Freemasons, Geelong	115
Freemasons, Melbourne	64
Friendly Societies, Geelong	118
Geelong Botanical Gardens	117
Geelong Fire Brigade	116
Geelong, Town Council of	67
Geelong, Town Council of (second address)	114
German Residents, Melbourne	111

	PAGE
ADDRESSES—continued. Gisborne and Lancefield Road Board	136
Guildford, Borough of	138
Hamilton, Borough of	75
Hampden, Shire of	121
Hebrew Congregation, Geelong	116
Hebrew Congregation, Melbourne	61
Hebrew Congregation, Mickva Yisrael	61
Hebrew Congregation and Residents, Sandhurst	145
Hotham, Borough of	71
Huntley, Shire of	147
Kyneton, Shire of	136
Ladies' Address, Geelong	116
Maldon, Shire of	70
Marong, Shire of	146
Maryborough, Borough of	125
Mount Rouse, Shire of	197
Melbourne, Corporation of	47
Melbourne, Corporation of (second address)	105
Melbourne Poesh	108
Ministers of the Gospel, Castlemaine	139
Oddfellows, M.U., Ballarat District	126
Oddfellows, M.U., Bendigo District	145
Oddfellows, A.I.O., Melbourne	65
Oddfellows, A.I.O., Melbourne (reply)	199
Oddfellows, G.U.O., Melbourne	65
Oddfellows, M.U., Melbourne	65
Old Colonists	175
Old Colonists, additional signatures	220
Orange (Loyal) Institute, Melbourne	66
Port Phillip Farmers' Society	98
Prahran, Borough of	73
Presbyterian Church, General Assembly of	60
Primitive Methodists, Melbourne	63
Prince of Wales Gold Mining Company	132
Poesh (Melbourne)	108
Queenscliff, Borough of	34
Queenscliff, Borough of (reply)	109
Raywood, Borough of	146
Rechabites, I.O. of, Melbourne	68
Rechabites, I.O. of, Sandhurst	144
Richmond, Borough of	106
Roman Catholic Church	220
Royal Society, Victoria	64
Royal Society (reply)	190
Sandhurst, Borough of	142
Sandhurst Fire Brigade	144
Sandridge, Borough of	41
Sebastopol, Borough of	128
Society of Blues	77
South Barwon, Borough of	119
Stawell, Shire of	196
St. Andrew's Society, Sandhurst	144
St. David's Society, Melbourne	66
St. Kilda, Borough of	71
Strathfieldsaye, Shire of	148
Strathfieldsaye, Shire of (reply)	190

	PAGE		PAGE
ADDRESSES—*continued*.		Collingwood, Children's Fête at	187
Table Bay Harbour, Commissioners of	20	Laying Foundation Stone of Mechanics' Institute	171
Tarnagulla, Borough of	197	Consuls, Reception of	151
Tallaroop, Shire of	72		
United Extended Band of Hope Company	127		
University of Melbourne	179	DOOKERBOOK and Wallan Wallan, Children's Fête at	185
Victorian Temperance Hall, Ballarat, Committee of	130	Duffield, Mr. William, Visit to, at Para-Para	26
Vinegrowers, Geelong District	129	Dunolly, Children's Fête at	186
Vinegrowers, Geelong District (reply)	220	Dunced, Arrival at	120
Wangaratta, Borough of	74		
Warrnambool, Borough of	122	EAGLEHAWK, School Treat at	192
Warrnambool, Shire of	76	Visit to	149
Wesleyan Body, Melbourne	92	Eckuen, Children's Treat given by Council	192
Williamstown, Borough of	76	Emerald Hill, Demonstrations at	42
Williamstown, Inhabitants of	181	Procession Formed at	44
Winchelsea, Shire of	129	Welcome given by the School Children	43
ADELAIDE—Agricultural and Horticultural Show	26	Essendon and Flemington, Children's Fête at	185
Athletic Sports	25		
Civic Banquet	26	FANCY DRESS BALL at Exhibition	156
Cricket Match	25	Fireworks in the Yarra Park	102
Dinner given to Crew of the *Galatea*	26	Fitzroy, Children's Fête at	200
Governor's Ball	50	Footscray, Children's Fête at	189
Grand Ball at the Town Hall	25	Visit to	185
Laying Foundation Stone of Prince Alfred College	25	Free Banquet at Melbourne	90
Laying Foundation Stone of Victoria Tower	23	GALATEA, H.M.S., Description of	35
Levee at Government House	23	Fête given to the Boys of the Ship	191
Sailor's Funeral at	25	List of Officers	35
Torchlight Procession	24	Passengers	35
Visit to St. Peter's College	20	Reception of, in Hobson's Bay	36
Volunteer Review	24	Gardiner (*see Madeira H.M.*)	
		Gawler, S.A., Visit to	25
BALLARAT—Albion Company's Claim, Visit to	126	Geelong, Arrival at	113
Banquet at the Alfred Hall	129	Address from Ladies of	119
Festivities at	124	Ball at	118
Fireworks at	129	Festivities at	120
Grand Ball at the Alfred Hall	131	Fête at Industrial Schools	185
Laying Foundation Stone of the Victoria Temperance Hall	129	Illuminations at	118
Levee at	125	Presentation of Book by King Jerry	118
Presentation of Addresses	123	Procession at	117
Regatta at Lake Learmonth	130	Regatta at	119
The Children's Welcome	131	Visit to the Botanical Gardens	118
United Extended Band of Hope Company's Claim, Visit to	127	Gisborne, the Duke at	196
Visit to	123	Glenelg, Arrival at	21
Barwon Park, Rabbit Shooting at	123	Landing and Public Reception	22
Benevolent Asylum, Melbourne, Dinner at	105	Rejoicings at	23
Black, Mr. Neil, Visit to	121	Glenormiston, Visit to	121
Brighton, Fête given to Children at	188	Governor's Ball at Melbourne	95
Funeral of Commander Wilkinson	134	Dinner at the Exhibition Building	154
Brunswick, Children's Fête at	185	Grants made to Towns by the Royal Reception Commission	33
Buninyong, the Duke at	155	Graving Dock, Williamstown, laying Memorial Stone of	181
CALEDONIAN GAMES at Melbourne	172		
Camperdown, Arrival at	129	HAHNDORF, S.A., Visit to	29
Cape of Good Hope, Festivities at	18	Hampden, Shire Council of Arch erected by	121
Cape Town, Laying Foundation Stone of Graving Dock	20	Haymarket Theatre, Visit to	171
Catherine Reef Company's Mine, Visit to	150	Henbane, Arrival at	122
Castlemaine, Arrival at	137	Highland Society's Fête, Melbourne	172
Ball at	140	Hobart Town, Arrival at	200
Levee at	138	Hobson's Bay, Arrival in	36
Visit to Botanical Gardens	140	Escort of Steam Flotilla	36
Chatsworth, Arrival at	122	Hotham, Children's Fête at	189
Children's and other Festivities	184	Hustler's Reef, Visit to	148
Church of England Grammar School, Distribution of Prizes	163		
City Council of Melbourne	106	ILLUMINATIONS at Geelong	118
Civic Banquet, Melbourne	107	Illuminations of Melbourne—Bourke-street	85
Colac, Arrival at	121	Little Bourke-street	91
Collegiate Schools' Speech Day	152	Collins-street	78
Collingwood, *see* East Collingwood		Little Collins-street	92
		Electric Lights	94
		Elizabeth street	82
		Fitzroy Gardens	94
		Flagstaff Gardens	94

Contents.

	PAGE
Illuminations of Melbourne—*continued.*	
Flinders-street	93
Little Flinders-street	92
King-street	93
Latrobe-street	94
Lonsdale-street	94
Market-street	94
Queen-street	88
Russell-street	90
Spencer-street	94
Spring-street	94
Stephen-street	93
Suburbs of Melbourne	95
Swanston-street	89
William-street	93
JOHNSTONE and O'Shannessy, Portraits of the Prince, taken by	194
KAPUNDA, S.A., Visit to	25
Keynes, Visit to the	21
Kyneton, Visit to	136
LEVEE at Melbourne, General Presentation	52
Names not included in list	159
Presentation of Addresses	59
Special Entree	52
Linton's, Arrival at	125
MADEIRA, Arrival at	18
Malvern Hill and Gardiner, Sports and Children's Treat at	192
Marseilles, Stay of the *Galatea* at	17
Melbourne, Arrival at Town Hall	46
Agricultural Show at	98
Aldermen and Councillors of	106
Caledonian Games	172
Children's Welcome	47
Civic Banquet	107
Cricket Match at	93
Dinner at the Benevolent Asylum	163
Distribution of Prizes, Collegiate Schools	152
Fancy Dress Ball	156
Fête given to the Châtelou by the Corporation	187
Fireworks in Yarra Park	162
Free Banquet	90
Botanic Gardens, Visit to	192
Gold Coin struck by City Council	107
Governor's Ball at	95
Governor's Dinner at the Exhibition Building	134
Illuminations	77
Laying Foundation Stone, Town Hall	104
Mayors of	106
Onerous Duties of the Police	193
Philharmonic Society, Concert by	193
Portraits taken by Messrs. Johnston and O'Shannessy	194
Presentation of Addresses at the Treasury	48
Presents to His Royal Highness	194
The Procession on the day of Arrival	46
Races on New Year's Day	174
Reception at	29
Royal Levee	50
Sailors' Home Ball	123
Scene in Collins-street on day of Arrival	47
Special Race Meeting	172
Supper given by the 14th Regiment to the Petty Officers of the *Galatea*	193
Torchlight Procession at	110
Visit to Police Barracks	172
Visit to Public Library	179
Visit to Princess's Theatre	180
Visit to University	179
Volunteers, Proficiency of	193

	PAGE
Melbourne—*continued.*	
Volunteer Review at	171
Walter Montgomery's Readings	193
Miscellaneous Items, Victoria	192
Moffat, Mr., the Duke's Visit to	122
Montgomery, Walter, Readings by	193
Moorabbin, Fête given to Children at	188
Mortlake, Arrival at	121
Mount Barker, S.A., Presentation of Address	28
Mount Morne, Arrival at	120
Murchison, Mr. John, presented to H.R.H.	192
NACHT-WACHT, Stay at, and Elephant Shooting	21
Northcote, Children's Feast at	192
OLD COLONISTS, Names Appended to Address	176
PARLIAMENT, Members of, Dinner given by Governor to	134
Pentridge, Fête given to Children at	188
Pioneer Crushing Works, Visit to	149
Plymouth to Tristan D'Acunha	17
Port Adelaide, Boat Races at	30
Port Phillip Farmers' Society's Show	95
Prahran and South Yarra, Children's Fête at	189
Presents to His Royal Highness, given in Melbourne	194
Prince Albert Vineyard, Geelong, Visit to	129
Prince's Bridge, Decorations of	45
Prince of Wales Gold Mining Company's Works, Visit to	132
Princess's Theatre, Melbourne, Visit to	180
Public Library, Melbourne, Visit to	179
QUEENSCLIFF, Arrival at	34
RACES at Flemington on New Year's Day	174
Special Meeting at Melbourne	172
Richmond, Children's Fête at	188
Police Barracks, Visit to	172
Riddell's Creek, the Duke at	135
Rio Janeiro, Grand Ball at	18
Robertson, Mr. (Colac), Visit to	124
Royal Appointments	105
Reception Commission	31
SAILORS' HOME Ball	173
Sandhurst, Arrival at	140
Ball at	150
Banquet at	142
Distressing Occurrence at	148
Fancy Fair at	142
Fire at the Alfred Hall	150
Illuminations	148
Levée at	142
Procession at	141
School Treat at	192
Sandridge, Arrival at	40
Demonstration by the Victorian Free Gardeners	41
Scarsdale, Arrival at	123
Schnapper Point, Hunting Party at	193
Scotch College, Distribution of Prizes	155
Sebastopol, Visit to	127
Sergeants of 14th Regiment, Supper given by, to the Petty Officers of the *Galatea*	193
Simon's Bay, Arrival at	18
Simon's Town, Amateur Performance at	21
Skipton, Arrival at	123
South Australia, Arrival at	22
Arrival at Mount Barker	28
Camping Out	30
Departure from	30
Presentation of Address at Hartley	28
Trip to the Lakes	27
Visit to Gawler	25

	PAGE		PAGE
South Australia—continued.		United Extended Band of Hope Company's Claim,	
Visit to Hahndorf	19	Visit to	127
Visit to Kapunda	25	University, Melbourne, Visit to	179
Visit to McFarlane's Station	28		
Visit to Wellington	28	Victoria, Arrival in	31
South Yarra (see *Prahran*)		Departure for Western District	112
St. Kilda, Children's Fête at	186	First Steps Taken for Reception	31
Visit to Bowling Green	174	Victorian Musical Association, Concert of	194
St. Patrick's College, Distribution of Prizes	154	Volunteer Review at Melbourne	171
Sunbury, Visit to	135	Volunteers, Victorian, Proficiency of	193
Sydney, Visit to	210		
		Wallan Wallan, (see *Donnybrook*)	
Tasmania, Arrival at	260	Warrnambool, Rejoicings at	109
Theatre Royal, Performance of Mr. Akhurst's Pantomime	175	Wesley College, Distribution of Prizes	153
		Western District (Victoria), Departure for	112
Visit to the Opera	135	Wilkinson, Commander, Funeral of	184
Toorak, Concert at	172	Williamstown, Claim made for the Prince's landing	32
Torchlight Procession, Melbourne	110	Departure from	184
Town Hall, Melbourne, Laying Foundation Stone of the	104	Visit to	180
		Willoughby, Hon. J. R. B., Death of	47
Tradesmen, Royal Appointments	195	Winchelsea, Departure for	119
Tristan D'Acunha, Visit to	18	Laying Cope Stone of Bridge	120

Visit of H.R.H. Prince Alfred.

Plymouth to Tristan d'Acunha.

ALTHOUGH the Governments of the several Australian Colonies had been led to anticipate the special honour of a visit from His Royal Highness the Duke of Edinburgh, it was not until July, 1867, that reliable information was received to confirm previous expectations. On the 11th of that month the Melbourne newspapers officially announced that the Government had just received, by the mail, despatches relative to the visit of His Royal Highness Prince Alfred to the Australian Colonies. The day of his departure from Gibraltar, where the ship was then staying, had not been fixed, but it was believed that the *Galatea* would leave early in June. The Colonies to be visited in succession were the Cape of Good Hope, Western Australia, South Australia, Victoria, Tasmania, New South Wales, Queensland, and New Zealand. Subsequently these arrangements were somewhat modified, the *Galatea* having called at Rio Janeiro, and Western Australia being struck out of the programme. The following account, published in the *South Australian Register*, contains the leading events connected with the voyage from Plymouth to Tristan d'Acunha:—

The *Galatea* was commissioned on the 22nd January, and left Plymouth on the 22nd February, for Lisbon. Having remained there a few days, she proceeded to Gibraltar, whence, after a short refit, she went on to Malta. At that time the Home Government had sent an ultimatum to Spain about the *Tornado* affair, and on the 6th March H.R.H. the Duke of Edinburgh was entrusted with despatches to be forwarded to Marseilles on that subject. After remaining there for some time, awaiting orders from England (the rumours of war with Spain having blown over), the Duke obtained leave of absence, and proceeded to Paris (to visit the Exhibition), England, and Germany, whence he returned on the 1st June, and rejoined his ship. During the stay of the *Galatea* in Marseilles she was moored in Napoleon Basin, which turned out to be an exceedingly unhealthy anchorage. All the sewage of the town empties itself into the dock, and there being little or no tide in the Mediterranean, the extreme filthiness of the place may be imagined. Fever broke out amongst the ship's company, and one of the patients (a first-class boy) died there; upwards of forty cases succeeded at intervals, many of them being rather severe, and several, including the surgeon of the ship, were long on the sick list. Just before going into Rio, a midshipman, the Hon. R. J. B. Willoughby, son of Lord Middleton, took the fever, and died the day after the ship's arrival there. From Marseilles the ship proceeded to Gibraltar to coal and make preparations for her start on her voyage round the world. On leaving that place, on the 11th June, the Duke (at the suggestion of Lord Clarence

Paget, the Admiral commanding the Mediterranean Squadron, who was there with a portion of his fleet) hoisted the royal standard, and commenced his cruise under a salute from the batteries and different ships in harbour. The *Galatea* arrived at Madeira on June 14th, and left again on the 18th for Rio, which, owing to adverse winds, she did not reach until the 15th July. During her stay there, a grand ball was given by the English Minister, and another by the English residents, at both of which the Emperor and Empress attended to meet the Duke. The Emperor inspected the ship before she left, and dined on board in the evening. On Tuesday, the 23rd July, she left Rio, and was driven down as far south as 37 deg. by strong S.E. winds, touching at Tristan D'Acunha on the 5th September. Here the Duke considerately supplied the islanders with the following articles of clothing and provisions, viz. :—34 yards blue cloth, 80 yards flannel, 40 yards serge, 15 lbs. tobacco, 9 gallons rum, 9 gallons vinegar, 500 lbs. sugar, 50 lbs. tea, 330 lbs. flour, 24 lbs. chocolate, and purchased supplies of fresh meat and vegetables for the ship's company. There were fifty-three persons remaining on the island, of whom sixteen had been born since the Rev. William Taylor had left them; they were baptised by the Chaplain of the *Galatea*, who went on shore for the purpose at the request of Mr. Green, the oldest remaining inhabitant. His Highness and suite, and a party of officers, landed and visited all the families, who were in good health and quite contented. It appears that a heavy westerly gale on the 10th May blew down two of their houses. . . . . The people from this time will call their village "Edinburgh," after the title of His Royal Highness.

The passage from Tristan D'Acunha to Simon's Bay occupied ten days, the *Galatea* having arrived at the Cape on the 19th of August.

The Cape of Good Hope.

The *Cape Argus* of 26th August furnishes the following description of some of the festivities provided for the entertainment of His Royal Highness:—

The ball given by the inhabitants of Cape Town and neighbourhood in honour of the Duke's visit, came off in the Market-house on Friday night. Nothing could have been more successful than the whole arrangements connected with it. The entrance to the ball-room was protected from the weather by a substantial balcony, under which the carriages drove for the purpose of setting down the guests, who were received immediately within the gates by the stewards. The ladies were at once shown into a retiring-room, while the gentlemen, after parting with their hats and cloaks, made their way into the reception-room, where they were shortly joined by their partners. The reception-room was fitted up in rustic style. It was thirty-three feet square, and the entire walls and ceiling consisted of trellis-work covered with the most beautiful Cape ferns. In the centre of the ceiling was a dome, the lower edge of which, as well as the cornice of the room, being decorated with golden fir-cones. From the ceiling depended four gas chandeliers, and an equal number of ornamental baskets, containing flowers of the choicest varieties. The centre of the floor was occupied by an ornamental fountain, from the base of which sprang a cluster of lilies and ferns, surrounded by a bed of moss, with the motto, in May blossoms, "Welcome to Cape Town, August 23, 1867." The basin of the fountain was thickly hung with glass prisms, which, lighted from the back by sixty gas jets, and with the water trickling over them, had a most brilliant effect. The floor, from about two feet from each wall, was converted into a flower-bed, from which sprang the various shrubs and names decorating the apartment. On the left of the reception-room were the private apartments of the Duke and of the ladies, while to the right were the refreshment and cloak rooms; all of which were roofed with flags, and gaily illuminated. From the reception-room access was obtained to the ball-room by three spacious doorways. This portion of the building was seventy-five feet long by seventy feet wide. The ceiling was covered with drapery in alternate bands of red, white, and blue, the end walls being of white and blue only. The galleries, which extended upon both sides, were fronted and covered with scarlet cloth, and displayed the crests of St. George, St. Andrew, and St. Patrick, upon shields. The stalls beneath, converted for the nonce into card-rooms, were hung with coloured drapery, and the outsides decorated with leaves of myrtle and sugar-bush. The spandrils of the iron pillars supporting the roof were decorated with shields, bearing the arms of England, Scotland, and Ireland, and the Cape, respectively. From the centre of the ceiling depended a sun-light, with an outer circle of eighteen burners, in addition to eight gas stars in different portions of the room. Over the principal entrance and inside the ball-room were the letters "V.R." and a crown in gas jets. Opposite to this was a dais, surmounted by flags, encircling a medallion containing a monogram of the Duke. The supper-room was forty-five feet wide by seventy feet in length.

The ball was opened at nine o'clock by the Prince, with Lady Hodges; and at about one o'clock the drapery separating the ball-room from the supper-room was drawn up, and H.R.H. sat down to supper, supported on the right and left by Sir William and Lady Hodges. After supper Sir William Hodges proposed "The Queen," which met with three hearty cheers. He next gave the toast of the evening, "His Royal Highness the Duke of Edinburgh," in a few appropriate remarks, coupling with it a wish for fair breezes to the *Galatea*, and also promising the royal guest another hearty welcome should he ever again visit this colony.

His Royal Highness, whose rising was a signal for renewed cheering, said:—"Ladies and gentlemen, I offer you my sincere thanks for the very cordial manner in which you have received the toast of my health this evening. I will take advantage of this opportunity to return my warmest thanks to you and to all the members of this colony for the reception that has been accorded me on the occasion of this my second visit among you. I have on previous occasions since my return, in reply to addresses I have received, expressed my thanks to the gentlemen; on this occasion I can return my thanks to the ladies. I need not tell you how much pleasure it gives me to have this second opportunity of visiting you. My former visit here made so much impression on me, and the kindness I received on all sides has been so well borne in mind, that I can heartily accept the invitation Sir William has given me, should it be in my power to accept it. I have also to thank you for wishing fair breezes to the *Galatea*, and hope that some day those breezes may blow her towards the Cape again."

His Royal Highness, after a pause of a few minutes, again rose, and said:—"Ladies and gentlemen, the toast I am about to propose I know you will all respond to heartily. It is a toast which has particular interest for all present. I wish to propose 'Prosperity—increased prosperity—to this Colony.' I know that since my last visit here it has been to you a time of considerable anxiety, but I hope that by this time—as, indeed, I have already heard many colonists here say—the crisis is over, and that you are now looking forward to better and brighter days. It would be needless for me to remind you of the interest which is taken in this colony, as well as in every other colony, by Her Majesty the Queen, and that this interest is most heartily shared by all the Royal Family, and I assure you that it is shared by myself in particular. In proposing this toast, I wish also to couple with it the name of His Excellency the Governor.' Ladies and gentlemen, 'Increased prosperity to the Colony of the Cape of Good Hope, coupling with it the name of His Excellency Sir Philip Wodehouse.'"

This toast was received with enthusiasm, and three cheers were given for His Excellency, which Sir Philip Wodehouse suitably acknowledged.

After supper, the Prince gratified the company by dancing a Scotch reel, with Mrs. Justice Bell as his partner, to an accompaniment by his own piper; Mrs. Van der Byl, Dr. Snell, Lord Newry, and one or two other ladies and gentlemen joining in the dance. His Highness gained the golden opinions of all by his unaffected and open demeanour and geniality. Dancing was kept up till a very late hour in the morning; but the Prince, together with His Excellency and suite, left about three o'clock.

On Saturday morning the Prince performed the ceremony of laying the foundation-stone of the graving-dock, at the breakwater. The sides of the dock and every available place where a view could be obtained were lined with thousands of spectators, who repeatedly cheered the Prince as he passed along. On their arrival at the site, the chairman of the Harbour Board requested His Highness to lay the foundation-stone of the graving-dock, and also presented the following address from the board :—

To His Royal Highness Alfred Ernest Albert, K.G., Captain of Her Majesty's frigate Galatea.

May it please your Royal Highness—The Commissioners of the Table Bay Harbour desire to congratulate your Royal Highness upon your revisiting these shores, and especially to express the pleasure it affords them to welcome you to these works.

Seven years ago, in a public assemblage in the largest city in the world, one whose memory is endeared to the whole empire by all that was great, and good, and noble, spoke in proud terms of the work in which two of his sons were then engaged in distant lands : one in inaugurating a stupendous work in the greatest of England's colonies ; the other in initiating a work intimately connected with the noble profession he had chosen, and whose object was to provide a safe harbour for ships of all nations rounding the Cape of Good Hope.

For more than forty years frequent though unsuccessful attempts had been made to provide a harbour of refuge in Table Bay; but it was only when Her Most Gracious Majesty had signified her permission that your Royal Highness should inaugurate the work, that all difficulties were surmounted, and thus auspiciously commenced its prosecution, which has hitherto been attended with every success ; the Breakwater already affording protection to the shipping in the bay, and the dock so nearly approaching completion that the commissioners have every reason to expect that it will be opened to the commerce of the world early next year.

In the original design no sufficient provision was made for the accommodation of a class of vessels which has now become so important a portion of the Imperial navy; but in anticipation of future arrangements, the commissioners have determined to make provision for the construction of a graving-dock, in the hope of thus securing for all nations the means of repairing iron-clads, and vessels of that class, at a port so conveniently situated for the purpose.

Whatever of interest or importance may attend the career of your Royal Highness, the colonists of the Cape of Good Hope will ever be mindful that the first public act of your life was the commencement of a work which will effectually prevent that destruction of valuable life and property which this bay has unhappily too frequently witnessed ; and since your Royal Highness is now so intimately associated with the rise and progress of these works, it is the earnest desire of the commissioners that your Royal Highness may graciously permit their being named after yourself, and thus add another link to the many which have connected the affectionate devotion of the colonists of the Cape of Good Hope with the person of your Royal Highness and the Illustrious House that claims their loyalty and devotion.

His Royal Highness replied as follows:—

Gentlemen—I accept with much pleasure your congratulations on my second visit to the scene of these labours, which confer as much credit on those who have been entrusted with the superintendence of these fine works as on the engineers through whose skill and energy they have been brought so far towards completion. The progress which has been made in the few years that have passed since I had the satisfaction of attending at the commencement of the undertaking far exceeds my expectations, and I am grateful to you for proposing that my name should be permanently associated with a work calculated to afford such great benefits to the ships and to the commerce of the world. I thank you for the expression of your loyalty and devotion to Her Majesty, and of your kindly regard for myself.

Cape Town, 24th August, 1867. ALFRED.

A blessing was pronounced by the Very Rev. the Dean of Cape Town; and, after the usual formula, Prince Alfred pronounced the stone to be well and truly laid.

His Royal Highness then returned to the landing steps, and proceeded to the Central Jetty, escorted by a procession of ten or a dozen of the amateur club boats. On H.R.H. disembarking, the crews "up oars," and gave him three ringing cheers, which were graciously acknowledged. His Highness next visited the Sailors' Home, and in the afternoon left for Simon's Town, where he intended staying until Tuesday.

The garrison ball in the evening was not the least pleasing and successful of the several public compliments that have been paid the Duke of Edinburgh since his arrival in Cape Town, and Colonel Ellis and the officers of the 9th Regiment, and their coadjutors of the 99th, may congratulate themselves upon the result of their labours.

The duty which necessitated the return of the Duke to Simon's Town, was, it is said, to preside at a court-martial on Saturday. He returned to town during the afternoon, and in the evening attended the performances at the Theatre Royal, which was re-opened that night under his special command and patronage. A peculiar interest was attached to this entertainment from the fact that the Hon. Eliot C. Yorke, one of the suite, kindly gave his assistance, and appeared in the closet scene in *Hamlet*. The following evening the Duke attended the Rev. Mr. Guard's lecture on "Body and Soul," delivered in the New Market. On Friday the Prince embarked in the *Petrel*, and proceeded to the Knysna. It is stated that the Duke's sport did not terminate at the Knysna, as Mr. A. Van der Byl, of Nachtwacht, in the Bredasdorp division, had invited him to spend a short time on the estate, which the Duke was graciously pleased to accept. The stay at Nachtwacht extended over three days, and there was no lack of capital sport. Here His Royal Highness added to his previous exploits by shooting a large elephant. The *Illustrated London News* of the 2nd and 9th of November contains some graphic sketches of the Royal party in their hunting excursions.

ARRIVAL AT GLENELG, SOUTH AUSTRALIA.

Leaving the Cape of Good Hope on the 2nd of the month, the *Galatea* arrived off Glenelg at 10 p.m. on Tuesday, 29th October. She was reported to have experienced westerly winds during the run, and as having sighted no land nor vessels on the passage, excepting the branch mail-ship *Alexandra*, which waited an hour to carry on letters from the Prince. In consequence of several false alarms, and more than one stupid hoax, the good people of Adelaide were slow to believe that the long-expected ship had really arrived at last, and the vessel had to select her own anchorage, having missed both the schooner *Beatrice* and the pilot-boat, which were stationed outside to signal her approach. The first persons to board the *Galatea* were five young men who had been boating in the Bay. The Mayor of Glenelg (Mr. E. W. Andrews) waited on H.R.H. in the morning, and was most cordially received. The Prince, hearing that he had been expected in Western Australia, stated that he had no instructions to visit that colony, and expressed his regret at the disappointment to which the people had been subjected.

The subjoined account of the

LANDING AND PUBLIC RECEPTION

on the afternoon of Thursday, 31st October, was telegraphed to the Melbourne newspapers by Messrs. Greville and Co., Reuter's agents, and was published on the 1st November:—

"In accordance with previous arrangements, His Royal Highness left the *Galatea* in his barge at two o'clock in the afternoon, escorted by several steamers, and, accompanied by his suite, landed on the Glenelg jetty, amid the cheers of the public in boats as well as on the shore, and under a royal salute fired by the *Galatea*, which was responded to by a battery manned by volunteers. Another salute was fired simultaneously at Port Adelaide. A military guard of honour was stationed on the pier. His Excellency the Governor and the officers of State, the Executive of the Reception Committee, members of both Houses of Parliament, foreign consuls, &c., received the Prince on the pier, and welcomed him to this part of Her Majesty's dominions. At the shore end of the pier His Royal Highness was received by the Mayor and Councillors of Glenelg, accompanied by the neighbouring clergy and some officials, who presented him with an address. A procession was then formed to escort the Prince to Adelaide, preceded by a small troop of cavalry. After the carriages of His Highness and suite, His Excellency and suite, and the others privileged to form this part of the procession, a considerable number of private vehicles and horsemen, who had formed into line in the streets leading off the main road, fell in, and the cavalcade moved on towards Adelaide. At the roadside inns and various private residences demonstrations of loyalty were made. On the arrival of the procession at the south-west corner of the city, where a large triumphal arch had been erected, an immense number of the inhabitants welcomed the Prince, and some time was occupied in getting the pedestrians into their places in the procession, the marshals experiencing some difficulty in effecting it. From this point along the south terrace the road was lined by crowds of persons of both sexes, extending to the south end of King William-street, where another triumphal arch was erected, and the platform (protected by a guard of honour), from which the Mayor of Adelaide read to His Royal Highness a loyal address, at the close of which the Artillery stationed at the Butts in the South Park lands bellowed out a royal salute, the Albert bells pealed forth from the Town Hall tower, and the now immense procession moved northwards along King William-street amidst great demonstrations of loyalty from the inhabitants on either side. On arriving at the north end of Victoria-square, the greatest popular display was presented. From that point to the north end of the town and the entrance to Government House, the street was lined by the military and volunteers. Banners waved from every house and from the public buildings, as well as from the flag-poles erected along the street. Balconies had been formed in front of the principal houses and places of business, most of which were tastefully decorated and filled with people, principally ladies, who were very demonstrative in their welcome, throwing bouquets at the Prince's carriage. At the corner opposite to the Government offices, and where the new post office is being built, three thousand school children joined in singing the National Anthem very effectively, and they received a marked recognition from the Prince. The most tumultuous demonstrations were made as the Prince moved on slowly towards the North-terrace, where he passed under another triumphal arch. The mass of the population of Adelaide and the suburbs appeared to have collected about this neighbourhood at the time the Prince drove into the grounds of Government House. The Adelaide Club, facing the Governor's grounds, was gaily decorated, as were also several of the residences along North-terrace. The entire reception was of the most cordial and enthusiastic description."

In his answer to the address of the Mayor of Glenelg, H.R.H. said he thanked the inhabitants for their hearty welcome, and for the proofs of their loyalty to the Queen. He regarded this as a very important part of Her Majesty's dominions. To the address of the Mayor of Adelaide, he said it would be his pleasing duty to communicate to the Queen the strong proofs which the whole city had given of their loyalty, and he thanked them cordially for their warm reception.

"The city was crowded with people, and gay with a mass of flags. Now that the Prince was on shore, the *Galatea* moved up the coast, and anchored off the Semaphore, where the embarkation was intended to take place, *viâ* Port Adelaide."

"The whole of the streets of the town were illuminated at night, and the effect was most imposing. The programme of the Reception Committee had thus far been well carried out."

On Friday, 1st November, the Duke held a levee at Government House. The guard of honour was composed of a number of the 50th Regiment, No. 1 company of Infantry (West Adelaide Rifles) and a portion of No. 2 company (Kapunda Rifles), under the command of Captain Tuckfield, assisted by Lieutenant Cunningham and Ensign Moore. The command of the whole was assumed by Captain Clarke, of the military. Noon was the hour fixed for the general reception, and half-past eleven o'clock for those gentlemen having the privilege of private *entrée*. His Royal Highness was dressed in naval uniform, and was attended by His Excellency Sir Dominick Daly. Major Lucas and Captain Deering acted as aides-de-camp in waiting. The Private Secretary acted in a similar capacity, and introduced the gentlemen having the private *entrée*. Before the doors were thrown open for the general reception, the addresses from the two Houses of Parliament were read, and replies given. At noon the doors were thrown open, and the general reception commenced, when a large number of gentlemen paid their respects. The general reception having closed, the Duke expressed his willingness to receive the addresses which it had been arranged to present to him. These were from the old colonists, the Civil Service, the Presbyterian and Methodist Churches, the Freemasons, Friendly Societies, Temperance Association, Farmers' Club, and the several Borough Councils.

The next ceremony on the programme of the day was laying the foundation stone of the Victoria Tower. This event was thus referred to in one of the Adelaide papers:—

"It was a happy coincidence that the Duke of Edinburgh was enabled to pay a visit to this city at a time when a structure which shall hereafter be numbered amongst our most prominent and important buildings had been just commenced, so that the foundation stone of the new General Post Office and Telegraph Station should be laid by the hands of royalty, and with all the *éclat* and ceremony which such interesting associations should call forth. A platform had been erected, upon which the 4000 or 5000 Sunday-school children stood on the previous day when they sang the National Anthem. The seats rose tier above tier to a height of twenty-five or thirty feet, and the whole was covered by an awning, the ceiling being gaily decorated with flags. A guard of honour consisting of cavalry was drawn up in King William-street, near the building, where also great crowds of people had assembled to catch a glimpse of the Prince. At half past two o'clock the royal standard was hoisted on the marquee as a signal that the Prince was approaching, the Albert bells ringing out a merry peal. His Royal Highness was met by the members of the Government and the Postmaster-General, and was attended by his equerries and suite. His Excellency the Governor was also accompanied by his private secretary and aides-de-camp Lucas and Deering. The Commissioner of Public Works (Hon. P. Santo) stepped forward and read the address, to which the Duke replied. Three cheers and one cheer more were then given for the Prince, after which Mr. R. G. Thomas, the architect, read the copy of the inscription contained in the bottle, which was placed under the stone. Besides this inscription there were deposited in the bottle the coins of the realm, and copies of the *Advertiser, Register,* and *Comet*. The mortar was then spread, and Mr. H. Brown, of the firm of Brown and Thompson, the contractors, presented the Duke with a very handsome trowel, made of pure gold, with which to perform the ceremony. The handle was composed of Echunga gold, of malachite from the Burra, and of silver; a silver cable encircled the malachite, beyond which was a monogram of the Prince; the end of the trowel was composed of solid gold, surmounted by a carbuncle worked up as a ducal coronet. The level which was used by the Duke was silver-plated, and the plumb-line was composed of blue silk, the mallet being made of colonial blackwood, and the handle formed of three or four native woods. The ceremony was concluded shortly before four o'clock, when His Royal Highness retired."

One of the grandest spectacles ever witnessed in South Australia was that presented by the German colonists in their torchlight demonstration. At nine o'clock the procession fell in on the west side of Victoria-square, and the torches were at once lighted and a start made. The procession was headed by a small party as an advanced guard, some having torches and others lanterns, with the word "welcome" inscribed upon them. The line of march was round the south and east side of Victoria-square, then down King William-street to Government House. The effect was extremely picturesque, and drew forth loud and continued plaudits. On reaching Government House, the Liedertafel and the band took up their positions on the lawn. The Liedertafel was under the leadership of Mr. C. Putman. While they were singing, the Prince appeared under the portico. The singing having concluded, Mr. C. Balk read an address, to which the Prince replied, expressing his gratification at the demonstration.

On the following morning the volunteer review took place. For the first time the volunteers were joined by the regulars; and after the inspection, the colours, presented by Mrs. Fuller, the Mayoress, were consecrated by the Lord Bishop of Adelaide. The ensigns then advanced and knelt before the Prince, who was thus addressed by the Mayor—" I have been deputed by the Adelaide Regiment of Rifle Volunteers to ask your Royal Highness's gracious permission that the regiment may henceforth be distinguished by the name of Prince Alfred's Rifle Volunteers, in commemoration of your most auspicious visit to this capital. Anticipating your Royal Highness's condescension, this title has been inscribed on the regimental colours, the gift of the Mayoress, which I hope your Royal Highness will now be pleased to present on her behalf." Having expressed acquiescence, His Highness formally touched the colours, which were then handed to the ensigns, and Lieut.-Colonel Mayo called for "Three cheers for the Prince." The National Anthem having been played, the ceremony closed.

The athletic sports, by the members of the Adelaide Amateur Club, took place immediately after the review, and as an exhibition of strength, endurance, and skill, the entertainment provided by the members was regarded as highly successful.

Early on Sunday morning the Duke proceeded in his carriage to the Semaphore Jetty, and went on board the *Galatea*, where he stayed during the day.

On Monday, 4th November, H.R.H. left the ship in the State barge *Delphinus* at 11 o'clock, landing at the Semaphore Jetty, where he was received by the President of the Marine Board and the Harbour-Master. After the usual greetings, he entered his carriage, which was drawn by his favourite greys, and drove to the town. On Tuesday, His Highness visited the Botanical Gardens for the purpose of planting memorial trees. Three trees were to have been planted by the Prince, but he requested that two of his friends, Lord Newry and the Hon. Eliot Yorke, should participate in the ceremony by each planting one, which was accordingly done. The Duke was escorted over the Gardens by Dr. Schomburgh, and expressed his great admiration of their general beauty, as well as of the excellent collection of Australian birds and animals, which form a very attractive feature in the grounds.

Later in the day the Duke laid the foundation-stone of Prince Alfred College—an institution connected with the Wesleyan Church. A massive golden trowel was handed to him, bearing the following inscription:—" Presented to H.R.H. the Duke of Edinburgh, K.G., on his laying the foundation-stone of Prince Alfred College, in connection with the Wesleyan Methodist Church, 1867." The ceremony was witnessed by a large concourse of people. On the evening of the same day, the subscription ball, which had been for some time in course of preparation, was held in the Town Hall, and proved a very brilliant success. The arrangements made by the committee were most perfect, and gave general satisfaction. King William-street, from the Government Demesne to the Town Hall, was again illuminated, and the Prince was loudly cheered by the large concourse outside on his arrival at the hall. The Duke's piper was in attendance in Highland costume, and his playing caused immense enthusiasm, especially when the Prince danced a Scotch reel. The banqueting hall was fitted up magnificently. The Duke conducted the Governor's eldest daughter to supper, and afterwards proposed the toast of " The Ladies." The ball terminated very satisfactorily. Guards of honour, consisting of the regulars and the volunteers, were in attendance until after the Prince's departure. The public buildings and principal streets were brilliantly illuminated, and attracted a large assemblage of persons.

On the following morning the Prince started on his northern trip to Kapunda and Gawler Town. He left by railway in a new state carriage, accompanied by the *élite* of Adelaide. His reception at Kapunda, where he arrived at noon, was thoroughly loyal and demonstrative, the whole of the town being profusely decorated, and the inhabitants enthusiastic in their welcome. An address was presented by the Corporation, to which a suitable reply was vouchsafed. Alighting from the train, the royal party drove through the town, and proceeded to Crase's Hotel, where a sumptuous luncheon was provided. Leaving Kapunda by special train at two o'clock, they next paid a visit to Gawler, and here again the most lavish preparations had been made for their reception. The whole town was profusely decorated, and a loyal address was presented by the Town Council. The unique casket containing the address, was a perfect working model in silver of Ridley's reaping machine. His Highness afterwards planted a tree in the park-lands, and the National Anthem was sung by a host of little children. The Prince subsequently visited the Gawler Institute, and inscribed his name in the visitors' book. Refreshments were afterwards served in the Oddfellows' Hall, upstairs, and the usual loyal toasts were given and responded to. He next visited Mr. William Duffield, at his residence, Para-Para, and finally returned by rail to town, arriving at Government House at six o'clock.

A most interesting event was the opening of the Show of the Agricultural and Horticultural Society, which took place on the 6th November, and at which the illustrious visitor was present. The President of the Society presented an address to His Highness, who returned the President a written reply, couched in highly complimentary terms.

On Thursday, 7th November, a dinner was given by the Reception Committee to the liberty men of H.M.S. *Galatea*, in the large building in the rear of the Town Hall, the caterers being Messrs. Hines and Son. The sailors and marines assembled outside the Town Hall, and after forming two deep, they entered the room, preceded by the *Galatea* band playing "Rule Britannia." When they had all taken their places, the Duke of Edinburgh entered, the blue and red jackets greeting him with three hearty cheers. After dinner, the Hon. the Chief Secretary proposed " The Health of the Queen," which was drunk with rounds of hearty cheers, and an expression on the part of the tars of " Long may she live."

His Royal Highness next rose and said—" My lads, after the kindness and civility which have been shown to us since our arrival in this colony, I ask you to drink ' The Health of the People of South Australia.' "

Whilst the company were preparing to honour the toast, a tar named Patrick Toohey caused a good deal of amusement by saying, "Wait a bit, sir ; our glasses are not full yet." As soon as the little defect had been rectified, the toast was drunk with enthusiastic cheering, led off by the Prince, a supplementary cheer being given for the ladies of South Australia. After a stay of nearly half-an-hour, His Royal Highness departed.

Jack and the red coats continued to discuss their repast, and after fully enjoying it one of the sailors proposed " The Pretty Girls of Australia." The toast was drunk with a round of cheers. Sub-lieutenant Mainwaring acknowledged the compliment in a few remarks on behalf of the ladies. Quartermaster Keneil proposed " The Health of the Chief Secretary," which was heartily responded to ; after which the Mayor invited the company to the hall above, where means had been devised to enjoy a dance. In compliance with the invitation, they adjourned upstairs, but not before giving three hearty cheers for His Worship for allowing them the use of the hall. The inspiriting strains from Chapman's band infused a spirit of joyous hilarity into the men, and a pleasant hour or two was spent ; the gallant fellows then separated, evidently well pleased with Adelaide hospitality.

On Friday, 8th November, a match between the South Australian Cricket Club and the officers and men of the *Galatea* came off, the ground having been specially prepared for the occasion. A grand stand, capable of accommodating five hundred persons, was erected, contiguous to which was a smaller one for the use of the Prince, who, accompanied by Dr. Young and Senior-Lieutenant Fane, arrived shortly after twelve o'clock, and was received by the president of the club, Mr. Justice Gwynne. The Prince remained for several hours, and was present at the luncheon.

On Saturday, 9th November, the civic banquet took place in the Town Hall. The Prince was received by twelve gentlemen-in-waiting the band playing the National Anthem, the guard presenting arms—who ushered him into the Council Chamber, where he was received by His Worship the Mayor. The Duke made his appearance in the banqueting chamber preceded by the stewards with their wands of office, each wearing an elegant rosette with a silver anchor attached, Piper Dickson marching in front in full Highland costume, and playing most lustily on the pipes. The gallery was crowded with ladies. The Prince was seated immediately on the right of His Worship the Mayor, who presided. Grace was said by His Lordship the Bishop. The Mayor proposed the toast of "H.R.H. the Duke of Edinburgh," which was warmly received and heartily responded to.

His Royal Highness, when the cheers with which he was greeted had ended, said : I thank you for the most enthusiastic manner in which you have responded to the toast of my health. I have received so many marks of your kindness since I have been here amongst you, that it is only hearing that cheer which I did just now that put, as I may call it, the finishing touch on the hearty welcome which you have given me. I thank you for the kind way in which you have drunk my health.

The toast of "The rest of the Royal Family" was then duly honoured, and was succeeded by one proposed by the Duke, "Increased prosperity to the colony of South Australia," coupled with the health of his Worship the Mayor of Adelaide ; to which the Mayor (Mr. Fuller) made an appropriate response. Mr. W. Townsend, M.P., proposed "The Army, Navy, and Volunteers."

The Duke of Edinburgh, in responding for the Navy, said he believed that the ship which he commanded—the *Galatea*—was the largest that had ever entered these waters. He hoped every facility had been given for all to pay a visit to her, as he thought they would find no ship in her Majesty's navy that would more truly represent the wooden walls of old England. It had been a source of pride to him—a pleasure that he had long looked forward to—to take the command of a ship ; but to have brought one to this colony afforded him still greater satisfaction ; and he hoped by the time the voyage home was completed, to have accomplished what Captain Cook had done—sailed round the world.

Several other toasts having been duly honoured,

His Royal Highness said the next toast was one that required no words of his to introduce it to gain a most enthusiastic reception ; he called upon them to give three good hearty cheers for the "Lady Mayoress and the ladies of South Australia."

Lord Newry responded on behalf of the Mayoress and the ladies :—After the flow of oratory poured upon their ears that evening, he felt somewhat nervous ; but he was honoured with a most pleasant task, that of returning thanks for the toast which the Prince had proposed, and which they had all drunk with that spirit and enthusiasm it so justly merited. He was about to say—and he hoped the ladies of South Australia would feel that he was representing them faithfully, when he said that they joined with all those whom he supposed the ladies called the weaker sex in the hearty and enthusiastic welcome the colony had given to the Duke of Edinburgh.

The Prince retired shortly after eleven o'clock.

The next morning (Sunday) the Prince went on board the *Galatea* to attend divine service, returning to town in the afternoon. His Royal Highness started on Monday, 10th November for the Lakes.

It had already been announced, in deference to a wish expressed in high quarters, that the trip of the Prince to the Lakes should be considered private, consequently the reporters for the press, who had so far accompanied him returned to Adelaide : it is therefore impossible to give anything like a detailed account of the Prince's movements during this part of his tour. On Wednesday night the Prince stayed at Campbell House. The next morning he and the party remaining with him resumed their sport, and at night reached a place known as the Tatiara Waterhole. Through some blundering, akin to that which characterised the management of other matters, the tents did not arrive until too late an hour to be pitched, and the Duke and his companions had literally to sleep *sub Jove*, without any covering but the blue canopy. Fortunately the night followed upon a day of intense heat, and the party were disposed to make the best of an adventure which, although a mere bagatelle to the hardy bushmen, of whom there were several, was an event worth remembering in the history of some few present. Two days out of the four spent in the Lake expedition were excessively warm, the thermometer being estimated at over 100 deg., and no precaution could save the countenances of the sportsmen from assuming an unpleasantly ruddy appearance. On Thursday, Mr. J. Dunn, M.P., who had only made preparations for a three days' stay, returned home, as also did Mr. J. D. Woods. On Friday evening the party reached Mr. M'Farlane's, a few miles from Wellington, and thus brought to a close their experience of roughing it in the bush. During the week the Prince was rewarded by some very good sport, and gained great credit, even among the crack shots attending him, for his dexterity in handling the rifle. Among his own peculiar spoils was a large kangaroo, besides numerous other specimens of birds and animals, with which it has been stated his Royal Highness contemplated forming the foundation of a museum of Australian natural history, as a trophy of his skill. The chief cause of regret connected with the excursion seemed to have been the inefficient arrangements made by the South-east Visiting Sub-Committee.

Between seven and eight o'clock on Saturday morning the Prince and party, having partaken of breakfast, started from Mr. M'Farlane's, intending to accomplish the ride to Mount Barker, a distance of forty-eight miles, in six hours. Wellington was reached in about an hour, and at a quarter to nine o'clock the start from Wellington, where there had been a brief halt, took place. The road was heavy in places, owing to the late rains, but very good speed was kept up. At Hartley an address was presented and graciously received, and a hearty welcome was given to the Prince by the people of Langhorne's Creek.

Mount Barker had all along been intended to be the principal station in the Prince's homeward journey, and the people had bestirred themselves to give his reception all the "pomp and circumstance" which could be looked for in so important an agricultural district. Shortly after two o'clock, the approach of the Prince, with his suite, and a long escort of horsemen who had gone out from the township to meet their illustrious visitor, was descried. Instantly windows and balconies were crowded, and as his Royal Highness drove by, the hundreds who lined the street from the Oakfield Hotel to the Telegraph Station sent up a cheer, which was repeated over and over again until the arch had been reached, where the band played "God Save the Queen." At the invitation of Mr. A. Bell, chairman of the district council, the Prince dismounted, and ascended the platform, followed by his suite, who, like himself, looked none the worse for their excursion, although they had been all, to a greater or less degree, embrowned and otherwise affected as to their faces by the sun. The district councillors and directors of the National Bank were also in attendance. Mr. Bell, in a few words, welcomed the Prince to Mount Barker, and Mr. F. I. Smith, clerk of the council, then read an address, which His Royal Highness received, and stated that a reply would be forwarded.

The Hon. A. Blyth, chairman of the directors of the Adelaide branch of the National Bank, then requested the Duke to partake of refreshments in an adjoining pavilion. The company sat down to a capital luncheon. The Hon. A. Blyth presided, supported on his right by the Prince and the Hon. Eliot Yorke; on his left by Lord Newry and the Hon. J. Morphett. After luncheon and the ordinary loyal toasts, the Hon. A. Blyth, having charged the company to honour the next toast with bumpers, said:—"Gentlemen: I will ask you to drink to 'The Health of his Royal Highness the Duke of Edinburgh.' There are very few men within fifty miles of Adelaide who have not come within the influence of his Royal Highness, and there are, I am sure, no ladies within that distance who have not been brought within it also. Wherever he has gone, he has won golden opinions from the people of the colony. I look upon the visit of his Royal Highness to South Australia as forming one of the most interesting pages in her history—an event which may do a vast deal of good. We have heard a great deal here of the Royal Family, but now we have had an opportunity, through seeing one member of it, of learning those graces which adorn every one of them, and none more than his Royal Highness. I ask you to drink 'The Health of his Royal Highness the Duke of Edinburgh.'"

The Prince replied:—"I thank you for the way in which you have drunk my health. As I have had the pleasure of meeting nearly every one of you before, it is needless to use many words. I thank you for the kind reception you have given me on this occasion, as well as on other occasions, and further words are unnecessary."

After a brief period spent in conversation, the party broke up, and, as soon as the carriages were ready, resumed the road, his Royal Highness leading with his team of four greys.

At the charming German township of Hahndorf, the inhabitants had made preparations on a scale worthy of a place having much more pretension to greatness. On his arrival the Prince was enthusiastically greeted by the inhabitants; whilst the children attending school, to the number of about two hundred, were drawn up, and as the Royal Duke neared them they eagerly held aloft their books to arrest his notice, and to indicate that they desired to show him more than a passing attention. His Royal Highness acceded to their wish, and reined in his horses. A circle was at once formed, and a basket of strawberries having been presented to the Prince by a little girl, and graciously accepted by him, the children sang a sweet German air, set to words of welcome, composed by Mr. Boehm, their teacher and conductor. At its close, Mr. Strenz, on behalf of the residents, addressed to his Royal Highness, in German, a few earnest and emphatic words. The Prince inclined his head, and was apparently about to reply, when the crowd opened, but the horses starting forward prevented his doing so. During the remainder of the passage through the townships signs of general rejoicings were everywhere visible. Between six and seven o'clock on Saturday evening his Royal Highness reached Adelaide, and drove direct to Government House, thus completing a six days' trip of more than ordinary interest.

On the following day (Sunday) his Royal Highness attended divine service, as usual, on board the *Galatea*.

In the afternoon the funeral took place of John Ware, the unfortunate seaman who met his death by falling overboard from the *Galatea*. The body was brought by the steamer *Eleanor* from the *Galatea* to the Port, attended by the officers and crew, and was taken to the Alberton Cemetery, the Prince walking with the rest of the officers in procession the whole distance (nearly two miles) and back to the Port. The deceased was buried with naval honours. A vast concourse of people assembled at the Port, and accompanied the procession to the place of interment.

The Prince expressed himself as greatly pleased with his hunting expedition. He was enthusiastically received at all the townships and roadside places throughout his trip. After dismissing the reporters, and when the party had been very much thinned in numbers, His Highness determined to have a night in the bush, and the party camped in the open air, sleeping without covering.

His Royal Highness paid a visit to St. Peter's College, where he was received by Canon Farr and a select party of ladies and gentlemen, with their pupils. He also visited the chapel of the College, and expressed his admiration of the stained-glass windows. His Royal Highness planted a tree in the College grounds as a memorial of his visit.

The new Masonic Hall, belonging to the lodge of the I.C., is to be called the Alfred Masonic Hall, by permission of his Royal Highness.

An old Trafalgar hero, named Stephen Williams, 87 years of age, was introduced to the Prince, who expressed great pleasure, and shook the old man very cordially by the hand.

On arriving at Port Adelaide the Prince was presented with an address by the Corporation. There were boat races and other sports, and the launching of a life-boat. The *Aldinga* conveyed His Highness and suite round from the Port to the *Galatea*.

The Governor's ball at the Town Hall was a magnificent affair, and terminated very satisfactorily. The Prince again gratified the company by dancing a Scotch reel to the music of the bagpipes. King William-street north and a few other portions of the city were once more illuminated, and the streets were thronged.

The Prince expressed his gratification at the manner in which Mr. Hines, the purveyor to the Parliamentary refreshment rooms, had managed all the catering for the public entertainments and the Lake excursions, stating that he never saw anything better arranged. In token of his approval, he presented Mr. Hines with a handsome gold ring.

The Prince was also greatly pleased with the way in which Tanner, the coachman, had driven him on State occasions, and gave him a pin of a sporting design. Tanner is the son of the well-known whip of that name, who drove out of London on the Hampstead-road for many years, and has himself been acknowledged as the best whip in the colony for many years past.

The Duke, before taking leave, paid a hasty visit to some of the public institutions, including the Museum and Library.

Captain Douglas, the Chairman of the Marine Board, had the honour of accompanying the Prince to Melbourne in the *Galatea*.

Thus terminated the visit of his Royal Highness the Duke of Edinburgh to South Australia—the first of the Australian group of colonies honoured by the presence of a Prince of the Royal Family of England. Of this circumstance the people of South Australia may be justly proud, and that such was the universal feeling of that community is demonstrated by the fact that there was no flagging or exhaustion on the part of the inhabitants in the round of festivities provided for the entertainment of their illustrious visitor, but, on the contrary, the most strenuous efforts were made to induce his Royal Highness to extend the period of his sojourn amongst them.

However much delighted and honoured the people of South Australia may have felt in the company of the Prince, it is well known that on his part he was equally as gratified and delighted as his bounteous entertainers, and it is not too much to say that the noble captain of the *Galatea*, his personal friends, his officers, and seamen, carried impressions from Adelaide which no subsequent reception in any other place could efface.

VICTORIA.

So soon as it became definitely known that the *Galatea* would visit the Australian colonies, and that upon Victoria would be conferred the honour of being the second colony to receive her illustrious captain, the Government evinced a most commendable zeal in initiating the necessary steps for giving the royal visitor such a reception as befitted his rank and relationship to our beloved Sovereign, whose name has been bestowed upon this dependency of her Majesty's dominions. The first official steps taken by the Executive to prepare for the important event, was to transmit a message from his Excellency the Governor to the Legislative Assembly, "to appropriate the sum of fifteen thousand pounds for the entertainment of his Royal Highness the Duke of Edinburgh, such grant to be exclusive of the amount required for alterations and additions to Government House." At the time of voting this specific sum it was understood and agreed to by the House, without dissent, that whatever amount was required by the Government or the purposes of suitably entertaining his Royal Highness during his stay in Victoria, would be freely granted by Parliament. The hearty concurrence of the Legislature being thus obtained, and *carte blanche* being virtually given to the Cabinet to do all that was required to uphold the character of Victoria in the contemplated reception, the next practical step was the appointment by proclamation of a Royal Commission for carrying out the wishes of Parliament in this respect, the following gentlemen being entrusted with the important duties:—The Hon. James M'Culloch, M.L.A., Chief Secretary, Chairman; his Honour Sir William Stawell, Knt., Chief Justice; the Hon. G. F. Verdon, C.B., Minister of Finance; the Hon. J. G. Francis, M.L.A., Commissioner of Trade and Customs; the Hon. Thos. Howard Fellows, M.L.C.; the Hon. John O'Shanassy; the Hon. A. Michie, Q.C.; the Hon. D. Moore, M.L.A.; the Hon. Charles M'Mahon, M.L.A.; the Hon. Sir James Palmer, Knt., President of the Legislative Council; the Hon. G. W. Cole, M.L.C.; Sir Francis Murphy, Knt., Speaker of the Legislative Assembly; his Honour Sir Redmond Barry, Knt.; William Williams, Esq., M.L.A. (then Mayor of Melbourne). Subsequently the names of the Hon. W. M. K. Vale, M.L.A., Commissioner of Public Works, and J. S. Butters, Esq., the newly elected Mayor of Melbourne, were added to the Commission. Mr. W. B. Gilbert was appointed Secretary, and Mr. J. G. Knight, F.R.I.B.A., the Agent to the Commission.

The appointment of the Commission exercised an immediate influence on the Victorian colonists, and almost every town of any magnitude or importance was on the *qui vive* to display its loyalty to the Queen in welcoming her son to the colony. A characteristic illustration of the feeling of the public is afforded by the following paragraph, taken from the *Age* of 25th September:—

"The Reception Commission met on Tuesday for the first time in the Executive Council Chamber, and settled the preliminaries of action. Their proceedings were brought within the *purview* of the Assembly on Tuesday by a notice of motion having for its object to make the Commission more representative in its *personnel* of the country districts. Composed entirely of Melbourne men, it was assumed that there would be displayed such a spirit of centralisation as would destroy all hope of any share in the vote of Parliament being obtained for any locality outside of the metropolis. The explanation of the Chief Secretary disabused every one's mind of such narrow and selfish notions characterising the actions of the Commission. The difficulty of naming gentlemen to act on the Commission without giving offence to some one could not have been better exemplified than by the proposal to include the Mayors of Ballarat East and West, Geelong, Castlemaine, and Sandhurst. Why not the Mayors of Sandridge, Williamstown, and Emerald Hill? and the list might have been extended to the representatives of other local bodies desirous of getting up a demonstration in the Prince's honour. These applications have been so numerous as to lead to the publication of the following notice, in which the Commissioners indicate their intention to confine their operations to the plans therein named :—' The Commissioners appointed by his Excellency to devise and carry into effect all necessary arrangements for a fitting reception of his Royal Highness the Duke of Edinburgh, and for paying suitable marks of respect to his Royal Highness during his visit to the colony, having had under their consideration numerous applications from country districts, are of opinion that, as his Royal Highness cannot be expected to visit every country town, it will be expedient for them to limit their co-operation to Geelong, Ballarat, Castlemaine, and Sandhurst, and to the city of Melbourne. The mode in which the co-operation of the Commissioners may be desired by the inhabitants of Melbourne, Geelong, Ballarat, Castlemaine, and Sandhurst, must be signified through their respective Mayors, who are requested with the least possible delay to communicate to the Commissioners their plans for the reception of his Royal Highness. The Commissioners consider that out of the money placed at their disposal they should contribute to the places before mentioned, having regard to the amounts locally raised. JAMES M°CULLOCH, Chairman. Executive Council Chamber, Melbourne, 24th September, 1867.'"

Although the machinery of the reception was thus far got ready for action, it was not to be expected that all the wheels would turn at the beginning with perfect smoothness, and the first symptoms of disarrangement were made manifest when the question was mooted as to where the Prince should land. Williamstown was the earliest to put in a claim, which was regarded as an act of usurpation by the indignant people of Sandridge, who sought the sisterly aid of Emerald Hill to defeat an attempt to deprive the port of Melbourne of its just rights and privileges. In the midst of the contention between Williamstown and Sandridge, a third competitor appeared on the scene, and for some days the paramount claims of St. Kilda, as a maritime depot, were fiercely advocated, and occupied a large space in the public journals. The natural beauty of this marine suburb was generally conceded as one of the points in its favour, but its jetty accommodation, although unique in its way, was considered scarcely adequate for the berthing of a ship of the size and tonnage of H.M. steam frigate *Galatea*. The anxiety for providing safe anchorage for the royal ship did not even stop at St. Kilda; the claims of Dromana finding many advocates, whilst the sage councillor *Melbourne Punch* came to the rescue with a graphic sketch showing his Royal Highness being borne ashore at Mordialloc on the shoulders of the stalwart but solitary boatman who constitutes the coastguard of that picturesque but somewhat desolate beach. As was naturally to be expected, the right of Sandridge as the principal *entrepôt* was recognised, the point of embarkation being conceded to Williamstown. Having settled that his Royal Highness should land at Sandridge, the next question was, by which route should he reach Melbourne? It was first arranged that he should be brought up by the Melbourne and Hobson's Bay Railway, and be formally received at the Flinders-street Station. This was too much for the pent-up loyalty of the premier and model borough of Emerald Hill, who forthwith appealed to the Commission to reconsider their determination, and after some negotiations the inhabitants were enabled to take that prominent part in the reception of the Prince which was so successfully achieved on the day of the royal landing. The rival claims of the jetties and lines of route did not, however, occupy all the attention of the public; no sooner was it definitely settled that the Prince would arrive in Victoria on a given time, than the daily papers were compelled constantly to devote several of their columns to the publication of suggestions upon all possible and impossible matters appertaining, or supposed to appertain, to the reception of the coming guest; and although it cannot be denied that a number of the proposals were crude and utterly impracticable, the fact of so many persons applying their time and intelligence to devising plans for celebrating the arrival of the royal visitor, is incontestible evidence of an ardent and earnest wish to do the fullest possible honour to the first member of the Royal Family of Britain who has visited these shores. As the time drew nigh for the advent of his Royal Highness from the sister colony, the duty devolved on the Reception Commission of arranging with those public bodies and institutions throughout the colonies who proposed to present addresses of welcome and congratulation to the Prince on his arrival in Victoria. For this purpose it became necessary that copies of the documents proposed to be presented should be submitted for approval, in order that no extraneous subjects should be introduced, or the addresses made too lengthy, and as the drafts were very numerous some considerable time was absorbed in their supervision. It must now, however, be a matter of congratulation to the colonists that every organised body of the slightest importance has testified in unmistakeable language to his Royal Highness the loyalty and devotion of the Victorian (and it may be added the Australian) community towards the throne and person of her gracious Majesty his royal mother.

As demonstrations of loyalty cannot be made without an expenditure of money, it followed as a matter of course that the Reception Commission would be pretty freely taxed in augmentation of local contributions for carrying out the various contemplated festivities. From all corners of Victoria applications for pecuniary aid poured in, and it may be fairly estimated that had the Commission been provided with unlimited funds to have responded to all these appeals, the carnival might have continued until 1870. Happily, however, for the calls of business, and much more happily for the health and comfort of his Royal Highness, the official rejoicings were limited to the towns already enumerated; nevertheless there was not a spot where a score of persons were resident, at which a day of festivity was not set apart for celebrating the happy occasion of the royal visit.

It was but reasonable to suppose that where the large towns proposed to expend considerable sums out of their own funds, they should be supplemented by grants in aid from the Government, through the Reception Commission. Recognising this principle, the following sums were allotted:—To the corporation of Melbourne, £2000; to Geelong, £1000; to Ballarat West and Ballarat East, £750 each; and to Castlemaine and Sandhurst also a grant of £750 each, making a total of £6000. It was subsequently determined that the contributions of these several municipalities should be supplemented to the extent of £1 for every £1 subscribed and expended, on the conditions already stated, instead of £1 to every £2, as previously resolved upon. Subsidies of £100 each were also passed to the boroughs of Emerald Hill, Sandridge, and Williamstown, on the same conditions as those to the country boroughs. In addition to the abovementioned sums, grants were made for residence expenses in the various country districts.

The general outline of the arrangements for the reception of his Royal Highness being decided upon, public attention was now turned towards the *Galatea*, as, reluctantly and regretfully, she bade adieu to South Australia, and was rapidly nearing the Port of Melbourne.

ARRIVAL OF THE PRINCE IN VICTORIA.

Fortunately for those who were officially charged with the reception of his Royal Highness, the electric telegraph furnished the exact time of the departure of the *Galatea* from Port Adelaide, and the authorities in Melbourne were thereby exempt from the risk of being caught napping, as in the case of the sister colony ; indeed, instead of being found unprepared for the arrival of the illustrious guest, it might be said that the farthest outlying picket was perhaps a little too forward in attesting its loyalty. According to the *Age* it appears that "after passing Queenscliff, the *Galatea* rounded to the South Channel, and was boarded by a Customs boat. In this craft was the gentleman who had charge of the lord of the manor's surprise, and for the information of the uninitiated, it may be mentioned that the lord of the manor is Mr. Thomas Howard Fellows. His surprise consisted of an address. It was said to have been prepared by the borough council of Queenscliff, and was presented by the Mayor, who had a seat in the boat. It was as follows :—

> We, her Majesty's most dutiful and loyal subjects, the Mayor, councillors, and burgesses of the Borough of Queenscliff, respectfully beg to greet your Royal Highness on entering the chief port of the colony of Victoria with a hearty welcome. Conscious that our progress in the works of civilization forbids a comparison of the material advancement of this colony with that of the United Kingdom, we, nevertheless, affirm that in loyalty to the Throne, in attachment to the person and family of our Most Gracious Queen, and in an earnest desire that Great Britain and Ireland, with all the colonies and dependencies of the Crown, may long remain one glorious, united empire, we are not surpassed by any of her Majesty's subjects. We feel assured that your Royal Highness, during your sojourn amongst us, will have ample proof that in crossing the seas the people of this colony have changed their skies, but not their disposition. Given under our common seal.
>
> CHARLES KENNEDY, Mayor.
> ROBERT JORDAN, Town Clerk.

There are a variety of stories afloat as to the way in which this address was received by the Duke. Some say he was very short with the presenters, and informed them that he thought it a very hard case he was not allowed to navigate his ship to port in peace. Be that as it may, Mr. Fellows can chuckle in his sleeve at the pleasant way in which he sold the Royal Reception Commission." Having received this first "loyal address" on the very threshold of the colony, his Royal Highness was allowed to wend his way without further interruption. The *Galatea* arrived exactly at the expected hour, and anchored in Hobson's Bay on Saturday, Nov. 23rd, 1867. The event is thus described in the *Australasian* :—

THE GALATEA.

H.M.S.S. frigate *Galatea*, the arrival of which had been eagerly and ardently looked for by thousands of Victorians, anchored in Hobson's Bay on Saturday evening, and had such welcome accorded her as must have greatly pleased her captain, who is not only a Prince of the Blood Royal of Great Britain, but is also reputed to be "every inch a sailor." The *Galatea* left Adelaide on the morning of the 21st November, was telegraphed off Cape Otway at half-past five a.m. on Saturday, and with great punctuality arrived at Queenscliff shortly before noon. At thirty minutes past ten a.m. on Saturday, and when about ten miles from Port Phillip Heads, she was descried from the pilot-cutter *Corsair*, of No. 1 Company. The wind during the night had been blowing strong from the S.W., and there was a high sea on, but the *Galatea* did not seem to feel it much. In the grey cloudy morning she loomed immensely large in the distance, but on nearer approach her apparently huge outline was qualified by eminently graceful proportions, and she looked a ship fit to be commanded by a royal captain. On nearing the *Corsair* the *Galatea* lay to, and was boarded by Mr. Pilot Bower, who had the honour of bringing the royal frigate into port. The advent of vessels of war to the waters of Port Phillip, although of not such frequent occurrence as in other British dependencies, has yet of late years taken place often enough to divest such circumstances of the charm of absolute novelty. Ships of war belonging to foreign powers have also anchored in Hobson's Bay, and in an exceptional instance—that of the Russian frigate *Bogatyr*—compared favourably in appearance with the representatives of the British navy; but it may be affirmed with safety that no ship of war like the *Galatea*, either British or foreign, has ever visited these waters. Her majestic proportions, her imposing armament, and her extensive array of the munitions of war, make her indeed a formidable vessel, and one not to be encountered unless on equal terms. Her hull has the appearance of immense size and undoubted strength, combined with exceeding gracefulness of outline and symmetry; her spars and rigging have a taut and light appearance, but a close inspection will show that they are in no wise disproportionate. Her exact dimensions are:—Length overall, 317 ft.; beam, 50 ft.; her gross tonnage is stated to be 3227 tons, and her steam-power is equal to 800-horse power. The rate of speed she attained when new, at the measured mile, was thirteen knots. Her engines are of the description known as Penn's trunk engines, from having one cylinder within the other, the lesser being 36 inches, and the greater 89¼ inches in diameter. Three feet eight inches is the stroke of the piston; and while the engines nominally are 800-horse power, they can work up to 3400 horses, consequently it is not astonishing that she speeds away at the rate of thirteen knots per hour in favourable weather. She is furnished with Griffith's patent feathering screw, which enables the pitch to be altered from 25 to 29, besides affording means of lifting it when under sail. The total weight of her machinery is 575 tons. There are 2756 tubes in the six boilers, which are supplied with fuel from bunkers capable of carrying 600 tons. Her draught of water (with three months' provisions on board) is—aft, 22 feet 7 inches, and forward 21 feet 8 inches. The height of her foremost ports above the water-line is 12 feet 9 inches, of the midship ports 10 feet 6½ inches, and the after ports 12 feet 5 inches. The armament of the *Galatea* is unusually formidable. It consists of thirteen guns on each side, or twenty-six in all. There are four 7-inch bore muzzle-loaders, weighing 6½ tons each, beautiful pieces, with carriage-gear, breeching, and tackling in such order as would do credit to any vessel. Then there are four 64-pounders, shunt muzzle-loaders, and eighteen 10-inch guns, each 87 cwt., and two 12-pounder Armstrong breechloaders for boating purposes, and one field-piece of similar character and calibre. In the arm racks are 172 Enfield rifles, 52 Colt's revolvers, and 172 cutlasses. As the *Galatea* has been only about a year in commission, her equipment is nearly altogether new.

The following is a list of the officers of the ship:—Captain his Royal Highness the Duke of Edinburgh, K.G. Commander—Hugh Campbell. Lieutenants—Charles G. Fane, George R. Heneage, Edward R. Forster, Wallace B. McHardy, Francis Romilly, Lord Phipps (acting). Master—William H. Bradley. Captain of Marines—Robert F. Taylor. First Lieutenant Marine Artillery—Francis H. Poore. Chaplain and Naval Instructor—Rev. John Milner, B.A. Surgeon—James Young, M.D. Paymaster—Thomas Bradbridge. Chief Engineer—John Sear. Sub-Lieutenants—Anthony Kingscote, John S. Halifax, George R. C. Eyres. Supernumerary—

Guy Mainwaring. Second Master—Sydney Smith. Assistant Surgeon W. L. Powell. Assistant Paymasters—William H. Symes (acting), Charles F. James, and Edmund H. Key. Passengers—Lord Viscount Newry, Hon. Eliot Yorke, and Mr. Brierly.

Reception of the Galatea and Escort to Hobson's Bay.

Since the day when the *Galatea* was known to have sailed from Adelaide for Victoria, the bustle in Melbourne, where innumerable preparations for public rejoicings were going on, doubled; and on Friday, when the first party started to meet the Prince, the city seemed in quite a fever of excitement. It was arranged that the *Victoria* should meet the *Galatea* at the Heads, to give her the first welcome; and it was impossible to restrain some show of enthusiasm at her departure, everything around—flags floating from thousands of masts, busy workmen erecting scaffoldings, and arches of evergreens, gay colours, and festive displays on every side—denoting the pervading spirit. The party on board consisted of his Excellency Sir J. H. Manners-Sutton, K.C.B.; Mr. Manners-Sutton, his private secretary; and Lieutenant Rothwell, his aide-de-camp; Sir Trevor Chute, K.C.B., commanding Her Majesty's troops in Australia; Lieutenant-Colonel Pitt, C.B., assistant military secretary; Lieutenant-Colonel Hyde Page, deputy quartermaster general; Major Baker, deputy adjutant-general; and Lieutenant Richardson, aide-de-camp; the Hon. J. M'Culloch, Chief Secretary; the Hon. G. F. Verdon, C.B., Treasurer; the Hon. J. G. Francis, Minister of Customs; Sir James Palmer, President of the Legislative Council; Sir F. Murphy, Speaker of the Legislative Assembly; Colonel W. A. D. Anderson, commandant of volunteers; the Hon. Captain Cole, M.L.C.; the Hon. A. Michie, late Minister of Justice; the Hon. John O'Shanassy, the Hon. R. D. Ireland, the Hon. H. Miller, the Hon. D. Moore, the Hon. J. B. Humffray, the Hon. James Service, the Hon. J. S. Johnston, the Hon. Hibbert Newton, the Hon. A. F. A. Greeves, the Hon. J. R. Bailey, the Hon. George Harker, the Hon. T. Loader, the Hon. J. F. Martley, and Professor Halford, of the Melbourne University. At first sight, too, it might be thought that among those who did attend, elements altogether too inharmonious existed, but fortunately there was no one willing to allow political opposition to influence their social intercourse, and all united in their desire to loyally receive the royal visitor. Queenscliff was reached in due course, and the major portion of the party went ashore to Adman's Hotel, prepared for their reception. There were plenty of flags flying; the Free Banquet of the morrow was ready, and only wanted laying; the public bonfire only wanted lighting; and it was whispered that the Mayor of Queenscliff and the Borough Council had determined to present an address to the noble captain of the *Galatea* when his ship entered the Heads; how they kept their word has been already narrated. The Prince having been telegraphed from Port Macdonnell, his arrival at noon next day seemed secure, and nothing remained for the people but to wait and hope. The next morning was windy and comfortless, and by nine o'clock the reception party, increased by the presence of Mr. J. S. Butters, Mayor of Melbourne, and the Hon. Mr. Sladen, were again on board. Ten o'clock came, and no *Galatea*. At half-past ten something like a steamer was seen in the distance, and the smoke of other steamers loomed on the northern horizon. At eleven a.m. the wind steadily abated. The *Victoria* was completely ready, not a pin was out of place, and she was dressed in flags fore and aft. At last, at fifteen minutes past eleven a.m., the wished-for signal was given from the outer lighthouse. The news quickly spread, and the lighthouses and flagstaffs at Queenscliff were in a moment afterwards streaming with gay-coloured bunting. The *Galatea*, as she steamed through the Heads, looked what she was—the finest specimen of marine architecture that ever entered our waters. Her massive hull loomed large, stately, and with a sort of majestic grace, the effect of which was heightened by her taunt masts, straight as arrows, her rigging taut and trim, and her line of white ports, beneath which the modern dogs of war protruded their terrible mouths. Not a sail was set, and nothing moved amid her yards and spars but a white ensign, indicative of the admiral of the white, to whose squadron she belonged, the thin folds of smoke from her two funnels, and snow-white wreaths of steam from her escape-pipe. An universal sentiment of admiration pervaded the beholders on board the *Victoria*, whose yards were by this time manned in honour of the new arrival; but the *Galatea* made no sign as she moved slowly, and with a sort of conscious grandeur, into Port Phillip Bay. A puff of white smoke and a distant boom then announced the first Royal salute given from the shore battery at Queenscliff, by the local corps, under the command of Captain Snee; but still our visitor lay silent and still. Then the *Victoria* thundered out her salute with yards still manned. It was given with admirable rapidity in three and a-half minutes, but the *Galatea*, now hove to, answered not a shot. It may be supposed that the Admiralty regulations were strictly complied with, but it seemed strange that the man-of-war should keep so cold and grim. Then the men came down from the *Victoria's* yards, and with commendable swiftness the pinnace was lowered and manned with a dozen stout oarsmen, and Commander Norman and Lieutenant Rothwell, the Governor's aide-de-camp, taking their seats in the stern, were rowed with all speed to the Royal vessel. But now the *Galatea* and *Victoria* were not alone. The steamers from Melbourne began to arrive to form the escort, and the air was darkened by their smoke. First came the little Government tug, the *George Rennie*, glorified with flags, her narrow decks crowded, and she, steaming under the *Galatea's* stern, her passengers cheering with all their might, received the first civility from the visitor, who dipped her ensign. The *Express* got the next dip, and the *Victoria* the third, whereat the passengers aboard rejoiced exceedingly. Other steamers came up in quick succession; the *Alddinga*, crowded with members of Parliament and their friends, her band playing loyal tunes and her passengers cheering lustily; the *Cooroug*, the *City of Melbourne*, the *Southern Cross*, the *Tasmania*, the *Derwent*, with many others; and, not least, the *Hero*, her decks and rigging one jam and crush of people, whose deafening hurrahs seemed to rend the air. Then the *Victoria's* pinnace was seen to return. What had passed was this: Captain Norman had been introduced at once to his Royal Highness, whom he asked to allow his vessel to be escorted to Hobson's Bay by the steamers which had come, and those which were coming. The Prince said he would willingly do so, but that he was hurried to get to his anchorage; and he asked whether Captain Norman brought any addresses? Then it came out that the eager folks of Queenscliff had done what they had threatened—had gone on board the *Galatea* and presented their congratulations. The Prince did not scruple to tell Captain Norman that he did not want any more addresses just then, having to attend to the navigation of his ship; however, he said he would wait awhile for the escort, and also expressed himself happy to meet his Excellency. The Governor and suite then proceeded on board the *Galatea*, Captain Norman accompanying the vice-regal party. The Royal steamer lay impressive and mute, not a man visible on her decks, save a marine standing sentry, three or four officers on her quarter-deck, and two figures on her bridge; but as his Excellency approached, there came suddenly a salute of seventeen guns, each fired at intervals of five seconds, with a rapidity somewhat startling. Before she had well done, the little *Pharos*, blazing with flags and her decks black with passengers, came up, and, with yards manned, fired off her salute with creditable speed and regularity. It was not long before Captain Norman returned without his Excellency, and then began the work of getting the escort into order.

First came the signalling. To any one unacquainted with the art of making signals at sea by means of little flags of bewildering variety of pattern, it must have been highly gratifying to notice the effective way in which the mysterious bunting performed its functions; how it was managed cannot now be said, but somehow or other the starboard and port lines were formed, and in very nearly the order of the programme. It was not easy to see which was which, but one could make out enough to say that besides the steamers already named, there were the *Tararua, Gothenburg, Edina, Rangatira, You Yangs, Resolute, Titan, Bendigo, Aldinga, Coorong, Bartson, Derwent, Hero, Southern Cross, Tasmanian, City of Adelaide*, &c. In the meantime the *Victoria* steamed close under the stern of the *Galatea*. A nearer view only increased the sentiment of admiration already formed. This was a vessel of war indeed, so serviceable, so clean, so neat, and so ready did she look. The Prince stood on the bridge, scarcely distinguishable save by the four stripes on his arm, and his occasionally raising his cap to acknowledge the cheering. In a few minutes more all was in order; the *Galatea*, greeted with sounding cheers and dipping ensigns, steamed majestically through the lines, and the whole fleet commenced the homeward trip along the Southern Channel. The wind had partially subsided, the sun had come out, and the spectacle became very interesting. It was soon evident that all the steamers could not keep up, and a few disorders occurred, which were remedied by the excellent feeling of the various captains, who promptly obeyed signals. At times the *Southern Cross* steamed too much ahead, and left the *Hero* behind, but in the end order was eliminated from the chaos of confusion. The *Victoria* and the other fast steamers went at slackened speed, and though many of the smaller boats could only put in an appearance on the horizon, the best part of the fleet managed to keep well together. Sometimes two vessels would come so nearly together as to be within earshot, and a few compliments were passed. But during all this time the *Galatea*, whose steaming powers appeared to be greater than those of any of the vessels forming the escort, had gone far ahead, and was at one time almost hull down. Some thought she would outstrip her escort altogether, but about four p.m., as the end approached, she stayed a while till the others came up. Upon this the *Victoria* signalled to the rest to come closer, and form their lines abeam. While in this order, the spires of Melbourne and the masts of the ships at anchor loomed through the haze, and the fleet entered Hobson's Bay.

With so much enthusiasm and such a collection of forces, the spectacle could not be otherwise than highly effective. A fleet, worth nearly half a million of money, and carrying 5000 or 6000 passengers, had come out to meet the Prince; and as the shore came more and more into view, it was found to be lined with masses of people, each of whom seemed to have a voice to cheer with, or a handkerchief to wave. The buildings appeared, even in the dim distance, to have lines and dots of colour, caused by the innumerable flags, and the ships and boats, large and small, seemed to have flags fastened to every rope and corner where they could be displayed. The air was filled with echoes of cheering, and when the *Galatea* cast anchor outside of the breakwater, she was instantly surrounded by a crowd of small sailing craft, whose passengers and crews cheered again and again, as they went under the stern. The major part of the escort was now pretty close up, and, wrapped in smoke and steam, waited to get near. Then came salutes from shore. The Williamstown battery fired hers, and shortly after a series of white puffs announced that the Sandridge battery was at the same work. The *Victoria*, with the other vessels of the escort half a cable's length off, next cast anchor, and manning her yards, fired a salute, the *Galatea* dipping her ensign in return. The little *Pharos* next fired off another salute, and then the crew of the *Victoria*, filling her rigging, gave cheers three times three. The other steamers followed suit, and as they steamed under the *Galatea's* stern, her ensign dipped her acknowledgments. Finally, it must have been found next to impossible to acknowledge each compliment. The crowd of vessels, large and small, thickened round the visitor, and the rush of passengers to one side of the decks made some to heel over dangerously. These loyal demonstrations lasted till nearly sundown.

The Reception at Melbourne.

The following description of the Royal progress from Sandridge to Melbourne is chiefly collected from the *Argus* and *Age* :—

Victoria had not known in her thirty years' life a brighter day than on Monday. A Royal Prince, son of the greatest and noblest Queen that ever sat on the Throne of the British Empire, had landed on her shores. The festivities belonging to our welcome began with the dawn, and as the metropolis woke to life, so did the people commence the work of celebration. Within a few hours of daybreak the city was alive with bustle, and as folks came abroad, the signs of the general feeling were manifested more and more. Long before ten a.m. the streets were full of passengers—many from the country were there to join the townsfolk in their gaiety. It is impossible to tell of the flags that waved from every roof, the festoons and arches of green that ornamented countless windows, balconies, and verandahs, or the other modes of ornamentation by which the loyalty of the people found expression. Looking down the vistas of streets was confusing work, so much was the eye diverted from the perspective by the broad masses of colour—chiefly red—on every side. The public stir was universal. Melbourne humanity seemed to be dressed in holiday clothing, and filling the thoroughfares. Those who had admission to the various choice points of view, hurried to their rendezvous. Volunteers, town and country, paced rapidly to their muster-grounds, and carriages, cabs, and cars dashed along the roadway; whilst even the policemen—and their name was legion—seemed to have forgotten their usual calm solemnity of demeanour, and betrayed their interest in the general proceedings. All this, however, was a mere preliminary to the after course of things. The formal current of affairs had not then begun to flow, and the only visible tokens of a pre-ordained arrangement of events were the gatherings in the bye-streets of the friendly societies. The holiday-keeping was without form, except perhaps at Parliament Houses, where the sudden summoning together of the Legislature to adopt addresses to the Prince, brought together not a few of those who were to take part in the Royal reception. Thither went the Governor and suite, and legislators, large and small, eager to get through the formal business, and be in time for the landing at Sandridge. His Excellency was escorted to and fro by the mounted police, and his and the Parliamentary equipages filled the reserve, where seemed to begin the labours of Captain Scott, the marshal of the procession, who, taking time by the forelock, was at hand to apportion to each vehicle its proper place. It is needless now to tell what Parliament did—how Ministerialists and Opposition alike displayed a high tone of feeling, and united to show of what loyal stuff our colonial politicians are made. By eleven a.m. there was a general streaming towards the various points of view, thousands and tens of thousands of people, all in holiday dress, pressing to their places, and animated by the universal sentiment. Long lines of school children (the girls in blue and white), volunteers in marching order, members of friendly societies glorious in rosettes and sashes, and men and women of all ages, dress, and degree, bent their steps in one direction, and from Melbourne to Sandridge was a scene of bustle, evergreens, flags, banners, arches, stands for spectators, policemen, horses, carriages, excitement, and cheerfulness. The day was fine, the wind blew cool, and all was blitheness, animation, rejoicing, and the flashing of many colours.

The Prince was to land at Sandridge, and great was the flutter of that port and her few thousand inhabitants. Exuberant loyalty displayed itself in groves of evergreens, and flags enough to stock a fleet. Besides these there were stands, private and public, erected for spectators, and each house seemed to vie with the other in its display. But all eyes and thoughts were turned to the pier, where the disembarkation was to take place. It was at this, the centreing point of the general attention, that there became visible the first fruits of the forethought and preparation of the officials, and to the police be the chief praise. At the railway station trains came and went without crowding or hindrance. Along the pier they might, if they chose, have been loading and unloading, as on ordinary days; but the space kept sacred for the Royal landing was clear, and reserved only for those whose position entitled them to that consideration. The gate of the railway reserve opening into Beach-street was the entrance, and from thence and the terminus to the ordinary landing-place of the Williamstown steamers, on the left side of the pier, was appropriated to the ceremony. A guard of honour of the 14th Regiment formed the two sides of an avenue along the space from the landing-stairs to where the carriages were in waiting, and the planked-floor was covered with light brown canvas. Round the stairs were judges, members of Parliament, foreign consuls, leading officials, ministers of religion, and distinguished colonists. Down the railway and town piers the crowded vessels alongside showed their colours, and looked gay; seaward the ships at anchor were ornamented with bunting of all colours; and near at hand, was the *Victoria*, looking every inch the serviceable little war-sloop she is, her yards manned, and her stock of bunting profligally displayed. In the distance lay the *Galatea*, her huge proportions splendidly prominent, and an almost countless number of small craft and steamers surrounding her like a cloud. At a few minutes before twelve it could be seen that the Prince was leaving his vessel; her yards were manned, her colours were flying, and a flash from her port side announced that the disembarkation had begun. Quick and prompt was the reply from the *Victoria*, and the answering salutes were fired gun for gun. For awhile the Royal vessel was lost to sight in the smoke of her firing; and when it cleared, the Prince's barge, carrying the Royal standard in her bow, and accompanying boats, were seen in full course for shore; soon the *cortège* reached the stairs, and the Prince disembarked.

The landing was as simple as might be. The crowd round and about hardly raised their voice as they saw a young gentleman, in morning costume, walk up the steps. A second glance realised matters, and the air pealed with the cheering. The Prince was very quietly dressed, and after being received by the Governor, walked up the pier to the carriages, members of the Government and Reception Commission, members of Parliament, and military and naval officers following. Every step he took was a signal for fresh cheers, and his was a Royal

Arrival in Victoria. 41

progress indeed. At the shore end of the pier he was met by the Sandridge Borough Council, the Mayor (Councillor Morley) in a furred robe, and the Town Clerk also gowned.

The Mayor advanced and said:—We, the Mayor and Council of this borough, wish, on behalf of the burgesses, to present you with an address, and with your permission I shall now request the Town Clerk to read it.

The Town Clerk (Mr. E. Clark) then advanced, and read the following address, which was tastefully engrossed on vellum, with heraldic devices, by Mr. G. F. Smith, and mounted on purple velvet:—

May it please your Royal Highness—We, the Mayor and Councillors of the municipal borough of Sandridge, desire to approach your Royal Highness with expressions of our sincere loyalty and attachment to the throne and person of Her Most Gracious Majesty, under whose wise and beneficent sway we enjoy so many blessings. We desire to congratulate your Royal Highness on your safe arrival on the shores of Hobson's Bay, and trust that your entry into this colony may be as pleasing to yourself as it is gratifying to us. We most heartily welcome your Royal Highness to this borough, but a few years since the home of the wandering aboriginal, now inhabited by a numerous and intelligent population, on whose behalf, also, we tender to your Royal Highness loyal welcome and congratulation. We sincerely trust that your Royal Highness in your progress through the colony may be gratified with the evidences which will doubtless be made apparent of the skill, enterprise, and intelligence of the general community, and that in the contemplation of the various literary, scientific, religious, and charitable institutions of the colony, your Royal Highness will be enabled to distinguish and appreciate the growth and development of all that adds grace and stability to a country, and thus perceive that the active pursuit of wealth has not caused the higher interests of our common humanity to be either forgotten or neglected. Further, we venture to hope that when hereafter your Royal Highness shall have left these shores, you may have many gratifying reminiscences of your sojourn in the thriving and energetic young colony of Victoria.

WILLIAM MORLEY, Mayor.
EDWARD CLARK, Town Clerk.

The following names were also appended to the address:—Councillors William May, Andrew Ross, Alfred Joseph Johnson, James Ker Beck Plummer, James Kelly, J.P.; David Thomas, J.P.; H. Charles Curtis, and Edward James Crockford.

After the reading of the address, the Mayor handed it to his Royal Highness, saying, "In presenting this address, permit me personally to welcome your Royal Highness to Sandridge, the seaport of this young and important colony, distinguished by the name of your royal mother, our most gracious and beloved Queen." The Prince then read the following reply, which he afterwards handed to the Town Clerk :—

GENTLEMEN—Accept my thanks for the expressions of loyalty and devotion to the Queen, and for the congratulations and kind wishes with which you have greeted my arrival on these shores. The present prosperous condition of this borough, which, as you inform me, has sprung into existence but a few years since, is already a substantial proof of the success which has crowned your enterprise and perseverance; and it is very gratifying to me to learn that the pursuit of wealth and material prosperity has not interfered with the cultivation of those literary, scientific and religious institutions which chiefly advance the civilisation of the nation. Let me assure you that I shall ever look back with the sincerest pleasure to the memory of the enthusiastic welcome that I have received in Victoria.
ALFRED.

To the Corporation of Sandridge.

In front of the platform where this ceremony took place there was drawn up a lodge of *Free Gardeners*, accompanied by forty-one young girls, dressed in white and blue, the daughters of the members. These were preceded by two boys, in Highland costume, carrying banners. One of the young ladies, Miss Elizabeth Marion Watson, advanced and presented the Prince with a very tastefully arranged bouquet, and the others strewed flowers in his path. On entering the carriage he was presented with another bouquet. The Prince seemed much pleased with these gifts, and courteously thanked the donors.

The Prince then proceeded to the vice-regal carriage, which was drawn by four bay horses. He was accompanied by his Excellency the Governor, General Chute, and the Hon. Mr. Yorke. The Mayor and Council of Sandridge, occupying three carriages, preceded the carriage of his Royal Highness through the borough, and the members of the Prince's suite, the Executive, and the Royal Reception Commission followed immediately behind. The escort consisted of a body of volunteer cavalry. The cavalcade was loudly cheered as it proceeded through the streets, and drove at a moderate pace until reaching

EMERALD HILL.

Long before the time appointed for the disembarkation of his Royal Highness the Duke of Edinburgh, the scene along the Sandridge-road, from the railway lines to the triumphal arch, was one of great animation and moving life. It having been decided that the children of the various local common public and private schools should take part in the official local reception of his Royal Highness in the borough, the scholars were mustered at their different schools, and marched in order to the place appointed them. The police arrangements at this point were under the management of Inspector Beaver, who exerted himself to the uttermost in preserving order and regularity. His Excellency the Governor drove past the grand stand in a closed carriage, but as soon as the livery of his servants was distinguished, a long and enthusiastic cheer was given by the congregation of spectators. Following the carriage of the Governor was one containing the Hon. Mr. M'Culloch and the Hon. Mr. Higinbotham. Other notables at intervals passed down the line, and were greeted with cheers. The Emerald Hill Artillery, officered by Major Krone, Captain Shepherd, and Lieutenant Sandilands, took up a position on the north side of the Sandridge-road, and their excellent regimental band played at intervals until the arrival of the Duke. The preparations made for the royal reception were on a most extensive scale, and reflected the greatest credit upon the borough council and committee who had the management of them. At the boundary line of the boroughs of Sandridge and Emerald Hill was erected a large and imposing triumphal arch, designed by Mr. Poulton. It had three spans, the centre one being forty-three feet wide by thirty-four feet high; the others, being over the footpath, were only sixteen feet wide by thirty feet high. The decorations were designed by Messrs. R. Shepherd and J. Ward, and the carrying out of the work was entrusted to Mr. James Stewart. The structure was richly decorated with heraldic, naval, and other emblems, the work of Mr. David Whitelaw. Appropriate mottoes of welcome were tastefully intermingled with the decorations. Leading from it to a distance of about two hundred yards up the Sandridge-road, on the north side, were erected a number of private stands. On the opposite side was also erected a monster stand, the centre being in the form of an amphitheatre, and specially appropriated to the accommodation of the school children. In front of the children was erected a kind of pavilion, constructed on a raised platform, suitably carpeted and furnished for the especial use of the borough councillors and their ladies. The building was erected by Mr. W. Ireland, from designs furnished by Mr. W. H. Ellerker. Leading from the platform was a raised dais, covered with scarlet cloth, from which it was intended the address should be presented. The pavilion and the barriers round were decorated with evergreens and flowers, and had an imposing effect. The school children were all similarly attired—the girls in white dresses and hats, with blue ribbons and sashes, and the boys generally in light clothes and straw hats. Every child wore the commemorative medal struck for the occasion by Mr. Stokes. There were nearly three thousand children on the stand, and their discipline and good behaviour were the subject of general remark. Rising tier above tier, in one compact mass, a prettier sight could not be seen. The credit for the precision with which they sang is due to Mr. Thomas Ford, who had spared no pains in making them perfect. The children were from the Church of England schools (St. Luke's), the Presbyterian, Wesleyan, and National Schools, the schools of St. Peter, St. John, and the two Orphanages, the Protestant Asylum, and the Asylum of St. Vincent de Paul. The Ragged School, and also the Sunday Schools of the Hill were represented, but these children took no part in the singing. After taking their seats they sang, by way of rehearsal, two verses of the National Anthem with such effect as to call for loud cheers and cries of encore. Punctually at a quarter-past twelve o'clock the advance escort was observed entering the Sandridge-road. The approach to Emerald Hill furnished a fine spectacle. Its triumphal arch was eminently handsome. Thousands on foot were waiting their chance to see the Prince, and all were waving hats or handkerchiefs, and joining lustily in the cheering. A guard of honour of the local Artillery corps, under the command of Major Krone, presented arms, their band played, and altogether the welcome to Emerald Hill was a magnificent one. The Mayor and Borough Council awaited the Prince beneath the handsome canopy referred to elsewhere. Hitherto, as the Prince had advanced, so had the reception increased in warmth and splendour, but in what followed "The Hill" more than maintained its ancient prestige. On the carriage containing the Duke passing under the triumphal arch, deafening cheers rent the air, which were repeated again and again until the state carriage stopped in front of the pavilion. On silence being obtained, the Mayor (Mr. W. Thistlethwaite), attired in his robes of office, advanced to the carriage, and in a few brief and appropriate remarks, expressed the satisfaction of the residents of Emerald Hill on his Royal Highness's safe arrival in the colony. The Mayor was accompanied by Councillors C. Roy (late Mayor), John Whiteman, M.P., T. Slead, John Nimmo, William Ireland, C. Skeats, B. N. Sandilands, and Patrick Ward; also the Health Officer of the Borough, Dr. Haig, J.P., and the Borough Surveyor, Mr. S. W. Smith, C.E. The Town Clerk (Mr. James Eville), clad in official robes, then advanced to the carriage, and read the address of the Borough Council, as follows:—

May it please your Royal Highness,—We, the Mayor, Councillors, and Burgesses of the Borough of Emerald Hill, greet you with a heartfelt welcome to the shores of Victoria as a Prince of great promise, and as the son of our beloved sovereign, for whose throne and person we feel the most devoted attachment, whose beneficent reign has contributed largely to the peace and prosperity of the British dominions, and whose many virtues and bright example have shed a lustre around monarchy well calculated to inspire the sovereigns of the world with high, pure, and noble impulses. We sincerely trust that your sojourn amongst us may be pleasant; and, when completed, that the good ship *Galatea* may convey you safe to the dear old land, where we pray God you may be long spared as an ornament of the Royal family to which you belong, and a blessing to that nation for whose physical, social, and moral welfare the late lamented Prince Consort, your gifted and noble father, laboured with unexampled and untiring assiduity.

WILLIAM THISTLETHWAITE, Mayor.
JAMES EVILLE, Town-Clerk.

His Royal Highness replied as follows :—

I thank you for the hearty welcome you have given me, and for the loyalty you have expressed to her Majesty, as well as for the kindly feeling expressed to myself. I am grateful for your good wishes for my safe return home. Nor can I be unmoved by the allusions you have made to the high examples set before me by her Majesty and my father.

ALFRED.

To the Mayor, Councillors, and Burgesses of Emerald Hill.

At the close of the reply of his Royal Highness, three cheers were given, and then the school children sang the two verses of the National Anthem, every one standing at the time. Hardly a sound was heard except the singing of the little ones, who kept excellent time, giving the music with such precision and power as to be heard at a considerable distance. Nothing could have been more effective, and when they finished a general shout of applause burst from the assembled crowd, his Excellency the Governor appearing visibly affected, and the Prince especially acknowledging the honour by half rising from his seat and bowing directly to the children. The carriage then drove on amid every possible demonstration of applause, which was continued for some time, and repeatedly renewed as the other carriages passed the stand. At a point at Emerald Hill, near the foot of Clarendon-street, the Friendly Societies, drawn up in long array, took their places in front of the procession in the following order :—

Manchester Unity Independent Order of Oddfellows,
Ancient Order of Foresters,
Grand United Order of Oddfellows,
United Ancient Order of Druids,
Order of Rechabites,
St. Patrick's Society,
Ancient Independent Order of Oddfellows,
Sons of Temperance,
St. Francis Society, and
Free Gardeners.

These bodies looked very well in their regalia and other ornaments, while the "Druids," cultivating the eccentric, contrived to be very comical in their appearance. They were dressed in long white linen gowns and cowls, and wore long stage beards, which made them appear like the priests in "Norma," without the advantages of paint, gaslight, and scenery. The entire procession being now complete, was composed (in addition to the members of it who proceeded on foot) of about fifty carriages in the following order:—

Carriages of the Melbourne Press.
The carriages containing His Royal Highness and the Governor, followed by two of the Governor's carriages conveying the personal staff, and the carriage of Major-General Trevor Chute.
The Members of the Government,
The Members of the Royal Reception Commission.
Members of the suite of His Royal Highness.
Members of the suite of His Excellency the Governor and the Consuls.
The Members of the Executive Council.
The Judges.
Members of the Legislative Council.
Members of the Legislative Assembly.
The Vice-Chancellor of the University of Melbourne.
The Mayor and Members of the Council of the Borough of Emerald Hill.
The Mayor and Members of the Council of the Borough of Sandridge.

Prince's Bridge.

At eleven o'clock, large numbers of persons began to assemble in the vicinity of Prince's bridge. The St. Kilda-road, as far as the Immigration Depôt, was thickly dotted with anxious visitors, and walking, or even riding, on the Sandridge-road was attended with great inconvenience. Near the junction of the two roads, which had been widened and improved by the Emerald Hill Borough Council at a considerable outlay, the children of the Industrial Schools were accommodated with seats on a raised platform. Four hundred boys arrived in town from Sunbury, in the care of Superintendent M'Farlane, Mr. Duross, and other officers of the schools, and, preceded by their band, they marched to Prince's-bridge, and were there joined by about three hundred and fifty girls. The boys wore blue sashes over their dresses, and the little white straw hats of the girls were trimmed with blue ribbon. Above their heads was fixed a large banner, with the motto, "A Children's Welcome," and placed at each end of the structure were two flags indicative of the institution to which the children belonged. On the opposite side of the road another platform was erected for the accommodation of the public. The arches erected on Prince's-bridge were elegant and tasteful; each spanned the whole roadway, and both were surmounted by flags of every description. The arches were surmounted with the following mottoes, viz.:—"Enter Royal Duke," "Welcome to Victoria," "Long may he Live," and "Welcome Alfred." The height of the arches in the centre were twenty-two feet: the piers rose thirty-two feet, and were painted with material representing red granite in a framework of marble, with gold mouldings, surmounted by emblazoned heraldry. The space between the arches on each end of the bridge, a distance of one hundred feet, was filled in with trellis work, from poles attached to which floated a rare display of bunting, the flags having been purchased by the corporation for the occasion. At the end of the bridge approaching from St. Kilda there was stationed a guard of honor, consisting of members of the Prince of Wales Light Horse; and still further down the road, a cadet corps, recently formed, and numbering above eighty pupils from Wesley College, together with over twenty from the private schools of Messrs. Pegus and Mann, were drawn up. The juvenile soldiers, dressed in a pretty uniform (dark grey with scarlet facings), and armed with carbines, presented a smart and novel appearance. All the balconies and verandahs in Swanston-street, from the bridge to Collins street, were crowded with spectators, and even the tops of many of the houses were occupied. At half-past twelve o'clock, Inspectors Hare and Dinsey, followed by a number of mounted police, galloped towards the bridge, and announced the approach of the royal procession. The road was then quickly cleared to allow the cavalcade to pass, and simultaneously every head was turned towards Sandridge. The procession was headed by the Friendly Societies. As the carriage in which His Royal Highness, the Governor, Major-General Chute, and the Hon. Mr. Yorke were seated, approached, the excitement became intense. The multitude cheered in the most enthusiastic manner, the cadet corps gave the usual military salute, and the children of the Industrial Schools sang the National Anthem with precision and accuracy. The length of the procession may be gathered from the fact that it was fully half an hour in passing the bridge, after the leading body reached the junction of the roads. In Swanston-street was stationed a detachment of the 14th Regiment, under the command of Colonel Trevor. When the Prince had crossed the bridge he was again greeted with deafening cheers and by the smiles of thousands of the fair sex, who occupied the various balconies and windows, and who continued to wave their handkerchiefs until he had almost disappeared, compliments which he repeatedly acknowledged by bowing.

THE TOWN HALL.

Here were gathered a large mass of persons on the stand erected by the City Council. Looking up and down Collins-street, as early as twelve o'clock, the scene presented was a most striking one. From each house hung decorations of every variety; high above the houses were flags flaunting in the breeze, of every color and of every nationality; while from the windows were to be seen adornments of the most picturesque kind. But, as seen from the Town Hall, the most pleasing sight was the children. There were thousands of them, the girls all dressed in white with blue trimmings, whilst the majority of the boys were attired in complimentary nautical apparel. Looking from Swanston-street, there was row upon row of bright young faces aglow with health and wreathed in smiles. A moderate estimate might compute the number of children at ten or eleven thousand. Through some mismanagement, the magnificent grand stand at the Town Hall got filled by those who were not amongst the invited. Many who had tickets for admission found themselves thrust out of any place by coming even a minute too late, and as a consequence there were complaints both loud and deep. However, by-and-bye, by the aid of friendly verandahs and pavements, and by a general subsidence into the positions left open, nearly every one was satisfied, and all that was left was to wait quietly the arrival of the Prince. In this hour of expectancy the line of route must have presented to even a careless observer a very impressive appearance. From Prince's Bridge to Bourke-street, Swanston-street was densely lined with people of every complexion and of every degree. These seemed as if they had only one object in view in life, and that was to obtain a sight of the Prince. Before one o'clock, the people on the look-out had the pleasure of hearing in the distance the strains from the bands accompanying the procession, and in a very few minutes the advance guard, in the shape of the members of the M.U.I.O.O.F., came trooping along. A few revolutions of old Father Time's hour-glass, and then the event so long looked for is a thing of the present. The Prince, seated next the Governor, had drawn up in front of the temporary halting place erected by the Council, and there was a huge cheer from the crowd, which was taken up and dilated on by the children, who seemed in the highest of high glee. There was a moment of silence after the state carriage stopped, and then the Mayor of Melbourne, accompanied by the Aldermen and City Councillors, attired in court costume, advanced to the side of the vehicle, and spoke as follows :— In presenting an address to your Royal Highness from the Corporation of Melbourne on behalf of the citizens, we beg to offer you our hearty congratulations on your safe arrival in the colony. We welcome you within the portals of our young and noble city with pride and pleasure, and hope your stay amongst us may be as gratifying to you as it is pleasing and honourable to us. Of our attachment and devotion to the person of Her Gracious Majesty the Queen, we doubt not you will have ample testimony ere you leave our shores. We are here for the purpose of presenting you with an address, which, with your permission, I will now read. The following address was then read:—

> We, Her Majesty's most dutiful and loyal subjects, the mayor, aldermen, councillors, and citizens of the city of Melbourne, respectfully offer to your Royal Highness our heartiest welcome to this city.
>
> We beg to assure your Royal Highness of our devoted loyalty to the throne of our Most Gracious Sovereign, and of our faithful attachment to her Royal person.
>
> Enjoying under Her Majesty's gracious rule the advantage of local incorporation, which has been with us for a quarter of a century, as amongst our ancestors for ages, the bulwark at once of liberty and order, we, as the oldest representative body in the colony, hail with enthusiasm the opportunity which the honour of your Royal Highness's visit affords us for expressing to a son of our revered Sovereign and of the wise and good Prince Albert, our deeply grateful sense of the benefits of good government and of public and private virtue and beneficence, which, whilst adorning the throne, have been fruitful in blessings to the empire, and have endeared Her Majesty, the memory of her illustrious consort, and the members of their august family, to Her Majesty's subjects throughout the world.
>
> We feel assured that amongst the pleasures of your Royal Highness's voyage (which we trust trust may be innumerable and unalloyed) none will exceed that of proving that these sentiments of devoted and affectionate loyalty are as wide spread as the ocean which you have traversed, and fervent at the antipodes as in the heart of Great Britain. (Signed)
>
> JAMES STEWART BUTTERS, Mayor.
> EDMUND GERALD FITZGIBBON, Town Clerk.

The address, which was bound in a superb morocco case, was then handed to the Prince, and his Royal Highness replied:—

> Mr. Mayor and Gentlemen,—I thank you sincerely for your very hearty welcome to the city of Melbourne, and for the expression of your devotion and loyalty to the throne and person of our Queen.
>
> I am pleased to find that the rapid growth of this colony, in a short space of years, from very small beginnings to an unwonted state of prosperity, is consistent with a just appreciation of and reverence for the institutions which have flourished in the mother country for so many centuries, and that, while proud of the liberty and freedom which those institutions guarantee, you so gladly come forward and assure me of the devoted loyalty to your Sovereign which I well believe exists in every heart in this colony.

In consequence of severe illness Mr. E. G. FitzGibbon, Town Clerk, was unable to be present to read the address, and Mr. S. Masters, Chief Clerk, acted as his deputy.

At the conclusion of the reply the signal was given, and the children, under the leadership of Mr. W. Bonwick, struck up the "National Anthem." They sang very correctly and with considerable power, and the obvious interest which the Duke took in their performance showed that to him it was not the least gratifying portion of the day's proceedings. At the conclusion of the anthem the procession again started amid the most enthusiastic demonstrations from the people. The Mayor and Corporation then entered their carriages, and fell in with the procession, the whole arrangements for which at this point were admirably conducted. The Mayor performed the duties of the occasion with dignity and tact, and may justly be congratulated on the first important appearance he made since he assumed the duties of the mayoralty.

After the ceremony at the Town Hall was completed, the procession was put again in motion, and was marshalled westward along Collins-street. The men of the 14th Regiment had hitherto assisted the police to keep the line clear, but now the volunteers began to do that duty, and they formed the guard of honour drawn up to receive the Prince. A handsome and stately arch had been erected by the City Council in Collins-street, at the intersection of

Elizabeth-street, fifty feet in height, and spanning the entire carriage-way, and was suitably decorated with flags and trophies. The imposing structure in a measure marred the *tout ensemble*, as it effectually deprived the cortege of the panoramic effect that it presented when in Bourke-street. The procession stopped for a moment outside the Bank of New South Wales, and to look back at the hill down which it had come was to see nothing but heads below and flags above; the bank was ornamented with crimson hangings and festoons and bunches of flowers, which harmonised with the general view. The length of the procession may be judged from the fact that as the Prince was passing Queen-street, the friendly societies were crossing the same street in the line of Bourke-street. Bursts of applause accompanied every step of the Royal advance, to which the Prince replied by bowing frequently. The line along the western end of Collins-street and William-street was kept by volunteers from Ballarat, Castlemaine, and Sandhurst, who did their duty most creditably. In William-street the appearance of the Prince was the signal for a peal of joy-bells from St. James's Church; but there was little to see till the procession turned by Goldsbrough's wool store and Menzies' new hotel, into Bourke-street, when the scene of Collins-street was repeated with scarcely abated impressiveness, though the people were not so numerous. There were, nevertheless, a great many stands, and most of them were full. Looking down the hill from the high ground opposite the horse-yards, the fine facade of the Post-office came out in splendid relief. The warmth of the people's welcome to the Prince never flagged. As he went forward, the cheers were renewed, and bands placed at frequent intervals heightened the general enthusiasm as they thundered out the tune every British heart loves so well. The modes in which the various business establishments put out their insignia of rejoicing were often as singular as they were successful. Messrs. Robertson and Moffat, the drapers, hung their ample balcony with Royal tartans. At Mr. Hosie's dining hall, the young waitresses were ranged in a row on the first-floor front, and formed a picturesque and not unattractive group. At the Wax-works were displayed excellent figures of the Prince and Princess, and a similar idea was carried out at Mr. Dwight's book-shop, where the busts of the Queen and late Prince Consort were prominently placed. The volunteers lined Bourke-street as well as Collins-street as far as Stephen-street, where the duty devolved upon the friendly societies, who did their best, and not badly. Turning into Spring-street, towards the Treasury, brought to view another enormous crowd awaiting the Royal arrival, and at a few minutes before two o'clock the procession reached the Treasury terrace.

Never before, and perhaps never again, will be seen anything like that which was witnessed in front of the Treasury buildings. On the terrace had been erected a superstructure of wood, with a canopied dais for the Royal party, and seats around for those entitled to that honour. These and the wide flight of steps in front were covered with crimson and blue cloth, all new and gorgeous, and on each side were masses of ferns and other fresh green shrubs. On either side were the Executive Councillors, members of the Legislature, the judges, heads of religious denominations, foreign consuls, members of the City Council, and some of the suburban borough councils; Commander Norman, of H.M.C.S. *Victoria*; Commander Wilkinson, R.N., of the Admiralty survey; the Vice-Chancellor and professors of the Melbourne University, and others; and behind them were benches for as many ladies as could be accommodated. Most of the gentlemen were in some sort of official costume; and the city aldermen and councillors appeared in their court dress and cocked hats. In front were in compact masses fully 30,000 persons, surging and waving backwards and forwards, as the police and soldiery strove to make them keep within bounds. The object was to secure space for the Prince's carriage, but it was only by almost superhuman exertions that this could be done. Concentrated masses of police, soldiery, and even the mounted police and the cavalry joined in the efforts made, and it must be said for both sides that they kept their temper admirably. As far as the eye could reach was nothing but a densely packed mass of human beings.

Tremendous cheers rent the air when the Prince left his carriage and took his stand on the dais. The Prince bowed his acknowledgments for a few moments, and then retired inside the building, where refreshments had been prepared in the Governor's apartments. While in the Governor's offices the members of the Ministry and the Reception Commission were presented to him, and in the long interval which ensued before he again appeared in public occurred the squeezing mentioned above. At last His Highness returned, and then for a few moments the deafening peals of cheering again rang through the air. When the enthusiastic plaudits had somewhat subsided, the members of the Legislative Council came forward, and the President read the following address:—

May it please your Royal Highness,—We, the Legislative Council of Victoria, in Parliament assembled, congratulate your Royal Highness on your safe arrival in this remote dependency of the British empire, which has the honour of being named after Her Most Gracious Majesty the Queen.

We assure your Royal Highness of our sincere loyalty, devotion, and attachment to Her Majesty's throne and person, and we rejoice to have this opportunity of bidding welcome to one of Her Majesty's sons in the person of your Royal Highness. We find it difficult to express the pleasure with which we regard your Royal Highness's visit to these colonies, and while we beg to tender to you our heartiest welcome, we desire also to express our hope that your visit will be attended with pleasure and satisfaction to yourself.

To this the Prince made the following reply:—

Gentlemen,—No answer that I can return to your address will sufficiently convey my thanks to you, or express the pleasure which I had derived from the manifestations of loyalty and affection to the Queen (my mother) by which I have been met upon my arrival in this province.

I shall never cease to rejoice that I have been enabled to visit this distant portion of the empire, to become acquainted with a people of whom I shall carry back with me most pleasing recollections.

It will be most welcome to Her Majesty to hear that this country is so prosperous and happy; and I shall not fail to convey to Her Majesty the expressions of your loyalty and devotion.

I thank you heartily for the good wishes with which you speed me on my way through this province.

Then the members of the Legislative Assembly presented themselves, and the Speaker (with whom was Mr. Palmer, sergeant-at-arms, manfully shouldering the mace, read the following address:—

May it please your Royal Highness,—We, the Legislative Assembly of Victoria, in Parliament assembled, beg leave to approach your Royal Highness with expressions of our loyalty to the Throne, and of our affectionate devotion to Her Most Gracious Majesty the Queen.

We offer your Royal Highness our hearty congratulations upon your arrival in Victoria, and we feel confident that the knowledge which your Royal Highness will obtain of the position and resources of this country will conduce to its highest interests as a part of the empire.

The visit of your Royal Highness affords us the most gratifying assurance of the interest with which Her Majesty is graciously pleased to regard these distant provinces of the Crown, and we express the universal sentiment of the people in bidding your Royal Highness welcome to Victoria.

The Prince replied as follows:

Gentlemen—The address you have presented to me, in which you proclaim your loyalty to the Queen and your attachment to the British Crown, demands my warmest acknowledgment.

For myself, gentlemen, I rejoice at the opportunity which has been afforded me of visiting this colony, whose growing prosperity offers a striking example of what may be effected by energy and enterprise, under free institutions.

The interest that Her Majesty takes in her Australian subjects is great, and I can with truth assure you of her anxiety for their happiness and prosperity.

Accept my hearty thanks for your kind wishes for my future happiness. In return, I wish you every prosperity.

The addresses over, Mr. M'Culloch came to the front of the dais, and called for three cheers for the Queen. It may be guessed with what heartiness the appeal was responded to, as also another on behalf of the Duke of Edinburgh, and a third for the Governor. The Prince then descended to his carriage, and drove off amid repeated demonstrations of applause.

All along the road to Toorak the same evidences of loyalty were exhibited in flags and evergreen decorations in honour of the princely visit. At the intersection of the Punt road a triumphal arch was erected; at the Bridge Hotel, corner of Chapel-street and Gardiner's Creek-road, flags and banners were shown over the road. There were not many folks about this part of the Prince's progress, for it seemed as if almost everybody had sought to present their loyal fealty in Melbourne. At Toorak, after a line of flags and banners, there came another triumphal arch of evergreens, and at this point just those few persons who could not reach Melbourne in good time mustered, and gave the Duke a hearty cheer as he passed. His Royal Highness then proceeded to Government House, where a dinner party—Ministers and friends—had been invited to meet him. In the course of the evening his Royal Highness, in company with his Excellency, visited the city, taking the route of Collins-street, and returning to Toorak before eleven o'clock.

THE ROYAL LEVEE.

The Levee of the Duke of Edinburgh, held in the New Exhibition Building on the 26th of November, was such a one as has never been seen in the colony before. All who desired to honour the Prince as we have honoured none who ever yet stood on Victorian shores, passed before him in thousands. The reception took place at the northern end, nearest the chief entrance, where a very handsome canopied dais had been erected. The floor was carpeted with crimson, from which sprang twisted columns of white and gold, supporting a canopy of gorgeous fretwork and crimson hangings, the inner ceiling of white and blue satin drawn into elegant folds. Beyond was the immense hall, its walls and roof in patterns of blue and buff, and broken by architectural details which robbed the aspect of any touch of sameness. Down the sides were rows of crimson-covered seats,

The Royal Levee. 51

and filling the southern end were some thousand or more ladies assembled to witness the proceedings. The space immediately before the dais was also laid with crimson cloth, and across it marched those who presented themselves and bowed their compliments. The sunlight shone gloriously through the stencilled windows, and though the vast interior was of no time-honoured stone, rich with the work of centuries in sculptured ornaments, it was not unfit for the Royal visitor, and told well of what had occupied us during our thirty years' life.

The Prince took his place on the dais precisely at noon, accompanied by the Governor. The former wore his naval uniform, with the broad blue ribbon of the Garter. His Highness's face, stamped with his mother's likeness, and a sufficiently noble bearing, added to the effect of his presence. At his right hand was the Governor in official uniform. Behind were the Prince's suite, his equerries, the Hon. Eliot Yorke and Mr. Haig, in uniforms of the Royal household, and Lord Newry in a yeomanry dress. To the right of the dais was a group consisting almost wholly of military and naval officers, Major General Sir Trevor Chute, K.C.B., and Colonel Pitt, C.B., Lieutenant-Colonel Hyde Page, Major Baker, a number of the officers of the *Galatea*, and others, including Mr. Brierly (a private friend of the Prince, and an artist of repute, who has accompanied him throughout his present trip). On the left hand was vacant ground at the commencement of the ceremony, but it was soon filled with colonial notabilities, admirably grouped. The presentations began as soon as the Prince took his place. First came the officers of the Executive Government and the members of the Executive Council, then the members of the two Houses of the Legislature, the judges, the clergy, the Vice-Chancellor and members of the University, of whom there was a great show; the military, both of the 14th Regiment and volunteer service, colonial naval officers, and, lastly, an indiscriminate array of Victorian gentlemen. Ever as eyes were turned to the gangways kept by the soldiery, who only let pass enough to keep up the stream, there was still an eager crowd pressing forward; still had the hoarse officials to call out the names of the new arrivals, and still had the Prince to bow as each Victorian loyalist bent before him. At last the flow slackened, and the aide-de-camp had no more to receive and read the imprinted pasteboards which previously had descended upon him like a gentle shower. There was first a lull, then a stoppage; at last the Prince retired for refreshment, and the presentations ceased for a brief interval.

On his return, his Royal Highness received addresses from different public bodies. It was supposed that they would be more numerous than they were, but as it was they were soon disposed of, for they were not read, but simply received and handed to the equerry. Replies were promised in due time. When they had all been handed in, there were a few more presentations, and the ceremony was over.

The Prince drove from Toorak in a coach and six, with outriders, accompanied by an escort of the Volunteer Light Horse, a hundred in number. As his entrance was made through the Public Library, the whole of Swanston-street front from Lonsdale to Latrobe streets was kept clear of foot and carriage traffic, and the way in which the police did their work cannot be commended too highly. When the Prince entered the city he was, being unexpected, met with but few cheers as he drove along; things however were different on his return. Thousands had collected to see him pass, and as he was whirled along the streets to the bridge—through rows of houses fringed and dotted with countless flags, and festooned with masses of evergreens—he was cheered with the greatest enthusiasm.

H 2

Visit of H.R.H. Prince Alfred.

The following gentlemen, having the special entrée, were first introduced:—

a'Beckett, Hon. Thomas Turner, M.L.C.
Agnew, G. F., Acting Vice-Consul for Spain
Amstel, J. W. Ploos Van, Consul-General for Netherlands
Amstel, D. Ploos Van, Vice-Consul for Netherlands
Anderson, Hon. Robert Stirling, M.L.C.
Anderson, Lieut.-Colonel, C.B., K.H.
Aspinall, Hon. Butler Cole
Bailey, Hon. Mr.
Berks, Gustave, Consul for Belgium
Biagi, Chevalier Guiseppe, Consul-General for Italy
Bindon, Hon. Samuel Henry, Minister of Justice
Brahe, W. A., Acting-Consul for Prussia
Brownless, A. C., M.D., Vice-Chancellor of the University
Campbell, A. J., Moderator of General Assembly of the Presbyterian Church of Victoria
Chase, Rev. S. L., Chaplain to Bishop of Melbourne
Cooper, R., Consul for Portugal
Damyon, James, Vice-Consul for Russia
De Castelnau, Le Comte, French Consul
Duffy, Hon. Charles Gavan
Fitzgerald, Hon. John Foster Vesey
Fullet, Henri, Vice-Consul for France
Goethe, Rev. Matthew, head of the Lutheran Church
Hall, Major Charles H., Superintendent of Local Military Store Department
Harker, Hon. George
Higginson, Rev. Henry, head of the Unitarian Church
Higinbotham, Hon. George, Attorney-General
Horne, ——, Deputy Commissary General
Johnston, Hon. J. S.
Kay, J. H., Clerk to the Executive Council
Loader, Hon. Thomas

Macartney, Very Rev. H. B., D.D., Dean of Melbourne
Macgregor, Hon. John, Minister of Mines
Michie, Hon. Archibald
Miller, Hon. Henry
Mitchell, Hon. William H. F., M.L.C.
Molesworth, His Honour Mr. Justice
Moore, Hon. David
Murphy, Hon. Sir F., Speaker of Legislative Assembly
M'Combie, Hon. John
M'Mahon, Hon. Captain Charles
Newton, Hon. Hibbert
O'Shanassy, Hon. John
Palmer, Hon. Sir James F., President Legislative Council
Perry, Right Rev. Charles, D.D., Bishop of Melbourne
Pohlman, Judge
Reid, Lieut. Col. R., Acting Brigade-Major of Volunteers
Rintel, Rev. Moses, head of the Hebrew Congregation
Rusden, G. W., Clerk of the Parliaments
service, Hon. James
Skinner, Judge
Sladen, Hon. Charles, M.L.C.
Standish, F. C., Chief Commissioner of Police
Stawell, Chief Justice, His Honour Sir William Foster
Strachan, Hon. James Ford, M.L.C.
Vale, Hon. W. M. K., Commissioner of Public Works
Waugh, Rev. James S., Chairman of Melbourne District of Wesleyan Church
Were, J. B., Consul for Denmark
Were, N. F., Vice-Consul for Sweden and Norway
Wilkie, Hon. David, M.L.C.
Wilkinson, Commander R.N.
Williams, His Honour Mr. Justice

The following were the general presentations:—

ABBOTT, David
Abbott, Robert Main
a'Beckett, Edward
a'Beckett, Edward F.
a'Beckett, Thomas T.
Acton, Rev. G. W.
Adams, J. D.
Adams, Robert
Adams, W.
Adet, Edward
Agg, Alfred J.
Agg, Edward J.
Agnew, P. A.
Agnew, Andrew
Aitken, Capt. John
Aitken, Thomas
Akhurst, W. M.
Albiston, Rev. Joseph
Alexander, Alexander
Alexander, M. A.
Alexander, Thomas
Alexander, Thomas Barry
Allan, George L.
Allan, George G.
Allan, Capt. J. H., E.C.R.

Allingham, J. Stratton
Allport, Curzon
Aloin, John
Alsop, David G. E.
Alston, Thomas
Alston, William C.
Alston, William Henry
Amess, Councillor
Amess, Mark
Amsinck, Commander, R.N.
Amsinck, Eugene C.
Amsinck, Frederick W.
Anderson, Alexander W.
Anderson, Arthur
Anderson, Major, V.V.L. Horse
Anderson, Rev. John
Anderson, Rev. John
Anderson, T. Y.
Andrew, H. M., M.A.
Andrew, J. W.
Andrews, Isaiah
Aplin, C. D'Oyly H.
Aplin, Dyson
Appleton, L. F.

Archbold, George
Arnold, T.
Arnold, Andrew
Arnot, Lieut. R.N.
Archbold, John
Archer, William Henry, Registrar-General
Armstrong, Thomas
Armstrong, William
Armytage, George
Asche, Thomas
Ashley, E.
Ashmore, William
Ashton, ——
Atchison, W. C.
Atkins, W. H.
Atkinson, J. P.
Atkinson, T. G.
Atkyns, Edward A.
Attenborough, ——
Attenborough, Thomas
Atwood, J. S.
Austin, G. B.
Austin, H. S.
Austin, Richard

Austin, Thomas
Avent, Nicholas

BACON, Thomas
Badcock, John
Bagley, Rev. John
Bagley, J. C.
Baillie, Thomas
Baillie, W. G., M.L.A.
Bailliere, F. F.
Baker, C.
Baker, John R.
Baker, Edward H.
Baker, Rev. Henry
Balfour, James, M.P.
Balharry, James
Ballantyne, Rev. James
Bamber, Thomas P.
Bance, Commander H. Prescott, R.N.
Barncliff, Edward
Banks, J. H.
Berdin, Rev. C. P. M.
Bashwell, Everett
Barbwell, T. H.

The Royal Levee. 53

Barker, Alexander S.
Barker, — clerk Legislative Assembly
Barker, Dr. Edward
Barker, Richard
Barker, William
Barlow, Rev. John
Barlow, Rev. Robt. Burrowes
Barnard, L.
Barnes, John G.
Barnett, Isaac
Barrett, W.
Barry, Rev. George V.
Barry, John M.
Barry, Sir Redmond
Bartine, H.
Bartlett, J. G.
Bartrop, G. F.
Basen, G.
Bastow, Henry B.
Bastow, W.
Bates, William
Batten, G. H.
Batten, H. J. L.
Battersby, Alexander
Baxter, B.
Bayles, William, M.P.
Beaney, Dr. James George
Bear, T. H.
Bear, J. P., M.L.C.
Beaver, F. E.
Becker, Rev. M. H.
Beckwith, Thomas William
Beer, Rev. Joseph
Beilby, Edwin T.
Bell, Benjamin
Bell, Edward
Bell, George
Bell, James
Bell, Major John Prince Wales V.V.L.H.
Bell, W. Moore
Bellin, John
Benjamin, B.
Benjamin, Elias
Benjamin, Moses
Bennett, John B.
Bennetts, William Rowling
Bennie, A. P.
Benson, William
Berry, G. B.
Berghoff, Charles
Berry, Henry
Best, Alban P.
Beveridge, J. A.
Beynon, John
Bright, Charles E.
Brook, Henry
Brooks, Henry
Biagi, Cavaliere Giuseppe, Italian Consul
Bickerton, R. F.
Bickford, Rev. James
Biddle, William Charles
Billing, B. Annesley
Binks, Rev. W. L.
Birchall, W. H[a]
Bird, Dr. Bougan
Bird, Rev. T. F.
Birkmyre, W.
Birkmyre, Wrixon William
Birnie, —
Bishop, James
Black, Neil
Black, Dr. Joseph

Blackburn, Gerard
Blackburn, James
Blackwell, Richard H.
Blackwood, J. H., M.P.
Blackwood, James
Blair, Dr.
Blair, George Gordon
Blair, James W.
Blanche, John F.
Bland, R. H.
Bland, James J.
Blamain, Alfred
Bleasdale, Rev. J. J., D.D.
Blundell James J.
Bogle, Andrew
Booker, —
Booley, Superintendent
Booth, Frederick O.
Bongman, H. C.
Bonford, G. W.
Born, James Ford
Boyista, Joseph
Boully, William
Bowen, William
Bowie, -
Bowman, Robert, M.P.
Bowring, J.
Box, Charles V.
Box, Henry
Box, Henry, jun.
Boyd, Rev. J. S.
Boynton, Alderman
Bradbury, Miles C.
Bradley, Capt., 14th Regt.
Bradly, Charles Ferdinand
Bradshaw Edward
Brady, Patrick
Braz re, J. De la Roche
Braham, —
Bramston, Thomas
Brennan, P. J.
Brett, Edwin
Brierly, John Phillips
Bright, S., jun.
Brock, James
Brodie, Philip
Brockleank, T.
Brodribb, P. C.
Brodribb, K. E.
Brodribb, William A.
Brodribb, W. Kennedy
Bromfield, —
Brooks, W. A.
Brooke Yates
Brotherton, Henry
Brown, Charles F. E.
Brown, Colin
Brown, Frederick
Brown, Gavin G.
Brown, G. H.
Brown, George
Brown, George
Brown, Gilbert Wilson
Brown, Rev. P.
Brown, J. P.
Brown, John
Brown, Seraphon Stather
Browne, Edward
Browning, Charles, M.A.
Browning, S. S.
Bruce, Henry A.
Bruce, M. F.
Bruce, J. L.
Brush, Samuel
Brunan, C. F.

Bryand, S. A.
Buchan, Capt. John J.
Buchanan, Alexander
Buckhurst, W. P.
Buckley, Marx
Budd, H. H.
Budd, R. Hale
Bull, Major
Bullivant, William How
Bunnett, Templeton
Bunny, B. F.
Burke, Edmund
Burke, James L.
Burnett, J. W.
Burrell, George
Burrow, William
Burrowes, R., M.P.
Burstall, B. B.
Burt, James
Burton, Capt. O. S., Local Staff
Bartt, J. G., M.P.
Buscombe, J. H. K.
Bushe, Robert
Butchart, George
Butler, Dr.
Butler, George W. G.
Butters, James Stewart, Mayor of Melbourne
Byrne, James P.
Byrne, Miles Garrett
Byrne, Robert, M.P.

CADDEN, C. J.
Cairns, John
Cairns, Rev. Dr.
Calder, Henry
Caldwell, Rev. James
Callaghan, James
Calvert, Samuel
Cameron, A.
Cameron, Daniel
Cameron, Denis J.
Cameron, R. R.
Campbell, Alexander
Campbell, Colin
Campbell, Capt. Charles C.
Campbell, D. Stodart
Campbell, James
Campbell, J. M.
Campbell, John
Campbell, Robert
Campbell, William
Candler, C.
Canterbury, John
Carpenter, W. H.
Capron, A. T.
Capper, Samuel
Carey, Capt.
Carlile, Edward
Carr, Robert C.
Carmichael, John
Carnaby, G.
Carpenter, Councillor
Carson, John
Carte, Surgeon-Major
Carter, Ernest
Carter, W. H.
Carter, Rev. William
Carter, —
Casey, J. J., M.P.
Castlemaine, Archdeacon of
Cattenach, Thomas
Caughey, Alexander

Caunter, Richard B.
Cave, Wm. St. John Midlane
Chalmer, G.
Chambers, Hugh J.
Chambers, J. S.
Chambers, Lieut. William
Champ, Lieut.-Col.
Charlwood, Charles J.
Chearley, Edward
Chase, Rev. S. L.
Clater, R. H.
Chauncy, Philip
Chew, Tom
Chiole, John
Chomside, Robert
Christie, E. P.
Christopherson, H. O.
Clark, Edward
Clark, George
Clark, Rev. John
Clark, H. Calvin
Clark, Thomas
Clark, Walter
Clarke, Lieut. H. A.
Clarke, Henry
Clarke, Joseph
Clarke, Marcus
Clarke, Richard
Clarke, William
Clarke, W. J.
Cloke, W. J. T.
Clauson, Wiliston
Clerke, Thomas Ford
Clery, James
Clipperton, Lieut.
Clipperton, —
Clutterbuck, V.
Clubb, Thomas J.
Cogdon, John
Cogle, James
Cogswell, E. H.
Cohen, Alderman
Cohen, A. J.
Cohen, L.
Cohen, Nathan Edward
Cohen, P.
Cohen, Samuel H.
Cohn, Jacob
Cole, J. R.
Cohen, Morris J.
Cole, Hon. G. Ward
Cole, Rev. Thomas C.
Colmer, H.
Colin, Leopold
Collings, Jonah
Colvin, Robert
Compton, Frederick
Compton, George Spencer
Comyns, Charles
Conder, Jones Henry
Connell, John
Considine, J. W.
Constable, A. H.
Cook, C. H. B.
Cook, Frederick
Cook, George
Cook, William
Cooke, Cecil Pybus
Cooper, Alfred
Cooper, Capt. J. S.
Coote, Frederick John
Cooper, Rev. John
Cooper, W. Henry
Cope, Edward
Cope, Rev. John

Visit of H.R.H. Prince Alfred.

Coppin, George
Corbett, Louis A.
Corcoran, W. P.
Corrigan, Dr.
Cosgrave, John
Coster, Frederick
Couchman, Capt. Thomas
Coulter, William
Courtis, John
Courtney, —
Couves, Alderman
Coward, Dr.
Cowderoy, B.
Cowderoy, F.
Cowell, Joshua
Cox, W. M.
Craig, James
Craig, M.
Craig, Robert, M.A. and LL.B.
Cramba, Dr.
Crawford, Commander
Crawford, D.
Craven, John
Creber, W. J. W.
Cresswell, Rev. A., M.A.
Cresswell, H. C.
Creswick, Henry
Crews, J. B.
Crichton, Robert
Cripps, A. J.
Crisp, Rev. J. W.
Crisp, T.
Crispo, Sydney Smith
Criswick, Charles F.
Crockford, Edward James
Crockford, John E.
Croft, Eugene
Croft, William
Crofts, Fortescue
Crooke, —
Crooke, Edward
Crooke, Robert
Crooke, Dr. W. E.
Cropper, S. R.
Cross, John
Crossen, Henry
Crouch, T. J.
Croxton, Rev. W. R.
Cruickshank, D. B.
Cumming, Donald
Cumming, James
Cumming, Rev. R. T.
Cunningham, Alexander
Curle, Capt.
Currie, Capt. Archibald
Currie, John
Currie, John L.
Curtain, Michael
Curtis, Capt.
Curtis, James
Curtis, Surgeon
Curtis, Frederick
Cuthbert, W. Wallace
Cuthbertson, P.
Cutts, Dr.

DAISH, W.
Dalgleish, Andrew
D'Alcourto, C.
Dalrymple, B.
Dalton, J. P.
Daly, James
Damme, Karl van
Dane, —

Dare, Paul
Daniel, Rev. C.
Denoon, H. S.
Deplaw H. B.
Dare, Jas. J.
Darling, Rev. Hugh
Dornal, E. Russell
Darcy, T.
Davies, B.
Davies, B. G.
Davies, Edward
Davies, J.
Davies, J. M.
Davies, John
Davies, J. T.
Davidson, G.
Davis, G. P.
Davis, G. W.
Davis, H. L.
Davis, J.
Davis, P.
Davis, P. Stevenson, M.A.
Davis, S.
Dawson, James
Dawson, Major
Day, C. W. H.
Dean, William
Deane, —
Defries, Dr. J.
Degraves, W.
Dennison, C. B.
Denailly, G. P.
D'Estro, A.
Detmold, W.
Devlin, A.
Dicker, C.
Dicker, T.
Dickinson, Rev. R. B.
Dickinson, J. W.
Dickson, Henry
Dickson, R. W.
Dickson, Thomas
Dickson, Thomas
Dill, George
Dillon, P. E.
Dishey, W. J.
Disney, R.
Dixon, C.
Dixon, J.
Dixon, Rev. M.
Doane, J. A.
Dobbyn, Dr. W. A.
Dobson, F. Stanley
Dodgson, J. H.
Dodgson, J.
Doig, R.
Don, J. W.
Don, Rev. R.
Donaldson, C. A.
Donaldson, H. B.
Donohoo, J.
Dougharty, J. G.
Douglas, A.
Dourlin, Emile
Dowden, E. A.
Dowling, A.
Dowling, Capt.
Downman, R.
Down, J.
Down, R.
Drummond, J. B.
Drysdale, J.
Drysdale, T. A.
Dubrayn, —
Duigan, —

Dugdale, Capt., 17th Regiment L. H. V.
Duncan, A. G.
Duncan, Gilbert
Du can, G. O.
Dunley, J.
Dunstone, T. O.
Dunn, R. C.
Dunn, Robert
Dunning, J. F.
Dwyer, J.
Dyte, C.

EARLES, Chester
Eaton, John
Eaton, H. P.
Ecroyd, William Joseph
Edmonds, H.
Edwards, John, jun., M.P.
Edwards, William
Ehrmann, F.
Elder, Capt. Douglas
Ebberton, Harry C. A.
Elkerker, W. H.
Elliott, S.
Ellis, John
Elliott, E. B.
Ellis, George G.
Emling, Dr., M.P.
Emmerton, Harry
England, Rev. Henry
Ettershank, John
Eva, John
Evans, Gordon H. J.
Evans, Gowen
Evans, J. C.
Evans, R. B.
Eville, James
Ewing, Rev. R. K.

FAGAN, Thomas
Fairbairn, George
Fairchild, J.
Falconer, J. J.
Falk, Sala
Farie, Claud
Farrar, Alfred
Farrage, Dr.
Farrar, J. W.
Farrage, R.
Farrell, James, M.P.
Farrar, T. H.
Fawkner, J. P.
Fellows, Rev. Walter
Fellows, Thomas Howard
Fenner, G. O. R.
Fenwick, Councillor
Fergie, Henry P.
Fernell, S. S.
Ferres, John
Fetherston, Dr.
Fowler, Lieut. John
Field, Rev. Benjamin
Finlay, C. C.
Finlay, John
Finlay, W.
Finn, Hugh J.
Firebrace, E. B.
Firth, R. J.
Fischer, W. Carl
Fisher, Burtie
Fisher, John
Fiskin, Archibald
Fitch, Reuben A.

Fitts, John
Fitzgerald, N.
Fitzgerald, T. Naghten
FitzGibbon, E. G.
Finnerton, John
Fleetwood, Thomas P.
Fletcher, Dr. E.
Fletcher, James
Fletcher, Rev. Wm. Roby
Foott, N., M.P.
Ford, Alfred
Ford, F. T. West
Ford, Thomas
Ford, William
Forster, Charles
Forster, W.
Forster, Edwin
Forster, James
Fox, William
Francis, Charles
Francis, J. G.
Francis, J. P. E., R.A.
Franklyn, F. B.
Fraser, Alexander, M.L.C.
Fraser, Henry C.
Fraser, Rev. Duncan
Fraser, Rev. T. M'Kenzie
Fraser, Rev. William
Fraser, Simon
Freeman, Alfred
Fry, James K.
Fullarton, Captain R.
Fullerton, James
Fulton, Dr.

GAHAN, John F.
Galbraith, D. Stewart
Gardiner, Rev. John
Gardner, H. S.
Gardson, Edward
Garton, James
Galbraith, William
Garbutt, John
Garlick, Rev. T. B.
Garrard, William
Garratt, J. M.
Gatehouse, James
Gaunson, Bruce
Gaunson, David
Gaunt, W. H., P.M.
Geake, James Edward
Geiger, William E.
Geelong, Archdeacon of
Gemmell, Hugh M. C.
George, Hugh
George, Joseph
Georgeson, William
Gershel, L. Charles, Treas. Mickva Yisrael Congregn.
Gibb, Dr., Depy. Inspector-General of Hospitals
Gibbs, —
Gibbs, Richard
Gibbs, S. Mountford
Gibson, Arthur
Gibson, Dr.
Gibson, Gavin
Gibson, Robert
Gibson, Robert
Gilbert, W. B., Sec. to the Reception Commission
Gill, Edwin, J.P.
Gill, G. D.
Gill, James
Gill, Robert

The Royal Levee.

Gillber, Captain H., Royal V.V. Artillery
Gilber, William, Surgeon-Major V V.
Gilles, Edmund F.
Gilchrist, Archibald, M.A.
Girdler, Joseph R.
Gladstone,
Glassford, J. L.
Glassford, Matthew
Glancy, Major J.
Gloster Captain
Godber, Charles
Godfrey, Frederic Bacn
Godfrey, George
Godfrey, William
George, Richard
Goldberg, A.
Goldstein, M.
Gomm, Alfred
Goodall, F. H.
Goodbist, Richard
Gr aham John
Goosier, D. J. C.
Goodwin, J. K., Staff Asst. Surgeon
G ohl T. G
Gosem, Henry
Gordon, F.
Gossam, Rev. Alexander
Gossage, Alfred H.
Goulding, Richard
Gouldstone, James P.
Gover, H. B.
Gowan, John D.
Graham Arthur
Graham, Dr
Graham, Edward
G abam, James
Graham, Rev George
Grant, G. W H.
Grant, Thomas
Grave, Wm , Geo , junr.
Gray, Charles
Greaveboa k, Josh
Greene, Charles Chapman
Greene Molesworth R.
Gregory, George
Gregory, John Barrdem B.A., LL B.
Gregory, Robert K.
Greenlow, William
Greeves, Hon. A F.
Greeson, Robert Christmas
Gregory, Dr.
Gregory, Samuel
Grey, Br. D. De
Grey, Rev. George
Grico, John
Grice, John, junr.
Grice, Richard
Griffin, Joseph
Griffiths, C Cecil
Grimwood, Thomas S , junr.
Grape, William
Groundwater, Rev James
Grover, William Alfred
Gruchy, B G. De
Guilemau, Robert
Guerard, Eugene von
Guerdon, William A.
Guest, Dr, Johannes W., Knight Legion of Honour
Gurner, Henry F.

Guthrie J., Inspector-Genrl. of Customs
Gwynne, F. A

HADLEY, T. R.
Hadley, Thomas H.
Hadden, Frederick W.
Haig, Dr. William
Haig, Robert George
Hailes, G. H.
Haine, T.
Halfey, John
Hall, A Keale
Halford, Professor
Hall, H. K.
Hallenstein, Michaelis
Ham, C melius J.
Ham, Theophilus J.
Hamburg and Bremen, the Consul for
Hammill, William
Hamilton, Rev R.
Hamilton, T. F.
Hamilton, William
Hammond, Henry T.
Hammond, R. K.
Hammond, R. W.
Hampshire, Rev. John
Hanbury, O. L.
Hancock, Theodore
Hadfield, F. O , Lieut. Commanding Naval Training Ship
Handfield, Rev. H H. P.
Hanna, Patrick, M.P.
Harcourt, Rev. John
Harcourt,
Hardie, William F.
Hardy, Dr.
Hardy, Assistant Surgeon C. P V V Horse
Harley, Edward Sloane
Harper, Andrew
Harper, John
Harper, William
Harrington, F. W , 14th Regt.
Harris, R J
Harris, Henry
Harris, W. G
Harrison, Commander, R.N.
Harris n, Horace W.
Harrison, E. G
Harston, Alfred W.
Hart, Asher
Hart, Henri J.
Hart, Hyam E.
Hart, Isaac
Hart, Jacob S.
Hart, John, jun , of Adelaide
Hartlett, W.
Harris,
Haywood, Thomas C.
Hassell, J N.
Hayes, J. F.
Hayes, Patrick
Hayman L.
Hayter, H. H.
Hayward, Rev. B.
Hayward, Charles H.
Healey, T. E
Hearde, Charles J., M.A.
Hearn, Professor
Heath, Capt.
Heath, Dr., M.P.

Heathcote, Robert William
Hedkin, George
Hedrick, John
Henderson, John C.
Henderson, James
Henderson, Rev. R.
Henderson, Samuel
Henderson, Thomas Percy
Hendren, Henry A.
Henri pen, Edmund
Henry, J. S.
Henty, E.
Henty, Henry, M.P.
Henty, S G
Hepburn, Charles J.
Hepburn, Thomas Robert
Hepburn, William Robert
Here, John H
Hetherington, Rev. I.
Hewbtt, T.
Heyde, W., Von der
Hickinbotham, J.
Hickinbotham, William
Hickie, James R.
Hicks, Robert
Hickub, Robert
Higgs, John
Hichett, William
Higinbothams, Thomas
Hibbteth, J. A.
Hill, John Thompson
Hill, Rev. William
Hill, T. A.
Hill, T. P.
Hill, Williams
Hill, William R.
Hillier, T , Assist Surgeon V V R Ballarat Rifles
Hines, William
Hinchon, John
Hind on, William
Hingston, James
Hirst, Charles, jun
Hitchcock, G. M.
Hobson Francis
Hocknell, Isaac R.
Hodgkinson, Percy C
Hodgkinson, Clement
Hogg, Edward F.
Hobson, Richard
Holsworth, Joseph
Holland, Frederick
Hollis, Rev. Josiah
Holroyd, Edward Duvelins
Holt, Edward B.
Hood, Dr. J. W.
Hood, J. H.
Hooker, Henry
Hope, George
Hope, Hon. Dr. R. C.
Hopkins, —
Hopkins, E
Hopkins, John H. A.
Hopkins, Rev. Francis
House, G. H. Hengist
Howell, Charles C.
Hoskins, H. Huntly, Mayor of Sandhurst
House, Samuel
Hooten, H. L. Van den
Howard, Frederick W.
Howden, Charles
Hewitt, Edward
Howell, W. S.
Howorth, J.

Hudson, George
Hudbart Peter
Hughes, Charles James
Hughes, Professor
Hughes, Samuel
Hughes, William
Hull, — , son.
Hull, H. N.
Hull, William H.
Humffray, J. B.
Hunter, Rev. Robert
Hunter, W. H.
Hurley, Alfred W.
Hurley, T.
Husband, William H.
Hutchens, William
Hutchinson, —
Hutchinson, R.
Hutten, J. B.

I'K, Rev. Thomas E., B.A.
Idle, Dr. N.
Inglis, Thomas A. F.
Ingle, Rev. J W.
Ireland, Hon. Richard Davis
Irving, Professor
Irvine, W. F. D'Arcy
Isaarson, Statoville J.
Isaacs, George
Isaacs, W B
Issel, John Thomas

JACKSON, James, M.D.
Jackson, T. W.
Jaffray, William R.
James, Elwin M.
James, T. R.
James, Samuel
James, Rev. T.
James, Dr J B.
Janes, John
Jameson,
Jameson, John Arthur
Jeffray, B. J
Jenkins, George H.
Jenner, Hon C. J , M L.C.
Jennings, J. G., jun.
Jennings, , M.L.C., N.S.W.
Jennings, J H.
Jennings, Henry, jun.
Jennings, Henry
Jeremy, John
Johnson, Ambrose
Johnson, Philip
Johnson, Henry
Johnson, Richard
Johnson, Walter R.
Johnson, Lieut. S.N.R.
Johnston, J. C.
Johnston, Rev Kerr
Johnston, D H , Lieut. R.N R
Johnston, Charles
Johnston, Robert
Johnstone, John, B.A
Johnstone, Robert de Bruce, Mayor of Geelong
Jonsson, Dr. Hermann
Jones, T Trevor
Jones, Philip F.
Jones, William
Jones, William B.
Jones, C. F
Jones, Benfield C.
Jones, Francis

Joseph, Raphael J.
Joshua, J. M.
Juske, Paul
Juske, Alexander
Jowers, Harry St John
Judd, Thomas

KATZENSTEIN, Jos. H.
Katzenstein, Isaac
Kay, Rev. D.
Kaye, Samuel
Keep, Edward
Kelly, Rev. Samuel
Kelly, Rev W., S.J.
Kelson, Horatio
Kemp, Samuel V.
Kendall, Franklyn B.
Kennedy, Charles
Kepworthy, Charles J.
Kent, Edgar G.
Keogh, Edmond
Kerferd, G. B.
Kerr, Robert
Kerr, P.
Kernot, W. C., M.A.
Kesterson, William
Kidney, Thomas
Kidston, Michael
Kilburn, Douglas T.
King, W. F.
King, M. L. M.P.
King, John C.
King, D. M.
King, Essington
King, Oliver
King, Edward
King, John B.
King, Henry James
King, Ernest
King, W. C
King, John
Kininmont, D. S.
Kininmont, Rev. A. D.
Kingsland, G. T.
Kinsman. N.
Kirkland, John Drummond
Kitchen, Richard W.
Klenau F. C.
Knight, J. G.
Knight, James M.
Knipe, J. H.
Koppen, R.
Krause, Ferdinand M.
Kursteiner, A. F.

LABERTOUCHE, Geo. E.
Labertouche, P. P.
Laby, Thomas J.
Lacey, Henry W.
Lambert, J. C.
Lamble, Rev. James
Laing, James B.
Lancashire, Samuel
Lang, Gideon S.
Lang, William
Langtree, Charles W.
Langtree, Henry, M.A.
Langtree, John
Langtree, Octavius
Lange, F. C.
Langston, Augustus
Langdon, H. J.
Langwill, P.
Langham, Rev. Joseph
Langlands, John
Langlands, H. W.

Langton, Edward, M.P.
Lang, George
Lankide, Robert
Lansly, Walter
Lavitt, R. W.
Lawrence, Frederick
Latham, Geo. G. B., Consul
U. S. America
Lawster, George T. A.
Lawrance, William
Lawrance, James B.
Lawrance, James
Lawrence, O. V.
Lawrence, W.
Laws, Robert
Laws, Horace
Lawes, Henry
Lawson, John D.
Lazarus, Samuel
Lazarus, Solomon
Learmonth, A. J. L.
Lecky, James
Lee, David
Leetch, Connolly
Legge, W Vincent
Lefferan, Rev W. D.
Lempriere, T. H.
Lempriere, C. M. D'A.
Lempriere, William G.
Leon, S.
Leplastrier, L. H.
Lethbridge, George
Levey, Oliver
Levey, George Collins, M.P.
Levey, William
Leveson, E. Ashworth
Levi, Nathaniel
Levien, Ernest
Levy, Goodman
Levy, Henry
Levy, E. P.
Levy, A.
Levy, Joseph
Lewers, Alexander
Lewellin, Dr
Lewins, Dr
Lewis, Stephen
Lewis, Robert E.
Lewis, James
Lewis, Louis L
Lewis, Arthur B.
Lewis, William
Leblie, Josh.
Lillesfield, Dr. B. B., M.D.
Lilly, George W.
Limares, Councillor
Lind. Rev William A.
Lindsay, Dr. Robert C.
Lintott, Stephen
Liston, John
Litchfield, Edwin
Littlewood, H. T.
Livingston, Dr. A. C.
Lloyd, John C.
Lloyd, J. P.
Lobb, W. J.
Loch, John D.
Logan, Thomas G.
Login, Rev. William Spence
Longmire, Francis
Looker, William R.
Lord, John
Lord, Samuel P.
Lorimer, James

Louden, James
Loughnan, Henry
Lovy, A , M.P.
Love, Duncan
Lowe, Ralph
Lowe, J. F.
Lowe, Edwin
Low, Rev. James Standey
Lowry, H. W.
Lucas, Charles J.
Luckey, Joseph
Luman, A.
Lyall, William
Lyall, James
Lyall, Rev James
Lyell, George
Lyell, Andrew
Lysland, W.
Lysa, Rev. James
Lynch, William
Lynch, Alfred
Lynch, John Denison
Lynch, George
Lyons, D.
Lyons, S.
Lyster, W. Saurin

MACARTNEY, —
Macartney, George
Macartney, Rev. Hussey Burgh
MacCullagh, Rev. J. C.
Macdonald, A. C
Macdonald, Allan B., M.D.
Macdonald, Rev. A.
Macdonald, Rev. D., M.A.
Macdowell, Swanston M.
Macfarlan, David
Macfarlane, Captain, Volunteer Naval Brigade
Macfarlane, J. A.
Macfarlane, John Horton
Macgregor, John
Macgregor, John Murray
Mackenzie, Enos
Mackenzie, James
Mackenzie, John
Mackenzie, M. J.S.
Mackie, Alexander
Mackie, Rev. George
Mackinnon, A. M.
Mackinnon, Hamilton
Macintosh, A.
Mackmeikem, Hugh
Maclean. D. P., Assistant-Surgeon, Naval Brigade
Macnamara, John
Macnaughten, Alexander
Macpherson, John A.
Macquarie, George A.
Macredie,
Macvean, Rev A
Madden, J , B.A. and L. L. B.
Madden, John
Magill, Daniel Magennis
Mailer, Robert
Maine, Crawford
Mair, Lieut. Colonel
Malleom, A. G.
Manifold, —
Manifold, James William
Manifold, Peter
Manifold, Walter S.
Mann, Thomas, B.A.
Manton, Charles

Many, Bartholomew
Maplestone, Charles
Ma grie, G.
Marine, Ludovic
Mark J., M.M.C. Hotham
Marks, H.
Marks, Edward
Marks, Henry
Marryat, G. Selwyn
Marsh,
Marshall, John, M.A.
Martin, Charles R.
Martin, D.
Martin, Dr.
Martin, George
Martin, John
Martin, John
Martin, Major
Martin. Peter J.
Martin. Robert
Martin, S. R.
Martin, T. Jacques
Martindale, Joseph
Marwick John G.
Merwood, M.
Mason, James
Mason, Thomas, J.P.
Massina, Lieutenant
Masterton, D.
Mathews, Alderman
Mathews, Barnard
Mathews, Captain B. R.
Mathews, J. Y.
Mathews, T. B.
Matheson, Alexander
Mattoson, Anthony
Matson. J. M.
Mattingley, Moxtem E.
May, W.
Mayne, James
Meachan, A. D.
Medlicott, W. S.
Meek, John
Meek, Rev. John
Meeks, Henry
Meese, John
Meiklejohn, Rev. D.
Merrifield, George
Menster, T.
Metcalfe, W. H., Lieut. and Adjutant Prince of Wales Light Horse
Middlemiss, John
Mibbleton, T. M.
Mier, Barras
Millar, B. B.
Miller, William
Miller, Edward
Miller, Henry
Miller, James D.
Miller, Rev. John S.
Miller, B. Crawford
Miller, William H.
Miller, W. M
Miller, Alexander
Mills, John, 14th Regiment
Milne, George M.
Milton, John H.
Minnett, Capt. V. C, 14th Regiment
Mitchell, Alfred
Mitchell, M. A
Mitchell, Matthew
Moffat, David
Mohr, John

The Royal Levee. 57

Moir, Rev. Charles
Moir, Rev. J. S.
Moline, Charles
Moline, Lewis Prichard
Molloy, Dr. William T.
Maloney, Patrick, M.B.
Montefiore, A. L.
Montefiore, E. L.
Montgomery, Walter
Moody, Frederick Alfred
Moody, J. J.
Moody, J. O.
Moody, Major Lesley Alex., Vict. Volunteer Rifles
Moore, Alfred E. C.
Moore, Dr.
Moore, Edward
Moore, F. F.
Moore, James
Moore, J. H.
Moore, Rev. Henry
Moore, Rev. Isaac, S.J.
Moorhead, Captain
Moore, Henry
Morgan, R. C.
Morley, William
Morris, John
Morris, William Selwyn
Morrison, Alexander, A.M.
Morrison, Christopher
Morrison, George, M.A.
Morrison, James Galt
Morrow, Thomas
Moss, Rev. William
Mosely, Henry
Motherwell, Dr.
Mount, Charles Alfred
Mouritz, George A.
Mowbray, Councillor
Mowell, J. Yorke
Moxham, W. J.
Mueller, Dr. F., F.R.S.
Muir, William P.
Mulcahey, P.
Mullaly, John
Munday, John
Munro, Donald
Munro, G. G.
Murchison, John
Muriet, J.
Murphy, Edward
Murphy, H. M.
Murphy, Hugh
Murphy, James
Murphy, Washington, M.D.
Murray, Andrew
Murray, Andrew
Murray, Dr. James P.
Murray, Hugh
Murray, John Gordon
Murray, Reginald A. F.
Murray, William G.
Myring, Joseph, Mayor of Castlemaine
M'Arthur, Peter
M'Bain, James, M.P.
M'Bride, Peter
M'Carthy, Dr.
M'Caw, Matthew
M'Cay, Rev. A. R. Boyd
M'Coan-, Francis
M'Comas, John Wesley
M'Comas, Richard N.
M'Combie, A. G.
M'Coy, F. H.

M'Coy, Professor
M'Coy, Robert Oliver, M.A.
M'Crae, Capt., late of H.M. 84th Regiment
M'Crae, — Chief Medical Officer
M'Crae, G. Gordon
M'Crae, John, M.L.C.
M'Culloch,
M'Culloch, William
M'Donnell, Edward
M'Donnell, S. McC.
M'Donegell, D.
M'Ewan, William
M'Farland, Patrick
M'Farland, Thomas
M'Fehen, William
M'Gauran, Dr.
M'Gee, John
M'Gregor, R.
M'Gregor, Samuel
M'Gowan, Samuel W.
M'Guigan, Henry
M'Guire, R. P.
M'Hagg, Andrew
M'Hugh, Patrick Hugo, Admiralty Survey
M'Intyre, J., Mayor of Sandhurst
M'Kay, George
M'Kean, James
M'Kenzie, Rev. D., A.M.
M'Lachlan, Duncan, 90th Light Infantry
M'Lachlan, Ronald
M'Mahon, Councillor
M'Meekan, James
M'Millan, Thomas L.
M'Millan, William
M'Nicol, Daniel
M'Nicol, Rev. A.
M'Niven, James
M'Pherson, Councillor
M'Pherson, James P.
M'Pherson, Rev. P., A.M.

NAGLE, Garrett Flood
Naylor, W. H.
Napier, James
Napier, T.
Nasmyth, Captain, Royal Engineers
Neighbour, G. H.
Neild, Dr. J. E.
Neill, Robert
Nell, Fred. Augustus
Nettleton, C.
Newbery, J. Cosmo
Newell, Andrew
Nicholas, W.
Nicholls, George M.
Nicholson, Dr.
Nicholson, Durham
Nicholson, Germain
Nicholson, John, B.A.
Nicholson, Joseph
Nicolson, C. H.
Nicolson, D.
Nicolson, Sir Arthur, Bart.
Ninnan, John
Ninmo, William
Nish, Rev. J.
Noall, William
Noel, —
Noone, John

Norman, Commander W. H., V.N.
Normoyle, John J.
Norris, James Francis
Norris, Richard A.
Noyes, Arthur E.
Noyes, A. W., 14th Regt.
Nunn, E. J. B.

OBIERS, W. H.
Officer, C. M.
Oter, Charles
Ogset, —
Ogilby, J. Fitzroy
Ogilvy, David
Oldham, John
Onslow, Richard
Oppenheim, Adolphus
Ormond, Francis
Ormond, James
Orr, James
Orr, John, M.P.
Orr, William A.
Ostler, Joseph
Otway, John Hastings
Outtrim, Frederick
Owen, Henry F.
Oxenbould, F. W.
Oxley, Arthur W.
O'Brien, Charles W.
O'Brien, Patrick
O'Brien, Thomas
O'Connor, D. F.
O'Connor, J. H., M.P.
O'Grady Thomas
O'Halloran, E.
O'Hea, George
O'Neill, Henry
O'Neill, Richard
O'Sullivan, S.

PACKER, Samuel
Paling, R. J.
Palmer, —
Palmer, Henry
Parmer, Henry P.
Panton, J. A.
Park, James
Parker, Arthur
Parker, Hugh
Parker, T. S.
Parnall, Captain, Volunteer Engineers
Pascoe, Charles E.
Pasco, —, R.N.
Pass, John de
Patterson, Dr.
Patterson, Harvey
Patterson, James
Patterson, L. O., Staff-Srgn.
Payne, M. T.
Payne, Thomas B.
Pearson, John W.
Pesse, J. C.
Peck, Hugh
Peel, Denis G.
Pegus, W. T.
Pein, C. William von
Pelletier, A.
Penell, Rev. John
Penfer, William
Penshanti, Rev. W. W.
Perkins, Horace
Perks, Rev. Charles T.
Petley, Charles P.

Permezel, Edward, B.A., L.B.
Perry, C. J.
Perry, George
Perry, G. W.
Perry, Rev. C. Stuart
Pettet, J. G.
Phead, J.
Phair, John
Phillip, Dr.
Phillips, James
Phillips, J. Walter
Phillips, Rev. A. P.
Phipps, Henry Francis
Pickerskill, Joseph
Picott, Henry Capel
Piley, George
Pinnock, Charles D. S.
Pinnock, J. Denham S.
Pinnock,
Pirani, F. J.
Prant, James Charles
Pitrace, Edward D.
Plaisted, Thomas
Platts, Rev. F. C.
Plummer, James K. B.
Plummer, W. , M P.
Plummer, W. A. Knight
Plunket, James
Plunkett, Charles T.
Plunkett, J. H.
Pohoray, Julius J.
Pollard, N. W.
Poolman, Frederick
Port, James
Porter, George Walfich
Porter, John A., the President of the Board of Land and Works
Potter, Rev. John
Potter, Rev. Robert
Potter, Rev. William
Powell, Charles R.
Power, Peter
Power, T. H.
Powning, W.
Poynter, —
Prangel, James T., C.E.
Prendergrast, Leonard
Price, Rev. C.
Price, Rev. C. S. Y.
Priestly, A.
Prince, Alfred H.
Prophet, —
Pryce, B. S.
Pryke, George
Puckle, Rev. Edward
Purcell, G. C. M.A.
Purdom, Captain
Purse, John
Purse, John

QUARTERMAN, —
Quinan, James
Quinlan, —
Quinn, James

RADCLIFFE, Lieut.-Col. G. T., Madras Cavalry
Rae, —, Assistant Surgeon Isaacho Mush Troop V. V. Light Horse
Ramsay, Rev A. M.
Randall, Charles E.
Randell, J. M.

Rankin, W. B., L.R.C.S.
Raven, Major J. C., Royal V. V. Artillery
Ray, Henry N.
Rayson, Harold
Read, Albert
Reed, Lieut.-Colonel, Local Staff
Reed, Frederic
Reed, Joseph
Rees, W. Carey, M.B.
Rees, W. Collins
Rees, David C.
Reeves, C. M.
Reeves, J. G., M.P.
Reeves, Abil
Reid, D. B., Assistant-Surgn. Geelong Artillery
Reid, C.
Reid, James
Reid, Stuart
Renard, Arthur
Renwick, John J.
Richardson, Albert
Richardson, John, M.P.
Richardson, J. Frederick
Riddell, Carre, M.P.
Rigby, J. V., M.D.
Riley, James
Rintel, Rev. Moses
Robb, William
Roberts, Charles Frederick
Roberts, P. Walker, M.T.C.
Roberts, William George
Robertson, Andrew
Robertson, Rev. Andrew
Robertson, A. S.
Robertson, A. W.
Robertson, George P.
Robertson, Dr. James
Robertson, James
Robertson, John
Robertson, J. Carle
Robertson, T. D. W.
Robertson, William
Robertson, William
Robertson, W.
Robertson, W., junr., B.A.
Robinson, Abraham White
Robinson, L.
Robinson, Dr.
Robinson, William
Robinson, W. V.
Robson, James L.
Robinson, J. D.
Roget, Henry Vidmore
Rolfe, —
Ronald R. B.
Rooktedge, Lieutenant, Volunteer Light Horse
Rose, John Octavius
Rosel, Lieutenant, Kyneton V.R.C.
Ross, Alex. M.
Ross, Alfred
Ross, Andrew
Ross, Charles G.
Ross, Clark S.
Ross, Hugh F.
Ross, Murray
Ross, Rev. William, M.A.
Rourke, Henry
Rowe, W. Wilson
Roy, Charles
Royce, James S. H.

Rudall, James T., F.R.C.S.
Russell, Edward
Russell, John
Russell, Phillip
Russell, Thomas
Russell, Thomas
Ryall, Edward B.
Ryder, Rupert

SABELBERG, Joseph
Salway, S.
Samuels, E. A.
Sanders, Councillor
Sanderson, H.
Sandiford, Edward
Sandilands, R. N.
Sandys, Rev. John Edwin
Sasse, Harry A.
Saunders, James H.
Saunders, William H.
Sawrey, Joseph
Sawell, James C.
Sayce, Joseph
Schmidt, Oscar
Schutt, —
Scott, Captain John
Scott, Capt. J. R.
Scott, James
Scott, James
Scott, R. D.
Scott, Robert
Scotchmer, Miller
Scurry, Frederick
Seabbon, Arthur
Seabbon, F. P.
Seabbon, Isaac C.
Seabbon, J. Sumner, B.A.
Seabbon, Rev. D., M.A.
Selby, G. W.
Selby, Prideaux
Selfe, James John
Sellar, Robert
Selwyn, Alfred R. C.
Serrell, W. H.
Sevren, H. A.
Sexton, John
Shackell, James
Shanklin, J. W.
Shaun, —
Shaw, Henry Steel
Shaw, James E.
Shaw, Joseph
Shaw, Joseph L.
Shaw, Walter Stephen
Sheahan, P. J.
Shee, E. O.
Sheffield, —
Shepard, Le-lie J.
Sherry, John D.
Sherwin, George
Sherwin, John
Shepherd, Richard, Capt. E.H.E.V. Artillery
Sheppard, Sherbourne
Shibbs, Andrew
Shier, Thomas
Shillinglaw, Malcolm L.
Short, William
Shuter, Charles
Shuttleworth, Fauconberg
Siddeley, William
Sievwright, Adolphus
Sievwright, Marcus
Simcoe, Howard
Simpson, G.

Simpson, Peter
Simpson, Rev. A.
Simpson, Robert
Sims, George John
Simson, James
Simson, John
Sinclair, P. S.
Singleton, J. W.
Singleton, Marshall, D.A.
Singleton, Rev. William
Singleton, Robert
Skeats, Charles
Skene, James W.
Slack, Edward
Slater, John
Sleicht, Edwin A.
Sloane, William
Smale, Arthur William
Smart, T. Stephen, Capt. Richmond Rifles
Smibert, James
Smith, Alexander John, Commander, R.N.
Smith, Brooke
Smith, Capt. Fred. Coape
Smith, Colonel, R.A.
Smith, Councillor A. K.
Smith, C. F. Digby
Smith, Francis Greg
Smith, Henry J.
Smith, James
Smith, James
Smith, John
Smith, John
Smith, John, jun.
Smith, John Clifford
Smith, J. T., M.P.
Smith, Louis L.
Smith, Patrick, M.A., M.B. and L.L.B.
Smith, Rev. Frederick
Smith, Richard
Smith, Robert
Smith, Robert
Smith, R. Murray
Smith, S.
Smith, Sydney W.
Smith, Thomas B.
Smith, William
Smith, William Jardine
Smithett, Albert L. C., B.A.
Smythe, Brough
Smyth, Charles A.
Smyth, F L., M.P.
Smyth, George
Snee, Captain
Snelling, William
Snowball, Joshua, M.P.
Snowden, —
Snowden, Edward G.
Somerville, Townsend
Souef, Albert Le
Southward, Joseph
Spence, John
Spensley, Howard
Spowers, James
Sprague, Edgar
Spurge, W. G.
Spyer, L. J.
Stampole, Adam
Stanley, Allen
Stansbridge, W. E.
Stanley, B. J., R.N.
Stark, Lieutenant J.
Stark, Malcolm Hannen

Stark, William E.
Stevenson, John
Steel, William H.
Steele, R. C., Captain
Steinfeld, E.
Stephen, J. Wilberforce
Stephen, Sydney James
Stephen, William Henry
Stephen, F. F.
Stephens, Henry Ernest
Stephens, Lieut. Frederick
Sterling, —
Sterne, Charles H.
Stevenson, George
Stevenson, William
Steward, Henry W.
Stewart, Duncan
Stewart, James
Stiles, Henry B. A.
Stilling, Edwin
Stilwell, J. S.
Stirling, William
Stokes, Capt W., R.V.V.A.
Story, Councillor
Story, Thomas
Strachan, John
Strachan, William
Strettle, Abraham
Stretcle, Stratford
Strickland, Robert, J.P.
Stone, Edward
Strubwicke, Capt. J. L., Brighton Artillery
Strutt, F. E.
Stuart, F.
Stubbs, Capt., Local Staff
Stubbs, Thomas, sen.
Stubbert, Rev. George
Sullivan, J F., M.P., Minister of Railways
Squimll, John
Summers, J.
Summerfield, J. W.
Summer, Theo. John
Sutcliffe, Richard
Sutherland, Charles
Sutherland, Joseph
Sutherland, Rev. Robert
Swallow, —
Swanson, H., 14th Regiment
Swindley, S. J.
Syder, Charles D.
Sykes, J. A.
Syme, David
Symonds, C. H.
Symonds, Edward S.
Symons, Rev. J. C.
Symnot, George

TALBOT, —
Tankard, John
Tatchell, T.
Taylor, Lloyd
Taylor, Enoch
Taylor, E. B.
Taylor, Frederick
Taylor, George H.
Taylor, G H.
Taylor, Herbert
Taylor, H.
Taylor, James D.
Taylor, J H.
Taylor, John
Taylor, Joseph

Taylor, Rev. Samuel
Teague, James P.
Tedlow, G.
Templar, H. F
Templeton, Capt.
Templeton, W.
Terry, Leonard
Testar, Thomas
Tetley, W. Anderson
Thistlethwaite, William
Thomas, D., J.P.
Thomas, Henry
Thomas, Rev. William
Thomas, Walter
Thomas, W. B.
Thompson, George, J.P.
Thompson, John Edward, Col. Com. Local Force
Thompson, J. H., M.A.
Thompson, Walter
Thompson, W. K.
Thomson, David E.
Thomson, John
Thomson, J.
Thomson, Rev. James
Thoneman, Emil
Thornton, Henry C.
Thorp, Samuel
Thwaites, Thomas Henry
Tibbing, James
Tipper, G. H.
Tobin, William A. B.
Todd, A. C.
Tolhurst, George E.
Toms, Revell, 14th Regt.
Topp, Charles A., B A.
Topp, Samuel
Tracy, Dr R. T.
Traill, G. Hamilton
Trangmar, James
Treacy, E. W.
Trenchard, Henry
Trenchard, John
Trenerry. E
Trevor, Lieut -Colonel, 14th Regiment
Trythall, Capt.
Tucker, Joseph J.
Tuckett, J. R.
Tucknell, Rev. James W.
Tulk,
Tulliett, Henry
Tully, J. H.
Turnbull, Robert
Turner, Caleb
Turner, Henry G.
Turner, John A.
Turner, Lieut. G. N., R V A.
Turner, Philip, Com.-Genl.
Turner, Thomas Edward
Turner, William
Twibill, —
Twentyman, R.

Tyler, J. Chatfield
Tyson, Charles
Tyson, Thomas
Tyson, G. R.

UPTON, William
Urquhart, George
Urquhart, W. S
Ussher, Rev P. R C.
Usher, Frederick W.

VAH, Edward L.
Valentine, George
Vaughan, O. R.
Veitch, Walter
Vieusseux, Lewis
Villiers, Lieut.
Vine, Henry
Virtue, E. P.

WADE, James
Wadeson, Herbert T.
Waldock, W. W.
Walford, F. Arthur
Walford, William F.
Walker, —
Walker, B. C.
Walker, Percy
Walker, Robert
Walker, Rev. R. S.
Walker, William Floggatt
Wall, Ross
Wall, William J.
Walls, John
Waller, R. R.
Wallace, Rev. William Campbell, M.A.
Walsh, Brevet-Captain A.
Walsh, Francis A.
Walsh, Frederick
Walstab, —
Walstab, George Arthur
Walstab, William
Walter, John C.
Ward, Martin
Wardill, Benjamin J.
Wardill, F. W.
Wartnaby, J., midshipman, R.N.
Warner, Ashton
Water, W. H.
Waterfield, W. P
Waters, W. H.
Watkin, Rev E. I.
Watkins, William M.P.
Watson, Edward
Watson, E. G.
Watson, G. E., B.A.
Watson, John
Watson, Rev. James
Watson, Rev. John H.
Watson, Robert
Watson, Robert Twells

Watt, John
Waxman, A.
Waynworth, Bryant
Webb, George H. K.
Webb, J. Heming
Webb, Rev. E. E., B A.
Webster, David
Webster, Joseph
Webster, William
Weigall, —
Weigall, Theyre
Weir, Daniel
Weire, A. L.
Weir, Arthur
Wells, Rev. W. P.
Were, W.
West, W. H.
Westby, E. Wright, LL.B.
Westley, Henry
Wetherall, W. A.
Wharton, George
Wheeler, D. Dickinson
Wheeler, J H.
White, F. Dennes
White, James
Whitford, R.
Whitehead, Edward
Whitelaw, G.
Whiteman, John
Whitney, John
Whitestone, Percy Bolfingham
Whittenbury, Edwyn C.
Whittendum, George
Whittingham, John
Whitton, Henry W.
Whitty, —
Whitworth, Robert P.
Wiblicombe, J.
Wicky, Middleton
Wild, Edward
Wilkes, Captain
Wilkins, Alfred
Wilkins, John F.R.C.S.
Wilkinson, Frederick
Wilkinson, Henry
Wilkinson, J. Bryce
Wilkinson, J. M.
Wilkinson, L. C.
Wilkinson, Rev. George
Wilkinson, Rev. Henry J.
Wilkinson, T., J.P.
Wilks, John
Willan, H.
Willan, H. H.
Williams, Hartley
Williams, H. A.
Williams, Hon. B., M L C.
Williams, H. James
Williams, W. H.
Williams, William
Williams, W. J.
Williamson, Dr. Walter

Williamson, E. W.
Willis, Charles
Willis, T.
Willoughby, Howard
Wilmoth, J.
Wilmoth, J. A.
Wilson, Dr.
Wilson, Dr. E. J.
Wilson, George
Wilson, James
Wilson, James
Wilson, J. L.
Wilson, Professor
Wilson, Ralph
Wilson, Rev. F R. M
Wilson, Samuel
Wilson, T. E., the Warden of the Senate of the University
Wilson, William, M.P.
Wilton, A L.
Wilton, J.
Winch, Frederick A.
Windsor, Arthur L.
Windle, G.
Wiseman, Arthur
Wisewould, James
Witchell, —
Wood, John
Wood, James W.
Wood, Rev. William
Wood, W. E.
Woodin, C. P.
Woods, A. T., jun
Woolcott, John S.
Wooley, Henry H.
Woolley, A.
Woolridge, Henry
Worthington, —
Wragge, Alderman
Wright, —
Wright, Edward Byam
Wright, Frederick
Wright, John
Wright, Thomas
Wright, Walter
Wright, W. H.
Wrixon, Henry
Wrixon, William
Wyburn, T. J.
Wyleigh, George T.

YOUNG, George
Young, George
Young, James
Young, John
Young, John Charles
Young, James
Young, Joseph
Young, R. M.

ZUMSTEIN, H.

The Presentation of Addresses.

The personal presentations being over, the ceremony of presenting the addresses commenced. None were read, but were simply presented by the official heads of the different public bodies, received by His Royal Highness, and handed by him to Lord Newry. It was intimated that a formal reply would be sent to each. Those subsequently obtained follow in order as received. These congratulations may be fairly taken as representing every public body in Victoria—religious, scientific, municipal, and friendly. An address, in which the Duke seemed to take special interest, was that from the Chinese. The Chinamen who presented it were in their full national costume, and with their head-gear done up in the most approved style. The first address presented was from the Bishop and Clergy of the Church of England. The Bishop of Melbourne, accompanied by his chaplain (Rev. S. L. Chase), the Deans of Melbourne, Geelong, and Castlemaine, and between forty and fifty of the clergy, were present. It was as follows:—

May it please your Royal Highness—We, the bishop and clergy of the United Church of England and Ireland in Victoria, beg most respectfully to offer you our cordial welcome.

The visit of your Royal Highness is a matter of rejoicing to the subjects of Her Most Gracious Majesty in every part of the British dominions which you honour with your presence; but to us the joy at your arrival is enhanced by its importance, as constituting an epoch in our colonial history. By it we are reminded that we are an integral part of the British Empire, and that, while we glory in our subjection to the sway of your Royal mother, it behoves us to reflect, as we trust we in some measure do, not only the energy, but also the domestic and social virtues, the loyalty, and the religion, of our fatherland.

Your Royal Highness will find the church in Victoria, in an external position, markedly contrasted with that which she occupies in England. Here she is not an established church; nor do we, in the circumstances of this country, desire for her any civil superiority over other religious communities. But God forbid we should ever be unmindful of what descent we come; and your Royal Highness will find us in all things maintaining a spiritual oneness with our mother church, to whose witness for the kingdom of God England in no small degree owes its pre-eminence.

As ministers of that church which acknowledges the Sovereign as her supreme governor on earth, we feel a peculiar gratification in testifying to your Royal Highness that there is no name so beloved and respected among all classes of men in our singularly independent-minded community as that of your Royal mother—a name which she has graciously permitted this country to bear.

Praying that the God and Father of our Lord Jesus Christ may bless your Royal Highness with all spiritual blessings, that He may carry you round the circuit of the world in safety, and in due time restore you to your home in peace, we beg to subscribe ourselves your Royal Highness's humble and devoted servants, &c.

The following was the reply of the Prince:—

My Lord Bishop and Gentlemen—I thank you for the interesting address which you have presented to me, and for the welcome with which you greet me.

I am heartily pleased to find that my arrival here has given occasion for the universal expression of love and loyalty for their Sovereign, of which every section of Her Majesty's subjects in Victoria has assured me.

It will indeed be a great satisfaction to the Queen to learn that Her faithful people of Victoria have lost nothing of those noble English feelings of true loyalty and of love for their old country; and that the Church of England, which for centuries has been the staunch upholder of the dignity of the Crown, is here changed only in external position; but that its faith, its doctrines, and its traditions remain the same, and its loyalty unshaken.

I return you my sincere thanks for the prayers that you have offered on my behalf.

(Signed) ALFRED.

The next address was from the General Assembly of the Presbyterian Church. It was presented by the moderator, the Rev. A. J. Campbell, who was accompanied by a number of ministers. The address was as follows:—

May it please your Royal Highness—We, the ministers and elders of the Presbyterian Church of Victoria, in General Assembly met, beg to congratulate your Royal Highness on your prosperous voyage from England, and to bid you a cordial welcome to Victoria.

We rejoice in the opportunity which is afforded us of uniting with our fellow-colonists in assuring your Royal

Highness of our loyalty to the British Crown, and our fervent desire for the continued maintenance of its supremacy.

In these sentiments of attachment to the throne we have been strengthened in a very eminent degree by our profound respect for the great qualities of your lamented father, the late Prince Consort, and our admiration of the personal virtues of Her Majesty the Queen, which have made the Royal palace the model of a Christian household.

We commend your Royal Highness to the protection of our Heavenly Father. May He guide you in your progress through these colonies, and in all your future career. May He enrich you with the blessing of His favour, and finally crown you with the joys of everlasting life, through Jesus Christ our Lord.

Signed in name and by authority of the General Assembly.   A. J. CAMPBELL, MODERATOR.

For reply to the above see Appendix, in which also will be found all those Addresses and Replies which did not arrive in time to appear in their regular order.

The following address from the president and wardens of the Melbourne Hebrew congregation was presented by the president, Mr. E. Cohen:—

May it please your Royal Highness—We, the president and wardens of the Melbourne Hebrew Congregation, for ourselves and the congregation whom we represent, dutifully offer to your Royal Highness, with heartfelt pleasure and devoted attachment, our congratulations on the happy event of your arrival in Victoria.

We hail with delight this opportunity of expressing to your Royal Highness our sincere and loyal attachment to our Most Gracious sovereign Lady Her Majesty the Queen, and to all the Royal Family.

We most earnestly pray that the future career of your Royal Highness may be bright and unclouded, and that your Royal Highness may be long spared to witness the advancing glory and prosperity of the British Empire.

(Signed)

A. F. ORNSTEIN, MINISTER.   A. A. COHEN, WARDEN.
EDWARD COHEN, J.P., PRESIDENT.   ISAAC BARENT, "
BENJAMIN BENJAMIN, TREASURER.   ISAAC JACOBS, "
EPHRAIM L. ZOX, WARDEN.   HENRY LEVY, "
SAMUEL LAZARUS, "   ELIAS SAMUEL, "
W. HEYMANSON, "   A. P. PHILLIPS, SECRETARY.

The Prince replied in the following terms:—

Gentlemen—I have received with much pleasure the expression of your congratulations on my safe arrival, as well as the assurance of your loyal attachment to Her Majesty and to the Royal Family, and I am duly grateful for your kind wishes and prayers for the happiness and success of my future career.

The Mickva Yisrael East Melbourne Hebrew Congregation, presented, through their President, Mr. Henri J. Hart, the following address:—

May it please your Royal Highness—We, the president, treasurer, minister, and committee of the Mickva Yisrael East Melbourne Hebrew Congregation, approach your Royal Highness with sentiments of profound respect for yourself, and of devoted loyalty and attachment to your Royal mother, our Most August Sovereign Queen Victoria.

We cordially congratulate you on your safe arrival in the metropolis of the colony which is honoured with the name of our gracious Queen. As Jews, we desire to express our grateful sense of the toleration which we share in common with all Her Majesty's subjects—a toleration springing from that glorious spirit of charity which has ever been fostered by our noble Queen and her lamented Consort, Prince Albert the Good.

Sincerely praying that the God of Israel may watch over your Royal Highness in your wanderings on the mighty deep, and restore you in safety to your native land, we have the honour to be, &c.

(On behalf of the committee)

HENRI J. HART, PRESIDENT.
L. C. GERSCHEL, TREASURER.
M. RINTEL, SENIOR JEWISH MINISTER.

The following was the reply:—

Gentlemen—It gives me the most sincere pleasure to receive from you, as from every section of the community, the assurance of devoted loyalty to Her Majesty the Queen.

I am also glad to find that you justly appreciate the happiness of living in our free English country, where the wisdom of our constitution allows every one to serve God after his own manner.

Accept my thanks for your congratulations on my safe arrival, and also for the prayers on my behalf which you offer to the One God whom we all worship.

The Rev. J. S. Waugh, the chairman of the Melbourne district, accompanied by Revs. John Harcourt, W. P. Wells, J. Dare, J. Albiston, W. D. Lelan, J. Cope, the Hon. A. Fraser, M.L.C., &c., presented an address from the Wesleyan body, as follows:—

May it please your Royal Highness—We, the ministers, office bearers, and members of the Wesleyan Methodist Church in Victoria, beg to approach your Royal Highness on this auspicious occasion with assurances of unfeigned and hearty welcome.

We gladly avail ourselves of this opportunity to express our most affectionate and devoted allegiance to the person and Government of your Royal mother, Her Majesty Queen Victoria, and rejoice in the visit of your Royal Highness to this colony, as tending to strengthen the bond by which this part of the empire is connected with the British throne.

Devoutly thankful to the gracious Providence by which your Royal Highness has been preserved from the perils of the sea, and guarded in safety to these shores, we trust that the stay of your Royal Highness among us will be one of much happiness, and that it may be ever associated by your Royal Highness, as it will be by us, with the most pleasing recollections.

We humbly add our devout and earnest wishes that your Royal Highness may enjoy health and length of days, followed by that better life which shall never decline or die.

Earnestly commending your Royal Highness to the continual favour and guardianship of Almighty God, we are, in the name and on the behalf of the Wesleyan Methodist Church in Victoria, your Royal Highness's faithful and most obedient servants,

        JAMES S. WAUGH, Chairman of District.
        WILLIAM L. BINKS,   "
        WILLIAM HILL,   "

His Royal Highness replied:—

Gentlemen—Accept my thanks for your kind welcome.

My visit among you will ever be most gratifying to me, not only on account of the pleasure it gives me, but chiefly because it has given occasion to the people of these colonies to assure Her Majesty of their loyalty and allegiance to Her throne and person.

I thank you sincerely for your congratulations on my safe arrival on these shores, as well as for the prayers you offer on my behalf to Almighty God.

The address from the Congregational body was presented by the Rev. J. M'Michael, the chairman of the Congregational Union. It was as follows:—

May it please your Royal Highness—We, the ministers and delegates representing the Congregational Union and Home Mission of Victoria, in general council assembled, desire to approach your Royal Highness with feelings of loyal respect.

We humbly desire to express devout thanks to Almighty God for having in His kind providence brought your Royal Highness in safety to these shores.

We desire to assure your Royal Highness of our unabated attachment to the Royal Family of Great Britain, and specially to the person and throne of our Most Gracious Sovereign the Queen.

We pray that your Royal Highness may during the remainder of your voyage enjoy Divine protection, and be permitted to fill for many years the exalted position in which your Royal Highness, by Divine providence, has been placed.

        JOHN CLUNIE M'MICHAEL, Chairman.
        CHARLES STICKERSON YAHRAH PRICE } Secretaries.
        ALEXANDER GOSMAN

The reply was as follows :—

Gentlemen—In thanking you for the address you have presented to me, I desire to assure you that I justly appreciate the spirit of loyalty to Her Majesty and attachment to the Royal family which has dictated it.

I must also return you my sincere thanks for the prayers you offer up on my behalf for my future protection and guidance.

The following address was presented on behalf of the Primitive Methodists by the Rev. G. Grey :—

Sir—We, the ministers and lay representatives of the Primitive Methodist churches in Victoria, assembled in committee, humbly beg to approach your Royal Highness with assurances of welcome to this colony, and to acknowledge the great kindness of Her Majesty, also that of your Royal Highness in foregoing the endearments of home to visit so distant a part of the British Empire.

And we would further humbly beg to assure your Royal Highness of our loyal attachment to the British throne, and loving devotion to the person, and prayers for the health and happiness, of Her Most Gracious Majesty. We have the honour to be, &c.,

GEORGE GREY, President.
JOSEPH LANGHAM, Secretary.

The Prince gave a reply as follows :—

Gentlemen—The address you have presented to me demands my warm acknowledgments, because it breathes the spirit of loyalty to the Queen and attachment to Her family.

On my part, I beg you to accept my thanks for your congratulations, and for your earnest prayers for my present and future happiness.
ALFRED.

An address from the Acclimatisation Society, together with a handsomely-bound copy of the Society's Reports, was presented by the president, Dr. T. Black :—

May it please your Royal Highness—We, the members of the Acclimatisation Society of Victoria, do ourselves the distinguished honour of approaching your Royal Highness with sentiments of loyalty and attachment to Her Majesty's throne and person, and we humbly offer our most sincere congratulations on your safe arrival in this distant part of Her Majesty's empire.

We presume it is unnecessary to remind your Royal Highness of the deep interest your late illustrious and ever-to-be-lamented father, the Prince Consort, took in the cause of acclimatisation, and also his Royal Highness the Prince of Wales, as evidenced by his Royal Highness's acceptance of the presidency of a kindred institution in Great Britain.

We further do ourselves the honour of presenting to your Royal Highness the published reports of our society, and we do so with the hope that you will find that our past labours have not been in vain. We have the honour to be, &c. Signed on behalf of the Society,

THOMAS BLACK, President.

REPLY.

Gentlemen—I duly appreciate the sentiments of loyalty which your address contains.

You are correct in supposing that I share in the interest taken in the cause of Acclimatisation by other members of my family, and I have no doubt that the success of your efforts in this colony must confer many signal benefits upon its inhabitants.

I accept with pleasure the public record of your past proceedings, and I trust that your future course may be attended with results as satisfactory as those which appear to have crowned your past labours.

The Civil Service address was presented by Mr. E. P. S. Sturt. It was as follows :—

May it please your Royal Highness—We, the officers of Her Majesty's Civil Service in the colony of Victoria, desire to approach your Royal Highness with the warmest expressions of our loyalty and devotion to Her Majesty's throne and person. To welcome and congratulate you on your arrival in Victoria gives to us the truest pleasure, and we joyfully hail this the first occasion afforded to us of tendering to a member of the Royal family our hearty tribute of loyalty and affection. We earnestly hope that health and happiness may attend your path, that your Royal Highness will be favourably impressed by your sojourn amongst us, and that you will carry away none but agreeable remembrances of the country, and of her Majesty's faithful subjects by whom it is inhabited.

The following reply to the address presented to his Royal Highness the Duke of Edinburgh by the officers of Her Majesty's Civil Service in Victoria was subsequently received:—

Gentlemen—I received with sincere gratification the warm expressions contained in your address of loyalty and devotion to her Majesty's throne and person. Your welcome and congratulations on my arrival in Victoria afforded me much pleasure, and I can assure you that my sojourn here has been most agreeable to me, and that it will ever be remembered by me with great interest and satisfaction.

The address of the Royal Society, presented by Mr. R. Ellery, was as follows :—

May it please your Royal Highness,—The Royal Society of Victoria humbly begs to offer its most respectful and dutiful assurances of the gratification afforded it by the presence of your Royal Highness in this colony.

The Royal Society, honoured by the special approbation of Her Most Gracious Majesty, seeks, in the paths of science, literature, and art, to foster those studies of which your lamented Royal father was so energetic a supporter and beneficent a patron.

The profession adopted by your Royal Highness is so intimately interwoven with a particular and important branch of study, as to give earnest hope that beneath your fostering hand science may rapidly expand, and the knowledge and enterprise possessed by Great Britain be disseminated throughout the world.

The Royal Society refers with great satisfaction to the circumstance of its labours having been largely characterised by an attention to those branches of science which have lately had a principal place in the studies of naval officers, and it is proud to regard this as a prominent reason for requesting the especial consideration of your Royal Highness.

Recognising the presence of your Royal Highness in this young colony as a further proof of the sympathy Her Most Gracious Majesty evinces towards her loyal subjects in this portion of her dominions, the Royal Society of Victoria humbly trusts that the visit of your Royal Highness to Australia may be a means of drawing still closer those bonds which unite us to the old country, and that the union it is so desirable to promote among the cultivators of science, literature, and art, in different parts of the world, may be thereby strengthened and permanently established. On behalf of the Royal Society of Victoria.

R. L. J. ELLERY, PRESIDENT.   R. WILLAN, HON. TREASURER.
T. H. RAWLINGS, HON. SECRETARY.   J. E. NEILD, HON. LIBRARIAN.

The following address from the Freemasons was presented by Captain Standish, grand master E.C.; Mr. J. T. Smith, grand master I.C.; and Mr. T. Reed, grand master S.C.

May it please your Royal Highness,—We, the brethren of the Ancient Order of Freemasons in Victoria, under the constitutions of England, Ireland, and Scotland, beg to offer to your Royal Highness our most sincere congratulations and hearty welcome upon your safe arrival in this colony. We desire to express to your Royal Highness our unwavering allegiance to our beloved Sovereign, your august mother—herself the daughter of a mason, and our reverent esteem for one who has long filled, and we fervently hope may be long spared to fill, the throne of the British empire with so much honour to herself and happiness to her people. We pray that, under the blessing of the Great Architect of the Universe, your Royal Highness may return to our fatherland in peace and safety; and that when you look back upon the many visits you have made during your tour, the remembrance of that to the colony of Victoria will not be among the least pleasant.

(Signed on behalf of the brethren.)

FREDK. C. STANDISH, DISTRICT GRAND MASTER, E.C.
JOHN THOMAS SMITH, PROVINCIAL GRAND MASTER, I.C.
T. REED, PROVINCIAL GRAND MASTER, S.C.

His Royal Highness the Duke of Edinburgh forwarded the subjoined reply to the Freemasons of Victoria :—

Gentlemen—I thank you, and all the members of the Masonic Order in Victoria, for the part you have taken in the reception which I have met with in this colony. I know that the loyalty of Freemasons is in all countries conspicuous for its sincerity, and I have heard this day, with the greatest pleasure, the expressions of allegiance contained in your address, which show that the Freemasons of Victoria are second to none in their devotion to Her Majesty. I feel sure that I shall always look back to my visit to this colony with pleasant recollections, where your prayers to Him who ruleth all things, for my safe return home, will ever remain graven on my heart.

The Royal Levee.

From the Ancient Independent Order of Oddfellows, the following address was presented by the grand master, Mr. W. Stirling :—

May it please your Royal Highness—We, the undersigned grand officers of, and on behalf of the members of the Ancient Independent Order of Oddfellows in Victoria, beg to congratulate you on your safe arrival in Victoria.

We desire, as members of an Order representing largely the industrial population of Victoria, to assure your Royal Highness of our devotion and fidelity to the person, dignity, and Throne of Her Most Gracious Majesty.

We also unite in heartfelt gratitude and loyalty towards Her Majesty the Queen for this distinguished mark of favour, as for the innumerable other privileges we enjoy under Her Majesty's beneficent sway, and in personal attachment and devotion towards your Royal Highness, as to every member of the Royal Family.

We sincerely hope that the present visit of your Royal Highness will prove no less pleasant to yourself than it is flattering and gratifying to us.

WILLIAM STIRLING, Grand Master.
JNO. W. DICKINSON, Deputy Grand Master.
JOHN HEDRICK, Grand Treasurer.
A. J. COHEN, Grand Secretary.

The address of the Grand United Order of Oddfellows, as follows, was presented by the grand master, Mr. W. Riddell :—

May it please your Royal Highness—We, the undersigned, on behalf of the Grand United Order of Oddfellows in Victoria, beg to tender our sincere and cordial congratulations to your Royal Highness on your safe arrival in this colony.

We desire to assure your Royal Highness of our continued devotion and loyalty to the person and Throne of your august mother, our most gracious Queen ; and we trust your Royal Highness's visit to this part of Her Majesty's dominions may strengthen these feelings, and may also be a source of pleasurable recollection to yourself.

WILLIAM RIDDELL, Grand Master.
THOS. J. MILBURN, Deputy Grand Master.
RICHD. THORN, Grand Treasurer.
HORATIO F. WILSON, Grand Secretary.

REPLY.

Gentlemen—Many thanks for your cordial congratulations, and for the assurance of your continued devotion and loyalty to the Throne and person of Her Majesty.

I trust that my visit to this colony may help to strengthen those feelings within you, and bind you nearer to the mother-country. For my part, I shall never forget my visit to Victoria, and in after years it will be a great source of gratification to me to look back upon the time I have had the pleasure of passing among you.

The Manchester Unity of Oddfellows, through their grand master, Mr. Henry P. Fergie, presented the following address :—

May it please your Royal Highness—We, the chief officers of the Manchester Unity Independent Order of Oddfellows' Friendly Society in Victoria, approach your Royal Highness with feelings of profound respect, and greet you with our hearty congratulations upon your safe arrival, and at the same time express our continued devotion to our most gracious Sovereign, your august mother.

United for purposes of benevolence and mutual help in sickness and distress, excluding all political and religious controversy, the bulk of the members of our society are of the industrial class, in whose welfare your lamented parent the late Prince Consort took so warm an interest.

We number throughout the world about half a million of members, of whom about 11,000 are resident in this colony. And our institution, by inculcating principles of self-reliance, foresight, and self-control, has not only proved a great boon to those for whom it is specially designed, but also tends to establish that spirit of independence, as well as obedience to law and constituted authority, which surely leads to the happiness and greatness of a people.

Sincerely hoping that your visit will be not only agreeable to yourself but advantageous to the whole empire, as manifesting the interest which our beloved Sovereign takes in the distant parts of her dominion; and sincerely wish you a safe voyage to your native land, and that you may be blessed with a long and happy life.

HENRY P. FERGIE, GRAND MASTER.
JOSIAH COLLINGS, DEPUTY GRAND MASTER.
JACOB S. HART, CORRESPONDING SECRETARY.

The following reply to the address of the Manchester Unity of Oddfellows has been received from H.R.H. the Duke of Edinburgh:—

Gentlemen—I acknowledge with sincere thanks your hearty congratulations upon my arrival among you. The invariable expression of devotion to the Queen's person which has greeted me everywhere during my visit to this portion of the empire has been highly pleasing to me, and I will not fail to make Her Majesty acquainted with every occasion when this devoted loyalty has been manifested. I understand and highly value the objects and results of your organisation; and I feel assured that so long as you keep steadily in view the principles upon which the foundation of your great society is based, and pursue a course of action wholly consistent with those principles, you may justly pride yourselves upon rendering great service to your adopted country, and shedding much happiness around you upon your fellow-colonists. I thank you for your good wishes and for this address.

The following address was presented from the St. David's Society by its president, Mr. J. W. Randall:—

TRA MOB, TRA BRYTHON.

May it please your Royal Highness—We, the President and Committee of St. David's Society, Melbourne, animated by profound sentiments of attachment to the throne and person of your illustrious mother the Queen, do cordially unite with all classes of our fellow-colonists in giving to your Royal Highness a heartfelt welcome to this colony.

We tender to your Royal Highness our best wishes for your health and happiness, devoutly hoping that under Divine Providence, the fullest measure of these blessings will be secured to you, and that your Royal Highness may long continue to adorn the glorious British navy, whose annals will derive additional lustre from your connection therewith.

REPLY.

Gentlemen—Your loyal and hearty address of welcome to me could not fail to give me satisfaction, and I sincerely thank you for it.

The unanimity and frequency with which kind wishes for my welfare, and loyal sentiments to the throne, have been tendered to me, have naturally caused me much gratification, and I shall bear away with me a warm recollection of it all.

The Loyal Orange Institute of Victoria presented, through its president, Mr. John Phair, the following address:—

May it please your Royal Highness—We, Her Majesty's dutiful and loyal subjects, the officers and members of the Loyal Orange Institution of Victoria, desire to approach your Royal Highness with feelings of devotion and loyalty to Her Most Gracious Majesty the Queen and the illustrious House of Brunswick.

We take the liberty of assuring your Royal Highness that the members of the Loyal Orange Institution—comprising, as they do, the Protestant nationalities of Europe resident within the colony hail your advent to these shores as the harbinger of that great and glorious future which awaits this distant appanage of the British Crown.

We feel it to be the highest honour of which freemen can boast, that we are the favoured subjects of a monarch whose social virtues and benign sway are alike the theme of journalist and historian, and we fervently hope that Divine Providence may long watch over and guard the best and noblest of Britain's sovereigns.

We sincerely hope that this visit may be as pleasing to your Royal Highness as it is gratifying to us, and we pray that, under the mercies of Divine Providence, your Royal Highness may enjoy a long life of health and happiness.

(Signed on behalf of the Loyal Orange Institution of Victoria.)

JOHN PHAIR, GRAND MASTER.
WILLIAM CLARKE, DEPUTY GRAND MASTER.
WILLIAM HINDS, GRAND TREASURER.
R. WALKER, GRAND SECRETARY.

The Royal Levee.

REPLY.

Gentlemen—The expression of your loyalty to the Crown, and the cordial welcome which you have tendered to me, demand my warm acknowledgments. In returning to you my hearty thanks for your address, I must not be misunderstood as implying the belief that any one religious denomination is exclusively or pre-eminently imbued with that spirit of loyalty to Her Majesty which I recognise with equal confidence and gratification in all Her Majesty's subjects in this part of the empire.

The Town Council of Geelong presented the following address through the Mayor, Mr. R. De Bruce Johnstone :—

May it please your Royal Highness—We, the Mayor, aldermen, councillors, and burgesses of the town of Geelong, desire, in approaching your Royal Highness on this most auspicious occasion, to offer you our sincere congratulations, and a hearty welcome to the colony of Victoria.

We beg to express our devotion, loyalty, and affection to the throne and person of our most gracious Sovereign, and our undeigned respect for your Royal Highness, and our high appreciation of the honour you have conferred upon the colony by your visit.

Trusting that this expression of our sentiments may not be unacceptable to your Royal Highness, we respectfully offer you our warmest wishes that your future progress may be crowned with every blessing.

ROBERT DE BRUCE JOHNSTONE, Mayor.
WILLIAM WEIRE, Town Clerk.

Reply of H.R.H. the Duke of Edinburgh to the two addresses presented to him (one in Melbourne on his arrival in Victoria, and on his visit to Geelong) by the Corporation of Geelong :—

Gentlemen—I thank you most sincerely for your congratulations, and for the hearty welcome which you gave me in Geelong. It will be my pleasing duty to inform Her Majesty of the universal sentiment of loyalty and affection for the throne which I have found wherever I have been in Victoria. The reception which has been accorded to me will be as gratifying to Her Majesty as it has been to me.

The following address was presented from the Chinese residents in Victoria, by Mr. Ho A Moi, who was accompanied by two of his countrymen :—

To the Illustrious Son of the Mighty Sovereign beneath whose Beneficent Rule it is Our Glory and Happiness to Abide, the Chinese Inhabitants of Victoria humbly bring their Tribute of Homage and Affection.

We pray your Royal Highness to lay at the feet of our gracious Queen the assurance that none of Her Majesty's subjects are truer in their loyalty, or warmer in their attachment, than the people of China abiding in this colony.

It is our high privilege to dwell amidst a great and honourable nation, and to enjoy the protection of just and benevolent laws. It is our joyful duty to live in obedience to these laws, to promote the blessings of order and tranquillity, and to follow the paths of peaceful industry.

We hail with delight this happy opportunity of addressing a prince so honoured and beloved.

We humbly beg that your Royal Highness will convey our sentiments of the deepest respect and devotion to the great Queen whose power excels that of all earthly monarchs, whose virtues illuminate the world, and whose happiness consists in the happiness of her people—that Queen whose subjects it is our pride to be accounted.

Address presented by the Victorian Society of Free Gardeners :—

May it please your Royal Highness—We, the members of the Victorian Society of Free Gardeners, beg most respectfully to offer to your Royal Highness our most cordial welcome to the shores of this colony. Enjoying as we do, under the benign and auspicious rule of our most gracious and revered Queen, the blessings which such a rule alone can confer, we esteem it a happiness as it is an honour to have the opportunity of expressing to one of Her Majesty's sons the gratitude, loyalty, and love we entertain for Her Majesty and her Royal House. We trust that the sojourn of your Royal Highness in Victoria and the other Australian colonies, will amongst other pleasures afford your Royal Highness the assurance that distance from the seat of empire does in no way diminish that ardent and honourable affection which the rare virtues of our Sovereign and of her children have engendered in the heart of every true Briton. We, therefore, as Free Gardeners, deriving our charter from the City of Edinburgh, desire to express to your Royal Highness the pleasure it affords us in being allowed to welcome your Royal Highness to this our adopted country; and that your Royal Highness may, during the remainder of your voyage, be attended by every blessing, is our most fervent wish.

GEORGE WATSON, Right Worshipful Master.
ISAAC ROBERTSON, Secretary.

The Victorian Free Gardeners received the following reply :—

Gentlemen—Many thanks for the cordiality of your reception, and for your congratulations on my arrival in Victoria. It is quite evident to me that distance does in no way whatever diminish your loyalty to Her Majesty and throne, and I shall not fail, on my return home to the mother-country, to convey to Her Majesty the assurance of your love and devotion to herself and Royal Family. It gives me the greatest pleasure to have had this opportunity of visiting you, and my only regret is that my stay amongst you is so limited. May every success attend you, and may all your endeavours meet with that reward which they so well deserve.

Address from the Ancient Order of Foresters :—

May it please your Royal Highness—We, the Executive Officers of the United Melbourne District of the Ancient Order of Foresters Friendly Society in Victoria, desire to approach your Royal Highness with every feeling of respect.

On behalf of the members of our ancient institution, comprising a large portion of the population of this colony, we beg to tender our sincere congratulations to your Royal Highness on your safe arrival in this our adopted country.

We desire to assure your Royal Highness of the feelings of loyalty and attachment entertained by the members of this Order for the person of our beloved Queen, the members of her august Family, and the Throne of that vast empire which Her Majesty has adorned for so many years, to the great advantage of her people and the world at large.

It is our earnest hope that the same wise Providence who has guided the path of your Royal Highness to this distant part of Her Majesty's dominions, may so watch over your future movements that you may return in safety to our dear and native land; and that your Royal Highness will be pleased to assure our gracious Sovereign of the hope entertained by the Members of this Order that Her Majesty's valuable life may be spared to her people for many years, to continue those good works which have endeared her gracious name to the hearts of Her Majesty's subjects all over the world.

CUNNINGHAM M'FARLANE, District Chief Ranger.
HYAM HART, District Sub-Chief Ranger.
FRANCIS LEPLASTRIER, District Secretary.
JOHN WHITEMAN, M.L.A., District Treasurer.
JAMES MADDOCKS, District Beadle.

REPLY.

Gentlemen—I beg to thank you for the hearty welcome you have given me to this country, and for the feelings of loyalty and attachment you have expressed towards Her Majesty and the other members of the Royal Family, and I shall not fail on my return home to England to convey to Her Majesty the assurances of your devotion to herself and Throne.

I came to this country with feelings of the greatest gratification, and shall leave it with deep regret, for since I first landed in Australia my visit has been one of continued pleasure and unabated interest.

The address from the Independent Order of Rechabites was presented by Bro. W. Bell, D.C.R., accompanied by Bro. Henry Meeks, acting D.D.R.; Bro. Joseph Goode, D.S.; Bro. William Robertson, D.T.; Bro. Robert Lormer, P.D.C.R.; and Bro. the Rev. H. Greenwood, P.C.R. (Steiglitz.)

May it please your Royal Highness—The undersigned office-bearers of the Victoria District Independent Order of Rechabites, on behalf of the District Council and the fifty-six branch societies connected with the order in this colony, desire in the name of the united brotherhood to congratulate your Royal Highness on your safe arrival in this golden colony, bearing the name of your illustrious and royal parent, Her Most Gracious Majesty the Queen.

We desire to express our sense of the high honour conferred upon the inhabitants of this portion of Her Majesty's dominions by the visit of your Royal Highness, which we hope may be as productive of gratification to yourself as it is of pride and pleasure to us, affording us, as it does, an opportunity of demonstrating, by our hearty and cordial reception of your Royal Highness, our devoted attachment to the throne and person of our beloved Sovereign, and to the members of the Royal Family.

That your Royal Highness may long be spared to cast additional lustre upon your royal parentage, and to uphold the honour of the noble profession which you have embraced, is the earnest prayer of your Royal Highness's devoted servants.

WILLIAM BELL, D.C.R.
DAVID BUCHAN, D.D.R.
JOSEPH GOODE, D.S.
WILLIAM ROBERTSON, D.T.

REPLY.

Gentlemen—I receive this address of the United Branches of the Order of Rechabites of Victoria with pleasure. My visit to the Australian Colonies has been a most interesting and gratifying one, and I have been glad to see that the progress of the colonists has been marked throughout by the establishment of many societies, of which yours forms one, and of others, all of which similar to yours cannot fail to benefit the community when conducted on the sound basis and principles which appear to me to govern them. Your welcome and reception have been most cordial and hearty, and from them I can well understand the sincerity of your loyal profession.

Address of the Baptist Association, presented to His Royal Highness the Duke of Edinburgh, &c., by the Revs. I. New (Chairman), W. Poole (Secretary), G. G. Lewis, D. Rees, and J. Moss:—

May it please your Royal Highness—We, the Executive Committee of the Baptist Association of Victoria, desire, on the part of those we represent, to congratulate your Royal Highness on your safe arrival in this colony, and in common with our fellow-colonists to tender your Royal Highness a most hearty welcome.

We embrace this opportunity of testifying the loyalty of the Baptists of Victoria to the British Throne, and their devoted attachment to your revered mother, Her Most Gracious Majesty the Queen, and to all the members of the Royal Family.

We rejoice in this visit of your Royal Highness, as we think it will strengthen and increase the many ties now binding this colony to the home land, and cement more closely the happy union at present existing.

We devoutly acknowledge the goodness of God, through whose protection your Royal Highness has hitherto been preserved, and would ever commend your Royal Highness to the benignity and guidance of the Almighty Ruler of all, the King of Kings and Lord of Lords.

(Signed on behalf of the Baptist Association.)

ISAAC NEW, CHAIRMAN.
W. POOLE, SECRETARY.

REPLY.

Gentlemen—I thank you very sincerely for your congratulations upon my safe arrival in Victoria, and for the hearty welcome you give me.

I shall have much pleasure in conveying to the Queen the assurances of your loyalty to the Throne and attachment to Her Majesty's person. It will ever be gratifying to me to know that my visit to Australia has been regarded as having strengthened the ties which unite England to her colonies. I am grateful to you for your prayers for my safety and prosperity.

Address presented by the Council of the Borough of Amherst:—

May it please your Royal Highness—We, the Mayor, councillors, and burgesses of the Borough of Amherst, feeling as we do the warmest attachment and loyalty to your Royal Highness's august mother—our most beloved Queen—desire to approach your Royal Highness with sentiments of affectionate regard, and to congratulate you upon your safe arrival in the prosperous colony which takes its name from Her Most Gracious Majesty. Trusting that your Royal Highness may long be spared by the Almighty disposer of events to enjoy the blessings of peace, and by your own bright example to influence the happiness of others, we have, with profound respect, the honour to subscribe ourselves your Royal Highness's most humble and obedient servants,

H. HUNTLY HOSKINS, MAYOR.
ISAIAH ANDREWS, TOWN CLERK.

REPLY.

Gentlemen—I thank you most sincerely for your address of welcome, presented to me on my arrival in this most influential and prosperous colony. I shall never cease to remember, with pride and gratification, your repeated expressions of loyal devotion to the Queen, which I shall have the greatest pleasure in repeating to Her Majesty on my return home. I thank you for your prayers and kind wishes for my future happiness in life.

Address from the Borough of Ararat:—

The Burgesses of Ararat, being desirous of expressing the feelings of loyalty and affection which they entertain towards the British Throne, would take the opportunity presented by the visit of your Royal Highness to this colony, to assure you of the unalterable attachment which they bear towards Her Majesty the Queen; and at the same time to express their sense of the pleasure which they experience on the occasion of your visit amongst them, and the hope that such an occurrence will yet further strengthen that feeling of respect and love for the Royal Family of England which has at all times distinguished Her Majesty's subjects in this colony. On behalf of the Burgesses of Ararat,

G. W. H. GRANO, Mayor of the Borough.
JAMES CAMPBELL, Town Clerk.

REPLY.

Gentlemen—The expression of your loyalty and devotion to Her Majesty's Throne and person has been received by me with sincere gratification, and I thank you heartily for your welcome to this prosperous colony.

Address from the Shire of Bet-Bet, presented by Councillors John Beynon, P. M'Bride, and the Secretary:—

We, the President and Councillors of the Shire of Bet-Bet desire to approach your Royal Highness with the assurance of our devoted attachment and loyalty to your august mother, our Most Gracious Sovereign Lady the Queen, and to all the Royal Family.

We beg to offer to your Royal Highness a fervent welcome to the land of our adoption, and tender our sincere congratulations on your arrival.

We earnestly hope and believe that during your Royal Highness's visit you will receive the most satisfactory evidence that the people of this colony yield to none in their loyalty to your Royal House—are proud to feel themselves subjects of Her Majesty, and deeply gratified at being able to salute you personally as our Prince.

We pray your Royal Highness to be assured that our joy on your arrival is enhanced by the knowledge that we are welcoming one whose princely virtues have even thus early added to the lustre of the Throne, and who has secured for himself an affectionate interest in the heart of every Briton.

We sincerely trust the voyage of your Royal Highness may prove in every way gratifying, and that under the care of an all-wise Providence you may return in safety to dear old England, there to adorn the high station to which you have been called—to win renown in the noble profession you have chosen—to become a solace and support to our ever beloved and widowed Queen, and a source of legitimate pride to all her subjects throughout the wide expanse of the British Empire.

We beg most respectfully to tender to your Royal Highness our devoted homage.

JOHN BEYNON, Councillor, for the President.
GEORGE COOK, Secretary of the Shire.

REPLY.

Gentlemen—I beg to assure you that I receive with much gratification your expressions of congratulation and attachment, and thank you sincerely for the warm welcome you have given me in this land of your adoption, where it affords me much pleasure to meet you, and to see for myself such great results of British energy and enterprise. I thank you for your sentiments of loyalty and devotion, which I will not fail to convey to Her Majesty on my return.

The following address, from the Shire Council of Maldon, was presented by Mr. Councillor Lawrence, to his Royal Highness the Duke of Edinburgh:—

May it please your Royal Highness—We, the President and members of the Shire Council of Maldon, beg to congratulate your Royal Highness upon your safe arrival to these distant shores, and to welcome your Royal Highness to one of principal goldfields in this Colony. We beg to assure your Royal Highness of our loyalty and attachment to her Most Gracious Majesty the Queen, and to all the members of the Royal Family.

We hope that the voyage your Royal Highness has undertaken will continue to be attended with safety and

The Royal Levee.

enjoyment, and that your sojourn in this colony will form not the least pleasing feature of your Royal Highness's reminiscence of foreign travel.

We desire to express our regret that circumstances should preclude Your Royal Highness from distinguishing our own district with the honour of your presence, which alone prevents its inhabitants from personally evincing their loyalty by giving Your Royal Highness a right hearty reception in their own Town and Shire.

On behalf of the Council of Maldon,
WILLIAM TAYLOR MILLER, PRESIDENT.
JOHN BRIDEMAN JONES, SECRETARY.

REPLY.

SIR—I beg to acknowledge and thank you for your address on behalf of the Shire Council of Maldon, expressing your loyalty and attachment to the Queen and members of the Royal Family, and for the congratulations it contains to myself personally. I regret that my brief stay in these colonies will not permit me to visit Maldon, but I desire to say through you that it has afforded me very much pleasure to receive this address from the Shire Council.

BOROUGH OF HOTHAM.

May it please your Royal Highness—We the Mayor, Councillors, and Burgesses of the Borough of Hotham, in the colony of Victoria, desire to express to your Royal Highness the pleasure we feel in being honoured with a visit from your Royal Highness to this colony, and to assure you of our attachment to Her Majesty's throne and family, and pray that your Royal Highness may enjoy a long life of health and happiness.

Signed on behalf of the Mayor, Councillors, and Burgesses of the Borough of Hotham, this 14th day of October, 1867.
JOHN BARWISE, MAYOR.
GEORGE EVANS, TOWN CLERK.

REPLY.

Gentlemen—It is very gratifying to me to receive so many proofs of the pleasure with which you have welcomed me to this colony, and to hear the assurances of your loyalty to Her Majesty, and of your attachment to the Royal Family, and I beg you to accept my thanks for your prayers for my future life and happiness.

BOROUGH OF ST. KILDA.

May it please your Royal Highness—We the Mayor, Councillors, and Burgesses of the Borough of St. Kilda desire to testify our joyful appreciation of the kind consideration of our gracious Queen, your august Mother, towards the inhabitants of this remote portion of her empire, by deputing you, her Royal Son, to undertake the long and perilous voyage to our shores.

We gratefully thank your Royal Highness for this auspicious visit, and confidently hope that your Royal Highness will be able to certify to her Majesty that here at the antipodes the hearts of her Majesty's subjects beat with as great enthusiasm to the throne and affection to her Majesty's person, as is felt by those whose privilege it is to have the Queen constantly near them.

Although many of the inhabitants of these Colonies have never seen Old England, yet they have never heard her spoken of except with affection and love; and this visit of one of England's Royal sons will be fondly remembered by us and by our children to the remotest generations.

In the name of the inhabitants of this borough we cordially and sincerely give your Royal Highness a most hearty welcome.

(Signed on behalf of the Council.)
JAMES PATERSON, MAYOR.
E. BRADSHAW, TOWN CLERK.

REPLY.

Gentlemen—My visit to your Borough, although short, was interesting to me. I thank you heartily for the expression conveyed to me, in your address, of your loyalty to the Queen and for your cordial welcome to myself.

BOROUGH OF BEECHWORTH.

We, the Mayor and Councillors of the Borough of Beechworth, in the Ovens District of the Colony of Victoria, beg most respectfully to approach your Royal Highness with deep feelings of loyalty and duty to your august mother, her Most Gracious Majesty Queen Victoria, and of respect and esteem towards yourself; and to offer our heartfelt congratulations on your safe arrival in this portion of Her Majesty's dominions.

We hope that during your stay amongst us your Royal Highness will become sufficiently acquainted with Her Majesty's subjects in this colony to be perfectly satisfied that they have displayed that talent, energy, and perseverance, in developing the resources of this new country, for which the British name is now so famous.

We sincerely trust that your Royal Highness will be so pleased with your visit to this remote dependency of the empire that you will be induced to look with leniency on our shortcomings, with satisfaction on our endeavours to progress (especially in those qualities which make a people great), and with pride and gratification on our unbounded loyalty and devotion to the throne of Great Britain; and that you may be enabled on your return to your mother country to express the pleasure you derived from your visit to and sojourn in Victoria. Should your Royal Highness deign to visit this distant but most important and interesting goldfields portion of the colony, we feel convinced that not only would your welcome by the burgesses of this borough and the inhabitants of the district generally be enthusiastic, heartfelt, and sincere, but you yourself would be highly gratified by witnessing the many peculiar and varied resources of the locality, as well as the beauty and picturesqueness of its unrivalled scenery. Wishing you every happiness that this world can give, we fervently pray that Almighty God may of His infinite mercy ever guard, guide, and protect you, and so control events that our beloved Queen may long continue to reign over these realms, and in the hearts and affections of her loyal and devoted subjects; and beg to subscribe ourselves your Royal Highness's most obedient servants,

JOHN JAMES BERESFORD BOWMAN, Mayor.   J. D. FISHER, Councillor.
HENRY LOUIS CHAS. RAECKE, Councillor.   GEORGE GRAHAM „
WILLIAM WITT   „   DONALD FIDDES „
EDWARD STEVENSON RUSSOM   „   JAMES COLLIER „
HENRY CLEMENGER   „   W. H. C. DARVALL, Town Clerk.

REPLY.

Gentlemen—I am deeply touched by the cordiality and warmth of feeling with which I have been welcomed by you. For your address I thank you, and heartily appreciate the sentiments of attachment to your Sovereign and her empire which you have expressed. I shall take every opportunity of making myself acquainted with the growing greatness of this colony, but I fear that the limited time at my disposal, and the numerous claims upon it will not admit of a journey so extended as the one to your town.

SHIRE OF TULLAROOP.

May it please your Royal Highness—We, the President and Councillors of the Shire of Tullaroop, welcome your Royal Highness to the colony of Victoria. We beg to assure your Royal Highness of our loyal and dutiful attachment to Her Most Gracious Majesty the Queen and all the members of the Royal Family. We sincerely hope the voyage your Royal Highness has undertaken will continue to be attended with safety and enjoyment, and that your sojourn in the Australias will be as agreeable and pleasant to yourself as it is the earnest desire of all classes of the community it should be.

SCRAFTON S. BROWN, President of the Shire of Tullaroop.
FREDERICK T. OUTTRIM, Secretary.

REPLY.

Gentlemen—It will be my pleasant duty to convey to the Queen your expression of dutiful attachment to Her Majesty and to the members of the Royal Family. I thank you for your good wishes for the success of my voyage, and for the enjoyment of my visit to Victoria.

BOROUGH OF EAST COLLINGWOOD.

May it please your Royal Highness—We, the Mayor, Councillors, and Burgesses of East Collingwood, beg to congratulate your Royal Highness upon your safe arrival in Australia, and to offer you a most cordial welcome to our adopted country.

We thank you for giving us this opportunity of expressing to your Royal Highness our heartfelt loyalty to the throne, and our devoted attachment to the person and family of Her Most Gracious Majesty your royal mother, Queen Victoria, and our deep and abiding reverence for the memory of your illustrious father.

We sincerely hope that your Royal Highness will, through a long, happy, and distinguished life, nobly emulate the example of your august parents, in goodness and in greatness pre-eminent; and that we, who now joyfully hail your advent amongst us, will, with our children, hereafter have pleasure and pride in the recollection of this auspicious occasion.

(Signed) SAUNDERS BAYNHAM, Mayor.   GEORGE DAVID LANGRIDGE, Councillor.
          JOSEPH PAUL BOWRING, Councillor. CHARLES ROBERT SWIFT   „
          BENJAMIN CLARK   „   JAMES H. TURNER   „
          G. GEORGE CRESPIN   „   GEO. H. VON BERG TURNBULL   „
          DANIEL ROSS HUNTER   „   GEORGE BENNETT, Town Clerk.

REPLY.

Gentlemen—Accept my thanks for your congratulations on my safe arrival in Australia, as well as for the cordial manner in which you have welcomed me here. It gives me great pleasure to receive these assurances of your loyalty and devoted attachment to Her Majesty, and of your reverence for the memory of my beloved father, whose noble example it will always be my earnest endeavour to follow. I thank you for the kind wishes for my future happiness, and I also trust that you all will, as I ever shall, look back upon my visit among you with sincere pleasure.

SHIRE OF BELFAST.

May it please your Royal Highness—We, the President and Members of the Council of the Belfast Shire, beg most respectfully to present our congratulations on your Royal Highness's arrival in Victoria, and avail ourselves of the present occasion to request that your Royal Highness will be pleased to convey to Her Most Gracious Majesty the Queen the expression of our most humble and devoted loyalty to her person and the empire at large.

SAMUEL BAIRD, President.
JAMES COX, Secretary.

REPLY.

Gentlemen—I thank you for your congratulations upon my arrival in Victoria. It will give me much pleasure to convey to Her Majesty the expressions of your loyalty to the Queen and the empire.

ADDRESS FROM THE SHIRE OF BEECHWORTH.

We, the President and Councillors of the Shire of Beechworth, beg leave, as the loyal and dutiful subjects of Her Most Gracious Majesty Queen Victoria, to offer our congratulations, and bid you a warm and hearty welcome on this your first visit to the colony of Victoria. We hope your Royal Highness will greatly enjoy your temporary sojourn amongst us, and may have many opportunities of witnessing that the prudence and energy of the people, which has shone so conspicuously in the past history of the British empire, has received fresh proofs of its inherent vitality and vigour in the marked development of the varied natural resources of this rich and promising dependency of the British Crown. We sincerely trust your visit to this and the other Australian colonies may be the means of strengthening and prolonging those ties of natural affection which bind us to the mother country; and we hail your visit as an earnest, on the part of Her Most Gracious Majesty the Queen, of the great interest she evinces in the welfare, happiness, and progress of those of her people who have made this distant colony their home. We hope your visit to this portion of the British Empire will ever have the effect of awakening in your mind a pleasing reminiscence of the past, when you again return to the shores of Great Britain; and we fervently pray that the blessing of Almighty God may be with you, and that you may long be spared to be an ornament to the high and honourable station you hold in your profession—a profession whose historical pages are emblazoned with a long line of illustrious names—names that will ever shine in the annals of the British Navy, not the least of which, we hope, will be England's Sailor Prince. Wishing you every happiness whilst here, and every prosperity for the future, we humbly pray that Almighty God will ever guard and protect you, and that Heaven's best blessing may descend upon Her Most Gracious Majesty Queen Victoria, your Royal Mother, and all the members of your Royal House; and that our beloved Queen may long continue to reign in the hearts and affections of a loyal and prosperous people. We beg to subscribe ourselves your Royal Highness's most humble servants—

RICHARD THOMSON, President.	ALEXANDER M'KINLY, Councillor.
HENRY BUSSELL, Councillor.	JAMES CRAWFORD, ,,
SAML. M'CLINTOCK ,,	CHRISTOPHER GILL ,,
WM. PETTIGREW ,,	JAMES IRVINE ,,
DAVID ALEXANDER ,,	

REPLY.

Gentlemen—Accept my best thanks for the address I have received from you, and for the warm expressions of welcome contained in it, which will ever be remembered by me with pleasure. The earnest feeling of loyalty and affection you have shown towards Her Majesty, is very gratifying to me. I regret that the limited time at my command will prevent the possibility of my visiting Beechworth, or it would have afforded me much pleasure to do so.

BOROUGH OF PRAHRAN.

May it please your Royal Highness—We, the Mayor and Councillors of the Borough of Prahran, in the colony of Victoria, approach your Royal Highness with dutiful assurances of our devoted loyalty to the throne and person of your august mother, our beloved Queen Victoria. We heartily congratulate your Royal Highness on your safe arrival in this colony, and hope that your visit will be a pleasant and satisfactory one, leaving such impressions as will result favourably to the future welfare of the Australian colonies. We trust that Providence will vouchsafe unto your Royal Highness a safe return to our mother country, when you will be able to lay before our most gracious Queen our expressions of loyalty to her Throne and attachment to her family.

GEORGE YOUNG, Mayor.
J. B. CREWS, Councillor.
H. W. LACEY, ,,
CHAS. BROWN, ,,
EDWD. L. VAIL, ,,
CHARLES OGG, Councillor.
J. H. KNIPE, ,,
ROBT. M. SMITH, ,,
AUG. F. WHITE, ,,
JOHN CRAVEN, Town Clerk.

REPLY.

Gentlemen—I thank you for the welcome you have given me, and for the assurances of your devoted loyalty to the Throne and person of Her Majesty, and for your attachment to the Royal Family. It is with pleasure that I see the growing prosperity of this colony, and I can assure you that I shall bear away with me a recollection of this remarkable country which will never be effaced from my mind. I shall not fail to convey to Her Majesty the expressions of your loyalty and attachment.

BOROUGH OF WANGARATTA.

We, the Mayor and Councillors of the Borough of Wangaratta, beg to express to your Royal Highness the deep sense of loyalty to the Throne and person of Her Most Gracious Majesty Queen Victoria, and the feeling of respect and esteem for you her son, with the other members of her Royal Family, entertained by the burgesses of this borough in common with all Her Majesty's subjects. We venture to hope that the present visit of a Prince of the Blood Royal to this distant part of Her Majesty's dominions, will result in the strengthening of those ties which now bind us to our beloved Sovereign and our mother country.

WILLIAM AUGUSTUS DOBBYN, Mayor.
JAMES DIXON, Councillor.
WILLIAM CLARK, ,,
D. H. EVANS, ,,
T. G. BULLIVANT, ,,
J. J. HALLETT, M.B., Councillor.
JOHN GRANT, ,,
F. C. MICHELL, ,,
W. WILLIS, ,,

REPLY.

Gentlemen—Accept my best thanks for your Address. I feel that the attachment which exists between these colonies and the mother-country, and the loyalty borne to Her Majesty the Queen, which have been so forcibly expressed in your address, are such that they can hardly be made stronger or deeper. That my visit here should be instrumental in doing good, will always give me the greatest pleasure.

BALLAN SHIRE COUNCIL.

May it please your Royal Highness—We, the undersigned, the President and Councillors of the Ballan Shire Council, beg to congratulate your Royal Highness on your safe arrival in this colony, and to convey to your Royal Highness the assurance of our loyalty and devotion to the throne and Her Majesty's person and Government. We are duly sensible of the great honour conferred on the Australian colonies by your Royal Highness's visit, and we regard it as a further proof of the kind interest which our beloved Queen feels in the welfare of this portion of Her Majesty's dominions. We hope that your Royal Highness will be so pleased with this the land of our adoption, that before long your Royal Highness will be inclined to pay us another visit; and we trust that your Royal Highness will remain with us a sufficient time to enable your Royal Highness to become acquainted with the value and importance of this portion of the British empire.

DUGALD MACPHERSON, President.
WALTER DUNCAN, Councillor.
DAVID MAIRS, ,,
WILLIAM ATKINSON, ,,
RICHARD CANTWELL, ,,
JOHN OSBORNE, Councillor.
JOHN GRAHAM, ,,
EDWARD BLAKE, ,,
JAMES MILLYARD, ,,
R. H. YOUNG, Secretary.

REPLY.

Gentlemen—In returning you my best thanks for the cordial welcome which you have given me on my arrival in this colony, let me assure you that I value greatly your expressions of loyalty towards Her Majesty and throne. It will be most welcome to the Queen to learn that this portion of the country is prosperous and happy, and I shall not fail to acquaint Her Majesty of that fact. I beg you to accept my thanks for your congratulations.

BOROUGH OF HAMILTON.

We, the Mayor, Councillors, and Burgesses of the Town of Hamilton, in the Colony of Victoria, respectfully beg to welcome your Royal Highness to Victoria and the Western District. We dutifully desire to express our continued and devoted loyalty to your august mother, Her Most Gracious Majesty the Queen. We trust that your stay in this colony will be productive of much gratification to your Royal Highness, and serve to draw yet closer the bonds of loyal affection which connect the people here with your illustrious family. And we desire further to express our most earnest wish that, when your thrice-welcome and most gracious visit to these colonies has terminated, your Royal Highness, carrying along with you the loyal sympathies of the colonists, may voyage peacefully and securely to the homely shores of Britain. (Signed, by request)

ALEX. LEARMONTH, Mayor.

REPLY.

Gentlemen — Pray accept my thanks for your welcome to Victoria. It will be my duty to convey to Her Majesty your expressions of continued and devoted loyalty to the Throne. My visit to Victoria has given me great pleasure, and I have seen with much gratification the richness and beauty of the Western District. I thank you for your good wishes for the rest of my voyage, and for my safe return to England.

BOROUGH OF FITZROY.

May it please your Royal Highness — We, the Mayor, Councillors, and Burgesses of Fitzroy, beg to offer you our heartiest congratulations on your safe arrival in this colony. We wish your Royal Highness much happiness during your stay amongst us. We avail ourselves of this opportunity of conveying to your Royal Highness our assurances of loyalty and dutiful allegiance to your royal mother, Her Majesty Queen Victoria. We trust Her Majesty may be long spared to reign in peace over her widely spread dominions, and through you may Her Majesty receive many demonstrations of esteem and affection from her subjects in the British colonies. Permit us to say, that your Royal Highness can receive from none more loyal and earnest wishes for Her Majesty's happiness than from the colonists of Victoria.

JOHN MICHAEL, J.P., Mayor.
EDWARD DELBRIDGE, Jun., J.P.
JOHN FALCONER.
ALBAN THOMAS BEST.
WILLIAM MILLER SCOTCHMERE.
THOMAS ROWE.
JAMES M'KEAN, M.P.
ALEXANDER GRANT.
GEORGE RUSHALL.
WILLIAM J. GILCHRIST, Town Clerk.

REPLY.

Gentlemen — Accept my thanks for your congratulations on my safe arrival, and for your kind wishes for my happiness. The hearty welcome which I have received here, as everywhere in Australia, will convince the Queen that the expressions of loyalty and devotion to her throne and person, which characterise every address presented to me, are not mere words, but the deep-rooted sentiments of all Her Majesty's subjects in these colonies.

BOROUGH OF DUNOLLY.

May it please your Royal Highness — We, the Mayor and Councillors of the Borough of Dunolly, in approaching your Royal Highness, desire most humbly to express our devoted attachment and loyalty to the Throne and person of your Royal Mother our Most Gracious Queen, and our fervent wishes that Her Majesty may, by the blessing of Almighty God, be long spared to rule her subjects, and that happiness and prosperity may continue to attend Her Majesty's reign. In common with all Her Majesty's loyal lieges in Victoria, we beg most heartily to welcome your Royal Highness to these shores, and to express our warm appreciation of the high honour your Royal Highness's visit to this colony will confer upon its people; and we feel assured that no other event could tend more strongly to cement the attachment felt by the colonists towards Her Majesty's Throne and the mother country. We regret most deeply and sincerely that, from the shortness of your stay, your Royal Highness will be able to visit only a few of the principal towns, and especially do we regret that you will be precluded from visiting the borough of Dunolly, which we have the honour to represent, and where your Royal Highness would have been accorded a most enthusiastic welcome, such as will greet you in every part of the colony honoured by your royal presence. With our fervent prayers that health, long life, and happiness may attend you, we beg to subscribe ourselves your Royal Highness's most humble and devoted servants,

JAMES CRAIG, Mayor.
CHARLES DICKER, Town Clerk.

REPLY.

Gentlemen — I receive with pleasure the assurances of your attachment to the Throne and person of Her Majesty, and return you my heartfelt thanks for the earnest wishes you express for the continued happiness and prosperity of her reign. I regret that the time at my disposal does not permit me to visit Dunolly, but trust that you will convey from me to the inhabitants of that borough my thanks for their welcome and congratulations, and for the kind wishes for my health and happiness which they send me through you.

BOROUGH OF BELFAST.

May it please your Royal Highness—We, the Mayor and Councillors of the Borough of Belfast in the Colony of Victoria, desire to assure your Royal Highness of our devoted and loyal attachment to Her Majesty the Queen and the Royal Family, of which you are a member. We esteem it a privilege to express to your Royal Highness feelings of the warmest welcome on this, your first visit to the colony of Victoria. In the hope that time will permit your Royal Highness to honour the favoured Western District of the colony with a visit. We are, your Royal Highness's devoted servants,

GEORGE HUTTON, Mayor.
ROBERT McMAHON, Councillor.   E. G. YORKE, Councillor.
C. VOISEY,   ,,   WILLIAM WEBB,   ,,
W. YOUNG,   ,,   P. McDANIEL   ,,
WILLIAM LOFTUS,   ,,   ROBERT ALLEN, Treasurer.
ANDREW BRUCE,   ,,   WILLIAM BARRETT, Town Clerk.

REPLY.

Gentlemen—I thank you sincerely for this address, and for its expression of loyalty and devotion towards Her Majesty and Throne, as well as for your feelings of attachment to the Royal Family. It gives me the greatest pleasure to visit this portion of Victoria, and my only regret is that I cannot stay longer amongst you. Accept my thanks for your kind wishes for my future happiness. In my turn, I wish you increased prosperity.

SHIRE OF WARRNAMBOOL.

May it please your Royal Highness—We the President and Councillors of the Shire of Warrnambool, in the Colony of Victoria, desire to approach your Royal Highness with an expression of our gratification at the visit you have been pleased to pay to these portions of the southern hemisphere, and to congratulate you on your safe arrival. We take the opportunity of your presence amongst us to express our unbounded loyalty to the Throne of England, and our personal attachment to the illustrious lady, your mother and our Queen, and to assure you of our fervent prayer that her reign may yet be long, as it has been good and glorious. We are accustomed to regard the resources of Victoria as almost unbounded. We believe that, great as they now are, they are, comparatively speaking, undeveloped, and we have taught ourselves to hope that this colony, now in its infancy, will rise to an eminence worthy the noble name it bears. In praying you to accept this our humble address, we venture to express the hope that, through your visit, these portions of Her Majesty's dominions may become more widely known, and we trust that in future days you will think with pleasure that countries, which in your early manhood expressed the sentiments we have embodied in this address, have retained their attachment to their mother country, and their devoted allegiance and affection to the illustrious family of which you are a member.

SAMUEL MACGREGOR, President.
ALFRED DAVIES, Secretary.

REPLY.

Gentlemen—Your hearty reiterations of welcome demand my warmest thanks. In the name of the Queen, my mother, I thank you for the expressions of loyalty and devotion towards herself and Throne, and for the just tribute you pay to the acts of her reign. In my own name also I thank you for the warm reception you have given me to Victoria, and for the earnest wishes you express for my happiness and welfare.

BOROUGH OF WILLIAMSTOWN.

May it please your Royal Highness—We, the Mayor, Councillors, and Burgesses of the Borough of Williamstown, loyal and devoted subjects of Her Most Gracious Majesty Queen Victoria, beg to tender to your Royal Highness our sincere congratulations on your safe arrival in this part of Her Majesty's dominions. It is with feelings of gratification and pride that we observe your Royal Highness engaged in the noble profession which has furnished some of the world's greatest heroes, whose deeds shed such lustre on the annals of our native land. We desire to express the hope that this visit of your Royal Highness to Victoria may be thoroughly enjoyed by you now, and in the future may be a source of many pleasurable reminiscences. We have the honour to be your Royal Highness's very obedient servants,

THOMAS MASON, Mayor.   RICHARD CLOUGH, Councillor.
JOHN COURTIS, Councillor.   A. C. LINDSEY,   ,,
RICHARD DOWMAN   ,,   JOSEPH DALGARNO   ,,
THOMAS HASLAM   ,,   PETER POWER   ,,
CHAS. FRANKLIN   ,,   GEO. F. SMITH, Town Clerk.

REPLY.

Gentlemen—I am sincerely gratified by the warm expressions of your kind feeling towards me, contained in the address I have received from you, and I thank you most heartily for your congratulations upon my safe arrival in this portion of Her Majesty's dominions. I am proud to belong to the profession which enables me to visit the Australian colonies in a vessel under my own command, and in which so many besides myself have the opportunity of seeing the loyalty, energy, and prosperity which characterise the people of this colony of the British empire, and of sharing in the welcome you have given me.

SOCIETY OF BLUES.

May it please your Royal Highness—We, the Committee of the Victorian Society of Blues, representing those of our fellow-colonists who have received their education upon the royal and ancient foundation of Christ's Hospital, desire to join with all other the loyal subjects of Her Majesty in this part of her dominions in tendering to your Royal Highness the expression of our cordial welcome to Victoria. We, retaining, in common with all our fraternity in various parts of the world, a strong feeling of affection and veneration for the noble institution in which we were reared, are associated together chiefly for benevolent objects. We are deeply conscious of the obligations under which that institution has been laid to Her Most Gracious Majesty, who, as well as other members of your Royal Family, have continued to bestow upon it the same fostering care which it has received from the Kings and Queens of England for three centuries. We, therefore, feel the more constrained to offer to your Royal Highness our dutiful homage. We trust that the interest your Royal Highness has manifested in these colonies may be maintained through many years of health and happiness; and praying that your Royal Highness's visit may prove of mutual advantage, by strengthening the ties that bind the affections of this people to the Throne and Family of Her Majesty, we beg most humbly to subscribe ourselves your Royal Highness's very dutiful and obedient servants.

B. COWDEROY, J.P., acting for E. WHITBY, J.P., PRESIDENT.
W. PERRY, DIRECTOR.
G. FOORD, ,,
C. MOULD, ,,

REPLY.

Gentlemen—I receive with deep gratification the address you have presented to me, and I thank you for the expression of your loyalty and devotion towards Her Majesty and Throne contained in your address. The welfare of this association has a particular interest for me, being myself a governor of Christ's Hospital, from which this association has its origin. I shall never forget my visit to these colonies, and I trust the interest that I have taken during my progress through this country will never be effaced from my memory. I thank you for your congratulations upon my safe arrival, and for your good wishes.

As stated previously, those addresses and replies which did not reach the Publishers in time for insertion here, will be found in the Appendix.

THE ILLUMINATIONS OF MELBOURNE AND ITS SUBURBS.

Scarcely recovered from the gaiety of the Prince's entry, the city was only half given to business on the following day, and as night closed in with every promise of fine calm weather—the night in which the city was to be lit up in honour of the royal visit—every one seemed prepared to give themselves over to the influence of the moment. The roads and avenues to the city were full of people in every sort of conveyance, and the expressions of surprise at what was seen, as well as evidences of ignorance as to localities, stamped a vast number of them strangers. As twilight deepened into darkness, so did the thoroughfares fill with passengers; and the lines of vehicles permitted by the police began to form. But the country folks were not left to themselves long; before nine the denizens of the metropolis commenced to issue forth, and then the streets began to assume the aspect they wore till the small hours arrived. In the centre proceeded the line of vehicles—cabs, carriages, carts, furniture-vans, lorries, hay-waggons, coaches, broughams, gigs, buggies, and every conceivable variety of conveyance—crammed to the utmost with men, women, and children, each adding to the prevailing noise by their exclamations. One seventh, at least, of the entire population of the colony were in Melbourne to see what was going on. Not one class, but all—artisan and merchant, labourer and civil servant, tradesman and agriculturist—either convoying women and children, or glorying in independence from such responsibilities, joined in the throng. It was hard work in places to get along, but people did move, even in the thickest throngs, and in sinuous course managed to see the show. Excellent order was preserved, and as a rule there was ample room for everybody. It is no exaggeration to set down the number of people in the streets at not less than one hundred thousand.

Early in the evening transparencies would not light up; designs in gas burnt patchy and scrappy; but as the wind calmed down, so did the lights improve, and everything went splendidly. From a height the effect was indescribably grand, and the light was reflected in the sky to a great distance. Bourke-street east seemed almost as bright as day, the dark background of the night giving the broad glare an effect like that of one of Martin's pictures of the nether regions, the lurid glow and smoke of the fire-pots on the roofs of some of the larger buildings increasing the similarity.

It is gratifying to record that the Prince, for whom was all this celebration, witnessed the splendid result. At about ten o'clock his Royal Highness, accompanied by the Governor, Lady Manners-Sutton and family following in another carriage, drove through the principal streets. They were cheered to the echo wherever they went, and a more unanimous exhibition of loyalty was never witnessed. At eleven o'clock his Royal Highness was entertained at the Melbourne Club, and while he stayed there it was impossible without difficulty to approach within five hundred yards of the entrance.

COLLINS STREET.

It was anticipated that this street would be the principal scene of the illuminations, being the locale of most of the banks, and containing the places of business of many of our chief citizens. Nor was the expectation so generally entertained disappointed. From one end of the street to the other, it was almost one continuous blaze of light; and all the designs that ingenuity could devise, or artists' skill could adorn, were there to be seen. In this street the greater part of Chevalier's transparencies were shown, and it is only justice to him to record that he expended an amount of skill that the ephemeral character of the productions scarcely justified. The large triumphal arch at the junction of Elizabeth and Collins streets somewhat interfered with the general view, and it would have been an improvement had its sombre aspect been relieved in some way. On the Treasury buildings the Royal Commission had expended the principal portion of their energies in the way of illuminations, and the designs were such as to bring the fine proportions of that building into prominent relief. The facade was one blaze of light from end to end, but it was chiefly on the centre that the decorations had been lavished, the chief of which was a colossal portrait of the Queen (painted by Chevalier), in her Royal robes, as on state occasions. The colouring was very beautifully done. The picture was a fac-simile of the one now in the Parliament Houses. On the other public offices but little labour was expended, the

Commission only illuminating them in order to show that they were Government buildings. The following is a list of the principal illuminations:—

Aarons, J., trade assignee—Gas illuminations in the form of an oval, containing between 3000 to 4000 jets; on top and bottom the words, "Welcome to Victoria," and letters, "P.A.," with anchor, and star at each side.

Alston and Brown, drapers—Transparencies of the Queen and Prince, Britannia and Neptune.

Annand's Chambers, offices of Mr. W. Cook, accountant; Mr. Ray, broker; and the shops beneath, Galvin, hatter, and Adamson, seedsman—Six large flags, surmounted by the union jack. The building was ornamented by large circles of evergreens, beneath a gilded entablature, "Welcome," in illuminated crimson letters.

Appleton and Twoddell, drapers—Windows encircled in gas jets, with letters "P.A.," over all a large gas star.

Argus Hotel—Transparency, a medallion portrait of the Prince surrounded by flags; motto, "Victoria welcomes the Sailor Prince."

Argus office—Large transparency, painted by Chevalier, a state barge, on which the Prince, dressed in full uniform, is standing; beside him Britannia introducing the Prince to the colonies. The supporters are two female figures, representing the colony and the City of Melbourne, Victoria surrounded by the foliage peculiar to the colony. In the distance is the Galatea approaching the Bay, with other ships following. The whole surrounded by a wreath, and beneath are a number of allegorical figures, representing literature, science, and art.

Audit Office—Transparency on glass, by Ferguson and Urie, the Royal arms; the windows illuminated with pyramids of candles.

Australian Alliance Insurance Co.—Transparency, the company's arms. In the fore-ground a sketch of the benefits derived from insurance, in back-ground a view of Hobson's Bay. At bottom the Royal arms, the whole surrounded by oak leaves, Australian flowers, shrubs, &c.

Australasian Insurance Co.—Transparency, painted by Chevalier. The "Galatea" in full sail. Over the transparency a gas star, in centre window a crown, and in those at the sides pyramids of candles.

Australian Mutual Provident Society—A star, and within it a transparency in glass.

Baillie and Butters, and Gemmell, Tuckett and Co.,— Transparency, figure of liberty, driven in a triumphal car; foreground, a female figure (Victoria) bearing fruit, flowers, &c., and a figure representing Asia.

Balderston, R., draper—Transparency, Victoria crowned with garlands. Motto, "Welcome to Victoria."

Bank of Australasia.—Transparency, by Chevalier, representing a colossal medallion portrait of His Royal Highness, encircled by a wreath of oak leaves, and supported by figures of Commerce and Maritime Navigation, and a royal crown in gas.

Bank of New South Wales—Lines of light arranged to give effect to the architectural features of the building, also lines around window openings and arches, connected to lower line of upper cornice by lines on keystones of windows. In centre windows were the letters "A.E.A." and a star in each of the side ones. From the balustrading were hung festoons.

Bank of Victoria—Transparency, painted by Campbell. This picture expresses the reception of the Prince by the people of Victoria.

Baptist Chapel (Rev. J. Taylor)—Reflector star, Duke's coronet in centre.

Batchelder and Co., photographers—Transparency, painted by Bottorill, representing four of England's chief naval heroes at different ages—Drake, Blake, Nelson, and Collingwood in frames; in the centre a bust of the Prince. Motto, "England's naval heroes and her hope."

Beaney, J. G., surgeon—Transparency, medallion portrait of the Prince, surrounded by wreath of oak leaves and surmounted by a crown.

Beauchamp and Rocke, auctioneers—Three reflector stars, each having a crown in the centre, with the word "Welcome."

Beaumont, J., draper—Star, with "A." in centre.

Benjamin, M.—Transparencies, the Prince in naval uniform, and a sailor.

Berghoff and Tonzel, tobacconists—Two rows of gas jets on the cornices.

Blair, Dr.—A number of lanterns, variegated colours.

Bradshaw, G. M., hosier—Brunswick star.

Briscoe and Co., ironmongers—Transparencies representing the Prince; a crown and two stars in crystal. The upper windows were lit by pyramids of candles.

Brown, Osborne and Co., carriers—Transparency, the Queen in her royal robes.

Brownless, Dr., Vice-Chancellor of University—Transparency, arms of the University, with the motto, "Postera crescam laude;" to the left, letters "A.E.," to the right, "D.E.,"—both surmounted by coronets.

Brush and Macdonnell, jewellers—Pyramids of candles.

Byrne, Robert, M.L.A., land agent—Handsome transparency of Prince Alfred's coat of arms, with mottos "Dieu et mon droit," "Tren and fest," and "Peace and plenty."

Buzzard, T. M., bookseller—Transparency, by Chevalier, containing a medallion portrait of the Prince in uniform, supported by two sailors.

Calvert, S., engraver—Transparency, the Prince in uniform.

Carnaby, George, tailor—Transparency on glass, an anchor surmounted by a crown and surrounded by oak leaves, at the bottom the word "Alfred."

Carson, John, boot and shoe importer—Brunswick star.

Cohen, S. H., and Co.—Two gas stars.

Criterion Hotel—Reflector star in gas, Duke's coronet in centre.

Commercial Bank—Transparencies representing Commerce, the Edinburgh Arms, and the Royal Arms; from the flagstaff, seventy feet high, floated a large number of flags.

Crown Law Offices—Transparency on glass, painted by Ferguson and Urie, Imperial crown; the windows filled with pyramids of candles.

Cuningham and Macredie, station agents—The front and the sides of the building festooned with lamps of various colours; in the windows of the second storey transparencies, containing each one of the letters of the word "Welcome."

Detmold, W., bookbinder—Rows of gas jets along the front of building.

Davidson, A., grocer—Star.

Duerdin, James, solicitor—St. George's star.

Duke of York Hotel—Transparency, bust of the Prince; over this a harp, with a wreath of shamrocks; on one side Britannia, and on the other a sailor; below, the "Galatea" in full sail.

Edwards, W., jeweller—Transparency of the Queen.

Eick, A., watchmaker—Transparency, Duke's coat of arms.

Ebridge, J., dyer—A star, with letter "A."

Ellis, J. E., outfitter—Brunswick star.

European Assurance Co.—Transparency, by Chevalier, emblematic of the business carried on by the company; over centre the word "Welcome" in large letters.

Evans Brothers, stationers—Transparencies representing the Duke in uniform and his coat of arms.

Fergusson and Mitchel, engravers—Transparency, Victoria and Great Britain shaking hands, in centre the "Galatea" coming up the Bay, the figures surrounded by flowers, fruit, &c.

Fraser and Co., auctioneers—Two large circles of gas, a large star, and two small circles containing anchors.

Gardner, F., furrier—Transparency, the city coat of arms, the Prince in the foreground, Britannia and Victoria on either side.

Garrard and Jaimet, surgeons—Transparency, star with motto, "Welcome, Prince Alfred."

Girdlestone, Dr.—Around windows and the arch of the door festoons of glass lamps.

Glen, W. H., music-seller—Star.

Goubl and Martin, chemists—Transparency, painted by Marsh, representing the Prince with his feet resting on a globe, sailors on one side and Australian natives on the other, with arms of the City of Edinburgh and Victoria, transparency bearing the legend "King of Australia."

Gowan, A., clothier—Transparency representing British flags surmounted by a crown and a ship in full sail.

Greig and Murray, auctioneers—Transparency, "Thousand welcomes to the Royal Sailor."

Grover and Baker's Sewing-machine Company—Transparencies representing the Prince and the ducal coat of arms; in the upper windows pyramids of candles.

Gunst, Dr. Transparency, the Royal arms, with "Welcome to Melbourne," and the Duke's and the City arms in a wreath on either side.

Haigh Brothers, outfitters—Reflector star, in centre a crown, with "Welcome" and an anchor.

Hall of Commerce—Star, "P. A." on either side.

Hart, furrier—Transparency, a wreath of roses, surmounted by a crown and surrounded by flags, with "A. E. A." in centre; round the building were a number of lanterns.

Henderson, Rev. A. M.—Transparency representing a lion supporting a shield of the Royal arms.

Henry, D., jeweller—Transparency, H.R.H.'s arms, supported by Cupids; beneath, a star.

Hetherington, C., saddler—Transparency of the Prince and the royal arms.

Hetherington, Rev. I.—Along the front of the manse a row of glass lamps, various colours.

Hickinbotham, W., carpet warehouse—Transparency, arms of Great Britain and Ireland, supported by kangaroo and emu; beneath, the Duke's motto, "Treu und fest."

Hill, W. R., chemist—Crown in gas; beneath it an anchor, also in gas.

Hope and King, importers of china—Transparency, the royal arms surrounded by flags, anchor beneath.

Howitt, Dr.—Transparency representing the "Galatea" in full sail; motto, "Welcome."

Hughes, C. J., confectioner—Reflector star, crown in centre.

Imperial Insurance Office—Transparency, arms of the company. In centre the royal arms; on either side a female figure, holding a cornucopia. Motto, "Victoria welcomes her noble Prince."

Insolvent Court—Transparency on glass, by Ferguson and Urie.

Kasner and Moss, opticians—Arch of gas jets.

Kilpatrick and Co., jewellers, and W. Bowen, chemist—Transparency, royal arms; at either side other transparencies representing stars.

King and Parsons, warehousemen—St. George's star.

Land Mortgage Bank—Two rows of gas jets along front of the building, star with letters "A. E. A." in centre, and a number of small stars.

Long, M., and Co., merchants—Pyramids of candles in windows.

Lange, Charles, dentist—Gas star.

Langwill, Craig and Co.—A circle of gas, within which was a gas star.

Law Brothers—Transparencies of the City arms, and those of the Duke.

Levi, N., an I Son—Gas star

Lewis, G., chemist—A star.

London and Australian Agency Company—The whole length of the building (65 feet) was illuminated with rows of gas jets; over the arch the letters "A. D. E.," on anchor, and crown; on either side the letters V.R. surmounting the crown; a star.

Lord and Co., merchants—Pyramids of candles in upper windows.

Lyons and Co., auctioneers—Transparency of "Galatea."

The Illuminations.

London Chartered Bank—Transparency, painted by Chevalier, a triumphal arch; beneath, the Prince received by Victoria, followed by Peace and Plenty; in the centre the arms of the Duke, the city of Edinburgh, and the city of Melbourne. On the top of the painting the arms of city of London, and at bottom maritime emblems.

M'Arthur, Sherrard and Copeland, merchants—Transparency, the Prince, attended by figures representing commerce, music, and painting; on either side, ships with sails half furled; at the top, the arms of the colony and the Prince.

M'Culloch, W., and Co., carriers—Transparency, the Murray River at Echuca; a steamer, laden with bales of wool, approaching the wharf. In the foreground one of M'Culloch and Co.'s waggons, laden with bales of wool. The picture surrounded by Australian trees, shrubs, &c.

M'Gill's Central City Hotel—Two gas stars.

M'Guigan, John, bookmaker—Transparency, coat of arms of St. Crispin; beneath, "Cead mille failthe."

Mackenzie, John, merchant—Transparencies containing mottoes in illuminated letters.

Maguire and Co., merchants—Pyramids of candles in upper windows.

Martin, P. J.—Harp in gas.

Mechanics' Institute—Star.

Melbourne Club—The royal arms in gas, with crown in centre. At bottom, in a ribbon, the words, "Ich dien Droit," at top, the motto, "Welcome, Duke of Edinburgh." The royal arms were surmounted by a star.

Melbourne Gas Co.—A crystal crown, beneath a rising sun surmounting the word "Welcome."

Melvin and Co., booktinters—Transparencies, the star of the order of the Scotch thistle, the crown of England, and harp.

Miller, R.U.—Circle of gas-jets, with "Galatea" and letters "D. E." on either side, surmounted by a small star.

Milton, J. B., and Co., drapers—Star.

Moore, S., fruiterer—Transparency of the Duke and the city arms.

Moubray, Lush and Co., drapers—Outline of building covered with gas jets; in centre a crown, with anchor beneath; letters "P. A." on either side.

Mullen, Samuel—Transparency, portrait of the Prince, surrounded by figures, the whole draped with union jacks; motto, "Tria ad fin."

Murray Brothers, tailors—Transparency representing the Duke of Edinburgh's arms; motto, "Welcome, our Sailor Prince."

National Bank—Transparency, Neptune in a car, the Prince beside him; the car drawn by four white sea-horses; the "Galatea" in the distance, in full sail. Beneath, in gas, crown, with the letters "V. R." on either side; four small stars.

Nicholls, G. M., tailor—A profusion of flags.

Nicholson, Germain, grocer—Transparency, a bust of the Prince, and above a view of Edinburgh Castle.

Northern Assurance Company—A transparency, painted by Mr. Farquhar, one of the officers of the company. In the centre a shield bearing the lion of Scotland rampant, surmounted by a crown, and over this the word "Welcome;" to the right and left anchors, interwoven with the Scottish thistle, and above these stars; at each side of the shield roses, and beneath it shamrocks, and the motto "Nemo me impune lacessit;" the whole surrounded by ropework.

Oppenheimer and Co., merchants—The windows illuminated with pyramids of candles.

Pacific Insurance Company—Transparencies representing Australia, and the "Galatea" entering the Heads.

Paling, R. J., musicseller—Harp in gas.

Pearson, J. W., engraver; and Girand and Co., confectioners—A pillar of revolving fire in gas, in various colours.

Power, Rutherford and Co., station agents—Round two sides of the building lanterns and coloured glass lamps; and anchor, with "A. E." on either side.

Powis, G. H., fine arts depository—Transparency, the Prince's arms.

Punch Office—Transparency, "Punch" seated on a cask.

Reed, T., fancy repository—A series of balls of gas, in shape of an inverted pyramid.

Robertson, Geo.—Transparency representing a medallion portrait of the Queen, supported by two Cupids; over the top an arch, which is again divided into three Gothic arches—the left containing a view of an English landscape by night; the right, an Australian landscape at sunrise; in the centre Britannia; motto, "Sub umbra sub si." The picture was painted by Freyberger, to illustrate the saying, "The sun never sets on the British dominions."

Robertson and Jacques, tailors—Transparency, a globe, the Australian arms beneath and the "Galatea" above.

Robinson, Leonard, draper—Star.

Sampson, T. W., mining agent—Star.

Sands and M'Dougall—Transparency, by Chevalier, representing the Prince at the moment of landing from his ship. In the background Hobson's Bay, and in the distance the lofty summits of the You Yangs. The three upper windows also contained transparencies.

Scott's Hotel—Transparency, by Chevalier, representing the Prince landing; to the left the arms of the City of Melbourne coupled with those of His Royal Highness. Beneath the transparency was an elaborate gas crown, on each side of which were Brunswick stars, and two smaller stars, with the word "Welcome."

Sleight, J., undertaker—Transparencies of the Queen the royal arms, and the Prince.

St. Paul Brothers, confectioners—Gas star.

Stokes, T., engraver—A transparency, painted by Roberts; bust of His Royal Highness; to the right, the "Galatea" in full sail.

Stubbs, Oatsby and Co.—Three transparencies representing Britannia, "Welcome, Prince Alfred," and the "Galatea."

Stanley and Co., tailors—Star.
Swasey, J. B., and Co.—Crown in gas.
Tasmania Insurance Company—Brunswick star, with "A" in centre.
Taylor, Joseph, and Co.—Crown in gas, with "A" on each side.
Temple-Court—Along the front of the building, sixty-six feet in breadth, three rows of gas jets ; the cornices lit up with small stars.
Thomas, Paul, bootmaker—Variegated lanterns.
Tracy, Dr.—In each of the openings of the balcony a transparency, painted by Miss Kennedy. In the centre, a large figure of Britannia; on one side Windsor Castle, and on the other Edinburgh Castle. On either side of these, transparencies representing the arms of the Duke of Edinburgh and those of the colony.
Union Bank of Australia—The upper parapet of the whole building fronting both Collins-street and Queen-street was decorated with flags. The lower portion of the building was decorated with flags and banners, in keeping with the upper. At the corner of the building was placed a magnificent anchor, composed of flowers and evergreens, entwined with a rope formed of red, white, and blue ribbons. The Illuminations of the Collins-street front embraced a handsome royal crown in gas, below which the word "Welcome ;" under it an excellent portrait of the Prince (transparency) by Mr. Campbell, representing the Duke in captain's uniform. Beneath this a beautiful double revolving star, 12 feet in diameter, and a very superior piece of mechanism. The effect of this star was very good, as the light appeared to radiate either from the axis or from the circumference. On the right and left of this star, the words "Prince Alfred;" and still nearer the ground, and below the star, the Duke's arms. On the Queen-street front, a gas anchor, nine feet high ; below the anchor a large transparency representing the "Galatea" under steam ; along the mouldings, oil lamps.
Union Club—The windows illuminated with Chinese lanterns.
Victoria Insurance Company—Transparency, the Prince surrounded by a wreath of laurels, surmounted by two female figures holding a crown ; at each side of the base, a British lion couchant.
Wade, James, and Co.—Star, with letters "A. A." on either side.
Walsh Brothers, jewellers—Brunswick star.
Watson, E., tailor—Star.
Whitehead, E., and Co., stationers—Transparency, a full-length portrait of the Prince in uniform ; in the background, the "Galatea" at anchor. Motto, "Welcome."
Whitehead, J., carver and gilder—Transparency, the British lion ; and beneath this another transparency representing sunrise, with ships in the horizon ; motto, "Victoria welcomes the Prince."
Whitney, Chambers and Co., ironmongers—In each of the nine windows of the second story a transparency, representing severally the stars of the orders of the Garter, Bath, Thistle, St. Patrick, St. George—the Britannia, Victoria, and Alfred stars, the ninth transparency representing the "Galatea." The parapet illuminated with variegated lanterns and lamps.
Wilkie, Webster and Co , music-sellers—Three festoons crossing the building of tri-colour drapery, festooned with stars and rosettes ; three large flags ; in all the windows pyramids of candles.
Wise, J., hairdresser—Star, with letters "A D. E." in centre.
Wraggo, George, chemist—Brunswick star.

ELIZABETH STREET.

In this street there being comparatively so few public buildings, the general display was necessarily not equal to Collins or Bourke-streets. The splendid facade of the new Post office was not interfered with by any devices placed on the exterior of the building itself, the design, by Mr. J. G. Knight, being on the French system, so as at once not to injure the structure, and yet to show off in its finest proportions the handsomest building yet erected in the city. On the pavement fronting Bourke and Elizabeth-streets were erected twenty-three decorated posts, each surmounted by large gasaliers, containing twelve large ground glass globes, and a still larger globe in the centre. The posts averaged eighteen feet in height, and were entwined with evergreens. The posts, which were about twelve feet distant from each other, were united with festoons of evergreens, eighteen inches in thickness in the middle, and diminishing in thickness at the ends. A double row of pierced piping, also connecting the pillars, threw a soft light on the festoons beneath, and cast a radiant brilliancy around. Each alternate post was surmounted by flags and bannerets. The face of the clock in the tower at the southern end was coloured in various devices. Along the two parapets fronting Bourke and Elizabeth streets were rows of fire pots, burning tallow, which, when lit up, added greatly to the effect of the illumination; and at the top of the tower were placed a number of pots containing similar material. In each of the windows were oil transparencies, painted to represent drapery and crimson hangings. The gas fittings were well executed by Mr. Brealey, of St. Kilda.

Adams, J., leather-merchant — Transparencies, St. Andrew's cross, and star.
Albion restaurant—Transparency, Edinburgh castle.
Archer, J.—Transparency, ship.
Age Office—Star, with "Welcome" in centre.
Barry, A., bootmaker—Transparency, crown and star.
Bates, T. Tompson, ironmonger—Three transparencies.
Beehive store—Reflector star, beehive in centre, silver rays.
Bowman, R., and Co., tea-merchants, and Lyell and Cowan, trade assignees—Transparencies, crown, a ship with the motto "Welcome, Alfred," and a medallion portrait of the Prince.
Briscoe and Co., ironmongers—Transparencies, Prince of Wales' feather, with letters "P. A."
Brooks, Henry, ironmonger—Star; beneath, "A. D. E." in gas jets.
Burns, G. H., grocer—Star.
Bush inn—Star.
Butchers' Arms Hotel—Transparency, Neptune guarding the "Galatea," with Victoria surrounded by the flags of all nations; on the right the City arms.
Carriers' Arms Hotel—Gas star.
City Arms Hotel—Transparency, City arms, and arch of gas.
Clarence Hotel—Transparencies, representing the City arms, the Prince in uniform, the Duke's arms, the "Galatea," and the Edinburgh arms.
Clarke, William, and Sons, sharebrokers—Transparency, St. George and the Dragon.
Colonial Bank of Australasia—On the balustrade, pots of fire, of red, green, blue, and orange colours alternately, were kept burning. From the flag-poles were hung a number of Chinese lanterns. All the windows in the top flat and the second story were beautifully lighted on a novel principle. Over the main entrance was a transparency representing a medallion portrait of the Prince. On either side, medallions of Britannia and Neptune; the "Galatea" in the distance. Over the transparency was a rising sun, with "A. D. E." in centre. On the Elizabeth-street frontage was a circle of gas, with the "Galatea" within it; beneath it the word "Welcome." Over the circle a crown and representations of the union jack, and on either side the letters "D. E." Beneath the circle was an anchor. On the Little Collins-street frontage were the letters "A. E. A.," in a double row of gas.
Colonial Wine Vaults—Star in gas.
Coutie, John, bootmaker—Large boot in gas.
Crouch and Wilson, architects—Transparency on glass, royal arms.
Donovan and Mulcahey, grocers—Crown.

De Pass Brothers and Co., embracing the offices of the Universal Marine Insurance Co. A handsome device on glass, illuminated in front by a wreath in jets of gas and four gas stars.
De Gruchy and Co., engravers, &c. — Transparency, the Duke's and the royal arms. Motto, "Victoria welcomes Alfred, England's Prince."
Draper, W., importer. "A. E. A." in gas.
Dublin Tavern—Transparency, harp, with motto, "Cead mille failthe."
Duke of Rothsay Hotel—Star.
Dunlea and Nicholson, grocers—Transparency, City arms, with mottos.
Eagan, J., butcher—Transparencies of Edinburgh Castle, with mottoes, "Welcome, Royal Duke," and "Alfred."
English, Scottish, and Australian Chartered Bank—Along the front of the building were rows of gas jets.
Fanning, Nankivell and Co.—A star, surmounted by the letter "A."
Full and Plenty Restaurant—Rising sun.
Glasgow Arms Hotel—Circle of gas, and gas star.
Harris, J., and Co., boot merchants—Pyramids of candles.
Heckin's Hotel—Transparencies: medallion portrait of the Prince; a ship in full sail; and the Duke's arms, with motto.
Horne and Co., agricultural implement makers—Transparency, the Prince in a ship, surrounded by flags and cannon, with the words "Welcome to Australia."
Hood and Co., chemists—Transparencies, representing Irish harp surrounded by oak leaves, shamrock, thistle, and rose; and Scotch thistle, surmounted by crown, with the Duke's arms at the bottom.
Hotel de France—Transparency, Britannia seated on a lion.
House, S., and Co., merchants—Transparencies, crown and star.
Isaacs, Moss, pawnbroker—"A.," in gas.
Jennings, grocer—Gas star.
Kennedy, D., plumber—Crown.
Lawrence and Adam, grocers—Transparency, Neptune in a car with Victoria at his side, drawn by sea-horses. The "Galatea" in full sail; beneath, Victoria bearing the Royal arms.
Lazarus and Co., importers—Crown, in gas.
Liphott, J., tobacconist—Star.
Liverpool, London, and Globe Insurance Company—Star of the order of the thistle, over this a line of gas jets, surmounted by ten lighted urns.
Louder, T., and Co., merchants—Transparencies, the Duke's arms, the royal arms, and the letters "A.E."
London Tavern—Crown, in gas, with letters "D. E." on either side.

Marks, H.—Transparency, medallion of the Prince, surrounded by rose, thistle, and shamrock.
Maynton and Co., stationers—Crown.
M'Donnell, J., and Co., grocers—St. Andrew's cross in gas, letters "A, D, E" on either side.
M'Dowell, J., bootmaker—Transparency, a crown and anchor.
M'Farlane, C., jeweller—Illuminated clock, and pyramids of candles in windows.
M'Ewan, James, and Co., ironmongers—A large glass transparency, Britannia seated on shield and union jack, and bearing the trident; figures in the background representing Commerce, Peace, and Plenty; the bottom panel having an anchor in medallion, surmounted by the Prince's coronet; the top panel filled in with ornamental work, and "Welcome" very neatly wrought in; the whole surrounded by an ornamental glass border. Also three well-executed glass transparencies, the centre one the Duke in naval uniform; on the right of this the Duke's shield; on the left the star of the Order of the Thistle; surmounting these, a fine cut crystal Brunswick star, brilliantly lighted. The glass transparencies were executed by Messrs. Ferguson, Urie, and Lyon, and reflect credit on the firm.
Melbourne and Hobson's Bay Railway Company—Transparency, Victoria, resting on a shield bearing the colonial arms, welcoming Prince Alfred. Different places about the station were hung with variegated lamps.
Mont de Piete—Anchor, in gas, with letters "P. A." on either side.
Mooney, W. E.—Gas star.
Native Oyster Company—Star.
Neave and Wiseman—Transparencies, the City arms and the royal arms.
Newing, Thomas R., oil-merchant—Gas star.
Nicholls, George, bookseller—Reflector star; steamer in centre, silver rays.
Norman, W. J., picture-dealer—Transparency, Victoria and Britannia greeting.
O'Connor's Chambers—Star.
Old Lamb Inn—Crown in gas.
Owen, Dodgson, and Arnell, tobacconists—Transparency, the British arms, surrounded by a wreath.
Perry, G. W., photographic artist; J. M'Kean, solicitor, S. Giflott, solicitor; Crouch and Wilson, architects—Grand display of the electric light.
Petty, Geo., butcher—Gas star.
Plummer, T., chemist—Star.
Post-office Club Hotel—Star.
Post-office Hotel—Transparency, sailor.
Railway Hotel—"Galatea" in full sail.
Rose, Thistle, and Shamrock Hotel (Grimwood's)—Transparencies representing volunteer artilleryman, volunteer rifleman, the "Galatea," and the Duke of Edinburgh.
Rish and Co., carriers—Gas star.
Rhodes, G., tinsmith—Circle of gas.

Robertson, Geo., bookseller—Transparency, by Chevalier. The prince seated on a triumphal car; Victoria presenting to him an olive branch. The car is accompanied by Literature, who is followed by Painting, Sculpture, and Architecture.
Royal Saxon Hotel—Transparency, the Prince in naval uniform, surrounded by guns, anchors, &c.; a view in the distance of the "Galatea" lying in the bay. To the left, Britannia with the national emblems; to the right, Neptune in his triumphal car, drawn by sea-horses, and surrounded by nymphs.
Sarton, Nicholas, oyster saloon—Transparency, British lion.
Scarlett and Marr, grocer—Transparency, medallion portrait of the Prince, supported by Britannia and Australia.
Scott, R., dentist—Transparency, crown.
Smythers, E., wine merchant—Star.
Spanish Hotel—Transparency, female figure, holding a wreath and a harp.
Stewart's Buildings—Containing in the block the warehouses of W. and S. Gardiner, J. and B. Callaghan, Hyam and Co., Paterson, Ray, Palmer and Co., and W. Young and Co.—All the windows lit up with pyramids of candles.
Tasmania Steam Navigation Company—Star.
Thompson, J. D., chemist—Transparency, "Galatea" in full sail.
Times Hotel—Transparency, the "Galatea," with the Duke's arms, and those of the City.
Topp, A. M., merchant—Transparency, Victoria and Britannia greeting.
Turner, R., tankmaker—Wreath surrounding the words, " Welcome our Sailor Prince."
Vernon and Co., leather-merchants — Transparency, crown and anchor.
Wallach Brothers, furniture dealers—Transparency, the royal arms supported by the colonial arms.
Weaver, William, and Co., merchants—Transparency representing the Duke's arms.
West, W. T., tobacconist—Gas star.
White, W. P., and Co.—Transparency on glass, the flags of Green's and Wigram's ships, and the A.S.N. Co.'s, with the ensign and union jack, surmounted by the letters "A. E.," the whole surrounded by gas jets representing a chain-cable; on the top of the flagstaff a small model of the "Galatea," wreathed in gas jets. The front of the premises decorated with flags.
Williams' Hotel—Transparencies, royal arms and City arms.
Wilson, Charles, tentmaker—Stationary and flowers, surrounded by a gas wreath in form of letter "A."
Wood, J., leather-seller—Transparency, medallion portrait of the Prince; on either side Edinburgh Castle and the "Galatea;" beneath, the Duke's arms.
Woolf Brothers, merchants—Star, in gas.
Wright, W., grocer—Transparency, medallion portrait of the Prince.

BOURKE STREET.

This, the great business thoroughfare of the city, made an appearance second only to that of Collins-street. The decorations used for the Parliament Houses were specially designed to hide the unsightly mass of unfinished brickwork at the top of that street. With this object in view, it was determined to cover the Spring-street front by erecting an opaque picture in oil, representing the front originally designed as a portion of the Legislative halls. The painting, which was on canvas, supported by a wooden framework, was 136ft. wide and 53ft. high, executed by Messrs. Pitt and Clarke. The windows of the mimic front were hung with crimson curtains, and at night they were lit up so as to resemble the windows of a London club. In the centre of the windows were painted heads of Walpole, Palmerston, Cobden, Pitt, Chatham, Peel, Mansfield, Canning, Burke, and Fox; and above was the portrait of the Queen. The whole structure was surmounted by twelve classic figures. The appearance of the street was brilliant in the extreme, the illuminations displaying the utmost variety, both of design and artistic merit.

Albion Hotel—A transparency, covering the greater portion of the upper story, Victoria welcoming the Duke of Edinburgh. The Prince, who has just descended from Neptune's car, is stepping on to a carpet, on which is inscribed the word "Welcome," spread at his feet by an aboriginal, and Victoria shaking hands with him. The "Galatea" in the distance; the car of the marine deity, drawn by sea horses and surrounded by tritons. The picture reflected great credit on the artist, Mr. Croft.

Allen's Gin Palace—Large portraits, Prince and Queen.

Anderson, T. Y., and Co., drapers—Transparency, a marine picture, depending from the hill of an albatross, whose outstretched wings cover the whole. A ship at sea, and an ornamental border of flags.

Artillery Hotel—Gas star.

Beaumont, S., wireworker—Large "A" formed of Chinese lanterns; and an illuminated church, composed of wire and painted calico.

Beehive Outfitting Establishment—Star, with reflector, having a beehive in the centre.

Bendigo Hotel—Star of St. Andrew, star of the garter, and Queen's crown in centre in gas.

Bennett, T. K., butcher—Transparency, painted in oil, by Watts, from a design by H. Oliver Nash, consisting of three pictures enclosed in wreaths, the centre a well-painted representation of the "Galatea" off Sandridge; the right of the picture, a figure of the Prince, in naval uniform, standing on the deck of his ship; the left, a portrait of the Queen, in robes of state.

Bickerstaff, L. F., draper—Transparency of the Prince.

Britannia Hotel—Transparency, figure of Britannia, with ship in the distance.

Broadbent and Kitchingman, grocers—Transparency, the Prince supported by Victoria and Britannia.

Bull and Mouth Hotel—A transparency (painted by Mr. Thomas Wright). Neptune apprising Victoria of the arrival of the "Galatea." Victoria appears seated on the beach, surrounded by various emblems of her products.

Bunet, G., tobacconist—Transparency of the Queen.

Buckley and Nunn, drapers—Transparency, Victoria welcoming the Prince on his landing, supported by figures of Britannia and Liberty.

Canterbury Music-hall—Gas anchor.

Citizen Restaurant—Transparency of ornamental design.

Charlwood and Son, printing office—"V. R.," with gas star, encircled by "Welcome Alfred."

Chiswell, confectioner—Transparencies of crown, and other devices.

Christian, Frans, tobacconist—Chinese lanterns.

City Buffet—Transparency, shoe, and figure of Britannia.

City Coffee and Chop House—Transparency, ship.

City Music-hall—Reflector stars.

Cockburn, confectioner—Gas star.

Colonial Wine Store—Gas star.

Cookson and Brown, clothiers—Transparency, the royal arms of Scotland, with red lion rampant on gold shield, with unicorns as supporters.

Crystal Palace Hotel—Large transparency, divided into compartments, the centre representing the Governor welcoming the Prince to Victoria. The right-hand cartoon represents two emus, surmounted by the colonial arms. The left-hand cartoon represents kangaroos, surmounted by the city arms. The painting was executed by Mr. William Handcock. Above was a large reflector star, and beneath a string of variegated lamps.

Cunliff, E., grocer—Transparency, the Prince on the deck of a man-of-war.

Cornwall Arms Hotel—Star, "A" in centre.

Creese, G. H., baker—Transparency, crown and "P. A."

Debit de Vin Colonial—Gas star.

Denis Brothers, jewellers—The front was dressed with garlands and flags, the French flag and the union jack being united; and also were disposed a number of coloured crystal globes. "Vive le Prince Alfred," in letters composed of flowers, and above appeared in coloured glass the words, "Welcome to Victoria."

Dickie, J., plumber—Thistle and "P. A." in gas.

Dalgety and Blackwood's warehouse—Transparency, painted by Messrs. Gill and Pain, the centre occupied by a moonlight view of a native corroboree, supported by figures of Britannia and Neptune; on the left, the shipping at the Sandridge Pier, carrying the flags of Dalgety and Co. From the upper corners of the central picture, flags of all nations; beneath, the British and colonial shields, with a representation of Edinburgh Castle; the whole surmounted by a crown.

Dinte, tailor—Painted stars on window, and bust of the Queen in front.

Domestic Bazaar—Transparency, Victoria going to meet the Prince in a car drawn by swans.

Dowling's Plough Inn—Masonic emblems in gas.

Dunkley, W. J., bootmaker—Transparency, the Royal arms.

Duerlin, James, solicitor—Six-pointed St. George's gas star.

Dwight's Book Store—Two coloured transparencies, one with "Welcome" at the top, "A. E. A." in the centre, and two anchors at foot; and the other, a crown, with the letters "V. R.," and some ornamental work.

East Melbourne Hotel—Transparency of the Prince, with a sailor on each side.

Ebler, jeweller—Illumination in coloured lanterns.

Evans, Thomas, tent and flag maker—Transparency, the centre group a painting of Neptune, drawn in a triumphal car by sea horses. On one side is Britannia, with the Prince on the other; a view of the "Galatea" in the distance.

Eve's City Baths—Gas star, and flag decorations.

Excelsior Hotel—Candles and lamps in the windows.

Flanner's White Hart Hotel—Transparency, royal coat of arms, and the front windows of the hotel, forty in number, lit up with candles arranged in pyramids.

Fletcher, hat-maker—Transparency, an exquisite; underneath, "Who's your hatter?"

Flying Scud Hotel—Transparency, Duke of Edinburgh.

Foggery's Colonial Wine Store—Rows of gas jets along the verandah.

Garrick's Head Hotel—Lamps in windows, and transparency, painted by Mr. Pitt—the British Lion.

Gascard, A., colonial wine rooms—Two transparencies, figure of Britannia, and the other filled with the several shields of the Swiss cantons.

Goebel, H., tobacconist—Large reflector star.

Goldsbrough, R., and Co., wool-brokers—Candles in each window, and a line of gas jets all round the first floor of the building, with large gas star in centre.

Gosling, P., draper—Gas star.

Great Eastern Dining-rooms—Transparency.

Hall, G., draper—Gas star.

Hanks, J., tea mart—Festoons of coloured lamps.

Hansen, B. J. W., draper—Transparency, Britannia, with lion and anchor.

Hatton and Laws, chemists—Transparency, Britannia.

Hickey, J., print shop—Transparency, His Excellency the Governor welcoming the Prince.

Higginbotham, W., wigmaker—Flags and Chinese lanterns, and transparency showing Fame welcoming Victoria's Son.

Hilton, F. J., grocer—Transparency, "Galatea," and Manchester coat of arms.

Hodgkins, T., draper—Gas star.

Hooker, —, clothier—"Welcome," in floral device.

Houle's Dining Hall—Transparency, the town of Edinburgh, and gas star in front of the verandah.

Howie, G. D.—Gas star.

Hummums Hotel—Transparency, the Prince surrounded by female figures typical of the various products of an agricultural country.

Imperial Hotel—Transparency of novel design, consisting of a framework with stars of various colours, and crystal anchor inside; the rose, shamrock, and thistle entwining the British oak painted on the exterior, with the motto "Welcome Alfred." On the Spring-street front of the hotel a transparency giving a view of Windsor Castle.

Jenkins, J., saddler—Gas star.

Johnston, G. K., auctioneer—Transparency, the Prince.

Johnstone and O'Shanassy's photographic studio—Three well-executed transparencies, the first containing the Governor, the second the Prince, and the third the Queen.

Jones, J., bootmaker—Star.

Jude, A., and Co., jewellers, and George Nowling, bootmaker—Transparency, Britannia crowning the Prince with a laurel wreath.

Kaye and Butchart, station agents—"A. E. A.," and star above, in gas.

King and Cuningham, stock and station agents—Transparency, Duke of Edinburgh, with the royal arms, &c.

Kleiner, W., jeweller—Gas star, and flags.

Langley, J. M., china and glass dealer—Transparencies, a ship and crown, and an anchor.

Lee, B., ironmonger—Her Majesty in regal robes, painted by Freyberger.

Lesh, G. G., grocer, and De Dollon, colonial wine store—Transparency, a French soldier shaking hands with a British sailor.

Leverett and Son, J., saddlers—Transparencies, the Duke of Edinburgh on board the "Galatea," and the British and Victorian coats of arms.

Leviathan Clothing Establishment—"Leviathan," in gas, with crown above.

Levy, J., tobacconist—Drapery, with initials "A. E. A.," "E. U.," and "D. E."

Levy Brothers, importers—Anchor between letters "A. A.," in gas.

Liverpool Hotel—Gas star and transparency of the Prince.

Lockyear, A., haircutter—Gas star.

London Chartered Bank of Australia—"A. E. A." in gigantic gas letters, and crown above.

Long and Son, chemists—Picture, painted by Chevalier. Subject, Victoria reclining under a fern-tree, while she gazes on a ship some distance from the shore.

The Illuminations.

Long and Co., sewing machine emporium—Transparency, the landing of the Prince, with Victoria extending her right hand to him. On the right, two miners, and the "Galatea" in the distance.
Lorimer, R., draper Transparency; the central figure, the "Galatea;" on one side a sailor, with union jack; on the other a Highlander, with flag of Scotland.
Lovell, W., furniture warehouse—Two transparencies.
Maguire, J. F., auctioneer—Transparency, the Prince.
Manners-Sutton Hotel—Gas anchor.
Market Hotel—Transparency of the Prince.
Marks, B. J., miscellaneous repository—Star.
Moss, Marks—Brunswick star.
Martin's Australian Hotel—Transparencies representing Victoria welcoming the Duke, His Royal Highness's coat of arms, and the British and Australian arms combined.
Mechanics' Restaurant—Star, letters "A.E.A."
Meares, Geo. and R., linendrapers—Transparency, painted by Mr. Roberts. Subject, Neptune's car, drawn by sea-horses; figures of Industry and Commerce on either side, with Victorian arms. The windows of the upper story were occupied by nine smaller transparencies of various designs.
M'Donald, A., photographer—St. George and the Dragon.
M'Farlane and Morris, tailors—Transparency.
M'Pherson, Thomas, warehouse—Transparency, the Duke of Edinburgh, supported by Victoria and Britannia, with royal arms above and colonial arms at foot.
Mirfin, George, plumber—Large reflector illuminator, star, and other designs, encircled by the words, "Thrice welcome, Royal Prince."
Menzies' new hotel was brilliantly illuminated. In the central portion of the middle story, facing Bourke street, were "A. E. A." in gas letters, and the windows on either side were occupied by as many gas stars, the design alternating. There was also a gas star in each of the windows facing William-street.
Monster Clothing Company—Crown and "Monster Clothing Company" in gas.
Muller, V. A., tobacconist—Reflector star.
Murray, James and Co., watchmakers—Gas star.
Muskett, C., bookseller—Transparencies, the Queen, and arms of the Duke of Edinburgh, and "Welcome" worked in coloured flowers—with festoons of lanterns.
National Bank of Australasia—Gas star, "P. A." in centre.
Newing, —, paperhanger—Two transparencies.
Newmarket Hotel—Three transparencies, severally bearing mottos.
Nissen's Café—Illumination of coloured lanterns.
North British Hotel—Transparency, the Duke of Edinburgh, the royal arms above, and a ship at each side. The windows were also lit up with pyramids of candles.
Original Scotch Pie-shop—Gas star, and festoons of Chinese lanterns.
Owston, W., and Co., flour importers—Transparency, the Prince.
Polytechnic Hall—Crown and star in gas.

Paterson, Ray, Palmer and Co.—Brunswick star, with "A." in centre.
Petty, George, butcher—painting on canvas, representing a native corroboree, with the Duke's arms and the Australian arms at the corners. Also gas crown, with letter "V." between letters "A. A."
Pierce, J. W., tobacconist—Transparency, the "Galatea," the Duke's coat of arms, and motto, "God speed the ship."
Phillips, P. S., china and glass warehouse—Pyramids of candles in windows, and festoons of coloured lamps.
Raine, Thomas, ironmonger—Transparency of the English and Edinburgh coats of arms.
Reaney, R., saddler—Illuminated with candles, with reflectors at back.
Robertson and Moffat, drapers—Transparencies painted in oil on glass, by Ferguson and Urie, consisting of a portrait of the Queen in her robes of state, a crown, and the royal coat of arms. These pictures had the appearance of stained glass.
Rodgers, G., tailor—Festoons of coloured lamps.
Rolfe and Co.'s warehouse—Crown in gas.
Rose of Australia Hotel—Crown in gas.
Royal Haymarket Hotel—Three stars of coloured glass, lit up with revolving gas-burners.
Royal Mail Coach Offices—Transparency, the Prince being conveyed ashore in Neptune's car; and a carriage drawn by six greys, in which the Governor and the Prince are seated.
Royal Mail Hotel—Transparency, containing three large pictures; the centre a representation of the Heads, with the "Galatea;" in the second panel a figure of Victoria and emblems of commerce; and in the third a digging scene, with miners and their implements.
Ruddell, J., provision store—Transparency of a man-of war's man.
Sanderson, G., and J., hat-manufacturers—Transparencies, the royal arms, with the Duke's coronet and motto, &c.
Sayers, J. W., printer—Crown and star on either side, in transparency.
Schobert, L. F., tobacconist—Reflector star.
Seymour, J. D., wood-carver—Pyramids of candles, with reflectors.
Skinner, —, draper—Gas star.
Skinner's Crinoline Emporium—Large frame of glass crystals, lit up from the back.
Smith, L. L., surgery—Transparency, the British lion defying an enemy; in front, two gas illuminations—a crown with an anchor on each side, and crown with a star on each side.
Solomons, A., outfitter—Star, with "A." in centre.
Southern Cross Hotel—Star, with "A." in centre.
Squoish Restaurant—Gas star.
St. Patrick's Hall—Harp in gas.
Streittle, A., and Co.—Transparency, representing a portion of the mythological history of Acis and Galatea, the whole surmounted by the word "Welcome," and underneath, the Duke's coronet and motto.

Stanford and Co.'s sewing-machine repository—The parapet of the building was encircled by white stars in glass, edged with gold; in every pane of the windows of upper story was a star, cut out of a crimson lake ground painted on the windows; and the middle story windows were filled with stars similarly designed, grouped in various forms.

Tattersall's Hotel—Crown and "Tattersall's" in gas.

Taylor, Enoch—Transparency, Victoria offering a crown to Prince Alfred, supported on the right by a figure of Plenty; on the left, boat, with sailors bearing union jack.

Temple of Pomona—"Alfred," in gas letters, and festoons of Chinese lanterns and flags.

Theatre Royal—A handsome transparency, painted by Mr. Hennings. Subject—Britannia, bearing a banner (on which is inscribed the royal arms), riding in a car drawn by sea-horses, round which are figures holding baskets of flowers.

Uncle Tom's Pawn-Office—Gas star.

Varieties—Gas illumination, "Varieties," with a crown at each side.

Vickers, George, hosier—Gas star.

Victoria Baths—Two anchors, with a star, surrounded by the word "Welcome," in gas.

Victoria Insurance Company—Transparency.

Victoria Wine Vaults—Illuminated bunch of grapes on coloured glass.

Warburton, T., iron-merchant—Three transparencies, the Queen in her robes of state, the Duke's crown, and the Duke's coat of arms.

Watts, G., boot store—Reflector star, with arms in centre.

Waxworks—Reflector star.

Wenzel and Enos, watchmakers—Gas star.

White House Hotel—Arches of fern-tree in front, lit up with Chinese lanterns, and transparencies in windows.

QUEEN STREET.

At the southern end of Queen-street almost as brilliant a show was made as in Collins and Bourke-streets, and there were one or two individual illuminations which were not surpassed elsewhere. The Oriental Bank was magnificently lighted, and mention may also be made of the illuminations of the Melbourne Banking Company and the London and Lancashire Insurance Company. The Government buildings in this street were very simply illuminated. At the offices of the Board of Agriculture was a design in coloured glass, exhibiting the Duke of Edinburgh's arms; and the building used for the purposes of the Mining Department was lighted up by candles, arranged in pyramids in each of the windows. The following is a list of the more prominent illuminations in this street:—

Abrahams, M., optician—Brunswick star.

Bell, Bruce and Co.—Transparency, portrait of the Prince.

Board of Agriculture—Transparency in coloured glass, Duke of Edinburgh's arms.

British Hotel—Brilliant illuminations in gas, and letter "A." in gas.

Carter, C., paperhanger—Four transparencies, the Queen and Prince in the centre, supported at the sides by Neptune and Albion.

Council Club Hotel—"D.E." with star and anchor, in gas.

Crisp, G., jeweller—Triple row of gas jets.

Franklyn, F. B., and Co.—Three very beautiful transparencies, painted by Mr. H. Gritten, two being shown in Queen-street and one in Flinders-lane; the whole of the windows festooned with a number of coloured lamps.

Gibbs, Ronald and Co.—Large crown in gas, and stars.

Harp of Erin Hotel—Harp, in gas.

Hosie, S. and Co.—The motto "God bless our Sailor Prince," in illuminated letters.

Kerr, J., butcher—Transparency, in coloured glass, of the royal arms.

Lang and Co.—Gas star.

Lilley Brothers, grocers—Transparency, consisting of the crown over harp, supported at the sides by the national arms.

London and Lancashire Insurance Company—Transparency, the royal and Lancashire arms enclosed in a wreath of laurel leaves, supported by lion and kangaroo, flags, bayonets, &c. At the top, "Advance Australia," within globe; and underneath, the motto "Victoria concordiâ crescit."

Loughnan's Hotel—Transparency of large Irish harp, with motto, "Cead mille failthe."

M'Culloch, Sellar and Co.—Handsome glass transparency, displaying the royal arms in coloured glass. On the left a similar transparency, consisting of a trophy of flags and naval insignia. On the other side a shield, with the Edinburgh arms and nautical emblems.

Melbourne Banking Company—Brunswick star.

Miller Brothers, coachbuilders—Transparency, royal arms, with Prince's motto; windows illuminated with candles and Chinese lamps.

Mining Department—Pyramids of candles in the windows.

Oriental Bank.—The pillars in front of the building, five in number, wreathed in spiral form with jets of gas, lines of gas along the cornice, and following the architectural features of the building, the mouldings of the pillars, &c.; at the summit of the building a number of flambeaux.

Queen Insurance Company.—A magnificent transparency in coloured glass, consisting of the Queen's portrait, surrounded by an ornamental border. On each side two small transparencies, also in coloured glass, showing the royal arms.

Sandhurst Hotel.—Two transparencies, portraits of the Queen, and royal arms.

Smith, J. T., butcher—Edinburgh Castle and the "Galatea" in two transparencies, and gas star.

Southern Insurance Company—Transparency, view of Queen-cliff, with the "Galatea" entering the Bay. The Prince represented being brought towards the shore by Neptune in his car, drawn by sea-horses.

Temple-Court Hotel—Anchor and letter "A." in gas.

The Victoria Sugar Company, Iceson, Williams and Co., and Moore, Hawthorn and Co. In the centre of the buildings a large transparency, consisting of the Queen's portrait, with motto "Victoria welcomes Victoria's Son." On each side, gas stars.

Webster Brothers, and W. Peterson and Co.—Transparencies in the six first-floor windows. In the centre, portraits of the Queen and the Prince, supported by the Royal arms and the arms of the Prince.

West Coast Hotel—Transparency, portrait of the Prince.

Western Port Hotel—Transparency, British and colonial arms combined.

SWANSTON STREET.

The Corporation spared no expense to make the Town Hall a great feature in the city illuminations, and they fairly succeeded in throwing everything near into the shade by the magnificence and success of their design, which accorded well with the architectural peculiarities of the structure, and the result was very striking. The massive front of the building, from basement to parapet, was literally ablaze, the whole facade being outlined in jets of gas, supplied by four-inch pipes. The central figure of the illumination was a coat of arms about 21ft. across and 14ft. high, flanked by the letters "A. E." and "A." In the freize of the entablature, running the whole length of the building, appeared the words "God Save the Queen;" and the whole was surmounted by a crown placed on the parapet. The Swanston-street front of the District Court House was illuminated with a thousand festoons and pendant coloured glass lamps. The illuminations on Prince's Bridge, the principal entrance to Melbourne from the south, were of a very noticeable character. Two triumphal arches had been erected from designs furnished by Mr. R. Wilson, of Crouch and Wilson, architects, a description of which was given in the account of the Prince's entry into Melbourne. On the Corporation Fish Market was a large allegorical picture, painted by Mr. O. R. Campbell. This transparency, the dimensions of which were very large, was much admired. On the Flinders-street front of the market were the initials "A. E. A.," in gigantic gas letters. The design selected by the Reception Commission for the Public Library consisted in the erection in wood and canvas of the portico of the building, as represented in the original plan of the still unfinished structure; the work executed by M. Kursteinel. After Collins and Bourke streets, this street attracted the largest share of public attention.

American Hotel—Three transparencies, with mottos of "Welcome to the Prince."

Barnett, I., jeweller—Gas star.

Batchelder and O'Neil's print-shop—Gas star.

Beers, C. N., bookseller—"Alfred," and crown in flowers.

Brown's Exchange Hotel—A likeness of the Duke, painted in transparency, and each window filled with various coloured devices on paper. The whole of the work was executed by Master Mier.

Burston, F., bootmaker—Crystal star.

Byrne, T., oil and lamp store—Lamps in windows.

Chapman, G., music-seller—Ornamental transparencies.

City Baths—Gas star, with motto of the garter.

Civet Cat toy-shop—Figure of a cat in gas.

Clark's Hotel—Two star, with "A" on each side.

Clement, T., luncheon rooms—Anchor, in gas, star at each side, and transparencies.

Cohen, A., china warehouse—Display of lamps.

Collingwood Gas Company—Gas star.

County Court Hotel—Transparency, the Prince.

Currie, J., grocer—Transparency of "Galatea," with the Prince, and a man-of-war's man.

Crystal Tavern—Transparency of Prince.
De Dollen's wine store—Transparency, Peace about to crown a Zouave and a grenadier.
Earl of Zetland Hotel—Transparency, the "Galatea" in the bay; also, a gas illumination, a crown between two anchors, on each side of the picture.
Erskine, James, plumber—Gas anchor.
Felton, Alfred, wholesale druggist—Line of gas jets along cornice, with gas star.
Foos's Hotel—Pyramids of candles in each window.
Ford, W., and Co., chemists and druggists—Transparency, the British shield supported by the lion and unicorn, with a soldier and sailor on either side.
Frahm, C., dairyman—Gas star.
Freemason's Hotel—Transparency.
Garten's Hotel—Gas star, with the word "Welcome" in centre, enclosing the letters "A. E. A.;" also rows of globe lamps.
German, J., fancy goods store—Crystal star.
Gittus, —, umbrella maker—Gas illumination, umbrella.
Goldberg, A., tobacconist—Gas star.
Goldstein, M., pawnbroker—Thistle in gas.
Greig, W., fancy warehouse—Transparency, star.
Guyatt, George, surgical instrument maker—Star.
Hann, C. J. and T., estate agents—Gas stars.
Heinecke, F. W., and Co., tobacconists—Gas stars.
Hoelskin, —, confectioner—Candles illumination.
Isard, W., fancy store—Two transparencies, Britannia and Victoria.
Law, Somner and Co., seedsmen—Transparent window-blinds, lighted from within.
Lucas and Sons, confectioners—Anchor.
Lyell and Brown, grocers—Crown, in gas.
M'Ewan and Co., merchants—Crown, with letter "A" on each side, in gas.
M'Lean, N., wholesale grocer—Transparencies, the Australian arms, Britannia, the "Galatea," and the Prince.

Manchester Unity Hall—Transparency, emblem of the Manchester Unity.
Maritime and General Credit Company—Brunswick star, with "A" in centre.
Mould, C., and Co., bootmakers—Wellington boot in gas jets.
Prince's Bridge Hotel—Transparency, the Prince surrounded by allegorical figures and emblems.
Prince George Hotel—Two transparencies, and candles in the windows.
Queen's Arms Hotel—Gas star.
Reynolds, J. N., seed stores—Flowers and evergreens, and lights in the windows.
Roberts, S. H., painter—Transparency, ship.
Royal Oak Hotel—Profusely decorated with flowers and evergreens, and ornamental lamps.
Rosecommon Arms Hotel—Transparency.
Schlamm, H., jeweller—Transparency.
Schlebach, E., tobacconist—"Welcome, Alfred," in coloured paper letters.
Solomon, S., furniture warehouse—Brunswick star.
Staff, C., paper-flower maker—Gas star on the verandah, "Welcome" in letters of flowers, with anchor and star.
Star Hotel—Gas star.
Stevenson and Elliot, coachbuilders—Flags and coloured lamps.
Strangers' Home Hotel—Candle illumination.
Talbot Hotel—Transparencies.
T. Tayler, ham warehouse—Transparency, ship.
Thurgood, W., baker—Transparency of the Prince and "Galatea."
Travellers' Home Hotel—Transparencies.
Walker, R., wine and spirit merchant—Gas star.
Willcox and Gibbs, sewing-machine depôt—Star.
Whitney, Chambers and Co.—Gas star.
Woolf, Marks—Ornamental transparency.
Youhlen, E., butcher—Gas star.

RUSSELL STREET.

The illuminations in Russell-street were far from numerous, and chiefly confined to that division of it lying between Collins and Lonsdale streets. The following were the principal illuminations:—

Alcock and Co., billiard-table manufacturers—Transparency, billiard-table surmounted by the royal arms.
A. M. Allard, butcher—Transparency, Britannia with her arm on a bust of the Prince, and a lion underneath.
Barnett, B., wholesale grocer—A magnificent Gothic star in every variety of coloured glass, surmounted by a crown in the same style, with the word "Welcome" under it. Below the star is the rose, the shamrock, and the thistle, with the letters "P. A." This illumination was executed by Mr. Nitch.
Bradshaw, Geo., dealer—Model of the "Galatea" in full sail and in motion; and a transparency, representing a soldier and a sailor.

Campi, J. and A., looking-glass manufacturers—Transparency, the "Galatea," with emu and kangaroo.
Crosby, John, gasfitter—Transparency, the Duke and the "Galatea."
Cross Keys Hotel—Illumination star, and figure of the Prince.
Courtet, Madame De, milliner and dressmaker—Transparencies, Queen Victoria and the Empress Eugenie.
Ebbret, Alfred, boot shop—Three stars.
Exford Hotel—Transparency, Britannia, with her arm on the Duke of Edinburgh.
Golden Fleece Hotel—Transparency, an English and a German welcome to the Prince.

The Illuminations.

Jacobson, S., pawnbroker—Portrait of Her Majesty the Queen.
New Exhibition Hotel—Transparency, Neptune and Britannia, with a figure of the "Galatea" surrounded by a wreath of flags.
Powell, J., jeweller—An illuminated clock, with circles of gas jets around; Chinese lanterns along the top of the building.
Bowden Brothers, tinsmiths—Chances and Venetian lanterns, pyramids of candles and flags.
Sitch, S., plumber—Brunswick star, with a glass transparency in centre, representing a quartering of the Duke's arms, surrounded by flags.
Trades' Hotel—Gas star with "A" in centre.
Warne and Webster, clothing manufacturers—six window transparencies.

LONSDALE STREET.

The Victorian Water Supply offices was one of the most effective displays of the night, the design representing a cascade illuminated by a powerful electric light, under the direction of Messrs. Vazie Symons and Francis. The other illuminations were as follow:—

Andrew, John, and Co., drapers—Crown.
Beehive Hotel—Star, and transparency of the Royal arms.
Black Eagle Hotel—Gas star, surmounted by eagle and crown.
British-American Boarding-house—Transparency, with anchor, &c.
Cornwell, H., butcher—Transparencies, portrait of the Prince, with Victoria and the letter "A."
Day, Charles, chemist—Transparency, "Galatea" and Duke's arms.
Ekman, B. A., furniture warehouse—Transparency, Neptune and Amphitrite, with the Prince behind them on a shell car drawn by sea-horses.
Galatea Baths—Star.
Hammond, Richard, dyer—Gas star.
Koppens, R., steam manufacturing works—Transparency, Britannia seated on a lion.
Maeller, John, and Co., ironmongers—Transparencies, the Duke, the Duke's arms, and the Queen.
Mueller, L., instrument-maker—Star.
Niagara Hotel—Transparency, the "Galatea" in full sail.
Plunkett, Charles, chemist—Star, with glass transparency in the centre, Edinburgh Castle.
Perry and Son, locksmiths—Brilliant gas constellation.
Prothonotary's Office—A crown in gas, and lights in the windows.
Prince of Wales Hotel—Gas star, with anchor in centre.
Public Works Office—A transparent crown in glass, and lights in the windows.
Robertson, John, dyer—Transparency, Balmoral Castle, surmounted by letters "A. E."
Rosengren, piano maker—Portrait of the Duke.
Sinclair's Hotel—Brunswick star in gas.
Snelgrove, Charles, draper—Transparency, the Prince being brought on shore by Neptune.
St. Francis Cathedral—Brilliant gas cross.
Stevenson and Elliot, coach-builders—This establishment was illuminated with Chinese lamps to represent the rigging of a ship. A pole sprung horizontally from the top of the building, and from the point of it ropes were stretched, hung with lanterns fore and aft, and on each side lanterns were employed; and carriage lamps suspended along the building gave additional effect.
Tankard's Temperance Hotel—Transparency, Neptune in a car drawn by sea-horses, accompanied by tritons and mermaids; on the one side Britannia, and on the other Victoria.

LITTLE BOURKE STREET.

THE CHINESE QUARTER.

This portion of the city had an illumination of its own, of a distinctive character. The Chinese residents combined together for the purpose of honouring the Prince with a display after the fashion of their own country. Two fine arches, lavishly decorated after the Mongolian manner, were erected—one at the intersection of Little Bourke-street with Swanston-street, and the other at the Russell-street end. There was a row of gas jets across each arch, the centre being topped by a large crown, in gas, with the letters "A. E. A." The sides were gaily painted and festooned with lanterns.

This locality was gaily decorated with Chinese flags, and the more prominent buildings had special illuminations. One of the largest business houses had a splendid gas star encircling the figure of a ship on a reflector. There were also large ornamental glass lamps, of Chinese manufacture. The Chinese Club-house, a very handsome stone building three-stories high, was made resplendent by a multitude of little coloured lamps, displayed in various devices.

Australian Arms Hotel—Three large lamps, with an oil painting on each pane.
Abercrombie, —, tinsmith—Gas star.
Attenborough's Restaurant—Chinese lanterns.
Burmeister, A., jeweller—A piece of mechanism, consisting of a rocking ship.
Commercial Inn—Transparency.
Enniscorthy Hotel—Lamps and candles.
Forster, —, saddler—Lanterns and evergreens.
Gannt, Thomas, jeweller and optician—Gas illumination, consisting of a star, with "P. A." in the centre; "A Grand," followed by an enormous pair of spectacles in gas, the illumination reading, "A Grand Spectacle."
Governor Arthur Hotel—Transparency, Britannia.
Horse and Jockey Hotel—Transparency, the Prince, with kangaroo and emu.
Brinckman, Otto, jeweller—Candles.
Rising Sun Hotel—Gas star.
Roberts, barber—Coloured lanterns.
Smith, A., gasfitter—Crown in gas.
Walsh, —, bootmaker—Transparency and coloured lanterns.

LITTLE COLLINS STREET.

Adam and Eve Hotel—Transparency, ship.
Alexander's Family Hotel—Transparencies: the Duke's arms, the City arms, and a ship in full sail.
Bray, —, china warehouse—Star.
Coop, James, lead-merchant—Anchor in gas.
Detective Office—Chinese lanterns.
Gepsler, F. C., Hunt Club Hotel—A wreath of gas in front of building.
Henty, J., and Co.—Reflector star.
Joske, A., and Co., wine merchants—Transparency of the Prince in uniform.
Kildare Hotel—Transparencies, the Prince, a harp, and a lion.
M'Cracken and Co., brewers—Brunswick star.
M'Donnell, John, and Co., grocers—Crown in gas.
M'Gregor's Colonial Bank Hotel—Rising sun.
M'Heraith, J., and Co., lead-merchants—Compass, star in gas, "A." in centre.
Paddington Hotel—Gas star.
Rainbow Hotel, Lowe—Rising sun.
Smith, John, plumber—In gas, the words "British Gems," surrounded by a wreath of the thistle.
Thorpe, D. T., vas-engineer—Crown.
United States Consulate, the Bishop's Registry, and L. Terry, architect—Candles.
Clisthorne and Co., grindery warehouse—Lanterns in gas.
Waterman's Arms—Gas star.
Watson, William, and Sons, warehousemen—Gas star.

LITTLE FLINDERS STREET.

Like the other smaller streets, this was illuminated only to a small extent, and the following were the more prominent:—

Cochrane and Brien—The windows lighted up with candles.
Connell, Watson and Hogarth—Crown above rising sun, in gas, with stars and the letters "P. A."; also, a row of gas jets the whole length of the frontage.
Davidson, J. and G., brassfounders—Gas crown.
Degraves's Mills—General illumination of the building by candles.
Dickson Brothers—Transparencies, portrait of the Prince, with the royal and colonial arms.
Galway Hotel—Transparencies, portraits of the Queen and the Prince, harp, and several stars in gas.
Laing and Webster—Transparencies filling the first-floor windows, the remainder of the front windows lighted with candles.
Malin and Co.—Brunswick star.
Mason, Firth and Co., printers—Brunswick star, enclosing letter "A."
M'Arthur, Sherrard and Copeland—Gas star, with transparencies.
M'Naughton, Love and Co.—Lines of gas jets along the cornices and pediment; above the pediment the letter "A." beneath a rising sun.
Norfolk Hotel—Gas star.
Paterson, Ray, Palmer and Co.—Windows lighted with gas burners.
Reid, I. and J.—Festoons of Chinese lanterns.
Royal Insurance Company—Transparency, showing the imperial arms and the arms of the company.
Savings Bank—Crown and anchor, in gas. At the Market-street and Flinders-lane frontages, Brunswick stars.
Spink, —, grocer—Star in gas.
Hen and Chickens Hotel—Gas star.
Weaver, W., and Co.—Pyramids of lamp candles in the front windows.

FLINDERS STREET.

The illumination at the Custom house was a transparency, placed in front of the brick pediment, representing the form of the building when finished; in the centre the figure of Commerce, in coloured glass.

Duke of Edinburgh Hotel—Large star.
Great Britain Hotel—Gas star, with letter "A."
Gough, J., and Co., maltsters—Brunswick star.
Harvest Home Hotel—Reflecting gas star.
Otago Hotel—Transparency, "Galatea" entering the Heads. Shields bearing English and Victorian arms. Above transparency, large star, with waving points.
Peninsular and Oriental Steam Navigation Company—Transparency, the "Galatea" entering the Heads; one of the company's steamers represented as crossing the "Galatea's" stern, and saluting.
Port Phillip Club Hotel—Line of gas jets.
Sargood, King, and Sargood, warehousemen—Ten large stars arranged in line in front of the first-floor windows.
Smith, J. C., produce-merchant—Display of candles.
Yarra Family Hotel—Star and anchor in gas.
Yarra Yarra Dining-rooms—Gas star.

KING STREET.

Government Stores—Gas crown, with flambeau pots on the parapet.
Ingram, J., draper—Gas star, and "A."
Kilkenny Hotel—Harp and coronet in coloured glass.
Krakowski, M., and Co., outfitters—Brunswick star.
Lilburne, James, produce store—Gas star.
M'Nicoll's Hotel—Brunswick star.
Nyberg, A., bootmaker—Six gas stars.
Plough Inn—Gas star.
Stevenson and Elliot, coachbuilders—Four transparencies, the first the royal arms, with the Prince's monogram; the second, device exhibiting the Victorian arms; the third, a portrait of the Prince; the fourth, an elaborately-painted design showing the arms of the coachbuilders, with their motto, "Triumphant, we bravely defend."
Terminus Hotel—Anchor and crown in gas.
Wilton, J., draper—Transparency, Britannia.

WILLIAM STREET.

Amess, Councillor—Brilliant design in gas of ship, with flags in gas on either side.
Barton's Hotel—Transparency representing the Prince approaching the shore; the "Galatea" at anchor in the distance.
Caughey and Dalzell—Candle illumination.
Cutts, Dr.—Candle illumination.
Johnson, G. and J., produce merchants—The windows lighted with candles.
Hanna, Peter, M.P. for Murray Boroughs—Gigantic letter "A" in Chinese lanterns, exhibited from flag-pole ninety feet high, forming a striking object from most parts of the city.
Lorimer, Marwood and Rome, and Holmes, White and Co.—Transparency, view of the Bay, with the "Galatea" and other vessels. In the windows, on either side, transparencies showing respectively the Royal, the Edinburgh, the Liverpool, and Glasgow arms.
Masterton, D.—Three transparencies—the "Galatea," portrait of the Queen, portrait of the Prince.
Metropolitan Hotel—Transparency representing Agriculture, with illumination of candles.
Office of Commissioner of Titles—Candles.
Roads and Bridges Office—Gas crown, &c.
St. James's Schools—Candle illumination.
Sydney Hotel—Large transparency, showing the "Galatea" entering the Bay.

STEPHEN STREET.

Allan, Robert, pawnbroker—Transparency, with the Duke of Edinburgh's arms. Britannia introducing the Prince to Victoria, with the "Galatea" in the distance.
Cornish Arms Hotel—Transparency of "Galatea."
Malcolm, John F.—Transparency, a ship locked in the ice, and crew leaving her in search of Franklin.
Melbourne Club Hotel—Transparencies, anchor and crown.
Olive Branch Hotel—Transparency, Britannia and the Prince.
Peacock Hotel—Candle illumination, with transparencies.
Protestant Hall—Transparency, William III., with Britannia on the one side and Victoria on the other.
Standard Hotel—Transparency, Victoria receiving the Prince.
Victoria Hotel—Pyramids of candles, and transparency representing the Queen.
Volunteer Office—A glass trophy and flags.
Young, John, and Son, jewellers—Design, painted by J. W. Burt, representing the Arts, with a view of the Bay and Port Phillip Heads.

LATROBE STREET.

Crown Lands Office—Pyramids of candles.
Duke of Kent Hotel—Royal Arms on glass.
Immigration Office—Pyramids of candles.
Liverpool Boarding-house—Transparency, "Galatea" entering the Heads.

Menzies' Hotel—Gas stars.
Royal Society—Every window was occupied by a transparency, each bearing a device suitable for the occasion.
Temperance Hotel—Gas star, with "A."

MARKET STREET.

In this street little display was made, the situation not being central, and many of the buildings being bonded stores. The premises of Messrs. Ross and Spowers, Messrs. George Martin and Co., and Messrs. Lange and Thoneman were however effectively illuminated with candles, while Messrs. White Brothers and Co. had a transparency consisting of a coat of arms, with the inscription "*Presto et persto*," and the motto of the Duke of Edinburgh.

SPRING STREET.

In addition to the Treasury and the Parliament Houses (which we have elsewhere described), there were no illuminations worth noticing, with the exception of the Model Schools, on which there was a brilliant display of light, consisting of a Prince of Wales' feather, and the letters "A. E.," in gas, with lighted flambeaux on every available part of the building.

SPENCER STREET.

With the exception of the Railway Terminus, which displayed two brilliant gas crowns, and a candle illumination at the Sailors' Home, there was nothing calling for special notice.

THE FITZROY GARDENS.

These gardens were illuminated on the evening previous to that of the general display, and the effect produced is almost beyond description. The natural beauty of the gardens, combined with the luxuriant foliage of the trees and shrubs, and the artistic arrangement of the various coloured lanterns, made for the time a fairy land on *terra firma*; and the general expressions of approval accorded by the thousands of visitors who were present at the fête, must have been a welcome and ample reward to the artists who undertook the labours of arrangement.

THE FLAGSTAFF GARDENS.

These Gardens were illuminated by means of Chinese lanterns, in the same manner as the Fitzroy Gardens on the previous evening. The general effect in the Flagstaff Gardens was equally beautiful with that of the Fitzroy Gardens. The electric light, which was exhibited at the old Observatory, also added to the beauty of the scene.

THE ELECTRIC LIGHTS.

One of the features of the illumination was the display of revolving electric lights by the Telegraph Department. These were exhibited from five points—the Parliament Houses, the Electric Telegraph Buildings, the Astronomical Observatory on the St. Kilda road, the Flagstaff-hill, and the Railway Sheds at Williamstown. They were all uniform in character, and were prepared under the direction of Mr. S. M'Gowan, the superintendent of the department. The greater portion of the apparatus employed was made in Melbourne by Mr. Robert Skilton, mathematical instrument maker at the Observatory, while the copper reflectors were manufactured by Messrs. Dykes and Edwards, coppersmiths. The electro-plating and burnishing was executed by Mr. Watt, of William-street.

The suburban boroughs of Collingwood, Fitzroy, Emerald Hill, Brighton, St. Kilda, Richmond, Hawthorn, Prahran, &c., all joined more or less in the demonstration. Space, however, will not admit of any detailed description being given.

THE CRICKET MATCH.

The Cricketers' Association, acting in concert with the Reception Commission, resolved to provide two days' sport which would be sufficient to justify a visit from His Royal Highness to the ground of the Melbourne Club. The meeting was arranged to extend over Wednesday and Thursday, 27th and 28th November, the sports to consist of a cricket match, in which those of colonial birth measured their strength against an eleven of the world; to be followed by an athletic exhibition, in which valuable prizes were offered for competition. A plain but neatly designed pavilion was erected for the accommodation of the Duke and his *suite* inside the members' reserve. The roof was lined and draped with green and white striped linen, with a trimming of scarlet fringe; and the floor, which was laid with green Brussels carpet, was amply furnished with blackwood chairs, covered in green wrap. The upholstery was supplied by Messrs. Beauchamp and Rocke. The match was announced to commence at noon on Wednesday. The ground did not assume a crowded appearance until past two o'clock, when there were in all from ten to twelve thousand persons present. At three o'clock His Royal Highness, accompanied by Lord Newry and Mr. Yorke, entered the ground, and was received by the president and office-bearers of the Victorian Cricketers' Association and Melbourne Club, and conducted to the pavilion prepared for his reception amid the most hearty cheering. The band of the 14th Regiment struck up the National Anthem, and cheers were also given for the Queen. The Prince remained in the pavilion a short time, and then retired to a marquee, in which refreshments were laid. The Prince was afterwards received by the players assembled in the middle of the ground, and then left, expressing his regret that engagements in connection with the departure of the mail prevented him making a longer stay. The match was resumed and finished on the following day, on which, however, the Duke's engagements precluded his attendance. The athletic sports included three events—a quarter mile race, won by Mr. Higgins; a mile race, won by Mr. A. D. Michie, and a steeplechase, in which Mr. H. C. Harrison was the victor.

THE GOVERNOR'S BALL.

The Ball given by his Excellency the Governor on the evening of Wednesday, 27th November, in honour of the arrival of his Royal Highness the Duke of Edinburgh, was on a scale of magnificence hitherto unsurpassed in the annals of the colony. The *Argus* thus describes this brilliant event:—

The scene of the *fête* was the new Exhibition-building, which, handsome before, had undergone a surprising transformation, and was greatly increased in beauty and convenience. Mr. J. G. Knight, the agent for the Reception Commissioners, had been hard at work many weeks in its ornamentation, and the result was a splendid success. At the northern end of the great hall stood the canopied dais, on which his Excellency and Lady Manners-Sutton stood, with the most illustrious of their guests, to receive the others. It was not unfit for the Royal presence. Supported by slender twisted pillars was a mass of filagree work in white and gold, surmounted by the Royal arms, gorgeously emblazoned, and hung with crimson, and ceiled with white and blue satin. The walls on each side were adorned with warlike trophies, composed of a thousand or so of swords and bayonets disposed in patterns on the walls. Below, and on the huge square pillars separating the nave and aisles, were large mirrors all along the room, and between were festoons of fragrant green shoots of tea-tree and roses. Beautiful shrubs served to occupy the vacant spaces, and break the monotony of the vista. The painted walls and roof of blue, buff, and etruscan red, needed no freshening up, and indeed the effulgence of the lustrous gas-burners would have covered a world of shabbiness. It was not the gas-sunlights only that illuminated the room, but there was a sort of lesser glory of stars. Depending from the ceiling were some hundreds of small gas-stars, which in the distance twinkled like Catherine wheels, and their scintillations produced an indescribably pretty effect. Opposite the dais rose the gallery, hung with green wreaths and crimson cloth, and that point commanded the best view of the dazzling scene below. Along the aisles were also rows of seats, draped in crimson. The octagon, whose elegant adornments and convenient shape always made it a favourite resort of visitors when the Exhibition was open, was now another surprise—its pillars wreathed with green and flowers, its sides and roof flashing with lustres and reflector-stars. There was dancing here as well as in the hall, the orchestra being raised conveniently opposite. But perhaps the most perfect thing of all was in the fountain court, now turned into a vast pavilion. It was a fairy scene of plashing waters, coloured lights, greenery, and flowers. In the centre, beneath a quaint pagoda, was an illuminated fountain, from which gushed water in jets, and inverted convolvulus shapes, resplendently glittering in variously-tinged lights, which, managed by hidden machinery, shifted continually. Here were provided magenta cloth covered seats, winding round spaces filled with turf, flowers, and shrubs, which were likewise set round the sides, interspersed with arches and tufts of huge fern leaves, and vases full of roses and geraniums. The whole was a charming bower.

Supper was laid in the old carriage annexe. The passage thither was hung with pink and white, set with rosettes in white metal. Anchors, shaped with roses, were suspended from the roof, and the place was lit with gas stars. In the room beyond were five rows of tables groaning with good things. The caterer was Mr. Miller (late Cockburn), of Collins-street, under the superintendence of Mr. Bartlett, his Excellency's butler, and things were managed to accommodate seven hundred guests at a time. The walls and wooden pillars were hung with pink and white. In lines along the ceiling were innumerable flags of all nations, the British in the centre, and Chinese lanterns, on which naval devices were painted. Cocoa-nut matting striped with crimson drugget covered the floor, and at the upper end was a dais, richly ornamented with hangings of crimson and gold. The arrangement and contents of the room were undeniably triumphs in their way. The National Art gallery afforded a delightful retreat from the noisy gaieties of the ballroom, and made an unequalled lounge. The music was provided by Mr. Zeplin, whose admirable band comprised thirty performers, and the programme included the Duke of Edinburgh Galop—a spirited and effective composition by the leader of the band.

The Governor's Ball.

The ball began at nine o'clock, by which time the train of carriages reached from Latrobe-street to Collins street—over half a mile—a state of things which continued some time. Two thousand eight hundred guests had been invited—two thousand five hundred had accepted their invitations, and it was no wonder there was a crush. The Prince, dressed in naval uniform, and wearing the ribbon of the Garter and other orders, was among the first arrivals, and opened the ball. It was a quadrille, and the first set was thus composed:—His Royal Highness and Miss Manners-Sutton, his Excellency and Mrs. J. G. Francis, General Sir Trevor Chute and Miss Mabel Manners-Sutton, Mr. Brierly and Mrs. Hogg, Lord Newry and Miss Cole, Mr. Haig and Miss Wilkinson, Mr. Vorke and Miss Pitt, and Colonel Page with a lady whose name was not ascertained. During the earlier hours, perhaps, the crowding was too great for comfortable dancing, but gradually as people found their way into the other rooms, the hall and octagon were greatly relieved. This must have been to the high gratification of the ladies, most of whom had adopted the modern fashion of trains—graceful, but so incommodious that, as the small hours of the night advanced, the triumphs of millinery seen in floating masses of gauzy or silken drapery were less and less, while the floor showed frequent signs of wrecked skirts. Such penalties—that is to say, the inconvenience to men, and the destruction to dress—were however, not too much to pay for the night's delight. Almost all that the colony had of worth and station were there to meet the royal visitor—the highest officials, chiefest politicians, foremost merchants, in fact, the ablest and best. There were present nearly every member of the Ministry, many Executive Councillors and members of both Houses of Legislature, officers, military and naval and volunteer, a large party from the *Galatea*, town and country mayors, presidents of shire councils, foreign consuls, and—what is unusual—a few clergymen. But these are only the outlines of an assemblage which was essentially comprehensive. It was not to be expected that the ladies were undistinguished either. They reached the highest colonial standard in female matters. Their toilettes were of the latest modes, the most exquisite elaboration. The sight from the gallery at the thousands of figures gliding through the dances was a great treat, and one probably never surpassed in the lifetime of the present generation.

At one o'clock the Prince and Lady Manners-Sutton, with the Governor following, led the way to the supper-room. The first batch of dancers being refreshed, his Excellency proposed a few loyal toasts, viz., the Queen, and the Prince and Princess of Wales, which were received with tremendous applause.

His Excellency, rising, said:—Ladies and gentlemen, I give you the Health of his Royal Highness the Duke of Edinburgh. In proposing this toast, which at all times and under all circumstances would be received with enthusiasm by you, we have the peculiar advantage, and we have the deep gratification, of having his Royal Highness among us, and I am sure his presence may be regarded by us as a proof of the interest which Her Majesty takes in her subjects in this part of her empire, and as a proof of his Royal Highness's desire to obtain a knowledge of the condition of some of his Royal mother's subjects in Australia, as well as a desire to promote their prosperity and union with the mother country. I need say no more, unless I take upon myself, as I shall with confidence, to express to his Royal Highness the deep and warm—I can hardly find words, indeed, to express the gratification we all feel. I call upon you to drink "the Health of his Royal Highness the Duke of Edinburgh, and the rest of the Royal Family."

The toast having been drunk with enthusiastic and repeated cheering,

The Prince said:—Ladies and gentlemen, I thank you sincerely, in my own name as well as those of the other members of the Royal Family, for the manner in which you have received this toast. If it is a source of gratification to you that I have paid this visit to Australia, I can only tell you that it has caused me the greatest possible pleasure to have been enabled to make this voyage, and visit this distant portion of Her Majesty's empire. I know from all that I have seen that I need not look far to find the most universal loyalty to Her Majesty's throne and person in every portion of these colonies. Ladies and gentlemen, I thank you sincerely for the kind way in which you have received this toast."

His Royal Highness and the Governor then left the table, and returned to the dancing room, when the Prince danced a Scotch reel with Mrs. Panton. Dancing during the interval amongst the guests was suspended in their admiration of his Royal Highness's agility, the musical accompaniment being played by the Prince's Scotch piper. The Scottish guests were particularly gratified, and gave vent to their appropriation in a marked manner. His Royal Highness and the Governor took their departure at about three a.m., but dancing was continued until a later hour.

PORT PHILLIP FARMERS' SOCIETY'S SHOW.

The grand day of this society's show was on Thursday, 28th November, when the anticipated visit of the Duke of Edinburgh drew a large number of people to the grounds. A platform was raised in the middle of the yard, covered over with an awning, under which to receive the Prince, and present him with the addresses which had been prepared for the occasion. On the arrival of His Royal Highness, who came in a close carriage, accompanied by his Excellency the Governor, the Hon. Eliot Yorke, and Lord Newry, he ascended the platform, and was received by the Hon. the Chief Secretary, the Hon. Messrs. Bindon, Sullivan, Sladen, Learmonth, and several other public and official personages. When the cheering had ceased, Mr. M'Culloch read the following address:—

> May it please your Royal Highness—We, the members of the Port Phillip Farmers' Society, approach your Royal Highness with the warmest expressions of our loyalty and devotion to our Most Gracious Majesty's throne and person. We respectfully tender to your Royal Highness our congratulations on your arrival in the colony of Victoria, and our acknowledgments of your condescension in honouring with your presence this exhibition. We feel that we are entitled to regard this mark of your Royal Highness's favour, not alone as consistent with the graciousness of your disposition, but as indicating that the lively interest manifested in all matters connected with agriculture and stock-breeding by the late lamented Prince, your father, is inherited by your Royal Highness. The Port Phillip Farmers' Society has, since its constitution in 1847, held annual shows of stock, implements and machinery; and during the last twelve years also of grain and general produce. From year to year the most marked improvement has been observable in the quality of every description of exhibit. These marks of improvement will, we trust, sufficiently demonstrate to your Royal Highness that Her Majesty's subjects in this part of Her Majesty's dominions are animated by that energy and self-reliance which characterise their brethren in all parts of the empire. It is to us a matter of much regret that owing to the advanced period of the season we shall be deprived of the pleasure of submitting to the inspection of your Royal Highness a large portion of our choicest stock, but we confidently hope that evidence will not be wanting to show to your Royal Highness that Victoria holds no mean place in Her Majesty's dominions, in regard to the particular industries which it is the object of our society to encourage.

His Royal Highness made no formal reply, but it was intimated that one would be forwarded to the society.

The Free Banquet.

Mr. T. Learmonth, M.L.C., then presented an address from the president and members of the Board of Agriculture, which was as follows:—

May it please your Royal Highness— We, the members of the Board of Agriculture representing the various agricultural societies in Victoria, desire to take this opportunity of adding one more to the many addresses of welcome which have already greeted your Royal Highness. In the old country the agricultural community has ever been conspicuous for loyalty and devotion to the Sovereign. We assure your Royal Highness that similar feelings towards Her Majesty the Queen exist among the agriculturists in this colony, and that they entertain a lively interest in the happiness and welfare of the Royal Family, and the maintenance of the integrity of the British empire. We thank your Royal Highness for honouring this exhibition with your presence. We are sensible that it can by no means compare with exhibitions of a like character in the father land; but we venture to hope that it may be pleasing to your Royal Highness to trace here, and in your visit to the interior, the progress in agriculture which has been made in a country where thirty-two years ago the white man was a stranger, and the ground was unbroken by the plough.

It was intimated with reference to this address also that a written reply would be returned.

After some more cheering, his Royal Highness went round the show, and examined the neat cattle and horse stock. He then partook of some slight refreshment, and left, after having spent about half an hour at the yards. All the time he was followed by a large crowd, who cheered him loudly as he departed.

THE FREE BANQUET.

Of all the events connected with the reception of his Royal Highness, that under the above heading was the only one that could not be pronounced a success. The failure should not, however, be altogether laid to the charge of the promoters. The origin of the undertaking was simply to provide a feast for the poor, and as the class under this category was known to be not a very large one, the first arrangements were of a proportionately moderate extent. As the scheme of the "Free Banquet" became more developed, the committee received such wholesale offers of assistance, both in money and kind, that it was resolved to depart from the original intention, and make it a free feast for the whole community. It is a matter of regret that the dimensions of the entertainment were eventually allowed to assume such excessive and unwieldy proportions, as without a large paid staff of well-drilled and experienced attendants, it would have been morally impossible to cater for such a mass of people as congregated in the Zoological reserve on the occasion referred to.

The *Herald* supplies the following account of the proceedings:—

By eleven o'clock the paddock was full of people eagerly making their way towards the reserve, and the railway trains stopping at the Cricket-ground Station were crowded to excess. Up to one o'clock the entrances to the ground where the banquet was to be held were kept carefully closed, policemen resolutely refusing admittance to all except those connected with the management of the feast. At one o'clock, however, these restrictions were removed, and the eager crowd entered the reserve intent on those two great passions of human nature —sightseeing, and eating and drinking. A strong force of police, mounted and foot, had been marched on to the ground some time before the opening of the gates, and under their management the approaches to the different tables were for a time kept tolerably clear.

The principal entrance to the grounds was by the gates near the superintendent's residence, and through this an immense crowd flocked continuously in. In the centre a canopy, decorated with flags furnished by the Reception Commission, had been erected. Close to this canopy, and within a railed-in enclosure, was the wine fountain, supplied from a five hundred gallon cask, furnished by Messrs. Knight, Bear, and Adams; and under the fountain was a tastefully arranged table covered with glasses and decanters, at which it was intended to offer to his Royal Highness a goblet of colonial wine. The goblet to be used for this purpose was an excessively elegant gold cup kindly furnished for the occasion by Mr. Edward Hart, of St. Kilda. A pavilion had also been prepared for the expected Royal visitor, the furniture having been supplied by Messrs. Beauchamp and Rocke. Other tents were also erected for the accommodation of the marshal (Mr. Gardner), the committee, the Press, and the storage of provisions, one of the largest of these being occupied by Mr. Grimwood, the caterer. In the rear of these was the culinary reserve, where since an early hour of the morning huge joints of meat and gigantic cauldrons of potatoes had been roasted and boiled. The bread, that important part of a good meal, had been baked by Mr. D. Cameron, of Victoria-street, from a large quantity of first-class flour furnished by Messrs. Degraves, Ramsden, Gibson, Walker, and others, in addition to 500 loaves supplied by other contributors. In the meat department the principal contributors were Messrs. Petty, Bignell, and Gardner; the two former furnishing two splendid barons of beef, and the latter a large quantity of mutton and lamb, in addition to a fine bullock, beautifully dressed for the purpose of being roasted whole. Over seventy tons of potatoes had also been supplied, and of pies, tarts, buns, lollies, fruit, &c., there was a goodly store indeed. The following, in fact, is a tolerably correct list of the contributions:—120,000 lbs. of meat, including beef, mutton, pork, and hams, besides 2800 lbs. sent cooked, the remainder being prepared on the ground; 4500 lbs. of plum pudding; 72 dozen of pastry, cooked on the ground; 5000 pies; 600 lbs. fish, cooked on the ground; 100 lbs. cakes. The whole of the provision department was under the charge of Mr. Hadley, and the kitchen under that of Mr. Maximilian and Mr. Louis Smith, the latter of whom had erected a patent oven for the especial cooking of Mr. Bignell's gigantic baron of beef. Of bulk ale there were six hhds., supplied by Messrs. Mitchell, Parker, Terry, and Allen; besides several cases of champagne and claret. Mr. James Young also furnished ten tons of firewood and one of coal, delivered on the ground. The long tables laid out for the occasion afforded a peculiarly pleasant sight, the ladies who had for the nonce assumed the *role* of waitresses, forming, in their neat uniforms of white and blue, an exceedingly attractive picture. Among these were Mrs. Clarson, Mrs. Langley, Mrs. Anderson, Mrs. Gotch, Madame De Bohm, Mrs. Campbell, Mrs. Hann, Mrs. and the Misses Moses, and others to the number of ninety. All these, uniformly dressed, at the hour appointed for the Prince's arrival formed four deep, and, marshalled by Mr. Dod, marched through the crowd, who willingly made way for them, and took their places under the canopy in readiness for the arrival—which did not take place, although the new flag was duly hoisted and a short speech made by the ladies' marshal.

And yet in spite of all these arrangements, in spite of the large quantity of food and liquor that undoubtedly had been provided, the affair was far from going off well, and out of the ninety-thousand faces present, very many were considerably elongated before their departure. That the food was there was beyond a doubt, for during some portion of the afternoon it was actually being thrown about; and towards the close of the proceedings the wine-fountain was made by some eccentric spirits to play upon the crowd; but for all this many in the throng never had the chance of either eating or drinking anything. Whose fault it was would be difficult and perhaps uncharitable to say; but from the moment they were opened, the tables, especially those where the colonial wine was laid on, were rushed by a crowd of decided roughs, prominent among whom was of course the colonial boy, and as a natural consequence the women and children wandered about the reserve utterly unable to obtain even a glass of water, unless when occasionally supplied from the committee and other sources. The bands, too, in attendance, including those of the 14th and the volunteers, complained that during the day they could get no refreshment, and the special constables employed murmured loudly to the same effect. By two o'clock there was, judging from the grumblings of the crowd, nothing whatever left to eat, and expressions of disapproval became louder than ever. Had his Royal Highness arrived at the time appointed, the attention of the people would, of course, have been diverted, and arrangements made for a second issue. Up to four o'clock the expectation of his arrival was kept up; and after that disappointment was changed to something very like anger, as the crowd contemplated at their leisure what they considered a decided hardship. The weather, too, was unfavourable, a strong hot wind blowing all the morning; and no man's temper is improved by having his eyes filled; and any food he may chance to get, peppered with considerably more than the peck of dirt each "frail son of Adam" is supposed to consume during his lifetime. Under all these combined circumstances, the invited guests began gradually to lose their temper, and shortly before five o'clock, when it had become generally known that the Prince was not coming, all the reserved tents were rushed, and—with the exception of the marshal's, temporarily preserved by the police and one excessively energetic volunteer—pulled down. The Press tent, of course, shared the general ruin, and after its destruction reporting became a task of considerable difficulty. Mr. Grimwood's tent, too, where a large quantity of wine and beer had been stored, was also rushed, and in a few moments the tent was levelled to the ground, and its contents distributed amongst the crowd, the unfortunate men in the tent being enveloped in the canvas, and generally jumped upon. After this the confusion became ten thousand times worse confounded. Some climbed into the tree where the cask of wine supplying the fountain was placed, and, cutting the pipes, distributed the contents pretty liberally over the crowd, far more of the ruby stream going over the heads of the people than into the pannikins and buckets that were held up to catch it. Others again managed to ascend the canopy erected over the table prepared for the Prince, and from that lofty position opened a heavy fire of chaff upon the crowd below, while the rest of the "invited" occupied themselves in discussing the liquor to which they had helped themselves. As for getting anything to eat it was by this time impossible, for the advertised miles of tables had long been cleared, and the fair waitresses dispersed, while the members of the committee, the stewards, and others had removed their distinguishing badges and mingled with the crowd; and yet with all this confusion there was no absolute ill-temper displayed, and the mob—with the exception of 200 or 300 persons, who, distinguished by small blue ribbons in their button-holes, were evidently acting in concert—seemed to think they were behaving in a perfectly justifiable manner. Perhaps, too, they were not without some reason for so thinking. After all, they were invited guests; and when one man asks another to his house, firstly to meet a distinguished guest, and secondly to eat a good dinner, the invited person has some reason to complain when he can neither see the one nor eat the other. Looking at the matter in this light, there are great excuses to be made for the people, but at the same time it would be wrong to censure the committee too severely. The confusion about half-past five o'clock reached a climax; and the remainder of the wine and beer having been sent off the ground under a guard of police, Inspector Hare, with a large force of mounted and foot, began to clear the reserve, and after a little time succeeded in doing so. Before half-past six o'clock their task was nearly completed; and numerous groups wending their way home were soon all that was left of the long-expected banquet. Before concluding this brief account of the Free Banquet, it is necessary to state the reasons why his Royal Highness did not attend as promised.

On leaving the Port Philip Farmers' Society's Show, the Prince drove at once towards Richmond, and was within a few hundred yards of the scene of the Free Banquet, when he was met by some of the police officials, who represented to his Royal Highness that in consequence of the enormous crowd there assembled, the excitement of the people who were unable to obtain refreshment, and the immense number of women and young children congregated about the pavilion erected for the reception of his Royal Highness, they (the police) were seriously apprehensive that his arrival in the midst of such a crowd might be the cause of serious injury to many of the spectators, and particularly the young. The Prince expressed himself as ready and anxious to keep his engagement with the public, and as perfectly easy in his mind as to his personal safety, but in deference to the strong remonstrance of those who were well qualified to advise, his Highness consented to go no further. In dissuading his Highness, as they did, the police authorities doubtless acted to the best of their judgment, having in view the protection of the lives of the public; and although it is much to be regretted that the Prince was not present at the Free Banquet, it would have been a matter of still more serious regret had his presence under the circumstances realised the apprehensions of the public authorities.

The Fireworks in the Yarra Park

On Thursday evening the 28th of November, Professor Brock gave the Melbourne public one of the finest displays of the pyrotechnic art ever seen in Australia. From first to last it was one uninterrupted success—the interest never flagging, and the crowd (one of the largest ever seen in Melbourne) kept in one continual simmer of good humour. Applause was bestowed as each more and more successful piece was discharged for their delight, until at last it almost seemed as if the spectators (especially the young folks) wanted words to express their wonder at the results achieved. The crowd, numerous as it was, was orderly in the extreme. The Military Store Department, under Major Hall, commenced the display by showing a variety of coloured fires, which excited the warmest approbation of thousands of those present amongst the spectators. The shells, with coloured fires, shown by this department, contributed greatly to the success of the evening. The programme was as follows:—Successive illuminations of Bengal fire and of red and green fire; then an aerial salute of maroon rockets; next a discharge of shells, with bright stars of all the colours of the rainbow. Multitudes of rockets filled up the spaces between the various displays of "pyrotechnic morceaux." Of the latter, first came a well-conceived composition, "The True Lovers' Knot," changing to a revolving sun amidst a sparkling fire. Presently there came a beautiful centre wheel of coloured fires, changing to resplendent figures of brilliant fire. Rockets with snakes, rockets with golden rain,

Danæ rockets, and cohorn shells filled up the time until Mr. Brock introduced his grand sun-piece, commencing with a rainbow wheel, changing to four vertical wheels illuminated with four more suns revolving in reverse. Then more rockets, shells, tourbillons, &c., and next was shown a Maltese cross in yellow and white, with three changes of brilliant fire. The compositions of the Professor which followed included the star of Brunswick, in yellow and white lances, with Saxon wheel in front, changing to a pretty device of brilliant fires; then, after intervals of rockets, &c., came a very fine composition of wheels, with three brilliant and beautiful changes. Presently was a very grand illuminated Saxon piece, with five-pointed stars in a device of brilliant fire. The last, and the crowning piece of the evening, was a picture one hundred and twenty feet wide by thirty feet high, representing Britannia, with H.M.S.S. *Galatea* in the distance, with the shamrock on one side, the thistle the other, with the rose, emblematical of England—the others, of course, representing Ireland and Scotland. In the composition, which was really artistic, were introduced transparencies of Her Majesty and her son Prince Alfred; on either side of them two revolving globes and five triplet stars, in coloured fires, with supporting columns of coloured Roman discharges. Then came discharges of mines, batteries, &c. Several hundreds of rockets with coloured fires were then discharged, and the finish was a brilliant device, "Victoria Welcomes Victoria's Son," followed by a parting word to the Victorian public, "Good night," in brilliant fire.

THE BENEVOLENT ASYLUM.

The same evening at the Benevolent Asylum (a suitable pavilion having been erected in front of the building), about four hundred and fifty of the inmates sat down to a good substantial dinner, the materials for which had been generously furnished by a number of ladies and gentlemen. The Hon. George Harker (chairman of the committee of management) presided, and a good many members of the committee were also present, among whom were Mr. Sturt, Mr. Marsden, Professor Wilson, Mr. Tankard, Mr. O'Brien, the Rev. M. Rintel, Mr. Barwise (Mayor of Hotham), &c. Dr. Nield represented the honorary medical staff. The sight was a particularly interesting one; for among the hundreds of poor creatures who tenant this admirable charity, there are the ex-representatives of almost every grade of social life. The toasts proposed and heartily responded to were—"The Queen," "The Duke of Edinburgh," and "The Governor," to which followed "The Superintendent, the Committee, and Honorary Medical Officers." Several of the inmates then sang some songs, and among the vocalists was an old man, aged ninety one, named Alexander Millar, who gave "Young Lochinvar" with remarkable spirit. An old man-of-war's man, some few years the junior of Millar, sang several comic songs, with much humorous accompaniment of action, and an old lady verging upon eighty sang three songs, accompanying herself on the accordeon. Another inmate, named Lloyd, delivered an eloquent oration on the visit of the Duke of Edinburgh to Australia. Whatever *contretemps* may have attended the other free banquet, this was admitted on all hands to be a great success—a success very largely due to the unflagging exertions of the excellent superintendent and matron, Mr. and Mrs. James M'Cutcheon.

Visit of H.R.H. Prince Alfred.

Laying the Foundation Stone of the New Town Hall.

On the afternoon of Friday 29th November, the ceremony of laying the foundation-stone of the new Town Hall, at the intersection of Collins and Swanston streets, was performed by his Royal Highness the Duke of Edinburgh. For some time before that appointed for the ceremonial to take place, a vast crowd, numbering several thousands of persons, assembled in the neighbourhood of the Town Hall. Every window, balcony, and housetop within sight of the building was thick with human life. The large stand erected by the Corporation was crowded from top to bottom with ladies, who were admitted by special ticket. Every colour and varieties of shade were blended amongst the vast concourse which assembled on the stand, and the ladies may feel gratified when they hear that the Prince said he never saw a finer sight. A strong body of police was drawn up in front of the building, and as barriers had been erected at various points, the crowd was kept well back from pressing on to the platform. The band of the 14th Regiment was stationed close to the entrance. At ten minutes to four a carriage containing his Royal Highness the Duke of Edinburgh, his Excellency the Governor, Lord Newry, and the Hon. Eliot Yorke, arrived at the principal entrance, where his Royal Highness was received by his Worship the Mayor and the members and officers of the Corporation, and by them conducted to the council chamber. The Misses Manners-Sutton were present, and occupied seats in the front of the stand. Punctually at four o'clock in a procession, in the following order, reached the platform, where the ceremony was to be performed:—

CONTRACTORS,
ARCHITECTS,
TOWN CLERK,
COUNCILLORS,
ALDERMEN,
THE RIGHT WORSHIPFUL THE MAYOR,
H.R.H. THE DUKE OF EDINBURGH AND SUITE,
HIS EXCELLENCY THE GOVERNOR AND SUITE,
THE LORD BISHOP OF MELBOURNE,
MAJOR-GENERAL SIR TREVOR CHUTE, K.C.B., AND STAFF,
THE MEMBERS OF THE CABINET,
THE ROYAL RECEPTION COMMISSION,
THE HON. SPEAKER OF THE LEGISLATIVE ASSEMBLY.

His Royal Highness was conducted to a position close to the stone about to be laid, and Mr. Reed, the architect, submitted for his inspection the bottle containing the records and coins to be placed in the cavity.

His Worship the Mayor then came forward and said—"Your Royal Highness, I beg to request your permission to give a few particulars as to the object for which we are at present met. From the early settlement of this colony, in 1835, the progress made in the city was very slow. In 1842, the then Government of New South Wales saw fit to endow the city with self-government. Up to 1851 the city was, indeed, small; but in that year the discovery of mineral wealth in Victoria caused the city to grow, as it were, by magic. The immense strain upon the funds of the Council and the Government at that time prevented the erection of a suitable building as a town hall, proportionate to the position of the city; but since the city has grown to such an extent, we found it our duty to erect a building which will be a credit to the city in

Laying the Foundation Stone of the New Town Hall.

years to come, and will at the present time meet the requirements of the country, and afford proper accommodation and convenience for carrying on the deliberations of this body. It is for that purpose that we are here to-day, and have invited your Royal Highness to lay this foundation-stone, and for your presence here we now beg to give you our thanks.

The Town Clerk (Mr. E. G. FitzGibbon) then read the following address:—

May it please your Royal Highness,—We, Her Majesty's most dutiful and loyal subjects, the mayor, aldermen, councillors, and citizens of the city of Melbourne, respectfully tender to your Royal Highness our sincerest thanks for the gracious favour accorded to us by your Royal Highness in consenting to perform the ceremony of laying the foundation-stone of the Town-hall of this city. Recognising, in the honour of your Royal Highness's presence in this most distant region of Her Majesty's dominions, an immediate and special indication in respect to us of the benignity, love for, and interest in the welfare of her subjects ever evinced by Her Majesty, and which have enshrined her in the hearts of her people, and in none more dearly than in those of the citizens of Melbourne; and confident that your Royal Highness is imbued with the like gracious sentiments, we venture to occupy your Royal Highness's attention with a brief outline of the local events which have preceded and led to the present undertaking.

Ten years prior to the birth of your Royal Highness the site of this city was a trackless forest, and the colony an unexplored wilderness. First occupied in 1835, in 1842 the town was incorporated, its burgesses being 543 in number, its revenue less than £3000, and its streetways dusty tracks and dangerous ravines, winding amongst growing trees and the uncleared roots and stumps of fallen timber.

With the public spirit fostered by its corporate council, the town aided in obtaining for the district of Port Phillip the boon of separation from New South Wales, and the elevation of the district into a new colony, founded by Her Majesty's favour and honoured with her royal name.

The immediately subsequent discovery of gold accelerated the progress of the city, and added so rapidly to its population, that public improvements for the convenience of the people became necessary simultaneously in all parts of the wide civic area of more than twelve square miles, and it was found expedient to place some portions of the outskirts under the care of minor corporations; eight of these, which were wholly or in part within the city, have now an aggregate population of 80,000 persons, and a revenue of £65,000 a year, while there remains to the parent city an area of seven square miles, 100 miles of well-made streets, a population of nearly 50,000 souls, and a revenue of £90,000 per annum. The progress of the city necessitated suitable buildings for the transaction of corporate business and the assembling of the citizens; a town-hall was planned, and the adjacent building, in which we have had the honour to receive your Royal Highness, and which is now about to be demolished, was erected some fifteen years ago as a part of the design. Public requirements have outstripped the provisions of that plan; it has therefore been found necessary to abandon it, to extend the area of the site, and to erect a larger structure. For this, designs have been prepared by Messrs. Reed and Barnes, architects; its erection is undertaken for £65,290, by Messrs Lawrence and Cain, builders; and the happy circumstance of your Royal Highness's visit to these shores has afforded us the singular gratification and honour of seeing its foundation-stone laid this day by your Royal Highness's hands. We hail the auspicious event as attaching new interest and distinction to the structure, and as twining a golden strand into the cords of loyal, proud, and loving associations and memories that bind to Her Majesty's throne and empire the hearts of Her Majesty's subjects in Australia. In recalling the occurrences of our short history, we reverently offer devout and humble thanks to a bountiful Providence for countless benefits vouchsafed to us for our enjoyment in this fair land. And we pray to the Almighty Giver of every good and perfect gift for long life and happiness to our Most Gracious Sovereign, and for His choicest blessings to your Royal Highness and to the other august members of Her Majesty's illustrious family.

JAMES STEWART BUTTERS, Mayor.
EDMUND GERALD FITZGIBBON, Town Clerk.

His Royal Highness made the following reply:—

Gentlemen—In thanking you for the very interesting address you have presented to me, I wish to assure you that it gives me great pleasure to perform the ceremony of laying the foundation-stone of the new Town-hall of this city, marking, as it does, another epoch in the increased and, I trust, increasing welfare of this capital. I am very glad that my visit to Australia has given me the opportunity of seeing the results of the wonderfully rapid progress made by this colony—results which only the experience of my stay among you could have enabled me duly to appreciate.

But that which gives me the sincerest gratification is to find that the pride which you must feel in the gigantic resources and prosperity of this province, so far from weakening your allegiance to the throne, has made you eager to impress upon me the assurance of your devoted loyalty to Her Majesty and your attachment to the mother country.

I heartily wish that every success may attend this building and the purposes for which it is intended; and that if it should ever meet with the fate of its predecessor, it may be from the same cause—the increased prosperity of the city of Melbourne.

The Lord Bishop of Melbourne having said a prayer suitable to the occasion, a bottle containing coins, a copy of the address, copies of the *Herald*, *Argus*, and *Age* newspapers, and a gold medal, struck in honour of the occasion, were then placed in the cavity of the stone, in which was also put the subjoined record :—

This Foundation Stone of the Town Hall of the City of Melbourne

Was Laid by the second son of our Most Gracious Sovereign Lady, Queen Victoria,

HIS ROYAL HIGHNESS PRINCE ALFRED, DUKE OF EDINBURGH, K.G., K.T.,

On the Twenty-ninth day of November, in the year of our Lord 1867, being the Thirty-first year of Her Majesty's Reign, and the Seventh Day of His Royal Highness's visit to the Colony of Victoria, and in the Governorship of His Excellency the Honourable Sir JOHN HENRY THOMAS MANNERS-SUTTON,

THE RIGHT WORSHIPFUL JAMES STEWART BUTTERS, J.P., MAYOR,

The Aldermen and Councillors of the several Wards being as follows :—

Lonsdale Ward.—Alderman EDWARD COHEN; Councillors WILLIAM BAYLES, THOMAS MOUBRAY, JAMES STEWART BUTTERS.

Bourke Ward.—Alderman JOHN THOMAS SMITH; Councillors THOMAS M'PHERSON, ORLANDO FENWICK, SAMUEL AMESS.

Gipps Ward.—Alderman GEORGE HUGHES; Councillors FLOCKHART, HENRY SANDERS, JOHN WALKER.

Latrobe Ward.—Alderman GEORGE WRAGGE; Councillors THOMAS REED, WILLIAM WILLIAMS, ALEX. KENNEDY SMITH.

Smith Ward.—Alderman JOHN HARRISON; Councillors JOSEPH STORY, ALEXANDER M'BEAN, ABRAHAM LINACRE.

MAYORS OF MELBOURNE:

1842—43. HENRY CONDELL.	1855—56. JOHN THOMAS SMITH.
1843—44. HENRY CONDELL.	1856—57. PETER DAVIS.
1844—45. HENRY MOOR.	1857—58. JOHN THOMAS SMITH.
1845—46. JAMES FREDERICK PALMER.	1858—59. HENRY SWALLOWS WALSH.
1846—47. HENRY MOOR.	1859—60. RICHARD EADES.
1847—48. ANDREW RUSSELL.	1860—61. JOHN THOMAS SMITH.
1848—49. WILLIAM MONTGOMERIE BELL.	1861—62. ROBERT BENNETT.
1849—50. AUGUSTUS F. A. GREEVES.	1862—63. EDWARD COHEN.
1850—51. WILLIAM NICHOLSON.	1863—64. JOHN THOMAS SMITH.
1851—52. JOHN THOMAS SMITH.	1864—65. GEORGE WRAGGE.
1852—53. JOHN THOMAS SMITH.	1865—66. WILLIAM BAYLES.
1853—54. JOHN HODGSON.	1866—67. WILLIAM WILLIAMS.
1854—55. JOHN THOMAS SMITH.	1867—68. JAMES STEWART BUTTERS.

Mortar having been spread over the bed of the stone, the Mayor presented a magnificent golden trowel to his Royal Highness, who took with it some mortar from a slab composed of colonial wood, decorated at the corners with emblematic devices in gilt. The Prince spread the mortar, and returned the trowel to the Mayor. The stone having been lowered by the builders, Alderman Cohen presented to his Royal Highness the plumb and level, while Alderman J. T. Smith presented the mallet, and the Duke of Edinburgh, having tried the level, gave the stone the customary three taps, and then declared the stone to be well and truly laid, amidst the cheers of those present.

The Mayor called for three cheers for the Queen, the Duke of Edinburgh, and the Governor, all of which were most enthusiastically responded to.

His Royal Highness, his Excellency, the Major-General, and those present on the platform, then returned to the Council Chamber, when, after partaking of some slight refreshment, the Prince took his departure amidst the enthusiastic cheers of the assembled crowds.

The gold medal which was struck in commemoration of the event is about the size of a sovereign. Upon one side is a bust of the Prince, in profile, with the inscription "H.R.H. the Duke of Edinburgh visited Victoria, 1867," and upon the reverse side is a representation of the new Town Hall, as it will appear when completed, with the sentence, "Laid Foundation Stone of Town Hall, Melbourne, 29th November." Six of these medals have been struck off; one for presentation to Her Majesty, and another was presented to the Prince. Two others were for his Excellency the Governor, and the Hon. the Chief Secretary; while, of the remaining two, one was placed in the cavity of the stone, and the other was sent to the Public Library, where it may be seen by the public, and will no doubt long be regarded as an interesting relic of the great and auspicious event which it was designed to commemorate.

The address, which was beautifully engrossed and illuminated, was bound in a cover of red morocco, and placed in a box manufactured of colonial woods, bound with gold clasps. The trowel was a most exquisite piece of workmanship, manufactured by Messrs. Brush and M'Donnell, of Collins-street, at a cost of £200. It was much admired by his Royal Highness, who handled it very daintily, and merely touched the mortar with the extreme edge. The designs for the building were furnished by Messrs. Reed and Barnes, architects, of Elizabeth-street. The contractors are Messrs. Cain and Laurence, and the amount of their contract is £65,000. The building, it is expected, will be finished in the course of two years.

THE CIVIC BANQUET.

The Banquet given by the Melbourne Corporation to his Royal Highness took place in the evening, in the Exhibition-hall, which had been specially prepared for the occasion. Shortly after seven o'clock, the time appointed, and when about six hundred guests had assembled, his Royal Highness arrived, and was ushered to the seat provided for him by the members of the Corporation. He was attended by the Governor and General Chute, with their respective staffs. The company further included Messrs. M'Culloch, Verdon, Francis, Grant, Vale, Bindon, Cole, and Sullivan, members of the Ministry; Mr. O'Shanassy, Mr. Fellows, and many executive councillors, besides the members of both Houses of Parliament, the principal military and naval dignitaries, the heads of departments, and many persons of distinction resident in the neighbourhood of the city. The Mayor of Melbourne presided, and had on his right hand the Prince, the Lord Bishop of Melbourne, the Hon. E. Yorke, and the Commissioner of Crown Lands. On his left were the Governor, General Chute, Mr. M'Culloch, and Lord Newry. There were six tables arranged down the large hall of the building, five of which were presided over by aldermen, and the sixth by the ex-mayor. Mr. A. K. Smith acted as toastmaster.

The first toast, "The Queen," was given by the Mayor, and was enthusiastically responded to.

The Mayor then proposed "The Prince and Princess of Wales," and the healths were duly honoured.

The Mayor next proposed the toast of the evening—"The Duke of Edinburgh." He said: Your Royal Highness, my Lords, and Gentlemen— In proposing this toast, I think it is hardly necessary for me to state to his Royal Highness the pride and pleasure we all, as Victorians, feel at having a member of the Royal family in our midst. We feel, as Victorians far removed from the mother country, that his visit here will do much to place this colony in her proper position in British eyes, which has not yet been done. I trust we have proved to his Royal Highness that Victorian loyalty is not superficial; but that what we feel on occasions like the present springs truly from the heart. I am quite sure that no effort will be spared during the remainder of the stay of his Royal Highness to make his time pass as pleasantly and agreeably to him as the Victorian public can make it; and I trust that when he leaves our shores, he will leave with the impression that the Victorians are a loyal and energetic race of people. I think I need hardly say more than ask you to drink right loyally to his Royal Highness the Duke of Edinburgh.

The Prince, who was received with loud and reiterated cheering, replied: My Lords and Gentlemen—I thank you for the cordial way in which you have responded to the toast which his Worship the Mayor has proposed. It is only a continuation of the enthusiastic welcome which I have received amongst you since my arrival here, and I look upon it not only as a reception which you have offered to me, but that you have offered it to me as a member of the Queen's family. I thank you again most cordially for your great kindness, and for the loyalty you have shown to Her Majesty the Queen.

The Mayor then proposed "His Excellency the Governor," remarking that the mention of his name was always a welcome signal to the people of Victoria. The Governor had, he said, during his stay amongst us, endeared himself to the hearts and homes of the people, and had filled the functions devolving upon him as the representative of Her Majesty to the satisfaction of every one in Victoria.

His Excellency replied: Mr. Mayor and Gentlemen—I am very deeply sensible of the very kindly, and I fear in some degree undeserved, manner in which you have responded to the toast just proposed. I am fully aware that any person who holds the office which I have the honour to hold will receive at all times from the people that support which they feel to be due to the representative of their Sovereign, and I entertain the gratifying feeling that I may hope—if I deserve it—always to receive that support. Gentlemen, I should now, under ordinary circumstances, abstain from saying one other word, but the Mayor has already said Her Majesty's subjects in distant parts of the empire but seldom have the gratification of seeing among them a member of Her Majesty's family. These opportunities have recently become more numerous than before, and I hope will be more numerous hereafter, and I should be doing injustice to my feelings if I did not avail myself of this opportunity of assuring you how sincerely, how firmly, I share in that deep gratification with which the people of Victoria have welcomed his Royal Highness.

The next toast, "The Army, Navy, and Volunteers," was proposed by the Mayor, who paid high compliments to all three services.

The Prince replied on behalf of the navy as follows: I return my best thanks on behalf of the navy. I think it is unnecessary for me to say much on the subject; the navy has achieved a name and a reputation, and I believe that the navy will always keep it up.

General Chute briefly replied for the army.

Colonel Champ, for the volunteers, confidently expressed his opinion that in no part of Her Majesty's dominions, peopled as they were by over one hundred million inhabitants, was there a deeper sense of loyalty and devotion to her Majesty than amongst the volunteers in this colony.

The Mayor proposed "Her Majesty's Ministers." The toast was well received, and was responded to by Mr. M'Culloch.

His Royal Highness proposed the next toast, "Prosperity to the City of Melbourne." He said: It is my pleasing duty on this occasion to propose to you this toast; but I will ask to modify it slightly. I find before me "Prosperity to the City of Melbourne." I wish to say, "Increased prosperity to the City of Melbourne." The proofs of the prosperity of this city we had to-day, when I had the pleasure of laying the foundation stone of a new town hall, the plans of which were sufficient to prove the large scale upon which everything is being done in this city. Gentlemen, I think there is very little more I need say, and I confess my inability to make a speech on this topic, in which I could not say sufficient if I said more.

The toast was heartily responded to, and the Mayor replied briefly.

His Royal Highness then proposed "The Ladies," remarking that the toast, like the first one proposed, required nothing to bring it into favour with Englishmen.

Lord Newry replied, stating that he felt overpowered by the enormous responsibility he had undertaken; but when he looked at that gallery and saw so many pairs of bright eyes, he was inspired to express the feelings of the ladies, by stating their appreciation of the honour his Royal Highness had on this occasion done them in proposing their healths, and their thanks to all present for the cordial manner in which the toast had been received. A most cordial reception had been given to his Royal Highness here, and the ladies would have him (Lord Newry) to tell them that they were much pleased at the manner in which they had conducted themselves; but he would also wish to impress upon them the fact that it had been the presence of the ladies which had rendered the meeting so complete. There was no champagne in the gallery, and therefore the ladies would drink to his Royal Highness and the gentlemen present "only with their eyes," since they had been "pledged with wine." They begged also through him (their most devoted though unworthy servant) to express their thanks for the manner in which their health had been drunk.

His Excellency proposed "His Worship the Mayor," referring to the onerous duties which had devolved upon him at the commencement of his year of office, and stating, that from the manner in which he had carried them out, they must feel that a successful choice had been made.

His Worship briefly thanked the assemblage, stating that he should endeavour to prove himself worthy of the city, and to conduct its business with credit to himself and some honour to the Corporation of Melbourne.

His Royal Highness and suite then left the hall, escorted by the Mayor, and repaired to the front of the Public Library

THE GERMAN TORCHLIGHT PROCESSION.

The account of this interesting and most successful exhibition of German loyalty is noted from the *Herald*:—

The German demonstration in honour of his Royal Highness was an undoubted and complete success from beginning to end. The arrangements of the committee who had the management of this brilliant affair seem to have been of such a character as to render any risk of failure beyond a doubt, and if any confusion did occur it was most decidedly no fault of theirs. The procession started from the Russell-street Police Barracks, the use of which had been allowed by the Government, and here, for some time before that hour, the Liedertafel torch and banner-bearers commenced to assemble, and precisely at nine o'clock the long procession commenced to defile from the barrack-yard, headed by the band of the 14th Regiment, supported in the middle and rear by the Collingwood Volunteer and the German bands. After the leading band, and between the two long lines of torchbearers, over a thousand in number, marched in procession the members of the Liedertafel, with their insignia, "the garlanded lyre," carried by Mr. Kursteiner, and preceded by the Southern Cross and other Australian banners. Behind these, at a short interval, the Imperial Eagle of Germany was borne aloft by Mr. Willms, and under its folds walked the deputation appointed to present the address, followed by Dr. de Baume, carrying the national colours of Germany. The rear of the procession was closed by other emblematic banners and devices, carried and supported by different members of the German community. Along Russell-street, down Collins-street, up Elizabeth-street, and on through Latrobe-street, towards the Public Library, marched the long procession, the lofty cressets blazing in the front, and the lurid glare of more than a thousand torches at the side; and, though an immense crowd collected on the pavement, occasionally joining in chorus to the airs played by the band, banners, cressets, and torches were borne without any attempt at a rush or the slightest disorder, until the head of the procession came in front of the Public Library, where the serenade was to take place. The band of the 14th, the members of the deputation, the Liedertafel, and about one hundred torchbearers entered the gates. Here the band was drawn up on one side of the lower terrace, the Liedertafel on the other, the members of the deputation being in the centre. The torchbearers filled up the interval between the terrace and the gates. By the time the whole were drawn up it was half-past nine o'clock. After a short delay, the Liedertafel, consisting of seventy performers, led by Mr. Sprinkhorn, commenced the serenade by singing Mendelssohn's "Der frohe Wandersmann." During the song several ladies and guests from the Civic Banquet came out under the portico, and greeted its rendering with loud applause. After this there was another interval of nearly twenty minutes, during which the torchbearers outside seemed to have rather a hard time of it; but at ten o'clock all symptoms of impatience were allayed by the appearance of the Duke on the stately flight of steps leading down from the artificial portico to the two couchant lions. In the centre of the space between these two his Royal Highness stopped, and stood full in view of the serenaders, the bright light of the torches shining brilliantly on his gold epaulettes and the decorations on his breast. His Royal Highness, who wore the uniform of a post-captain in the navy, was accompanied by his Excellency the Governor, Major-General Chute, the Chief Secretary, and other members of the

Ministry, the Mayor of Melbourne, the officers of his personal staff, Lord Newry, Mr. Brierly, several naval and military officers, and a large number of other gentlemen, Lieut. Rothwell, and Mr. Manners-Sutton being in attendance on his Excellency the Governor. As soon as his Royal Highness appeared, the Liedertafel sang "Des Deutsche Lied," his Royal Highness and those around him applauding loudly; and after this Mr. Brahe, the Prussian Vice-Consul, introduced the deputation, consisting of Mr. Pokorny (secretary), Dr. Lilienfeld, Dr. Mueller, Dr. Jonasson, and Messrs. Cleve, Gelbrecht, Wenzel, Von Guerard, and Martin; and requested his Royal Highness to receive an address from the German inhabitants of Melbourne. The Duke having bowed his assent, Mr. Pokorny read the address as follows:—

May it please your Royal Highness—We, the German residents of Melbourne and the delegates of the Germans in Victoria, approach your Royal Highness to offer you our hearty welcome, to congratulate you on your safe arrival in this country, and to tender the sincere expressions of our devotion and loyalty to Her Most Gracious Majesty the Queen, your august mother, to Her throne, and to the Royal family. Under the benign rule of Her Majesty the Queen we have here established a new home, and have always been ready to take a fair share in the peaceful contest by which this country, scarcely known to a previous generation, has been subdued by means of labour, enterprise, arts, and science, rendered a fit abode of free men, and led to so high a development of civilisation. Your Royal Highness is destined at some future day to become still more closely connected with Germany; and we beg most respectfully to express our sincere conviction that, following the example of your noble father, you will always endeavour to strengthen still more the ties of friendship which unite the two great Teutonic nations—England and Germany—both claiming with equal pride and justice your Royal Highness as their own. We have the honour to sign, on behalf of the Germans of Victoria, your Royal Highness's truly devoted and most obedient servants, the deputies.

(Signed)

Melbourne, 29th November, 1867.

J. J. POKORNY, SECRETARY.
W. A. BRAHE, PRESIDENT.

His Royal Highness replied in German, expressing a few words of thanks and appreciation. The address, beautifully mounted on red morocco, and ornamented at each end with silver ducal coronets, having been handed to the Prince, the deputation retired. His Royal Highness descended the steps to his carriage, the Liedertafel singing, at the request of the Prince, Becker's "Frisch die ganze Compagnie." The appearance of the Prince outside the gates was the signal for renewed cheers, amid which he drove down the lines of torch-bearers towards Prince's Bridge, the band, the Liedertafel, and the deputation following him. The route was then continued, with bands playing and banners waving, down Swanston-street, past the illuminated Town-hall, to Flinders-street, and so on to Spring-street, where in front of the Model Schools the torches were one by one flung down, and a huge fire soon blazed merrily away, shedding a bright light on the immense crowd collecting, and throwing the Houses of Parliament into a dark shadowy background. The Liedertafel then sung Reichardt's "Was ist des Deutschen Vaterland," and as the soul-stirring words of Arndt rung through the night air, the crowd listened in admiring silence, applauding loudly at the conclusion. The demonstration terminated by the singing of "God save the Queen" to the band accompaniment, and the large crowd dispersed in the best possible temper. And so ended the German torchlight procession, a demonstration neither Prince nor people are soon likely to forget. The Germans had every reason to congratulate themselves upon it as a success, and all connected with it, including the committee, Dr. de Baume (who was intrusted with many of the most important duties), Mr. John Hennings (who designed and painted the banners and devices), and Messrs. Kelly and Lewis, who supplied the torches.

Special Race Meeting.

Not the least attractive of the entertainments provided for the royal visit was the Special Race Meeting, which took place on Saturday, the 30th November. The excellent programme put forward by the committee, and the knowledge that his Royal Highness the Duke of Edinburgh was to be present on the ground, had created even more than the usual excitement of a race-day in Victoria. At about twelve o'clock the outriders of the vice-regal carriage and the glittering accoutrements of the constabulary escort, were seen in the distance. In a few minutes the calvacade drew up in front of the grand stand, where a gate was thrown open for the entrance of the distinguished visitor, who was accompanied by his Excellency the Governor and two officers of his personal suite—Lord Newry, Mr. Manners-Sutton, and others having arrived previously in a drag. Lady and the Misses Manners-Sutton came on the ground in one of the Governor's close carriages. As soon as his Royal Highness had alighted, he was conducted to that portion of the grand stand railed off for his accommodation, and in the decoration of which the committee had evidently expended considerable trouble. Tasteful, however, as were the decorations, the prettiest sight among them was afforded by some flowers, kindly furnished by Mr. Hugh Glass, who, on the application of Mr. Bagot, placed his hot-house at their disposal. The selection and arrangement were made by Mr. Ferguson, Mr. Glass's head gardener, who with his assistants had worked during nearly the whole night in making the floral decorations. A handsome lunch, provided by Mr. Scott, was laid out for the private refreshment of the Prince, the Governor, and their personal staff. It is gratifying to be able to say, too, that after the Duke had once entered the stand he was left entirely to himself, and not in any way intruded upon. Captain Standish was in attendance on his Royal Highness during the entire day, and it would have been difficult to find a better qualified guide to the Melbourne racecourse; but, with this exception, the Duke walked, talked, and betted like one of the crowd, and there is reason to believe enjoyed immensely the racing that followed. The Duke viewed most of the races from the stewards' position over the weighing-room. Shortly after the last race his Royal Highness entered his carriage with the Governor, and was driven away amid loud and hearty cheers.

The announcement that the Duke of Edinburgh would pay a visit to the Princess's Opera-house in the evening to hear the opera of *Faust* was in itself sufficient to fill the theatre. At nine o'clock the Duke of Edinburgh and suite arrived, and were conducted to a private box on the right of the dress circle. The special feature in the opera was the part taken by the band of the 14th Regiment in the "Soldiers' Chorus," which was applauded and encored.

During Sunday, 1st December, the Prince remained on board the *Galatea*. Leaving the ship at 6 p.m., he landed at Sandridge, and drove to Toorak, where he joined the vice-regal dinner party, and afterwards returned to the ship.

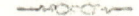

The Departure for the Western District.

The Duke of Edinburgh, having enjoyed just one week of the hospitalities of the capital, took his departure early on Monday, 2nd December, for Geelong, where he began one of the provincial tours which had been arranged with the view of giving his Royal Highness a more perfect knowledge of the resources of the colony than he could acquire in Melbourne. The

Reception at Geelong.

Prince had left the Spencer-street station for Williamstown, by special train, at eleven o'clock the previous evening, and passed the night on board his vessel. A special train conveyed his Excellency the Governor and suite to Williamstown, at half-past eight o'clock on Monday morning, and the vice-regal party was at once taken on board the *Victoria*. On receiving the Governor on board, the *Victoria* fired a salute and manned yards. The Naval Training Ship also manned yards and dressed ship, the latter mark of respect being repeated by the reformatory hulks and the barque *Jeannie Oswald*. The *Victoria* then got under steam, advanced slowly towards the *Galatea*, and received the Prince on board. Captain Nicholson, harbour-master of Geelong, was on board to pilot the vessel to her destination. There was no public demonstration either at Sandridge or Williamstown; and before the *Victoria* was out of sight, the decks of the *Galatea* were crowded with visitors, who had availed themselves of the privilege of inspecting so noble a ship.

Quoting from the *Geelong Advertiser*, the following are the principal features that marked

THE PRINCE'S VISIT TO GEELONG.

Never have the loyal citizens of Geelong and the surrounding district witnessed a greater sight in the second town of the colony of Victoria, than that which took place on Monday. The visit of his Royal Highness the Duke of Edinburgh was one of those bright scenes that will form a green spot in the memory of all who were fortunate enough to witness it. At a very early hour in the morning gaily dressed visitors poured into the town, and continued to arrive until two o'clock, at which hour the streets were lined on either side with men, women, and children, anxious to give a hearty greeting to the son of our Queen. The weather was delightful. Thousands of yards of bunting waved in the breeze, Moorabool-street being especially gay; balconies, verandahs, windows, and posts were tastefully decorated with evergreens, grass-trees, and choice flowers, and triumphal arches were to be seen in every direction. Between eleven and twelve o'clock the smoke issuing from the funnel of the *Victoria* was seen in Bellerine Bay, the steamer steering for the ship channel, and all hastened to the Yarra-street wharf and slopes of the eastern beach to witness the approach and arrival of the Royal visitor. Everywhere was excitement and bustle, but the order kept throughout the day by a strong body of police under the command of Mr. Superintendent Bookey and Sub-Inspectors Macnamara and Ryall, was admirable. The main body of the procession formed on Corio-terrace. An avenue was kept clear by means of ropes, and at the time the Prince arrived there could not have been less than twenty thousand persons congregated. At the end of the Yarra-street wharf nearest the town appeared a very neat triumphal arch erected by the Corporation, and on which was inscribed the motto:—"Welcome to Geelong." Railings kept the crowd from trespassing upon the space through which the Prince was to pass, the central avenue being covered with matting right up to the rich and handsome crimson dais provided for the occasion by Messrs. Ashmore and Sons, and situated in the centre of the wharf, about fifty yards from the landing-place. The dais was surmounted by a rich cornice and graceful canopy, on the top of which appeared a gilt and crimson crown. On the right-hand side of the wharf the clipper ship *Lamarkshire* was gaily dressed in bunting; on the left side, the *Damascus* and the *Salamander*, and the barque *India*, were similarly decorated. The most interesting feature to be seen was the children's platforms, on which were seated over three thousand boys and girls, each of whom had been presented with a medal struck in honour of the Duke's visit to Victoria. At half-past twelve a guard of honour of volunteers, selected from the Volunteer Artillery, were marched past the dais under the command of Captain Heath, and took up a position at the end of the wharf. Among the officers present were Lieutenant-Colonel Rede, Major Dawson, Captains Rashleigh and Smith, and Lieutenants Macklin and Price. About the same time the *Victoria* was seen making her way through the ship channel and approaching the wharf, having the Royal Standard at the main, and the Prince's ensign at the peak. Shortly after this the Mayor and Town-Clerk of Geelong, in robes of office, and accompanied by the members of the Council, the Mayors of South Barwon, and Newton, and Chilwell, and other members of those Councils, the presidents and members of the various Shire Councils, the chairmen and members of the several road boards in the Geelong district, the clergy of every denomination, members of the Legislative Council and Legislative Assembly, members of the legal and medical professions, and the leading men among the Friendly Societies, congregated near the dais, and were marshalled into line facing the volunteers, thus forming an avenue in the centre of which appeared the Mayor of Geelong ready to walk up and receive his Royal Highness at the temporary steps erected at the end of the platform. The *Victoria* anchored at the eastern end of the wharf, and as the Prince placed his foot in the captain's gig, the yards of the *Victoria* were manned, and her guns and also those of the beach battery, under the command of Lieutenant Hague, thundered forth a Royal salute. The landing of the Prince on the wharf was the signal for immense cheering, the clear ringing voices of the three thousand children being heard above all. He was received by his Worship the Mayor, and conducted to the dais. The Duke appeared to be pleased with the reception given him, and when he took his stand on the dais he received a hearty ovation of cheering. His Excellency the Governor occupied a position on the stand, as did also Lord Newry and the Hon. Mr. Yorke.

The Mayor, approaching the Prince, said:—" May it please your Royal Highness, I have the honour, on behalf of the town and Corporation of Geelong, to present you with an address of cordial welcome to our town, and to convey to your Royal Highness our expression of loyalty and devotion to the throne of our beloved Sovereign the Queen, and our high appreciation of the honour conferred upon the colony by your visit, which I feel assured will, under God's blessing, greatly tend to the advancement of this distant portion of Her Majesty's dominions. With Royal Highness's permission, I will call upon the Town Clerk to read the address which I now have the honour of presenting."

The address was then handed to the town clerk (Mr. W. Weire) who read, as follows:—

May it please your Royal Highness—We, the Mayor, Aldermen, Councillors, and Burgesses of Geelong, respectfully offer our heartiest welcome to your Royal Highness, on this your visit to our town, and rejoice in the opportunity of again expressing our feelings of devotion and loyalty to the Throne of our Most Gracious Queen, and of affection and attachment to her Royal person. As the chief representative body of Geelong, and the oldest municipal corporation (with but one exception) in Victoria, we highly value the important privileges attached to local self-government, instituted in remote ages by our ancestors for the maintenance of tranquillity, the security of property, the encouragement of industry, and the preservation of property. These privileges are the more highly prized by us seeing that under the beneficent and gracious rule of Her Majesty they have, by wise and enlightened policy, been greatly extended. We, therefore, have the high honour in the presence of yourself, a son of our beloved Queen and her illustrious and lamented Consort, of expressing our grateful appreciation of the many blessings which, under Divine Providence, we enjoy, in common with our fellow subjects in all parts of Her Majesty's dominions, through the bright and glorious examples shown by your Royal parents, which has conduced so eminently to the advancement and stability of the Throne, and thereby tended to improve the religious and social condition of all classes of Her Majesty's subjects, and rendered the foundation of the national prosperity more firm and sure. Deeply sensible of the great honour you have by your visit conferred upon our town, and sincerely trusting that it

Reception at Geelong.

may be a source of enjoyment to you, we again respectfully offer your Royal Highness our heart-felt wishes that your future progress may be attended with unalloyed happiness and pleasure.

ROBERT DE BRUCE JOHNSTONE, Mayor.
WILLIAM WEIRE, Town Clerk.

Given under the Corporation seal of the Town of Geelong this 2nd day of December, 1867.

The address was a beautiful specimen of illuminated writing on vellum, artistically executed. The Mayor having handed the address to the Prince, his Royal Highness replied, "I am highly gratified at this reception, and will reply to this address as soon as possible." His Royal Highness subsequently forwarded a reply to this and the other address presented by the Corporation of Geelong at the levee held in Melbourne, in the account of which it will be found.

Mr. Harwood then presented the following address from the Freemasons:—

May it please your Royal Highness.—On behalf of the members of the Ancient Order of Free and Accepted Masons resident in Geelong, we beg to offer to your Royal Highness our congratulations and welcome on the occasion of your visit to the colony and to our town. We rejoice at the opportunity now afforded us of expressing to a son of Her Most Gracious Majesty that loyalty and devotion to the person and throne of the Sovereign which throughout every portion of her dominions is a prominent characteristic of our Order, for whether its members be peers or peasants, whether it be presided over by an humble colonist or by a Royal Duke, attachment to the Queen, obedience to the law, and brotherly love everywhere prevail. We wish your Royal Highness every happiness which this world can afford, and if in the fulness of time it should please you (following the example of some of your royal ancestors) to seek admission within the mystic portals of the craft, we, and all Masons throughout the universe, will rejoice in the privilege of greeting you as a brother.—We have the honour, &c.,

THOS. C. HARWOOD, P.M. of Lodge No. 545, E.C., and No. 366, S.C., and P.M. Grand Principal, Z.
R. J. BRADLEY, W.M. of Lodge No. 545, E.C.
EDWD. KNIGHT, R.W.M. of Lodge No. 366, S.C.
M. S. LEVY, M.E.Z., of R.A.C., No. 81.

This address was splendidly engrossed by Mr. Carpenter.

The Friendly Societies, represented by Mr. Christey and Mr. Bannister, then came forward and presented their address, beautifully written and illuminated on vellum by Mr. W. Birdsey:—

May it please Your Royal Highness,—We, the District Officers, on behalf of the members of the Friendly Societies of this district, respectfully approach your Royal Highness to offer our sincere congratulations on the occasion of your visiting Geelong. Loyalty being one of the chief characteristics of our Orders, we gladly avail ourselves of this opportunity to express to your Royal Highness our devoted loyalty and attachment to Her Most Gracious Majesty the Queen and Royal Family. We trust your Royal Highness may long continue in the enjoyment of health and happiness, and that you may return safely to our Fatherland to take the position your Royal Highness is so well calculated to adorn. We have the honour to be your Royal Highness's most obedient and humble servants,

A. CHRISTY, G.M.; J. BAILIFF, D.G.M.; W. G. CLUTTERBUCK, C.S.
—M. U. Independent Order of Oddfellows.
R. B. MALEY, D.C.R.; H. MORE, D.S.C.R.; H. BANNISTER, D.S.—
Ancient Order of Foresters.
J. F. GRIGGS, P.G.M.; W. H. BENNETT, D.P.G.M.; J. C. MOGG, P.G.S.
—Ancient Order of Oddfellows.
GEO. MARTIN, D.M.W.P.; JOSEPH E. LANDER, P.W.S.; W. BOX, P.G.S.—Sons of Temperance.

REPLY.

Gentlemen I feel very grateful to you for your kindly congratulations, and I fully believe that they are expressed towards me with all sincerity, and in a spirit of loyalty which appears to pervade this community. Your useful society aiding, as it does, the cultivation of all those sentiments among you which must promote good citizenship, proves, I am quite convinced, the correctness of your statement, that loyalty is one of the characteristics of your Order. I thank you for your good wishes for the prosperity of my voyage. ALFRED.

Visit of H.R.H. Prince Alfred.

The Ancient Order of Foresters incurred considerable expense in decorating a triumphal car, on which appeared a young lady in the character of a shepherdess, and leading a milk white lamb; she was supported on each side by juvenile Foresters attired in the green costume of the Order. The Oddfellows provided new regalia. Mr. J. E. Lander acted as marshal.

The next feature in the programme was a novel and interesting one, being an address signed by four hundred ladies of Geelong, who were represented by the Hon. C. Sladen, M.L.C., and Captain Haimes.

The Hon. C. Sladen, M.L.C., addressing his Royal Highness, asked permission to read the address.

His Royal Highness said he would not trouble Mr. Sladen, as he had seen a copy of the address, and would forward a written reply to it. In the meantime he asked Mr. Sladen to inform the ladies that he regretted that it was not in his power to comply with their request; his ship had been moored in Hobson's Bay, and arrangements had been made for her remaining there during his stay. The following is the Ladies' Address:—

May it please your Royal Highness,—We, the undersigned most loyal and affectionate subjects and countrywomen of your Royal mother, Queen Victoria, beg to congratulate you on your arrival on these shores. We can hardly express the profound satisfaction and pleasure we feel in welcoming you to this distant but important and flourishing colony. The presence of your noble ship in these waters gives us assurance of security, and makes us feel that we are guarded by the Queen of that great empire on whose dominion the sun never sets. Your countrywomen most anxiously desire that your Royal Highness will be pleased to allow the *Galatea* to visit Point Henry for a brief period, so that the people of Geelong, Ballarat, and the populous Western District may have the privilege and gratification of inspecting the finest ship of war that has ever entered Port Phillip Heads. In conclusion your countrywomen most fervently pray that your Royal Highness may enjoy long life, health, and happiness, and that your voyage round the world may be accomplished with safety and pleasure.

Mr. Leon presented the following address from the members of the Jewish congregation:—

May it please your Royal Highness,—We, the president and members of the Jewish Congregation of Geelong, beg to express the pride and pleasure we feel in being able to welcome the son of our beloved and gracious Queen to this our adopted city.

Your sojourn among us will, we fear, be but short, though long enough we trust to assure your Royal Highness of our loyal and dutiful attachment to Her Majesty's throne, convinced that, under her protection, we have perfect security for the equal freedom of our people as other sects; and to assure your Royal Highness that, though separated by many thousands of miles, and years have elapsed since we left our native land—the mother country—we still maintain the same affectionate and loyal feeling to Her Majesty as ever; and to you as the son of our gracious Queen, words can but feebly express the hearty welcome we would fain offer.

S. LEON, PRESIDENT.
M. FINK, TREASURER.
J. STONE, MINISTER.

REPLY.

Gentlemen—I thank you most sincerely for the cordial reception you gave me in Geelong, and I regret that the shortness of my visit to Australia prevented me from staying with you longer. The feelings of loyalty and affection you entertain for the Queen shall be made known to Her Majesty, who will be deeply gratified by the manner in which I have been received in this country.

Mr. Knight, foreman of the Geelong Volunteer Brigade, presented the following address:—

May it please your Royal Highness—We, the officers and members of the Geelong and Newtown and Chilwell Volunteer Fire Brigades beg most respectfully to offer our hearty congratulations on the auspicious event of your Royal Highness's visit to Geelong; we humbly beg to state that the Geelong Volunteer Fire Brigades have, as public bodies, ever distinguished themselves for their loyalty, and while giving yourself a fireman's hearty welcome, we humbly request that we may be permitted to avail ourselves of the memorable occasion of your presence to express the continuance of our devoted attachment to the person and throne of your august mother.

her most Gracious Majesty the Queen. We trust your Royal Highness may live long and enjoy every blessing this world can give you, and wish you a safe and pleasant passage back to our fatherland.

E. KNIGHT, FOREMAN GEELONG VOLUNTEER BRIGADE.
E. SEELEY, FOREMAN NEWTOWN AND CHILWELL VOLUNTEER FIRE BRIGADE.

The following address was also presented :—

The Trustees of the Geelong Botanical Gardens beg, in all loyalty, to approach your Royal Highness, and to welcome you to the Gardens. It being the intention of the Trustees to erect handsome gates, they respectfully request that you may be pleased to christen them the "Prince's Gates," and do the town the honour of planting a tree (*Wellingtonia Gigantea*) as a memorial of your Royal visit to Geelong.

CHARLES IBBOTSON, CHAIRMAN.

REPLY.

Gentlemen—Accept my thanks for your address. It affords me great pleasure to visit the Botanical Gardens of Geelong, and I most willingly accept the permission you desire to have the gates you intend to erect named after myself.

This concluded the presentation of addresses, and the Mayor then invited the Prince to inspect the town of Geelong. His Highness, accompanied by his Excellency the Governor, the Mayor, and followed by the members of the two suites, and the gentlemen who had occupied positions near the dais, walked down the centre of the wharf between two dense lines of people, the children singing the National Anthem. His Highness stopped for a few seconds opposite the children, in acknowledgment of the juvenile welcome, and on arriving at the end of the wharf passed under the triumphal arch, where a carriage drawn by four greys ridden by postillions was waiting for him; the carriage, a very handsome landau, being lent for the occasion by A. B. White, Esq. The members of the fire brigades, friendly societies, and other public bodies having been drawn up in line opposite Mack's Hotel, the signal was given by the marshal, Mr. W. T. Morris, to proceed, and the Royal progress through the town of Geelong commenced. The advance guard was formed by the Prince of Wales Light Horse, and then came the members of the two volunteer fire brigades with their three engines. Then followed the Rechabites, who mustered strongly, and appeared to great advantage in their new regalia. The Sons of Temperance came next, and were succeeded by the members of the following orders, viz.:—Ancient Order of Foresters, Ancient Independent Order of Oddfellows, Manchester Unity Independent Order of Oddfellows, Members of Road Boards, Members of Shire Councils, Municipal Councils, Reception Committee, Corporation of Geelong, Clergy. An advanced guard of the escort proceeded immediately in front of the carriage containing the Prince, the Governor, Lord Newry, and Mr. Yorke, the carriage being guarded on either side by an escort of the volunteer cavalry. The royal carriage was followed by private carriages, and as the long line turned round into Moorabool-street, the sight was a magnificent one. The firemen's arch, erected at the junction of Great Malop and Moorabool-streets, was a great credit not only to the brigade, but to the town, and a triumph in the art of decoration. As the cortege was returning down Malop-street, the fire-bell commenced to peal an alarm. The services of the Fire Brigade, it appeared, were required in Skene-street, and, leaving the line of procession, the three engines, each drawn by two of Mr. Kerley's powerful horses, proceeded to the scene of the fire. The departure of the firemen and their engines detracted somewhat from the appearance of the procession, which then passed along Great Malop-street. The Prince returned to Mack's Hotel, where the Royal party partook of a luncheon provided in Mr. Trear's best style.

During the stay of the Prince at Mack's Hotel, the Mayor and Town Clerk had an interview with his Excellency, and presented him with a book, with a request that he would hand it to the Prince. The book (a copy of Mr. Bunce's "Language of the Aborigines") was handsomely bound in blue morocco, the interior containing a portrait of King Jerry, and bearing the following inscription:—

> Presented by King Jerry, the remaining representative of the Geelong, or the Pun-dan-nock, tribe. This book is, with the deepest respect, presented to his Royal Highness, as a specimen of the language of his [King Jerry's] own and other tribes of Australasia.

His Royal Highness the Duke of Edinburgh did not leave Geelong without paying a visit to the Botanical Gardens. It had been suggested that he would probably consent to plant a tree in the gardens to commemorate his visit to the town, and the Prince at once kindly acquiesced. On his entering the gardens, the Mayor, addressing his Highness, said:— "Upon the marriage of your illustrious brother with the Princess Alexandra two trees were planted here to commemorate that auspicious event. I now have the honour and pleasure of requesting your Royal Highness to plant a tree in remembrance of your visit." Mr. Bunce, the curator, then handed a spade to the Prince, who turned the earth, and planted a very handsome tree of the Wellingtonia Gigantea species. The Prince then drove through the gardens, and returned to his hotel.

At night the town was illuminated, and the streets were crowded with spectators, many of whom had come from a considerable distance. The weather was everything that could be desired. The illuminations commenced at seven o'clock, and an hour after the town from one end to the other was a blaze of light. Chinese crackers, and other descriptions of small fireworks, were fizzing and banging in every direction; rockets towered high, bursting in showers of brilliantly coloured stars. Nearly every place of business could boast of either a transparency or a design illuminated with jets of gas, the ships in the harbour were lit up with blue lights, and the general appearance of the town was very striking. A pretty scene was presented by the Market-square Gardens, which were illuminated with festoons of innumerable gaily-coloured Chinese lamps. The Town Hall grounds, the numerous triumphal arches, and the front of the Chamber of Commerce, were also illuminated in the same manner, and had a good effect. The departure of the Prince from Mack's Hotel to the Ball was announced by a fine display of blue lights. Those inhabitants who were unable to obtain gas, or had been too late with their orders for transparencies, made up for it with thousands of candles, arranged on angular stands or in coloured glass lamps.

The Ball at the Mechanics' Institute in honour of the Prince's visit was another of the many successes of the eventful day. The committee had been indefatigable in their exertions to conduct the ball on such a principle that all classes of the community of good repute could be present, and make it eclipse all others previously given in the town, for which purpose they engaged the whole of the Mechanics' Institute, and removed the platform in the hall to make more room for the expected large number of dancers. The hall was decorated under the superintendence of Mr. Wheatland, secretary to the Institute, and Mr. Bunce, curator of the Botanical Gardens. The entrance was from the principal door in Ryrie-street, and the floor from there to the landing, and the stairs leading down to the hall, was covered with crimson baize. On entering the ball-room the scene was very striking. Around the room, in the recesses of the windows, were ranged large mirrors, and on either side of the mirrors were vases of choicest flowers, the pilasters being elegantly decorated with floral ornaments. The cornices were covered with festoons of drapery representing the national colours of England—red, white, and blue. At the upper end of the hall was erected the dais, and at the other end a platform for the musicians, on the barrier of which were the words "Welcome Alfred," under a gas star.

The reading-room was fitted up as a ladies' retiring room, and the library as a card room. As early as eight o'clock the company began to assemble; but it was not until ten o'clock that his Royal Highness made his appearance, accompanied by his Excellency and their respective suites. As the Duke entered the ball-room the band played the National Anthem, which being concluded, a quadrille was danced, a double set being formed, as follows:—The Duke and Mrs. Strachan, his Excellency the Governor and Miss Murphy, Lord Newry and Miss Chirnside, the Hon. Eliot Yorke and Miss Murray, Sir Francis Murphy and Mrs. A. B. White, Mr. Brierly and Miss Chapman. After this the Duke joined in a galop with Miss Murphy. At eleven o'clock the company, headed by the Duke and suite, proceeded through the covered passage to the Council Chamber at the Town Hall, where supper was laid, provided by Mrs. Bedford, of the Terminus Hotel. After supper, the Mayor, R. de B. Johnstone, Esq., proposed the health of Her Majesty the Queen, which was drank with enthusiasm. The health of the Prince and Princess of Wales was next drank; after which the Mayor said: The next toast I have to propose is one that I am sure you will all respond to with heart and soul. It is the health of his Royal Highness the Duke of Edinburgh, and the other members of the Royal family. To this the Duke replied: Ladies and gentlemen—I thank you most heartily for the manner in which you have responded to the toast of my health. I need not tell you with what pleasure I accepted the invitation of this visit to Geelong, being as it is a starting point for the western portion of the colony; and while I return you thanks for your expressions of regard to myself and family, I have also to return you thanks for the appreciation in which you hold the naval service, with which I am connected, shown by the address of the ladies of the town, presented to me this day, asking that the *Galatea* should visit Geelong, and remain off Point Henry. I am very sorry that such cannot be done, as my orders are strict that she shall not leave her present anchorage until I leave the colony. Ladies and gentlemen, again I beg to return you my best thanks for your kind expression of regard. The Mayor then proposed the health of his Excellency the Governor.

His Excellency responded, expressing the satisfaction he felt at finding that with all the differences that had arisen with regard to politics, the colonists of Victoria were loyal to the British throne. The company returned to the ball room, and at one o'clock the Duke left. Dancing was then recommenced and kept up until morning, when the company separated.

It was hoped that the Prince would extend the time of his departure until two o'clock p.m., in order that his presence might have graced a good portion of the Regatta, but he was anxious to get on his way, and, through his Excellency the Governor, signified to the Regatta Committee that unless the first race took place early, he should be obliged to leave for Barwon Park. The Committee having advertised the time for the first race, were unable to alter the arrangements, but ultimately his Royal Highness very kindly delayed his departure. At half-past ten he was driven to the Yarra-street wharf, and as soon as his presence was made known, a gun was fired from the *Pharos*, which acted as the flag-ship, and the Regatta commenced. After remaining a short time, the Royal visitor left, escorted by a detachment of the V. L. Horse, under the command of Lieutenant Isard, and proceeded through the town *en route* for Winchelsea. Passing Barwon Iron Bridge, the Prince was met by the Mayor and Councillors of the Borough of South Barwon, who presented the following address:—

May it please your Royal Highness—We, the Mayor, Councillors, and Burgesses of the Borough of South Barwon, beg most respectfully to offer our sincere feelings of respect for yourself, and our hearty welcome to this part of the colony of Victoria. We desire to express our undiminished loyalty to the throne and person of Her Most Gracious

Majesty the Queen, and our high appreciation of the honor we have had conferred upon us by being thus privileged to convey this feeling of loyalty to a member of the royal family personally. We trust this expression of our sincere feelings may be graciously accepted by your Royal Highness, and that after a visit of unalloyed pleasure to this part of the British Dominions you may have a safe return to the old country, and carry with you pleasing recollections of the loyalty and progress of the people of this and the other colonies you may have visited.

Council Chambers, South Barwon, 2nd December, 1867.
WILLIAM BATTEN, Mayor.
JOHN RICHARDSON, Town Clerk.

REPLY.

Gentlemen—I receive with satisfaction this expression of your heartfelt loyalty to the Throne and person of Her Majesty. I thank you for the hearty welcome, and for your good wishes for my safe return to England; and I assure you that I shall carry with me the most pleasing recollections of the loyalty and progress of the people of Victoria.
ALFRED.

The festivities at Geelong were successfully concluded by a free banquet, a children's picnic, and a treat to the inmates of the Infirmary and Benevolent Asylum.

Leaving Geelong and its suburban dependencies, the next object of interest visited was the Prince Albert Vineyard, where the following address from the vinegrowers was presented by Messrs. Hanson, Pettavel, M'Kenzie, and Heirick:—

We, the vinegrowers of the Geelong district, natives of various countries of Europe, are unable to express in words our delight at being permitted to welcome in this beautiful valley, amidst the scenes of our industry, the second son of our beloved Queen. The remembrance of the gracious acceptance by your Royal Highness of this simple display of our loyalty will long be cherished by us and by our children.

(Signed) GEORGE HANSON.
D. L. PETTAVEL.
ALEX. M'KENZIE.

The Duke then proceeded on his journey. On arriving at Duneed another demonstration took place. Mr. Cotton, a local storekeeper, had gallantly maintained the credit of his district by erecting an arch of evergreens, by treating the school children to a free banquet, and by other hospitable services. At Mount Moriac the Prince stopped for refreshment, afterwards going on to Winchelsea. A triumphal arch had been thrown across the road, and Mr. Elkington's store was tastefully decorated. Nothing more of note happened during the journey till the arrival at Winchelsea, at which place the Shire Council had been building a stone bridge over the Barwon, and that this should be opened by royalty was the earnest desire of the residents. The Prince consenting, drove down to the bridge, which consists of three spans, erected at a cost of £4500. The structure was ornamented with two arches of evergreens, bedecked with flowers. Here H.R.H. was met by the Council, with their president, Mr. Thomas Austin, at their head; an address was presented, and then the event of the day took place. The Prince duly laid the cope-stone of the bridge, having been presented by the President with a handsome silver trowel, suitably inscribed, for the purposes of the ceremony. The following is the address presented by the Council to his Royal Highness:—

May it please your Royal Highness—We, the Council of the Shire of Winchelsea, rejoice to have this opportunity of welcoming your Royal Highness in Victoria, and of assuring you of our sincere loyalty and affection to Her Majesty's throne and person, and attachment to the Royal family. Proud of the distinguished honour conferred on this district by one of the princes of the blood royal, we venture to ask your Royal Highness to be pleased to lay a stone in the parapet of the bridge, with an inscription commemorative of your Royal Highness's presence on this occasion, and of the opening of the bridge for traffic.
THOMAS AUSTIN, President.

REPLY.

Gentlemen—Accept my best thanks for the address you have presented to me, in which the expressions of loyalty to the Queen are sure signs of the real attachment which you bear to Her Majesty and the great kingdom of which Victoria forms so important a part. It has given me great pleasure to be able to leave a visible and tangible token of my visit to your district of this colony, where I hope all success will attend the building, and an increased traffic prove the utility of the undertaking.
ALFRED.

The formalities of the reception being disposed of, his Royal Highness and party were driven to the Barwon Hotel, where a few bumpers of champagne were drank, and the *cortège* then proceeded to Barwon Park, the residence of Mr. Austin. In the afternoon, the Royal party went out rabbit shooting, and had some very remarkable sport. In three and a-half hours 805 had fallen to the guns of the sportsmen, 416 of the number killed having been shot by the Duke.

The following day (Wednesday) after more rabbit shooting, the Prince left, about three p.m., for the residence of Mr. W. Robertson, near Colac, where he passed the night. The only township on the route was Birregurra, where the Prince stopped and received an address from the inhabitants, which was presented by Mr. Albert Clark, postmaster. A few miles further on was a triumphal arch, erected by Mr. Beale, of Bleak House, a neighbouring home station.

At Colac a public holiday had been declared; the shops were shut, the school children were paraded in dresses of white and blue, half a dozen triumphal arches had been erected, and a number of gay flags were flying. Members of the friendly societies were called out, and a space in front of the shire hall, where the address was to have been read, was reserved for the ladies. But unfortunately all was in vain, the Prince driving through at full gallop, neither stopping nor drawing rein. The expressions of regret, as might reasonably be expected, were loud and frequent; but there was a cause for it—H.R.H. was suffering from sand blight, in consequence of having been exposed to the blinding dust for several hours.

The Prince left Mr. Robertson's residence at seven o'clock on the morning of Friday, 6th December, *en route* for Mr. Neil Black's station, near Camperdown, which was reached at noon, and where he was met by about two thousand people, on horses, in carriages, and on foot. A triumphal arch of great beauty, designed by Mr. Keddie, had been erected by the Shire Council. Mr. D. Mackinnon, the President of the Shire Council, accompanied by Messrs. Fergusson, P. Macarthur, Curdie, T. Shaw, jun., D. D. Scott, Paton, Pimbleth, M'Nicoll, Walls, and J. L. Currie, presented the following address, which was graciously received:—

May it please your Royal Highness.—We the inhabitants of the Shire of Hampden, beg most respectfully to approach your Royal Highness with a sincere expression of the deep interest we entertain to your Royal Highness as the son of our Most Gracious Sovereign the Queen. It is with feelings of ardent loyalty and devoted attachment to her Majesty's Person, Throne, and Government, that we now welcome her son to our inland homes; and it is with fervent gratitude we recognise in this visit evidence of the solicitude and regard which her Majesty extends to her loyal subjects in this remote portion of her dominions. It is little more than twenty years since the foot of civilised man first trod these fertile plains; and it is truly gratifying to us to be thus early honoured by a visit of a Prince of the Royal Family. We beg to assure your Royal Highness that this most welcome visit will be held in grateful remembrance, and it will be our earnest wish and prayer that your Royal Highness may be long spared to be a blessing and ornament to our country and t the honourable profession to which your time and distinguished talents are devoted.

Hitherto the Royal party had been escorted by the Geelong police, but they now returned, and H.R.H. was accompanied by Port Fairy troopers.

His Royal Highness journeyed to Mr. Neil Black's, at Glenormiston, by a cross country route. Leaving Glenormiston at eleven, he proceeded to Mortlake, where he met with a most enthusiastic welcome, the Shire Council and the Local Reception Committee taking an active part to ensure not only a splendid demonstration in honour of the Prince, but a due regard to the feelings and convenience of his Royal Highness—matters which in many other places were entirely overlooked. Amongst the gentlemen who promoted the success of the Royal reception at Mortlake should be mentioned Mr. Grieve, Mr. Kerr, Messrs. Jones, Despard, and Hayes, marshals; Mr. Cumming, Mr. Puckle, and Mr. Thomas Shaw, jun.

Visit of H.R.H. Prince Alfred.

The Prince arrived at Hexham at half-past five o'clock in the afternoon. A handsome triumphal arch had been erected, and he met with a splendid reception. He went on at once to Mr. Moffat's station—Chatsworth, and reached there at seven o'clock. The very short notice given to Mr. Moffat as to the day on which the Prince would arrive at Hopkins-hill, rendered it impossible for him to make such preparations for the entertainment and amusement of his distinguished visitor and his own private friends as he would otherwise have done; but only those who knew what those intentions were, could miss anything in the arrangements, which, so far as the reception and comfort of the Prince were concerned, were on a scale of princely magnificence.

Amongst other gentlemen awaiting the arrival of the Prince were Mr. R. Hood, Mr. Routledge, Mr. M'Knight, Mr. E. Henty, Mr. F. Henty, Mr. Richmond Henty, Mr. Onslow (midshipman of the *Galatea*), Mr. Ibbetson, Mr. Charles Larnach (manager of the Bank of New South Wales, Geelong), Mr. Sanderson, Mr. Bree, and Mr. Fox. At eight o'clock dinner was served, Mr. Moffat presiding.

During the Prince's stay at Mr. Moffat's mansion, his Royal Highness planted a tree in the grounds directly opposite the house. Several ladies and gentlemen who had not been invited to dine, enjoyed the privilege of sitting down at table with the Duke at luncheon on Sunday, and Mr. and Mrs. Gray, of Nareeb-Nareeb, near neighbours of Mr. Moffat, were present by command of his Royal Highness. The dinner party on Sunday was more numerously attended than on the previous occasions, and during the evening several gentlemen were introduced, including the Mayor of Hamilton (Mr. Alexander Learmonth), and the ex-Mayor (Dr. Govett). During his stay his Royal Highness received the following address from the Council of Warrnambool, Messrs. Jamieson, Aitkin, Boyd, Bromfield, Cramer, Dooley, Hider, King, and Murray, having travelled upwards of fifty miles to present it:—

May it please your Royal Highness—We, the Mayor, Borough Council, and Burgesses of the town of Warrnambool, county of Villiers, in the colony of Victoria, most respectfully venture, upon the occasion of your visit to the colony of Victoria, to offer to your Royal Highness our most sincere and fervent expressions of loyalty and regard. We would wish to convey to your Royal Highness, as an illustrious member of that noble family whom we all reverence and esteem, our great satisfaction in welcoming you to the shores of this colony. Forming perhaps the most distant portion of that vast empire over which floats the glorious flag of dear old England, we would assure you that in no part of the Queen's dominions has Her Majesty subjects more loyal or devoted. To yourself, personally, as an officer of the Navy which has ever been the glory and might of Great Britain, and the boast of Englishmen, we would beg to accord our liveliest feelings of attachment; and we pray earnestly that your Royal Highness may be long spared to be an ornament to the distinguished profession you have chosen, and a source of pride and gratification to the illustrious lady our most gracious Queen.

WILLIAM W. JAMIESON, Mayor.
HENRY T. BEAD, Town Clerk.

The address was beautifully engrossed by Mr. Henry, and mounted on blue and satin by Mrs. Cramer.

REPLY.

Gentlemen—I am deeply touched by the warmth and cordiality with which I have been welcomed to this colony, and thank you most heartily for your Address. It will be my most pleasing duty to inform Her Majesty of the proofs which you have given me of your feelings of loyalty and devotion to her throne and person, and to assure Her Majesty that in no part of her vast dominions is there a people more attached to the British Constitution, and more sensible of its privileges. I beg you to accept my thanks for imploring the blessings of Heaven on my behalf, and it is my earnest prayer that I may prove myself worthy of the noble profession I have chosen.

On the night of the arrival a number of bonfires were lit, and there was a display of fireworks. On the following morning there was a kangaroo hunt. The Prince shot thirty, several of which were skinned and prepared as trophies. The Prince remained at Chatsworth during Sunday, and left early the next morning, breakfasting at Streatham. H.R.H. drove across the plains, a strong hot wind blowing. He reached Skipton at one o'clock, where he stopped for refreshment. From Linton's, where the Prince lunched, and received several addresses, almost every hotel was ornamented with a triumphal arch. Scarsdale was also very demonstrative in that respect.

ARRIVAL OF THE PRINCE AT BALLARAT.

The account of the visit of the Prince to Ballarat, and the enthusiastic reception given to him by its inhabitants, has been condensed principally from the *Ballarat Star*:—

His Royal Highness the Duke of Edinburgh made his entry into Ballarat on the afternoon of Monday, the 9th of Dec. Happily, the weather was all that could be desired. The Prince started from Streatham at eleven o'clock, and was expected to arrive at Ballarat about five p.m. His Excellency the Governor arrived from Melbourne by special train at noon. The Mayors of Ballarat and Ballarat East, the two Borough Councils, the Mayor and Borough Council of Sebastopol, the President and Members of the Council of Buninyongshire, assembled at the Alfred Hall, where carriages were waiting to convey them to the western end of the town, as his Royal Highness was to make his entry from the Smythesdale road. In the meantime the Ballarat Rifles, with band playing, marched from their orderly-room past the hall *en route* for Pleasant-street, there to await the arrival of the Prince. The Rifles mustered over two hundred strong, and were under the command of Captains Smith and Sleep. Towards four o'clock the municipal bodies started in their carriages for Craig's Hotel, proceeding by way of Mair and Doveton streets, to Gibbings's stables, where the Royal carriage, built by Messrs. M'Cartney and Co., was ordered out, for the Governor to proceed in to meet the Prince. The Royal carriage then drove up, two postilions, in Royal scarlet, riding, and the vehicle being drawn by four of Gibbings's well-matched bays. Some little difficulties in the way of organising the procession having been got over, and the patience of the inhabitants, who for several hours had been waiting for the Royal visitor, having been sorely tried, at length the news of the arrival of the Prince was communicated, and that his Excellency the Governor and the municipal authorities had gone to meet him. At six o'clock the booming of the artillery announced the approach of the Prince. His Royal Highness drove up to the triumphal arch in Pleasant-street in the Royal carriage. The Rifles presented arms, and the band played the National Anthem as his Royal Highness came up. Beneath the triumphal arch erected at the corner of Pleasant and Stuart streets, the Mayors and Councillors of Ballarat and Ballarat East were waiting to present their joint address. Upon his Royal Highness approaching, the Town-Clerk of Ballarat (Mr. Joseph Comb) read the address, as follows:—

May it please your Royal Highness.—It is with feelings of the deepest satisfaction that we, the mayors and members of the borough councils of Ballarat and Ballarat East, in our names and in the names of our fellow townspeople, beg to tender your Royal Highness our warm and hearty welcome to these boroughs. Animated, as all the inhabitants of the colony are, with sentiments of the utmost reverence, admiration, and affection for our much-loved Queen, it is peculiarly gratifying to us to have the opportunity of testifying our loyalty, afforded by the visit of one so closely connected with the throne, and who has otherwise so many claims upon our esteem as your Royal Highness. While our earnest prayer is that Her Most Gracious Majesty may, in the Providence of Almighty God, be long spared to reign in peace and prosperity over us and our fellow subjects throughout the British empire. It is also our heartfelt wish that the blessing of God may ever rest upon your Royal Highness, that you may be long preserved to be an ornament to the honourable profession which your Royal Highness has chosen, and one of the chief supports to the British throne. In conclusion, we hope this visit of your Royal Highness to the land of our adoption will be as agreeable to yourself as it is gratifying to us.

THOMAS DAVEY, Mayor.		EMANUEL STEINFELD, Mayor.	
GILBERT DUNCAN, Councillor.		GEORGE GLENDINNING, Councillor.	
JOSEPH A. DOANE	,,	ANDREW ANDERSON	,,
JAMES McDOWALL	,,	JAMES DODDS	,,
DAVID ROBERTSON	,, BALLARAT.	GEORGE R. FINCHAM	,, BALLARAT
THOMAS COWARD	,,	JAMES EDDY	,, EAST.
GEORGE F. LOVITT	,,	JOHN JAMES	,,
CHARLES D. CUTHBERT	,,	EDWARD EASTWOOD	,,
JAMES HUNT	,,	WILLIAM B. RODIER	,,
JOSEPH COMB, Town Clerk.		E. CHARLESWORTH, Town Clerk.	

The address was enclosed within morocco covers, on one of which was a plate of solid gold nine inches in width by seven inches in depth, and bearing the inscription of presentation to his Royal Highness. It was engrossed and illuminated on parchment by Mr. William Thompson, secretary of the Water Supply Committee, and was beautifully executed. The address having been read and handed to the Prince, H.R.H. made the following reply, which he observed would be sent in due time in a suitable form to the two councils :—

Gentlemen—I offer you my most hearty thanks for the welcome you have given me to Ballarat. I gratefully acknowledge your assurances of loyalty and devotion to Her Majesty's throne and person, and I am proud of the privilege which has fallen to my lot of being the first member of the royal family who has visited this most interesting and important part of Her Majesty's dominions. I thank you for the blessings you invoke upon me, and for the good wishes you express for my welfare and success.

As soon as the presentation of the address was over, the procession started on its way along the south side of Sturt-street. It was headed by the Chief Marshal, Major Wallace, who was assisted by three smart sub-marshals (Messrs. Greene, F. C. Moore, and Vance) attired in blue uniforms with silver facings. The municipal carriages came next, the Royal carriage following; afterwards the gallant fire brigades of Ballarat and Ballarat West, the Friendly Societies, Chinese residents, &c. Flags were floating everywhere; the gardens were crowded with people; galleries, balconies, windows, and housetops were lined with spectators. The progress was necessarily accommodated to a walking pace, and Marshal Wallace was everywhere. His sub-marshals were posted variously, Mr. Greene in the van, Mr. Moore with the Royal escort, and Mr. Vance hovered about the rear. As the procession moved down Sturt-street the full force of the ovation given to the Royal guest became more and more apparent. The great surging crowd rolled along with the procession, shouting welcomes wherever the Prince was visible. As the cavalcade arrived at the intersection of Sturt and Lydiard streets, the spectacle was magnificent. All around the buildings were brilliantly lighted up, and over the wide expanse of Ballarat East the whole air seemed tremulous with multicoloured motion. House tops, towers, arches, masts, galleries, balconies, all were bright in colours of waving drapery and bunting. But still the immense crowds were ever the greater spectacle. The total number gathered within the field of view must have been forty or fifty thousand, a number equal if not superior to the display in front of the Treasury in Melbourne on the occasion of the Prince's official reception.

At Craig's Hotel, where the Prince's quarters were, the royal standard was floating. Here his Royal Highness and suite alighted, and passed in amid the acclamations of the crowd.

Reception at Ballarat.

The Torchlight Procession of the German residents of Ballarat and the surrounding districts was very successful, and added considerably to the general illumination which so loyally and effectively characterised the arrival of the Prince in every part of the town. The procession was formed at the Eastern Town-hall, Mr. Louis Seiffert officiating as marshal, and Mr. Theodor Kawerau acting as musical conductor. The Germans lighted the Prince to and from the Theatre Royal, to which he paid a brief visit; and upon his return to Craig's Hotel, an address was presented by the German residents. The address was contained in a very beautifully finished box, made of colonial lightwood, composed of over five hundred different pieces, and bearing a suitable inscription on a gold plate inside. The box was the work and gift of Mr. Schrieber, Main road. Mr. Luth, who officiated as spokesman, addressed his Royal Highness in German, and read the address, on receiving which his Royal Highness replied briefly in the same language, stating that he was highly pleased at the interest taken by the German residents of Ballarat in his visit, and he would in due time send a suitable reply. After the presentation of the address, the Duke was serenaded. The Mayors of Ballarat and Ballarat East, together with Captain Sherard, of the Volunteer Light Horse Troop, dined with the Prince at Craig's Hotel, the Governor being also present. Captain W. C. Smith was also among the invited, as representing the Volunteer Rangers. In the evening the two boroughs were brilliantly illuminated on a scale of unprecedented magnificence, and thus finished up a day ever to be remembered in the annals of Ballarat.

The following day (Tuesday, 10th December), the Prince proceeded to the Alfred Hall to hold a Levee at eleven o'clock. The streets leading from Craig's Hotel to the hall were crowded with spectators, all anxious to obtain a glimpse of the Royal visitor. One thousand ladies (the exact number) attended as spectators, and filled the gallery and the body of the hall. A number of addresses were presented to the Prince, after the levee presentations had taken place, and amongst others was one from the Ballarat Caledonian Society. That received from the Borough of Creswick, is appended:—

May it please your Royal Highness—We, the mayor, councillors, and burgesses of the borough of Creswick beg to assure your Royal Highness of our continued loyalty and devotion to the person and throne of our beloved Sovereign. We most heartily congratulate your Royal Highness on your safe arrival in this colony, and sincerely hope that your visit to this distant part of the empire will prove a personal gratification, and afford your Royal Highness abundant proof of our unchanging attachment as a people to Her Most Gracious Majesty, and our high regard for yourself personally as an illustrious member of the royal family. We most cordially unite in wishing your Royal Highness every personal happiness; and we pray that amongst the many illustrious names that have been and are still connected with the royal navy of England, that of your Royal Highness may ever occupy a high and conspicuous place. (signed) JOHN THOMAS JEBB, Mayor. WILLIAM GARDINER, Councillor.
THOMAS COOPER, Councillor. JOSEPH HARRIS ,,
GEORGE WILLIAMS ,, HENRY STOREY ,,
ANTHONY PASCO ,, JOSEPH MOORE ,,
Dec. 10th, 1867. JAMES ROGERS ,, JOSEPH REED, Town Clerk.

REPLY.

Gentlemen—I thank you for your congratulations upon my safe arrival in Victoria, and for your expressions of loyalty and devotion to the Queen, which it will be my duty to convey to Her Majesty. The good wishes which you offer for my personal happiness and for my success in my profession are very grateful to me, and I heartily thank you for them.

The Mayor and Town-Clerk of Maryborough attended, and presented the following address on behalf of the Burgesses of that place, to which the reply is appended:—

May it please your Royal Highness—We the Mayor and Councillors of the borough of Maryborough, in the colony of Victoria, approach your Royal Highness with mingled feelings of the deepest respect and joy upon this most auspicious event, your first visit to this colony. It is most gratifying to know that in all the places which you have honoured with your presence, you have been greeted with those expressions of loyalty so justly due to our beloved Queen; and your Royal Highness may rest assured that there are none who more heartily appreciate and welcome your visit, than the inhabitants of the Maryborough district, who earnestly wish that your sojourn amongst us may be as agreeable to yourself, as we sincerely desire that it should be.

ALEXANDER LOWENSTEIN, Mayor.
CHARLES TOUTCHER, Town Clerk.

REPLY.

Gentlemen,—I assure you that it has given me the greatest pleasure to have had an opportunity of visiting this most important colony. The cordial reception that has been given me, and the reiterated expressions of loyalty to Her Majesty the Queen, and of attachment to the old country, which I have heard on all sides, will lead me ever to look back upon my short residence here with feelings of unmixed gratification. I thank you most sincerely for the part you have taken in the general welcome which I have received in Victoria, and for the kind wishes on any behalf contained in your address.

Addresses were also presented from the Mayor and Town-Clerk of Clunes, on behalf of the residents of that place; by Mr. R. H. Bland, for those of Bungaree; by Mr. H. Clark, for the Rechabites; and from the officers of the various Lodges of Odd Fellows, Druids, and Foresters. The following is a copy of that from the Odd Fellows:—

May it please your Royal Highness—We, the members of the Ballarat District M.U.I.O.O.F., beg leave, as most loyal and faithful subjects of Her Most Gracious Majesty Queen Victoria, to tender our sincere congratulations on your safe arrival in this colony, and especially for your visit to Ballarat, one of the richest of all the goldfields in Her Majesty's dominions. As members of the largest Friendly Society in the world, whose branches spread through every country in which the English language is spoken, as well as in many other parts of Europe, and numbering in our ranks men of every station from the peer to the peasant, our objects being those of philanthropy and charity, the relief of each other in sickness or distress, and to assist the widow and orphan, without reference to the religious or political feelings of any, further than a loyal attachment to the Throne of Her Most Gracious Majesty, we feel the highest honour conferred on us in thus being allowed to approach your Royal Highness with the most humble assurance of our attachment to the crown of Great Britain. That your Royal Highness may ever enjoy the love and esteem of all Her Majesty's subjects, and may long live in the enjoyment of a life of honour and virtue, as unfolded in the history of your illustrious parents, is the sincere wish of the loyal Independent Order of Odd Fellows, Manchester Unity.

RICHARD KENT, Prov. G.M.
WM. ROBERTSON, Prov. D.G.M.
WM. NELSON, Prov. C.S.

Ballarat, Victoria, December, 1867.

REPLY.

Gentlemen,—I pray you to accept my hearty thanks for your congratulations upon my safe arrival at Ballarat. I am glad to find that the societies which have done so much in other parts of the world for the relief of sickness and distress, are so well represented here. I shall have great pleasure in making known to Her Majesty the assurance of your attachment to the crown.

ALFRED.

The President, Treasurer, and Secretary of the Jewish Society of Ballarat, as representing that body; the Mining Board, by the hand of its President; the Chairman, accompanied by several members of the Ballaratshire Council; Captain M'Dowall, on behalf of the Ballarat West Fire Brigade, and Master Scurby, on behalf of the Students of the Ballarat College, also had the honour of presenting addresses. The Duke was also presented with a copy of a local musical production by Mr. Lennox, entitled "The Duke's Welcome to Australia."

It had been arranged that H.R.H. should start at two o'clock to visit the Band of Hope Company's claim, thence to the Sebastopol Town Hall, thence to the Prince of Wales Company's claim, and thence to the Albion Company's claim, returning afterwards to his hotel. The proceedings were to be finished by the attendance of the Prince at the Alfred Hall, to open the banquet. The Prince, accompanied by members of his suite, took their places in the carriage, and the Duke, taking the reins, proceeded down Lydiard-street at a pace which promised a speedy arrival at their destination.

Shortly after two o'clock o'clock his Royal Highness arrived at the claim. He alighted at the No. 2 shaft, where a very large number of persons were congregated. Inside the gates leading up to the shaft and machinery there were drawn up, in lines two deep, the men employed on the mine. The Prince was met at the gate by the chairman of the Board of directors, Mr. Caselli, and by him he was conducted to the mines, where the working committee of the board met him, and showed him round the machinery. For his enlightenment four of the machines, which had been kept loaded with washdirt for the occasion, were put in motion, and he was initiated into some of the mysteries of washing up. The machinery having been inspected, the Prince and his party prepared to descend the mine. The works are always lit with gas, but on this occasion there had been extra burners put on, and here and there were placed stars and other devices. In one of the drives there were tables, laid out on which a light refection was spread. The directors had provided for the royal party a number of suits of clothes, into which they were duly inducted, and then the process of lowering commenced. Arrived at the bottom of the shaft, the party proceeded through the drives. H.R.H. stopped at several points, and with an ordinary pick went to work to dig out for himself some of the treasure which has been so richly scattered by nature throughout this company's claim. He was not unsuccessful in his researches, for he unearthed several pieces of gold of tolerably large size. After spending about an hour and a half in the mine, the party were drawn to the surface, and such a sight as they presented when they came into the full light of day, will not easily be forgotten by those who saw it. With faces begrimed, hands encrusted with mud, and garments all stained with the earth, they looked like ordinary miners emerging from a day's work. Safely landed, there was a short adjournment to the dressing-rooms, and much merriment was caused by his Royal Highness insisting on every one keeping their dress and their mud on, in order that they might be photographed together. The artist requiring a few minutes for preparation, there was another visit to the works, when the process of washing-off was illustrated to the Royal visitor by the manager. A most handsome nugget of gold, beautifully interspersed with crystals of quartz, was then presented to his Royal Highness. Its weight is 22 oz. It was enclosed in a handsome morocco case, which, on a silver plate, bears the following inscription:—
"Presented to H.R.H. Prince Alfred, Duke of Edinburgh, on the occasion of his visit to the United Extended Band of Hope Company's mine, Ballarat. H. R. Caselli, chairman; A. J. Forbes, manager. 10th December, 1867." The following is an abridgment of the history of the United Extended Band of Hope Mine, presented to His Royal Highness by Mr. Thomas Carpenter, mining engineer:—

I am commissioned by the directors of the United Extended Band of Hope Company to give your Royal Highness a description of their mine—the richest gold mine in this or any other country. The company was registered in 1856, and obtained a concession of some 5540 feet on the course or trend of the Golden Point Lead. Other concessions of a very extensive character have been registered on the course of other leads; on the Frenchman's some 5140 feet, and the complement allowed to sixty men on the Redan, Inkermann, and Suburban Leads. The capital subscribed was £64,000, with power to increase to £80,000. The workings are very large, and at the outset were prosecuted against obstacles of a very severe and trying character. At present the productive workings are on the Golden Point Lead, or, more correctly speaking, on some large river bed, which is composed of quartzose boulders, pebbles, and sand, intermixed with iron pyrites. Through this the gold is more or less distributed. The principal portion is always found near or on the bed-rock, or in its interstices, in nuggets or pepitos of various shapes and weight down to the finest dust, and in a state of great purity, the fineness being 23 car. 2 grs. 6/7, and 23 car 3 grs. The course of this river is south of west, as far as it is worked, a distance of some 1100 feet. Its average breadth is 200 feet, and thickness from 5 feet 6 inches to 7 feet. This is all more or less auriferous. Overlying this diluvium or wash there are eight distinct strata, four of igneous rock and four of aqueous. The igneous is basalt, or trap; the aqueous sedimentary, chiefly clay, slate, and marl, all the result of some more recent deposit. The older formation upon which all this reposes is traversed with many rich veins and lodes of golden quartz, the source from which we have obtained all our gold, and the one upon which we shall have to depend for our future permanent wealth. The metallic deposits are analogous to the stanniferous deposits of Cornwall. The thickness of the overlying matter is some 380 feet. The lead is reached from a shaft and a gallery. The shaft is 420 feet deep; closely timbered and divided into compartments for lowering and raising the workmen, draining the works, and hauling up the broken ground. The main gallery, traversing the ground below the river bed, is 2500 feet in length. Its transverse dimensions are 7 feet by 7 feet. It is timbered with heavy frames, traversed with a double line of tramway, and is lighted with gas. From this gallery several small shafts are raised at convenient distances, from which small galleries are driven to intersect or form the ground (the river bed) into blocks. The quantity of ground broken from these and sent to surface each 24 hours amounts to some 1800 small waggons or trucks, the transit of which is so managed that their contents are not disturbed in their passage from the faces to the washing mills. Twelve horses suffice to work the trucks. The quantity of ground excavated and washed amounts to some 2,500,000 cubic feet. The gold extracted from the same in ounces is 151,000, which has realised some £908,000.

The general character and extent of such very extensive workings require considerable skill and care on the part of those entrusted with the management, and that such care and skill has been at all times exercised is known from the fact, that not one single life has been sacrificed. The mine is directed by a board of gentlemen of considerable experience in the class of work they direct :— Messrs. H. R. Caselli (Chairman), F. Treasury, P. Brennan, M. Loe, J. M'Cafferty, D. Brophy, J. Wheelan, R. Jones, and W. Canning.

The company's property and finances are in charge and under the general management of their Chief Officer, Mr. A. J. Forbes. Mr. Ward is the Mining Manager at No. 2 Works, Mr. Davey at No. 3 Works, and Mr. Salkield, the Engineer.

The aggregate horse-power employed for drainage, lowering and raising the miners, raising the stuff, ventilating the subterranean works, and extracting the gold, all of which is done by steam power, amounts to that of 349 horses. The number of men employed, of all classes and grades, is 350. The amount paid monthly in wages is £3500. The general cost of timber, material, and light, for the same period, is some £3500. The total value of machinery is £70,000.

The photographs having been taken, and the miners' habiliments doffed, the party proceeded in the direction of Sebastopol, at which place the Mayor and Councillors of the borough presented the following address :—

May it please your Royal Highness— We, the Mayor and Members of the Borough Council of Sebastopol, beg to approach your Royal Highness with the most sincere feelings of loyalty and affection towards the throne and person of Her Most Gracious Majesty Queen Victoria; and towards yourself personally, as the son of our beloved Sovereign, we desire to express our warmest regard and esteem. In the name of the Burgesses of Sebastopol, we give you a most hearty welcome to this renowned mining town, and we trust that your visit here may be one of pleasure and interest, and hope it will not fail to make an indelible impression on your mind of the national importance of the gold mines in this district. And we pray that the Almighty may endow you richly with wisdom from above, to enable you to perform the onerous duties of your high station. We are your Royal Highness's loyal servants,

ISAAC VICKERS, Mayor	NICHOLAS KENT, Councillor.
JOHN EDWARDS, Councillor	JOHN WHITTAKER ,,
THOMAS SAYLE ,,	GEORGE TAIT ,,
WILLIAM BELCHER ,,	ISAAC GRANT ,,
THOMAS DICKINSON ,,	JOHN WALE, Town Clerk.

REPLY.

Gentlemen – I thank you for the welcome you have given me to this important mining district, and for the expressions of personal regard which you offer me. I will not fail to lay before Her Majesty your assurances of loyalty and affection. I have gladly availed myself of the opportunity my visit to Australia has afforded me of seeing the mining districts which have done so much for England. ALFRED.

The Prince then drove off to keep his third appointment of the afternoon, at the Albion Company's claim. As he left the Town Hall a shower of bouquets was thrown at him by a bevy of damsels dressed in white and blue. The Prince arrived on the works of the Albion Company at about half-past six o'clock in the evening, where he was received by the directors, who presented him with the following address :—

May it please your Royal Highness—We, the directors of the Albion Gold Mining Company, on behalf of the general body of the shareholders, beg to express our pleasure in welcoming to the metropolis of the Victorian gold-

Reception at Ballarat.

fields your Royal Highness, and assure you of our loyalty and attachment to the throne and person of Her Majesty. We venture to hope that, taking into consideration only sixteen years have elapsed since gold was first discovered in this colony, you will feel pleased at the magnitude and extent of the works of the mining companies which you have visited and are about to visit. The following is a brief outline of the history of the company :- The shaft was commenced in 1856, and, after many difficulties and delays, through flooding out, &c., gold was struck five years afterwards—viz., in November, 1861, and the first dividend declared in December of the same year ; since which they have been paid regularly, amounting at the present time to £90,921 15s., the total yield of gold since its first discovery being 61,626 oz., of the value of £230,031. The company employ 500 men, at a weekly expenditure of about £1,300, thus distributing a large sum per annum. We hope that your Royal Highness will be gratified with your visit to Australia, and return in health and safety to your native land.

  J. H. HAMMOND, Chairman, DUNCAN CAMPBELL, Director.
  F. R. MICHINSON, Director. J. POULES, "
  CHARLES SEAL, " JOHN CAMERON, "
  DONALD SHAW, "

In the evening the Banquet in honour of the Duke's visit was held at the Alfred Hall, which since the levee in the morning had been promptly prepared for the purpose. Mr. Miller, of Collins-street west, Melbourne, was the "Gunter" for the occasion, and it is only just to state that he fulfilled his contract in a very creditable manner. The Mayor of Ballarat (Mr. Thomas Davey) and the Mayor of Ballarat East (Mr. Steinfeld) received the distinguished guests. His Royal Highness and the Governor advanced to their places on the dais, and the chair was taken by the Mayor of Ballarat East. Mr. Oliver, of Buninyong, officiated as toast master. At the conclusion of the dinner the usual loyal toasts were drunk, after which

The Chairman proposed "The guest, his Royal Highness the Duke of Edinburgh, and the Royal Family," which was responded to most enthusiastically.

His Royal Highness acknowledged the toast, and said:—"Mr. Mayor and gentlemen, I thank you for the hearty manner in which you have responded to the toast of myself, so ably proposed by the Chairman. It has caused me the greatest pleasure to pay this visit, and to have witnessed the immense progress made by the colony in so short a time, and to be able from my own observation to carry away with me an opinion of how important the discovery of gold has been to this city, adding so much to the prosperity of the colony and to the wealth of the world."

The next toast was "His Excellency the Governor," to which his Excellency replied.

His Royal Highness the Prince proposed the next toast, "Prosperity to Ballarat," coupled with the names of the Mayors of Ballarat and Ballarat East. He said : Mr. Chairman and Gentlemen—I think there is no one has any doubt of the thriving and prosperous condition of the colony of Victoria, and more particularly the district of Ballarat. I have had the pleasure to-day of viewing the mineral riches of the district underground, and to-morrow I purpose visiting Learmonth, one of the most important agricultural portions of this colony, in which I hope to see the same prosperity above ground. I have, therefore, much pleasure in proposing the toast of "Prosperity to Ballarat," coupling with it the names of the Mayors of Ballarat and Ballarat East.

The last toast, "The Ladies," was proposed by his Excellency the Governor ; shortly after which the Prince and the Governor retired.

Mr. Prescott gave a grand display of Fireworks on the Cricket Ground during the evening, and a truly splendid show it proved.

On Wednesday, 11th December, his Royal Highness laid the Foundation-stone of the Victoria Temperance Hall, in Lydiard-street. Although the rain came down in torrents, it did not deter a large assemblage from being present. Upon arriving at the place, the Prince proceeded within the enclosure, accompanied by the Hon. W. M. K. Vale, the members of the Royal Commission, the Hon. T. Learmonth, M.L.C., Mr. C. E. Jones, M.P., and others. Mr. Davey, the Mayor, presented to his Royal Highness Mr. Gray, the President, and other members of the Temperance League. His Royal Highness then proceeded to the dais, when the President of the Society presented the following address :—

May it please your Royal Highness,—We, on behalf of the Committee of the Victoria Temperance Hall, Ballarat, desire to welcome you with a loyalty as sincere as the principles of temperance are pure, and to express our devoted attachment to the throne and person of your Royal mother, than whom no monarch ever reigned more firmly in the love and affection of a people. We desire to express our appreciation of your gracious condescension to lay the foundation-stone of this building, which will be devoted to the sacred cause of temperance. We feel assured that your Royal Highness will recognise in the erection of this hall evidences of the growing prosperity of this young district, as well as of the improved and improving social, moral, and intellectual status of the population, as also promise of its future happiness. The hall will bear the name of our much-beloved Queen, in recognition of those high moral virtues which have been, and are now, the glory and lustre of her reign. That she may long live to happily witness the social and material advancement of her vast dominions, that every member of her illustrious family may enjoy a future of unclouded prosperity, and that your Royal Highness may, through a long and happy life, dignify and maintain the honour of the noble profession of your choice and the high character of the British navy, and that the genius of peace may so control the affairs of nations that the noble *Galatea*, or any other vessel which your Royal Highness shall command, may be required to be employed for no purpose more severe than a messenger of "goodwill to man," is the fervent prayer of your Royal Highness's most devoted and humble servants.

JOHN WHITEMAN GRAY, PRESIDENT.
Ballarat, 11th December, 1867.   JAMES BAKER, HONORARY SECRETARY.

After an address from the Hon. Mr. Vale, the stone was lowered amid strains of music. A magnificent gold trowel was presented to the Prince by the Hon. T. Learmonth, M.L.C.; and a bottle, containing copies of the Melbourne and Ballarat papers, the coins of the realm, and other memorials, was deposited in the cavity of the stone. His Royal Highness then used the trowel, applied the spirit-level and the plumb, and declared the stone to be well and truly laid. The trowel which was used by his Royal Highness was composed of gold contributed by the Albion and Prince of Wales Mining Companies, and was very tastefully made. It bore the following inscription :—" Presented to his Royal Highness Prince Alfred, Duke of Edinburgh, at the laying of the foundation-stone of the Victoria Temperance Hall, Ballarat, and manufactured from gold presented by the Albion Gold Mining Company (J. W. Hammond, chairman) and by the Prince of Wales Mining Company (W. Davies, chairman). J. W. Gray, president ; James Baker, hon. sec. ; Frederick Poeppel, architect." The trowel was enclosed in a handsomely-made box of colonial wood, and was the workmanship of Irving, Clover and Co. The ceremony of laying the foundation-stone being over, the Duke took his departure.

The Regatta at Lake Learmonth was the next event of the day, but all enjoyment was marred by the unfavourable state of the weather.

The Duke of Edinburgh departed from Craig's Hotel about twelve o'clock. At the boundary of the Ballarat Shire a large body of farmers, on horseback, were in waiting to receive his Royal Highness, and hearty cheers greeted his arrival. He was received by the president of the Ballarat Agricultural Society, Mr. Learmonth, and an address was presented. The Royal party then drove on to Learmonth, where they were received with the greatest enthusiasm. The Duke was met by Mr. T. Bath, the president of the Regatta Club, and the members of the committee, and conducted to the Court-house, where the members of the Ballarat Shire Council and the Talbot Shire Council were assembled. Addresses were presented from both of these bodies, which were accepted, and a reply promised. The Royal party then proceeded to the shores of the lake, but the unpleasantness of the weather rendered it impossible for them to remain any length of time. After a short stay they went to the marquee, where lunch was served. The health of the Duke was proposed and drunk with loyal enthusiasm, and briefly acknowledged by his Royal Highness. This concluded the visit of the Royal party to Lake Learmonth.

In the evening a dinner, partaking of something of a public character, was given by his Royal Highness the Duke of Edinburgh at Craig's Hotel. There were present, in addition to his Royal Highness's suite, the Hon. Mr. Verdon, the Hon. Mr. Vale, Captain M'Mahon, Messrs. Jenner, M.L.C., Dyte, M.L.A., Jones, M.L.A., the Mayors of Ballarat and Ballarat East, the Mayor of Melbourne, and Captain W. C. Smith. The day's rejoicings were finished up by a ball at the Alfred Hall, which began shortly after ten o'clock, when the Prince and suite were received by the Mayors of the two boroughs, and conducted to the dais. The opening quadrille was formed as follows:—The Prince danced with the Mayoress of Ballarat at the top, and the Mayor of Ballarat with Mrs. Robertson danced at his side. At the bottom the Mayoress of Ballarat East, who was *vis-à-vis* to the Prince, danced with Captain M'Mahon, and Mr. and Mrs. Embling formed the other couple. At the right side, the couple next the top was Mrs. Clissold and the Hon. Eliot Yorke, and the Mayoress of Melbourne and Mr. Brierly formed the other couple. At the left side the corresponding couples were Mrs. R. B. Gibbs and Mr. Henderson, and Mrs. Mitchison and Captain W. C. Smith. The Prince afterwards danced with the Mayoress of Ballarat East and Mrs. Clissold, and in the Scotch reel his partner was Miss Williamson.

On Thursday morning the Prince visited the Alfred Hall to receive the address from the children of Ballarat, and the scene presented was another proof of the marvellous transformations the interior of the building was capable of being subjected to when everybody was bent on loyalty in its most festive and various forms. The glittering beauty of the previous night's ball had all vanished, and the whole area of the hall was filled with children, including those of the Benevolent Asylum, under the care of Mrs. Boughen, the matron. About five thousand little ones were mustered, and presented a sight not soon to be forgotten by those who witnessed it.

The arrival of his Royal Highness the Prince being announced, his entry at once took place, the big army of little people looking on in quiet wonder. Two constables headed the Royal progress, then came sixteen young girls dressed in white with blue scarfs and trimmings, an anchor being visible on their scarfs. Each of this pretty bevy of little ladies carried a basket of flowers, and as the Prince walked up the nave they spread his path with their floral offerings. When the Prince and party had got half-way up the nave, Councillor M'Dowall, from the orchestra, gave a sign, and a storm of cheers at once broke out all over the hall, the children giving full tongue to their juvenile loyalty, delighted at being able to have at last a regular burst out. As soon as silence had again been obtained, the following fourteen young ladies, representing all the denominations in Ballarat, approached the Prince, with the address from the children of that township—Eliza Ann Ainley, Mary Duffy, Sarah Ann Thorpe, Barbara Johnson, Martha Wallis, Lucy Lake, Edith Mary Williams, Emma Jane King, Kate Solomon, Mary Eliza Sim, Mary Scott, Eliza Snelling, Sarah Ann Eastwood, and Alice Hart. Miss Ainley was selected to read the address, which was as follows:—

We, the children of Ballarat, are greatly pleased at being permitted to welcome your Royal Highness to our town and country, and we feel sure that you will accept this address, though presented by children, as graciously as if it were from our parents. Our parents and teachers have taught us to love and revere your noble mother, our

Visit of H.R.H. Prince Alfred.

Most Gracious Queen, and we thank you for coming to this distant part of her empire to assure us of Her Majesty's favour and affection. We have also heard much of "Albert the Good," your lamented father; and we assure you that we shall never cease to remember the great honour we have had of seeing and addressing the son of such illustrious parents. We shall never forget the visit of your Royal Highness, and we venture to hope that, wherever Providence may lead you in future life, you will sometimes remember the children of Ballarat. In conclusion, we pray that God may grant you a safe and prosperous voyage home again, and that your Royal Highness, with the other members of the Royal family, may long be spared to fulfil with honour the high duties entrusted to you.

The Prince, having taken the address from the little lady, said, in a loud voice, to the children :—" I thank you for your address, which is one of the most interesting I have received in the colony. I have been delighted by your appearance, and I wish that you may all enjoy your holidays. I will not detain you now by saying much; but if you ever should think in time to come of my visit, pray remember that I shall never cease to have an interest in your welfare, and in the welfare of your parents, by whose industry and perseverance this colony has attained the prosperity and happiness it now enjoys, and whose example I trust you all will follow."

The conclusion of the Prince's reply was greeted by fresh peals of cheers, and when silence was restored, Mr. A. T. Turner gave the signal to the children for singing the National Anthem, which was well done, and in capital time. As soon as the music was over the Prince and his company left the hall by the way they came, the Prince's egress being saluted by fresh cheers from the thousands of little ones in the hall.

After the children's welcome, his Royal Highness proceeded to visit the works of the Prince of Wales Mining Company. The Royal carriage was escorted by the Troop of Ballarat Light Horse, under the command of Captain Sherard, and by a force of mounted police under the charge of Mr. Sub-inspector Ryall. On arriving at the claim, his Royal Highness entered the company's office, which had been suitably decorated, having an arch in front of the doorway. Here an address from the company, worded as follows, was presented and acknowledged :—

To Captain His Royal Highness Alfred Ernest Albert, Duke of Edinburgh, Knight of the Garter.—We, the Chairman and board of Directors of the Prince of Wales Gold Mining Company, Sebastopol, approach your Royal Highness with feelings of the highest esteem and respect, and with assurances of our devoted loyalty to Her Most Gracious Majesty the Queen. We heartily thank your Royal Highness for the opportunity afforded us of showing you the works and claim of the Prince of Wales Company, and to express our sense of the high honour conferred on us by your visit. The following particulars of this mine may not be uninteresting to your Royal Highness. The company commenced operations in 1857, and first obtained gold in 1861, since which time 75,000 ounces of gold, of the value of £300,000, have been obtained, out of which £152,000 have been paid in dividends. The company is at present working the alluvial deposits and quartz reefs, and employs 450 men. We venture to express a hope that your Royal Highness will enjoy your visit to Ballarat, and in particular to the claim of the Prince of Wales Company; and wishing your Royal Highness long life, happiness, and prosperity, we subscribe ourselves your Royal Highness's most faithful and obedient servants,

WM. DAVIES, CHAIRMAN.	JOHN MUNRO.
J. R. BALLANTYNE.	WILLIAM MORGAN.
HENRY LEWIS.	DUNCAN CAMPBELL.
JULIAN BROOKE.	ALEX. DEMPSTER.
SAML. KINGTON.	FREDK. W. TATHAM, MANAGER.

A very clever piece of draughtsman's work, executed by Mr. F. Ive, was then presented. It gave a section of the No. 3 shaft, and a portion of the underground workings; also the surface works, and the various strata intersected by the shaft, with their relative thicknesses, and coloured as they actually appeared when struck in sinking. His Royal Highness proceeded to inspect the plant, first entering the battery-house, where the use of the ripples and blankets were explained by the chairman of the company. The action of the stampers was then inspected, and attention was drawn to the mode in which the quartz tailings were treated after they left the stamper-boxes. The shoots into which the quartz is thrown, and from whence a steady supply passes under the stamp-heads, were pointed out, and also the simple means by which the stampers are made to revolve; the engine-houses were next visited, and the mode of winding up washdirt and quartz, with the powerful engine used for that purpose, minutely examined and explained. Then an adjournment to the office was made, where refreshments had been provided. The healths of the Queen and the Prince and Princess of Wales, and the Duke of Edinburgh, were proposed by Councillor Lovitt. Mr. W. Dempster, one of the company's directors, in responding to "Success to the Prince of Wales Company," referred to the pleasure and pride the shareholders felt at being so honoured by his Royal Highness. The party then went to the No. 3 shaft, and entered the engine-house, where the double-cylinder vertical winding-engine (designed by Mr. Matthews, the company's engineer, and made by Messrs. Hunt and Opie, of Ballarat) was at work. The principles on which the engine had been constructed were explained. At the sluices a parcel of over 200 ozs. of gold was seen, just as it had been won from the mine, and several small nuggets were pulled out and handed to members of his Royal Highness's suite. The yield was then passed through a riddle or sieve, and the coarser particles were left in it, the finer gold passing through. The rough gold, weighing about five ounces, was distributed as keepsakes of the visit. At the office, his Royal Highness was presented by Mr. Tatham, the company's manager, with a very handsome nugget, in which some pieces of white quartz set off the rich colour of the gold.

The Prince next proceeded to Buninyong, where the local Borough Council presented an address couched as follows:—

May it please your Royal Highness—We, the Mayor and Councillors of the Borough of Buninyong, on behalf of its residents, hail with joy this opportunity of greeting your Royal Highness, and welcoming you to this the oldest inland town in the colony of Victoria, and also the site of the first discovery of gold. We assure you Royal Highness of our loyalty and devotion to Her Majesty's throne and person; and we rejoice to meet in this distant portion of Her Majesty's dominions the son of our beloved and Most Gracious Queen.

JOHN BISHOP, Mayor.
PETER HEDRICK, Councillor.
DAVID BRAYSHAY, ,,
ROBERT ALLAN, ,,
ROBERT GRAHAM, ,,

WILLIAM SAUNDERS, Councillor.
CHARLES SEAL, ,,
HENRY TURNER, ,,
EDWARD NETTELL, Town Clerk.

REPLY.

Gentlemen—It has given me much pleasure to visit your interesting town, upon the site of which gold was first discovered in Victoria. I will gladly express to the Queen the loyalty and devotion you entertain for Her Majesty's throne and person.
ALFRED.

The Buninyongshire Council also presented an address in these terms:—

May it please your Royal Highness—We, Her Majesty's dutiful and loyal subjects, the President and Councillors of the shire of Buninyong, beg leave to approach you on this eventful occasion, to offer you on behalf of the ratepayers, of whom we are the representatives, that respectful homage which is due to your Royal Highness as the son of our well-beloved and Most Gracious Sovereign. We hail your appearance amongst us as a happy omen of the glorious future which we trust yet awaits this colony, and cheerfully bid you welcome to this portion of Her Majesty's dominions. We beg to assure your Royal Highness of our unalterable attachment to your illustrious house, and pray that the Almighty Giver of all good may watch over you with a fatherly care, and make your career one of honour to yourself and glory to the country of your birth.

ROBERT LAMB, President.
GEORGE INNES.
BENJAMIN BROWN.
GEORGE ARTHUR HALE.

WILLIAM HOCKING.
CHARLES C. SCORER.
WILLIAM CLARKE, Secretary.

Address by the Highland Society of Buninyong : —

May it please your Royal Highness—We, the President, Officers, and Members of the Buninyong Highland Society, desire to express our loyalty to our Queen, through her much-loved son, and feel highly gratified in being enabled to accord to your Royal Highness a hearty Highland welcome; and, although so many thousand miles distant from our native land, to express our warmest love and attachment to your Royal person. Trusting God, in His great mercy, will protect, preserve, and bless you, during your stay with us, and through a long and happy life. In name and by their authority,
THOMAS PURVES, PRESIDENT.

REPLY.

Gentlemen—It will be very gratifying to Her Majesty to receive through me your expressions of loyalty and affection. I thank you most sincerely for the Highland welcome you have accorded me. ALFRED.

At the luncheon, Mr. Brayshaw acted as toastmaster, and Mr. Bishop, the Mayor of Buninyong, proposed "Her Majesty the Queen." The next toast was "The Prince and Princess of Wales." The Mayor, in proposing the health of the Duke, remarked that, although they were unable to give him such a demonstration as had been done at other places, he would assure him that there was no more genuine loyalty in any part of the colony than in Buninyong.

Shortly after the return of his Royal Highness to Ballarat, Mr. Philip Davies, mining manager of the Prince of Wales Company, presented, on behalf of the company, a very handsome piece of quartz, weighing about thirty pounds, having gold thickly distributed through it.

Amongst the presents received by his Royal Highness at Ballarat was a carriage built by Messrs. M'Cartney and Aldred. The Prince expressed his intention of sending the carriage to England for his own use. Messrs. M'Cartney and Aldred were generally congratulated on having turned out a carriage that has met with such marked approval.

It had been arranged that Prince Alfred should start for Melbourne by special train at five o'clock, about which time he drove off rapidly for the station. A guard of honour under the command of Captain Smith was drawn up opposite the train, and saluted as his Royal Highness passed. In saying farewell, his Royal Highness thanked the Mayors for the reception he had received, and asked the Hon. Mr. Vale to express his intense satisfaction with the reception, and intimated his intention of coming to Ballarat again to enjoy himself privately at the races. The train started amidst the cheers of a large concourse of people, and made a rapid journey to Melbourne.

Friday, the 13th December, was memorable in the history of the Royal visit. It was the first day, since his arrival, that the Prince had to himself. His Royal Highness did not appear in public, it being the anniversary of the death of his father, Prince Albert.

Having spent a quiet day on Friday, his Royal Highness went on board the *Galatea* on Saturday, and remained there till Sunday afternoon, when he returned on shore.

During Monday the Prince attended the funeral of Commander Wilkinson, R.N. In the evening his Excellency the Governor gave a dinner at the New Exhibition Building to the members of both Houses of Parliament, at which his Royal Highness was present. The party was strictly confined to members of Parliament and the suites of the Prince and his Excellency the Governor. The accommodation of so small a number of guests in so great a hall required some skill, and in order to obtain the effect of an appropriately small space, 120 feet in length by 30 feet in width was completely embowered with evergreens and draped with flags. The organ gallery was filled by ladies who possessed *entrée* cards. His Excellency the Governor was seated in the middle of the hall, facing the rotunda, having on his right his Royal

Highness, and Mr. Verdon and Mr. Macgregor. On the Governor's left hand were Messrs. M'Culloch, Cole, a'Beckett, and Grant. The President of the Council and the Speaker of the Assembly immediately faced the Governor and his Royal Highness. No speeches were made, and the only toast proposed was "The Queen," which was drunk without comment. The caterer was Mr. Scott. His Royal Highness left the building about twenty-five minutes to nine, as had been previously arranged, in order to be present at the Opera.

The Theatre Royal was well filled in every part on the occasion of the Royal visit. The Prince and party occupied the centre box. The opera of *William Tell* commenced when the Prince and the Governor arrived, so that they were enabled to witness the whole of the performance.

VISIT TO CASTLEMAINE AND SANDHURST.

The Duke of Edinburgh proceeded on Tuesday, 17th December, to Castlemaine by train from the Spencer-street station. The time fixed for leaving Melbourne was nine o'clock, and a little before half-past nine the Royal train, preceded by a pilot engine, started on its journey.

The first stoppage was at Footscray. The station was very tastefully decorated, and there was the usual pretty sight of blooming children (dressed in white, with the accompanying blue trimmings) mustered in great force on the platform, who sang the National Anthem. The following address was presented by His Worship the Mayor (Mr. John Brown):—

May it please your Royal Highness—We, the Mayor and Councillors of the Borough of Footscray, grateful for the distinguished favour granted to us in this the visit of your Royal Highness, eagerly embrace the opportunity of expressing our devoted loyalty and strong attachment to Her Most Gracious Majesty Queen Victoria, her Throne and her Government, and to all the members of her illustrious Family. We welcome you to our shores as the son of our beloved Queen, whose exalted virtues and bright example have shed their salutary influence over the whole civilised world. We welcome you as the son of an exalted Prince, whose memory we revere, and under whose benign influence you have been trained to fill the high position in life which you are called to occupy. We welcome you on your own account, and hail you as our Sailor Prince, destined, we believe, from the profession you have chosen, to be the grand link which will bind this far distant colony in loyalty and permanent attachment to the Throne and Government of our much-loved Queen. We earnestly pray that you may be long spared to exhibit, from time to time, the influence of that high moral and intellectual training and example which you so richly enjoyed in the happy home of your childhood and youth. We now desire to commend you to the gracious care of Him who "rules the raging of the sea, and when the waves thereof arise, stilleth them again."

JOHN BROWN, Mayor.
HYAM HART, Town Clerk.

REPLY.

Gentlemen—It will be my gratifying duty to convey to Her Majesty the expressions of loyalty and attachment which your address contains. It will be a source of great pleasure to me if my visit to Australia should tend in any degree to bridge over the distance which divides these colonies from the mother-country. I thank you sincerely for your good wishes for my future happiness.

The next stoppage occurred at Sunbury, where a *contretemps* occurred which seemed to render nugatory the preparations made for the reception. The children of the Industrial School were present, the station was decorated, and the address was ready, in the possession of Mr. Robertson, of Sunbury, although not presented. It had been understood that the Hon. J. G. Francis would present the address, but he was not there. The train stayed, and his Royal Highness stood in the doorway of the saloon evidently expectant of the usual programme. The apparent lapse at length excited the attention of the Hon. J. F. Sullivan, who, upon being informed of the absence of the intended presenter, undertook to explain the matter to the Prince, and the train shortly after left the station.

The reception at Gisborne was a pleasant one, and excellent taste was displayed in the decorations. Stepping from the carriage on to the platform was like stepping into a conservatory of flowers. Mr. Thomas F. Hamilton, with the members of the Gisborne and Lancefield Road Boards, were in waiting, and handed Prince Alfred the following address:—

It is with feelings of the deepest satisfaction that we, the members of the Gisborne and Lancefield Road Boards, on behalf of the inhabitants of those agricultural districts, beg most heartily to welcome your Royal Highness on this occasion; and to assure you of our loyalty and attachment to Her Most Gracious Majesty the Queen, and of our well-wishes for your happiness.

T. F. HAMILTON, Chairman.	J. RIDDELL, Chairman.	
W. HAMILTON, jun., Ex-Chairman.	J. P. WRAGGE, Ex-Chairman.	
H. HUSSEY, Member.	R. S. GRAHAM, Member.	
H. CAMPBELL ,, Gisborne	R. T. BEASLEY ,,	Lancefield
H. WILSON ,, District.	D. MACKAY ,,	District.
M. BRADY ,,	T. KEENAN ,,	
T. H. LIGHTFOOT, Clerk.	T. GANNON, Clerk.	

The Prince received the address, and promised that a reply should be forwarded.

After the presentation of the address, the children present, to the number of seven hundred, led and accompanied by a brass band, sang the first verse of the National Anthem. When this was concluded, a little girl, daughter of Mr. G. W. Knight, of Riddell's Creek, stepped forward and offered for his Royal Highness's acceptance a basket of fruit. The contents were very tastefully arranged, and the ripe fruit nestling amongst the green leaves looked refreshingly cool. The little possessor of the basket, too, seemed to be proud of her burden, and very neatly re-arranged the fruit after it had been disturbed by the Prince and his Excellency partaking of it. Another present was also made to the Royal visitor here in the shape of a bouquet, tendered by a little daughter of Mr. Hamilton. Both gifts were conveyed to the royal carriage. The Prince and his Excellency and suite then proceeded to an apartment in the station, and partook of some wine, the produce of Mr. Knight's vineyard. As the train moved off, preparations, in an adjacent paddock, could be observed for the enjoyment of an *al fresco* entertainment.

The arrangements at Kyneton, although evidently on a large scale, were scarcely equal to those just left. On stepping from the train, the Prince and those accompanying him were met by the President and members of the Shire of Kyneton, and received the following address, to which the reply (since forwarded) is appended:—

May it please your Royal Highness—We, the President, Councillors, and inhabitants of the shire of Kyneton, desire to express our gratification at the auspicious visit of your Royal Highness to this colony. We trust that your progress through these colonies will be as productive of pleasure and enjoyment to yourself as it will be in us of increased attachment to the Throne and person of our Most Gracious Majesty the Queen. We fervently wish prolonged health and happiness to your Royal Highness; and trust that you will carry with you, to that land which we delight to call the "mother-country," a firm assurance of the loyalty and devotion of the people of this colony. Sealed with the corporate seal, the seventeenth day of December, A.D. 1867.

W. THOMSON, President.
J. APPERLY, Secretary.

REPLY.

Gentlemen—It will be my pleasing duty to convey to Her Majesty the assurance you offer me of your loyalty and devotion to the crown, and of your affection for the mother-country. I thank you for your good wishes.
ALFRED.

After the address was read to the Prince, the children sang the National Anthem, at the close of which the Royal party proceeded on their way.

Reception at Castlemaine. 137

At Malmsbury it was intended that the Prince should visit the waterworks, and carriages were in waiting for the purpose of conveying him there. Mr. Christopherson, the chief engineer, was also ready to conduct the Royal party over the works, but, owing to the lateness of the hour and the necessity of proceeding to Castlemaine, his Royal Highness could not undertake that part of the day's programme.

CASTLEMAINE.

So soon as the train, with the Royal standard flying from the engine, entered Castlemaine station, it was perceived that the platforms on both sides of the line were crowded with anxious observers. In the open ground in Templeton-street, fronting the railway station, a guard of honour was furnished by the 1st Castlemaine Rifles, while a cavalry escort was present under the command of Captain Ryland. The Mayor of Castlemaine (Mr. Myring) presented the following address, which was read by Mr. Joseph Davies, the town clerk :—

May it please your Royal Highness—We, Her Majesty's most dutiful and loyal subjects, the Mayor, Councillors, and Burgesses, have extreme pleasure in giving your Royal Highness a cordial welcome to Castlemaine. Permit us to express our loyalty and attachment to our Most Gracious Sovereign the Queen, and the Royal Family of England. We further desire to express our pride in having a Prince who has nobly imposed upon himself a long and fatiguing voyage, by which means alone he could make himself personally acquainted with the several parts of Her Majesty's dominions, being assured that the same desire will direct his liberal views and powerful influence to aid the prosperity and happiness of Her Majesty's subjects in each part of the world. We shall always retain a grateful sense of the honour which your Royal Highness has conferred upon us on this occasion, and beg leave to express our earnest hope that you will so enjoy yourself, that your visit to Castlemaine may form an item in your travels to which your Royal Highness may refer with emotions of pleasure. We are impelled by every consideration to wish you a pleasant voyage and safe return to your native land, and to those who are most dear to you; and, further, to express our hope that the life of your Royal Highness may be prolonged in the full enjoyment of each temporal blessing.

JOSEPH MYRING, Mayor.
JOSEPH DAVIS, Town Clerk.

The address was also signed by the following members of the Castlemaine Borough Council :—Messrs. W. H. Ross, E. P. Newcombe, F. Hirschi, J. Matheson, W. E. Richards, J. Temple, A. Callaway, T. Bannister.

His Royal Highness subsequently made the following reply :—

Gentlemen—I thank you for your cordial welcome to Castlemaine. It will give me much pleasure to convey to Her Majesty the expression of your loyalty and devotion. I am glad to avail myself of the opportunity my voyage affords of making myself personally acquainted with these distant but most important parts of the empire. It will be ever a source of the highest gratification to me, if my visit to Australia should conduce in any degree to its advancement and prosperity.

After the reading of the address, the Prince took his place in the carriage provided for him, and a procession was then formed. At the junction of Barker and Moyston-streets the school children, several hundred in number, were collected, and as his Royal Highness passed along they sang the National Anthem with capital effect. Just after the procession had started from the railway station, the horses in the Royal carriage became restive and unmanageable; the scarlet-coated postilions were unable to control them, and after the horses had run against a triumphal arch, his Royal Highness and the Governor were obliged to alight, and occupy another carriage. A feature in the procession was the demonstration made by the Chinese residents, who were decked out in garments of various descriptions, and presented a picturesque appearance. Upon arriving at Murphy's Castlemaine Hotel, his Royal Highness was received by the Mayor, Councillors, and Town Clerk of the borough. The people cheered most heartily. Several triumphal arches had been erected along the line of route taken by the procession, and it was evident that the people of Castlemaine were bent, so far as possible, upon giving to the son of the Sovereign a loyal and hearty welcome.

At two o'clock his Royal Highness proceeded to the Market Hall, and held a Levee. The hall had been expressly fitted up for the occasion, and most tastefully, and indeed artistically, decorated with flowering shrubs, ferns, and other festive kinds of ornamentation. His Royal Highness was attired in plain dress. The members of the borough council were first presented by his Worship the Mayor, the general presentations following. The names were announced by Mr. Superintendent Winch. Addresses from public bodies were afterwards presented. These, so far as they have been obtained in time, with the replies thereto, are here appended :—

Address from Campbell's Creek.

May it please your Royal Highness—We, the Chairman and Members of the Corporation of the district of Campbell's Creek, do, on behalf of the inhabitants, most heartily welcome your Royal Highness, and must express the gratification your presence affords in giving us an opportunity of renewing our assurance of loyalty and devotion to Her Most Gracious Majesty the Queen ; and we trust your stay will be as agreeable to your Royal Highness as it is the desire of all classes of the community it should be.   S. W. PAULSON, CHAIRMAN.
HENRY LONDON, CLERK.

REPLY.

Gentlemen— Accept my thanks for the welcome you have given me to Campbell's Creek. I will gladly convey to the Queen the expressions of loyalty and devotion which your address contains.   ALFRED.

Address from Guildford.

May it please your Royal Highness—We, the Mayor, Councillors, and Burgesses of the Borough of Guildford, earnestly desire to express the sincere pleasure we feel in welcoming your Royal Highness to this district, and to assure your Royal Highness of the loyalty and attachment we have to our Most Gracious Majesty the Queen. We also desire to express the esteem we feel personally towards your Royal Highness, and that we shall always retain a lively and grateful recollection of the honour which you have conferred upon the district on this occasion.

JAMES NEWMAN, MAYOR.
JAMES MILLIGAN, TOWN CLERK.

REPLY.

Gentlemen—It will be my pleasing duty to convey to Her Majesty your assurances of loyalty and devotion. I am very glad to have an opportunity of visiting Guildford, and I thank you sincerely for the cordial welcome you have given me.   ALFRED.

Volunteer Fire Brigade.

The Castlemaine Volunteer Fire Brigade, with profound respect and loyalty, approach your Royal Highness, humbly to join in the congratulations of our fellow-citizens on being favoured with your benignant visit. The advance made by this town from canvas to solidity in the brief space of thirteen years, the period of existence of this body, though the oldest in the colony, with the settlement even of our artisans on their own freeholds, evinces the true beneficence of the reign under which we glory to live; and we would desire to convey to our gracious Queen our unbounded sentiments of fealty and devotion. May your Royal Highness please to accept our felicitations on the noble career you have embraced; and whilst now on a mission of peace and goodwill, we rest assured that in England's need you would nail your colours to the mast like a true old British Admiral, and

Naught shall make us rue
If England to itself do rest but true.
May every blessedness attend you.

Your Royal Highness's most humble and dutiful servants,

EDWARD GORDON WELCH, CHAIRMAN AND TREASURER.
ROBERT JAMES CHURCH, CAPTAIN.
JOHN WORN, FOREMAN.
EDMUND ASHER YANDELL.
HENRY FAWKNER.
WILLIAM MILLAR.
JOHN STEER CHRISTOPHERS.
CHARLES LEE, ENGINEER.
HENRY CHRISTOPHERS, HON. SEC.

REPLY.

Gentlemen,—I thank you for your congratulations upon my visit to Castlemaine. It is very gratifying to learn from your address that from the beginning of the town there has been a Volunteer Fire Brigade. The public spirit which has maintained so useful an institution, will secure for Victoria the greatness and prosperity for which she seems to be destined.

ALFRED.

From the Ancient Order of Foresters.

May it please your Royal Highness,—We, the undersigned, on behalf of the Members of the Ancient Order of Foresters resident in Castlemaine and District, beg to approach your Royal Highness with feelings of devoted loyalty and attachment to Her Most Gracious Majesty, Queen Victoria. We esteem as a high honour and privilege the visit of your Royal Highness to this distant portion of her Majesty's dominions, and we assure your Royal Highness that, although separated so far from the parent land, we still possess and shall ever retain the most ardent attachment to her Majesty's Throne and person. We heartily welcome your Royal Highness to Castlemaine and District, and that you may long live, and by your many virtues sustain the honour and dignity of the Illustrious house of which you are so distinguished a representative, is the sincere desire of every member of the Ancient Order of Foresters.

(Signed) JOSEPH GOLDSMITH, C.R., Court Castlemaine.
CHAS. C. HOULT, C.R., Court Campbell's Creek.
D. F. MARTIN, Sec., Court Tarradgower.
HENRY W. GREEN, Sec., Court Castlemaine.

REPLY.

Gentlemen,—Nothing in connection with my visit to Australia will be more gratifying to the Queen than the assurance you offer me, and which I have received universally, that the distance which separates you from the mother-country serves to increase rather than to diminish the loyalty and devotion of the people to her Majesty's Throne and person. I thank you for your good wishes and for your welcome to Castlemaine.

ALFRED.

From Ministers of the Gospel.

May it please your Royal Highness,—The Ministers of the Gospel residing in Castlemaine and the neighbouring towns, and subscribing this Address on behalf of themselves and their respective congregations, hail with unbounded joy the visit of your Royal Highness to this part of the British dominions, and bid you most heartily "God speed" throughout the remainder of your contemplated tour. They avail themselves also of the present opportunity of testifying their unwavering loyalty to their gracious Sovereign the Queen; their unfeigned reverence for the noble qualities which have invariably distinguished her in every department of life; their appreciation of the great privileges and particularly the civil and religious liberty enjoyed under the beneficent sway and personal influence of her Majesty; and their prayerful hope that her valuable life will long be spared to the Royal Family, and the empire on which the sun never sets. And they desire likewise to express their ardent attachment and devotion to your Royal Highness, and to every member of the Royal Family, praying that long life and prosperity here and eternal happiness hereafter may be the portion of all.

ANDREW ROSS BOYD McCAY, B.A.
HUGH STOCKMAN CRAMER.
GEORGE TUDOR HALL.
FREDERICK JOHN PITMAN.
ALEXANDER ROBB.
DAVID MORTIMER DAVIES.
FRIEDRICH MUNZELL.
EDWARD KING.
EDWIN DAY.
J. O. COOME.
CHARLES DUBOURG.
WILLIAM TRANTER.
EVAN LEWIS.
WILLIAM HOPKINS.
WILLIAM F. MAYNE.
JOHN ANDERSON.

REPLY.

Gentlemen,—I thank you sincerely for your assurances of loyalty and devotion towards her Majesty, and for the hearty welcome you have given me to this country. I trust that your efforts, in common with those of your fellow-labourers, may, through the blessings of Providence, be rewarded by Du rearing up under your care of a population fearing God and honouring the Queen. I thank you, gentlemen, for the prayers you have offered up to Almighty God for my prosperity, long life, and future happiness.

ALFRED.

An address from the Chinese was presented by three Chinamen, gorgeously dressed, and with splendid pigtails. The address, which was rather lengthy, was very quaintly written. It was translated into English by Mr. C. P. Hodges, of the *Mount Alexander Mail* office. The addresses were merely formally presented, and no replies were made.

After the Levee, the Prince proceeded in a carriage, with four greys, driven by Mr. Robertson, on a visit to the Ajax Mine. The cavalry, under Captain Ryland and Staff Captain Burton, with the mounted police, furnished the escort. The honour of showing the party over the claim fell to the Mayor of Campbell's Creek. The Prince inspected the plant and machinery, witnessed some quartz-crushing, and went up one of the leaders. He was afterwards presented with some rich specimens of gold-bearing quartz, as a memento of his visit to the Ajax mine. The Royal and vice-regal visitors were then driven back to Castlemaine, and reached the hotel shortly after half-past three o'clock. There was a dinner party at night at the Castlemaine Hotel, at which covers were laid for seventeen. The Mayor and Town Clerk, the Mayor of Melbourne, Hon. N. Fitzgerald, M.L.C.; Lieutenant-Colonel Rede, Local Staff; Captain Burton, Staff Officer, and Captain Ryland, were amongst the guests. At night the town was brilliantly illuminated, the Market Square being particularly well lighted.

The day's festivities were concluded with a grand ball given in the Market Hall. The *élite* of the town and suburbs were present. The Prince opened the ball with Mrs. Myring, the Governor dancing with Mrs. Fitzgerald. At half-past eleven the Prince and his Excellency took their partners in to supper, where the usual toasts were drunk with the customary enthusiasm. The Royal guest, however, ventured upon no more words in reply to the toast of his health than, "Ladies and gentlemen, I thank you." His Royal Highness, who was fatigued with the day's laborious proceedings, retired early. Mr. Goodwin was the caterer for the occasion, and gave general satisfaction to the guests.

The following morning (Wednesday, December 18th), the Prince, having previously planted a tree in the Castlemaine Botanic Gardens, entered a special train for Sandhurst about noon. Messrs. Jeremy, Tetley, and Christie were in attendance to secure the perfect carrying out of the arrangements, and the journey was accomplished in less than thirty minutes. The only wayside welcome was at Harcourt, where some fifty or so persons assembled, and cheered as the train swept through.

SANDHURST.

The glorious reception given by "Old Bendigo" to His Royal Highness is abridged from the *Bendigo Advertiser* of Thursday, December 19th.

Precisely at 12.30 was heard the whistle of the approaching special train, which, under the conductorship of Mr. Jeremy, the traffic superintendent, conveyed the Prince and his suite from Castlemaine. Drawing up at the platform opposite the entrance, H.R.H. the Duke of Edinburgh alighted from the Royal carriage, accompanied by His Excellency the Governor, the Hon. Eliot Yorke, the Hon. Mr. M'Culloch, the Hon. Mr. Sullivan, Lieutenants Rothwell and Haig, and the Mayors of Melbourne and Geelong. As the Prince placed his foot on Old Bendigo, he was received by the Mayor and Councillors and members of the local reception committee, while the volunteer guard of honour, under the command of Colonel Bull and Captains Taylor and Joseph, presented arms, and the volunteer field battery fired a royal salute. It was not, however, until he had entered the carriage at the porch of the station facing the approach that he received such a welcome cheer as must have convinced him that the people of Bendigo had not forgotten the mode of evincing their welcome to a visitor, and their loyalty to the British Throne.

A procession having been formed, it proceeded under the triumphal arch, and turned down Mitchell-street. The excitement amongst the crowd lining the street was intense. On the rising ground towards the bridge, and on the north side of Mitchell-street, the female population were in force; and on the south side the Duke must have been struck by the novel, though not elegant, sight of hundreds actually "sitting on a rail," for the fence of the railway reserve proved a capital perch. The marshal, Mr. O'Keefe, headed the procession. A rushing, pushing, cheering crowd of men gathered around the Prince's carriage, and the crowd increased in strength as the procession moved on. For gaiety and picturesque effect, the view of the town along Mitchell-street was most effective. From every house waved coloured flags in great variety. Strings of bunting were suspended in various places from one side of the street to the other. On the tops of the houses, at the windows, and on the verandahs, and indeed in every favourable position for a view, were clusters of people, and they, as the Prince passed along, cheered again and again, while the ladies waved their handkerchiefs with feminine vigour. At Charing Cross, strings of gay-looking flags were hung across the wide space. Up View-street the festooned floral decorations had a charming effect, while the green trees of the Camp Reserve and the private garden on the Ironbark Ranges added to the picturesqueness of the scene. As the procession headed into the Camp Reserve, there was a great crush of people. The central large gates were guarded by the police, but a rush took place, and it was with difficulty room was kept for the procession to pass. As soon as the Royal carriage arrived opposite the place where the school children were assembled, there was a halt of the procession.

The scene in the Reserve at this moment was one of the most interesting and animated description. The brow of the hill had been cut into terraces, seated and covered with grass to keep down the dust, and on these terraces were seated about six thousand school children from all parts of the district. It was a magnificent and thrilling sight, as these young Australians— the girls tastefully dressed, for the most part in white with blue ribbons—rose at a signal from the conductor, Mr. J. T. Davies, to sing. With wonderful precision their young voices swelled forth "God Save the Queen," with a volume of sound and sweetness of expression that must have influenced every heart of the immense gathering of people around, variously estimated at from ten to twenty thousand. When the last note of the anthem was sung, three thrilling cheers were given by the children, and the last merged into long-continued cheering and waving of handkerchiefs, during which the procession again moved on.

A novel and attractive feature in the reception was the introduction of a miniature *Galatea*, with steam up, and little sailors at their posts. It was indeed a pretty picture, and a grand feature in the procession. The kilted members of the St. Andrew's Society came in too for a share of regard, and the Chinese portion of the display, with its rich and curious dresses and warlike instruments, was a novel attraction.

Along the Mall, the crowds of people under the verandahs, over the verandahs, at the windows, and on the housetops, cheered heartily as the royal carriage passed, and the Prince at intervals acknowledged the welcome by raising his hat. The procession proceeded up Mitchell-street, at the corner of which the people on Birtwistle and M'Leod's stand had another view of his Royal Highness, and thence along Hargreaves-street to the Town Hall, where a guard of honour was formed by the Volunteer Rifles, and with the assistance of the police and the cavalry a clear space was kept in front of the building. An immense crowd had gathered at this point, and as His Royal Highness stepped from his carriage, enthusiastic cheering burst forth. He was received on the steps by the Mayor, and was conducted with his suite into the Town Hall to the banquet. At the principal table, at the head of the hall, the Mayor of Sandhurst was seated; on his right sat the Duke of Edinburgh, and on his left the Governor, at each side of whom were the Hon. Messrs. M'Culloch and Sullivan, Eliot Yorke, and Messrs. J. Halfey, J. J. Casey, and P. Burrowes, M.P.'s. Amongst the guests at the other two tables were Lieuts. Rothwell and Haig, the Hon. Mr. N. Fitzgerald, the Hon. Mr. Fraser, Colonel Rede, Captain Burton, Colonel Bull, Captain Taylor; the Mayors of Melbourne, Geelong, and Eaglehawk; the Presidents, Chairmen, and members of the neighbouring Shire Councils and Road Boards; and several of the most influential of the Sandhurst citizens, the total number of guests being about a hundred.

After the banquet, the Prince proceeded to a Fancy Bazaar, held in the Volunteer Orderly-room, in aid of the building fund. His Royal Highness was received at the entrance by the volunteers, drawn up in double line, and having taken his seat on the dais erected at the eastern extremity of the building (his Excellency the Governor being on his left hand), he proclaimed the bazaar to be opened. He then took a tour of the handsomely decorated room, stopping occasionally at the different stalls, which were arranged from the chief entrance in the following order:—On the right was a compartment presided over by Mrs. Heffernan and Mrs. Cheyne, presenting a very gay appearance with its collection of bijouterie, vertu, and fancy work. The next stall was occupied by Mrs. Buttry and Miss Davis, of Kangaroo Flat, and contained many objects of interest. Mrs. Burtrop, assisted by Miss Wrixon, was surrounded by wares of many kinds; amongst others which attracted considerable attention were an ottoman, two doll's houses, and a footstool made and presented by Staff Sergeant Fly, the wool-work on the ottoman being by Mrs. Tolmie, and that on the footstool by Mrs. Bartrop. Mrs. Miles and Mrs. John Watson presided over a varied collection of fancy articles, a tea service of old china, presented by Mr. Hartley, being much admired, as was also a leather-worked frame given by Mr. Carkeet. The stall of Mesdames Latham, Sibley, and Macartney overflowed with fancy goods of all descriptions—artificial flowers, juvenile apparel, and a peculiarly handsome photographic album. The handsome variegated lanterns, with vases and engravings, in Mrs. Taylor and Mrs. Betham's department, were not without admirers. Mrs. A. Aldworth and Mrs. Howard made a good display of toys, dolls, and various knickknackeries. The wax flowers which adorned the stall of Mrs. Forbes were beautiful in the extreme. Mrs. Blackham and Mrs. Brown had some nicely arrayed pot plants and cut flowers, with shrubs of various descriptions, and Mrs. Woodward had a large collection of toys. At the western end of the room Mrs. Benson presided over a wheel of fortune, while at the eastern end Mrs. Moore Hill, assisted by Miss Scott and Miss Stead, gracefully supplied the refreshments. Upon the entrance of the Prince to the Orderly-room, the National Anthem was sung by the Misses Roberts, Lee, Regan, M'Lachlan, and Mesdames Ellis, Benson, Betham, and Messrs. Fowler, Casey, Daly, Pitman, and Roberts, in a manner which seemed particularly to attract the attention of H.R.H. After the ceremony of opening the bazaar had been completed, the Prince returned to the Shamrock Hotel, and at four o'clock was driven to the Town Hall, where he held a Levee, at which the following addresses were presented:—

From the Borough of Sandhurst.

May it please your Royal Highness - We, the Mayor, Councillors, and Burgesses of the Borough of Sandhurst, approach your Royal Highness with sentiments of the profoundest respect, and tender to you our heartfelt welcome to the colony of Victoria, and to our loyal borough. We beg through you to convey our sincere thanks to Her Most Gracious

Reception at Sandhurst.

Majesty our beloved Queen (whose noble virtues and example have added such deep reverence in the hearts of her subjects to the loyalty due to her exalted station) for affording us in this remote portion of the British Empire the kind consideration of a visit from her son. We trust that every success will attend the tour of your Royal Highness, and that you will carry away pleasant and interesting memories of our country and its progress, and of the devoted affection of its inhabitants to Her Most Gracious Majesty and her family.

JOHN M'INTYRE, Mayor.
R. BURROWES, M.L.A., Councillor.
GEORGE ASPINALL, ,,
JAMES BOYD, M.D., ,,
JOHN HOLMES, ,,
JOHN HOLDSWORTH, Councillor.
DUGALD M'DOUGALL, ,,
EDWARD GARSED, ,,
JOHN LATHAM, ,,
GEORGE AVERY FLETCHER, Town Clerk.

From the Shire of Strathfieldsaye.

May it please your Royal Highness—We, the President and Councillors of the Shire of Strathfieldsaye, beg to approach your Royal Highness with feelings of the deepest respect, and offer to you our hearty welcome to this district. We beg to tender through you our devotion and loyalty to the Throne and person of your Royal mother our Most Gracious Queen, and to proffer our heartfelt thanks to her for permitting us to receive the high honour of a visit from your Royal Highness. We trust that the tour of your Royal Highness will be a pleasant and happy one, that you may be favourably impressed with the progress and resources of this country; and that you will be spared to return in health and safety to your Royal home, is the sincere prayer of your Royal Highness's humble servants,

ROBERT BLACKWOOD SIBLEY, President.
JOSEPH BELL, Secretary.

From the Freemasons of Bendigo.

May it please your Royal Highness—On behalf of the Freemasons of Bendigo, we have the honour of expressing our gratification at your visit, and of bidding you a hearty welcome to Sandhurst. We gladly embrace the opportunity of conveying to you our sentiments of loyalty and attachment to the throne and person of Her Most Gracious Majesty, and our feeling of high regard and esteem for yourself personally. Loyalty and respect for authority are part of our traditional teachings, but we approach your Royal Highness with far warmer feelings than that of mere duty. Your noble ancestry have been members and patrons of our order, and your illustrious relative the late Duke of Sussex was Grand Master of the craft; therefore we have especial pleasure in your visit, and we fervently pray the Most High that He may so direct your steps in the paths of truth and virtue as to make you to discharge your duties in a manner pleasing to Him and worthy of your exalted position.

T. H. HENDERSON, W.M., Golden Lodge.
J. BUCKLEY, W.M., Corinthian Lodge.
J. DOWLING, W.M., Eaglehawk Lodge.
S. P. HOGG, W.M., Zenith Lodge.

REPLY.

Gentlemen—I thank you for the expression of your loyalty and attachment to the Throne and person of Her Majesty. Although I am not a member of the craft, I recognise with pleasure the extensive charities and the fraternal sympathy with each other of the Freemasons of every land. I tender to you my hearty acknowledgments for the welcome with which you received me on my visit to your district. ALFRED.

From the Chinese Residents of Sandhurst.

We, the Chinese residents of Sandhurst, humbly and respectfully congratulate the second son of the Queen of the great nation of England on safely arriving in this country. It displays the great wisdom of your Royal Highness in travelling abroad, because by that means you are enabled to judge of the various forms of government in every portion of your great mother's dominions. As you do now, so did many of our former enlightened and intelligent princes. We obey the benign laws of your royal mother, and it is a joyous duty for us to do so, for although aliens, we are equally benefited with the other inhabitants. We rejoice very much that you have visited us, to bear our affection to the Great Queen. Your visit will cause all waters to flow with fragrance, all grass and trees to be radiantly green; all places will glow in the effulgence of the great light shed by your Royal Highness, and your visit and travels will, in our history, reach to a myriad of ages. May the Great Spirit watch over your Royal Highness, and bear you in safety back to your native land. Dated this 23rd day of the 11th month of the 6th year of the reign of Tong Tsze, of the Tsi being dynasty. Signed on behalf of the Chinese residents,

WAT A CHEE, and Others.

Visit of H.R.H. Prince Alfred.

REPLY.

Gentlemen—Your congratulations on my arrival in this part of Her Majesty's dominions were very pleasing to me, and I have received with satisfaction the assurance of your respect for Her Majesty the Queen, and that you recognise the benefits which you, while residents here, derive, in common with Her Majesty's subjects, from obedience to and an impartial administration of the laws. I thank you for your good wishes for my safety and welfare.

ALFRED.

From the Sandhurst Volunteer Fire Brigade.

May it please your Royal Highness—We, the members of the Sandhurst Volunteer Fire Brigade, respectfully beg permission to express our feelings of loyal and devoted attachment to Her Most Gracious Majesty the Queen, and to tender to your Royal Highness our cordial and respectful welcome to Sandhurst. In thus venturing to present ourselves to your Royal Highness, we are encouraged by the hope that the objects for which we are voluntarily associated, namely, the saving of life and property from fire, are such as your Royal Highness will deign to regard with interest and approbation.

MICHAEL MEAGHER, Captain.		JOHN KERR, Hon. Sec.
THOMAS HARRIS, Foreman.		GEORGE WEBB, Hon. Treasurer.
JAMES HICKEY, Assistant-Foreman.		GEORGE OWEN, Apparatus Officer.

MEMBERS.

R. R. PEEL.	RYLAND J. HOWARD.	ROBERT PEEL.	JAMES ROBERTSON.
SAMUEL GARSIDE.	SAMUEL LINNETT.	PATRICK M'GRATH.	WILLIAM BOLTON.
RICHARD WOOTTON.	SAMUEL MACORD.	JOSEPH WALKER.	PETER BURRELL.

REPLY.

I thank you for the expression of your loyalty to the Queen, and your welcome to myself. The beautiful display with which you greeted me, when visiting your district, was attended with circumstances which will be remembered with sorrow by us; but I do not the less recognise the benevolence of the objects of your voluntary association, or the extensive benefits which are derived from it by the community.

From the Bendigo St. Andrew's Society.

May it please your Royal Highness—We, the officers and brethren of the Bendigo St. Andrew's Society, beg leave to express the feelings of pleasure we entertain on your visit to Sandhurst. The presence of the son of our beloved Queen in this distant part of Her Majesty's dominions we feel to be an especial honour, and we desire to convey through your Royal Highness our sentiments of attachment and loyalty to the person and Throne of Her Most Gracious Majesty the Queen. We trust that your Royal Highness may be long spared, a graceful and honourable support of Britain's maritime bulwarks. As a Scottish society in Victoria, we crave to be permitted to express our gratification in welcoming a Scottish Peer in our midst.

REPLY.

Gentlemen—I thank you warmly for your address welcoming me to this part of Victoria, and expressing your devoted loyalty to the person and Throne of Her Majesty. In my own name I thank you for your kind wishes for my future happiness, and in return wish you every prosperity.

ALFRED.

From the Independent Order of Rechabites.

May it please your Royal Highness—We, the officers and brethren of the Independent Order of Rechabites in the district of Bendigo, beg to congratulate your Royal Highness on your safe arrival in the colony of Victoria, and heartily welcome you to Sandhurst and to the district of Bendigo. As an order, we have no political nor religious creed. We are united together to assist each other in sickness, and to do all in our power to relieve our common brotherhood from the degrading influences of intemperance. We, therefore, come unitedly to assure your Royal Highness of our attachment to our beloved Queen (long may she live), and of our desire that this colony may be an ornament to the British Crown, by possessing a united, sober, loving, and industrious people. Trusting that your Royal Highness may enjoy health and happiness while in this colony, and be long spared to add additional lustre to your Royal parentage, we have the honour to subscribe ourselves on behalf of the order. Signed in name of the society, &c.

REPLY.

Gentlemen—I am much pleased with the very loyal address you have presented to me on behalf of the Independent Order of Rechabites. I thank you heartily for this expression of your welcome and good wishes, and I trust that your society may be instrumental in forwarding the best interests of this noble colony, of which I shall ever retain the most pleasant remembrance.

ALFRED.

Reception at Sandhurst.

From the Jewish Residents.

May it please your Royal Highness—On behalf of the Jewish residents of Sandhurst, we approach your Royal Highness to proffer our sincere congratulations on your safe arrival, and to welcome you to this part of the southern hemisphere. Not only as loyal subjects do we welcome you, son of Britain's beloved Queen, but for the love and admiration you have already inspired throughout Her Majesty's dominions. As Jews, we hail with joy the opportunity that the presence of your Royal Highness affords us to acknowledge our deep attachment and devoted fealty towards the Royal Sovereign who sways the British sceptre. Her Gracious Majesty may justly claim the devoted love of Her Jewish subjects; we owe it, Royal Prince, to the throne and country whose flag in the cause of civilisation and humanity wields its protecting influence over the suffering and persecuted, and has created in the breasts of every son of Israel a love and admiration to England's Throne, and Britain's peerless Queen. In bidding a farewell to your Royal Highness, we fervently pray that Divine Providence, who protected your noble ship through the vast ocean, and conveyed her precious freight in health, will continue to watch over you; and that when you shall be pleased to return to Britain's shores, you will there receive the expectant love of a loyal people, with the more endearing greetings of your Royal Mother.

J. FRIEDMAN, Minister.
GEORGE P. JOSEPH, President.
M. SAMUEL, Treasurer.
A. ALEXANDER, Member of Committee.

REPLY.

Gentlemen—I thank you for your congratulations upon my arrival in Victoria, and for your welcome to Sandhurst. It will give the Queen great pleasure to receive from every portion of the community so warm an assurance of the affectionate devotion to Her Majesty's Throne and person as that which your address contains. I am grateful for the good wishes you offer me for my safe return to England. ALFRED.

The Sandhurst Mining Board.

May it please your Royal Highness—We, the Chairman and Members of the Sandhurst Mining Board, desire, on behalf of the Sandhurst Mining District, to congratulate you upon your safe arrival in this colony, and to accord to you a warm welcome to this goldfield. We have very great pleasure in being thus afforded an opportunity of expressing to your Royal Highness in person our loyalty and attachment to the Throne of your august mother, Her Most Gracious Majesty the Queen; and, while we trust that your visit to Victoria may be productive of pleasure to yourself, we feel assured that the honour conferred upon us by the visit of one so nearly related to Her Majesty, will but serve to draw closer the warm ties which already bind us to our beloved fatherland. We beg to tender our respects to your Royal Highness, and would venture to express a hope that this will not be the last occasion on which you will honour this portion of the empire with your presence. We trust that your Royal Highness will view with feelings of interest the progress which has been made in the development of the vast mineral resources of this colony, and from personal observation be able to estimate at its true value the importance of this country as a portion of Her Majesty's dominions. With warmest wishes for your future welfare, and that of the other members of the Royal Family, we have the honour to subscribe ourselves your Royal Highness's most obedient servants,

ROBERT OGILVIE SMITH, Chairman.
JAMES BURNSIDE, Clerk.

REPLY.

Gentlemen—I thank you most sincerely for your congratulations upon my safe arrival in Victoria, and for the cordial welcome you have given me to this district. It will ever be a source of the highest gratification to me that my visit to Australia should have evoked so many assurances of loyalty to the Crown, and of the deep affection with which the people regard the fatherland. No one who has seen this and other goldfields can restrain his admiration of the progress which has been made in the development of the vast mineral resources of the country, or fail to recognise the importance of this part of Her Majesty's dominions. ALFRED.

The Order of Oddfellows.

May it please your Royal Highness—We, the members of the Manchester Unity Independent Order of Oddfellows, Bendigo District, approach your Royal Highness with feelings of the most profound respect, and beg to offer you our hearty congratulations on your safe arrival in the colony, and our sincere thanks for the great honour you have done the district by your visit to it. We recognise in your presence amongst us another strong proof of the great interest which your Royal Mother, our beloved Queen, takes in the welfare of her people, even in the most remote part of her dominions; and pray that your Royal Highness may convey to Her Most Gracious Majesty an assurance that the Independent Order of Oddfellows will ever be found loyal and attached subjects to the throne.

Your Royal Highness will graciously please to accept our expression of deep respect and devotion to yourself, as also to the other members of the Royal Family, and most sincere wishes for a happy and favourable voyage on your return to England. May it please your Royal Highness, we subscribe ourselves your devoted humble servants, on behalf of the Bendigo District, M.U.I.O.O.F.,

        MICHAEL DOYLE, Prov. G.M.
        HENRY WILLIAMS, Prov. D.G.M.
        ADOLPHUS ROBERT BARNETT, Prov. C.S.

REPLY.

Gentlemen—The expressions of hearty welcome and congratulation on my safe arrival among you, conveyed to me in your address, demand my warmest acknowledgments, as well as do your kind wishes for my safe return to England. It will be a pleasing duty to me to convey to the Queen the assurance of your loyalty to her Throne and person, and it will be very gratifying to Her Majesty to learn that you receive my visit among you as an earnest proof of the love which her Majesty indeed bears to you and all her subjects, however remote from England. ALFRED.

Borough of Raywood.

May it please your Royal Highness—We, Her Majesty's most dutiful and loyal subjects, the Mayor and Councillors of the Borough of Raywood, beg leave to approach your Royal Highness with assurances of our devoted loyalty to the Throne and attachment to Her Most Gracious Majesty and the members of the Royal Family. Permit us most respectfully to offer to your Royal Highness our sincere welcome and congratulations upon your safe arrival in Victoria, and to express the hope that your Royal Highness may experience no feelings but those of gratification and pleasure in connection with your visit to this colony.

        JAMES RATCLIFFE, Mayor.
        GEORGE BRITTEN KING, Town Clerk.

REPLY.

Gentlemen—The expression of your devoted loyalty to the Throne and of your attachment to Her Majesty, has been received by me with great satisfaction. For your congratulations on my arrival in Victoria, and for your good wishes, I heartily thank you. ALFRED.

Address of the Foresters.

We, the District Chief Ranger, Officers, and Brothers, representing over 1300 Members of the Ancient Order of Foresters, Bendigo United District, in approaching your Royal Highness to tender you our welcome to the Borough of Sandhurst, do so, not only with sentiments of the most profound respect for yourself, but also with feelings of the deepest veneration for our beloved Queen, who has thus graciously permitted us, in this remote portion of the world, to receive a visit from her son; and for this great honour we beg, through you, to tender our thanks to Her Majesty, and to assure you of the deep feelings of loyalty and respect we entertain for her, our Most Gracious Sovereign. May the tour of your Royal Highness be attended with every imaginable success; and we trust you will return to England favourably impressed, not only with the climate and productions of this flourishing colony, but also with the loyal feelings of the inhabitants of this important district.

     THOMAS NORTON HENSHALL, District Chief Ranger.
     JOHN WILLS, District Sub-Chief Ranger.
     JAMES THOMAS HOLL, District Secretary.

The Shire of Marong.

May it please your Royal Highness—We, the President, Councillors, and Inhabitants of the Shire of Marong, avail ourselves with pleasure of the opportunity afforded us by the visit of your Royal Highness to this district, to offer you our sincere congratulations on your safe arrival in this colony, and to give you a hearty welcome. We accept the visit of your Royal Highness as a distinguished mark of the consideration of Her Most Gracious Majesty the Queen for the inhabitants of her Australian colonies, and we assure your Royal Highness that all classes in this shire are actuated by a strong feeling of loyalty and attachment to the person and Throne of Her Majesty. We trust that the voyage on which your Royal Highness is at present embarked, may prove as pleasant to your Royal Highness as your presence in our midst is gratifying and welcome to us; and we desire to express our sincere attachment and devotion to your Royal Highness, and every member of the Royal Family. We have the honour to be, your Royal Highness's most obedient humble servants,

        WILLIAM ROGERS, President.
        J. PARIS, Secretary.

REPLY.

Gentlemen—I thank you for your congratulations upon my arrival in Victoria, and for the hearty welcome you offer me to the Shire of Marong. The Queen will be glad to know that my visit to Australia is regarded as an expression of Her Majesty's deep interest in the well-being of her people in this distant part of the empire.

              ALFRED.

The Shire of Huntly.

May it please your Royal Highness- We, the President, Councillors, and Ratepayers of the Shire of Huntly, beg to offer our cordial congratulations to your Royal Highness on your safe arrival on these shores, and to accord to you a warm welcome to the Bendigo goldfields. We avail ourselves with pleasure of the present opportunity to express to your Royal Highness our devotion and loyalty to the Throne and person of our well-beloved Queen, and to assure your Royal Highness of our attachment to the laws and constitution under which we have the privilege to live. We look upon your Royal Highness's presence amongst us as a proof that Her Majesty regards her Australian subjects with affection and interest; and we trust that the reception accorded by all classes of the community to a son of our Queen, will be accepted not only as a mark of respect to your Royal Highness, but as a proof of our appreciation of those principles of genuine liberty which we enjoy by virtue of our position as a part of the British empire.

(Signed) JOHN PETER NOLAN, PRESIDENT. JOHN ROBERTS HOSKINS, COUNCILLOR.
THOMAS BRITT, COUNCILLOR. GEORGE SKURRIE, ,,
FREDERICK SEBBES, ,, JOHN MATCHETT, ,,
JAMES WARREN, SECRETARY.

REPLY.

Gentlemen—I pray you to accept my thanks for your cordial congratulations upon my arrival in Victoria, and for your welcome to the Bendigo goldfields. I will convey to Her Majesty your expressions of loyalty to the Throne, and your attachment to the laws and free constitution which you have brought with you from the mother-country. It is unnecessary that I should assure you of the deep and affectionate interest with which Her Majesty regards her Australian people. ALFRED.

Bendigo Benevolent Asylum.

May it please your Royal Highness—We, the President and Members of Committee of the Bendigo Benevolent Asylum, have the honour to congratulate your Royal Highness on your safe arrival in Victoria, and to assure you of our attachment and loyalty to your Royal mother the Queen, and our devotion and respect to the members of the Royal Family. We are certain you will view with feelings of pleasure the establishment of charitable institutions, erected for relief of suffering humanity in these remote dependencies of Her Most Gracious Majesty. As your voyage up to the present time has been exceedingly prosperous, we sincerely hope that, under the guiding hand of a kind Providence, you may return in safety, and that you may live long to adorn that position which your exalted station entitles you to; and in after years, when reflecting on the incidents of your voyage, they will afford an amount of pleasure which could scarcely be anticipated. We would specially thank you for the honour of this visit, and we offer you a sincere and heartfelt welcome. We beg most respectfully to subscribe ourselves your Royal Highness's most obedient servants,

JAMES BURNSIDE, PRESIDENT.
GEORGE ASPINALL, VICE-PRESIDENT.
J. N. JONES, TREASURER.
JAMES BOYD, M.D., SECRETARY.

REPLY.

Gentlemen Accept my sincere thanks for your congratulations upon my arrival in Victoria. It is one of the highest proofs of your national progress that such liberal provision has been made throughout the colony for the relief of the sick, and for the care of the poor and the infirm. ALFRED.

From the Foresters of Echuca.

May it please your Royal Highness—We, the brethren of "Court Hearts of Oak," of the Ancient Order of Foresters, at Echuca, on the River Murray, in the Colony of Victoria, hail your Royal Highness's visit to this distant part of the colony with sentiments of the heartiest welcome. We earnestly hope that your Royal Highness will believe in the sincere and deep loyalty we feel for the person and Throne of your Royal mother, our most gracious Queen. The remembrance of your Royal Highness's visit will be cherished by us as a further cause of endearment to our loved Queen and the Royal Family. That your Royal Highness may ever enjoy health and happiness, is the fervent prayer of the brethren of this court at Echuca.

JAMES LEONARD, CHIEF RANGER.
JOSEPH WM. BURRIDGE, SUB-CHIEF RANGER.
RICHARD GEO. LEWIN, SECRETARY.

REPLY.

Gentlemen—I thank you for the welcome from your court at Echuca. Your expressions of loyalty to the throne will be very gratifying to Her Majesty, and it will give me great pleasure to know that the remembrance of my visit to Australia will knit still more closely the ties which unite the colonies to the mother-country.

After receiving the addresses, the following gentlemen were presented to H.R.H.:—

Joseph H. Abbott, G. Adams, George Aspinall, Theodore Ballerstedt, Charles E. Barker, Alexander Bayne, John Ball, T. Benson, Henry Elbein Bower, Joseph Brittain, D. Bishan, William Aston Bucknall, J. M. Burridge, Joseph Butterfield, Rev. Dr. Backhaus, J. C. Campbell, Robert Cay, H. M. Coumley, Lieutenant H. A. Clarke, P.V.V. Artillery, Jacob Cohn, Julius Cohn, E. Craigie, M. Doyle, G. Edward Davis, John C. Donvan, Frederick Ellis, T. Eyre, E. N. Emmett, Dr. Eadie, John Fader, Thomas Farnie, W. Martin Flegg, J. Giles, R. E. H. Getschmann, J. Gabriel, Edward Garsed, John Hayes, James Thomas Holt, J. A. C. Helm, T. N. Hensdall, Edward Holton, C. Houston, William Hughes, W. M. Dyndman, Dr Hickson, John Jones, W. Kier, A. M. Lloyd, J. L. Leonard, J. W. Lewis, Rev. W. B. Lewis, Alexander M'Cullough, Alfred E. Moore, Angus Mackay, A. A. Munroy, Captain Muschead, D. MacDougall, Hugh M'Coll, H. Marks, Thompson Moore, Montgomery P. H. MacGillivray, W. Meakell, William M'Millan, William Murcott, John T. Moffit, James M'Culloch, John O'Milley, J. B. Pounds, District Coroner; George Beale, William Robertson, secretary St. Andrew's Society; Charles Robinson, J. T. Sanders, Charles Sayer, John Shale, J. P. F. Schurmann, A. G. W. Scott, James Stirling, N. G. Stephens, Hugh Sutherland, John Turnbull Strong, Dr Seeley, Dr. Stilwell, M. Tolmie, A. Thunder, Captain John Hamlet Taylor, Bendigo Rifles; W. C. Valdwel, E. P. Victor, R. S. Walkley, John Wagner, John White, J. A. Woodward, Andrew Williamson, and Mr. Charles Yeo.

At the conclusion of the presentations his Royal Highness and suite returned to the Shamrock Hotel, where they remained during the rest of the evening. The illumination in honour of the Prince was very effective. The banners used in the daylight celebration still floated from the houses and hung in festoons across the thoroughfares; and the triumphal arches, with the rest of the varied ornamentation which was so conspicuous in the morning, lent additional interest to the spectacle. But the great feature of the evening was the Miners' Torchlight Procession, which numbered about a thousand torches. The miners of the whole district entered into the affair with great spirit. The procession formed in the reserve at the Survey Office at about eight o'clock, and as it passed through View-point, with bands playing, banners waving, torches flaming, and innumerable little paper lamps painted with various coloured devices, carried by some of the men, the appearance presented was both novel and effective. When the procession halted opposite the Shamrock Hotel, the Prince appeared in the balcony, and bowed his acknowledgments to the repeated cheers of the crowd. In full view of the hotel was the Camp Reserve, where a display of fireworks was going on, in the midst of as effective an illumination of its kind as could be wished.

When the excitement was at its height, an unfortunate catastrophe occurred. The model of the *Galatea* (which filled a prominent part in the morning's proceedings, and whose crew had been discharging blue lights and rockets in front of the Shamrock Hotel) suddenly rushed through the crowd—its canvas, bulwarks, and wooden decks all a-blaze. By some means or other, the fireworks on board had ignited, and the conflagration was so rapid that all the boys in the ship were more or less burned before they could be extricated. Three, who were seriously burned—Wm. Langston M'Grath, aged eleven; Thomas Walters, aged nine; and Sylvester Francis Cahill, aged nine years—were at once removed to the hospital, and only survived their injuries a short time. The Prince evinced the liveliest concern for the sufferers on hearing of the sad mishap, and sent Mr. Yorke, his equerry, to the hospital, to inquire how they were progressing. Soon after they had been conveyed to that institution, the Mayors of Melbourne and Sandhurst also visited the unfortunate boys. Thus, in the very height of the rejoicings, the shadow of the cypress was thrown over the celebration.

Shortly after ten a.m. the following morning the Royal *cortège* left the Shamrock Hotel for Hustler's Reef, escorted by a troop of the Bendigo Light Horse, under Captain Stewart. Before leaving town his Royal Highness, accompanied by his suite and several gentlemen, called at the shop of Messrs. Joseph and Co., Pall-mall, and there inspected the beautiful little model of a quartz-crushing machine in silver, exhibited at the Intercolonial Exhibition.

The Bendigo Mines.

The party then proceeded to the celebrated claim of Latham and Watson, at Hustler's Reef. The preparations for the Royal visit were considerable. A triumphal arch adorned the entrance; a fair display of shrubs and flowers gave a holiday appearance to the neat office buildings; and the Bendigo Volunteer Rifles Band was collected on the brace. The Prince inspected the ripple-boxes, the eight batteries of stampers, the steam-engine, and other accessories of the mine. Having seen the quartz crushed, the process of amalgamation, and all the varied means by which the precious metal is extracted, he was next invited to witness a huge retort being taken red-hot from the furnace, which, when opened, was seen to contain a cake of gold weighing some 300 ounces. The Prince, equipped in a scarlet shirt, then prepared for his descent. The first stoppage was at the 400-ft. level, the Royal visitor exploring some of the tunnels, and when in the bowels of the earth the proprietors presented him with a trophy, enclosed in a box inlaid with nearly a hundred pieces of local woods, and manufactured at Sandhurst. The trophy was a collection of curious specimens from the mine, arranged in a cone, some rich in gold, but all exhibiting in a curious way the presence of various minerals—iron pyrites, antimony, bismuth, &c.—which being obtained at so great a depth have a more than usual interest to the geologist.

The party next proceeded to Long Gully, to inspect Mr. M. E. Koch's Pioneer Crushing Works, and afterwards started for Eaglehawk.

The Duke's visit to Sandhurst would have failed of part of its object had it terminated without a trip to the borough of Eaglehawk, which embraces a most important portion of the mining district of Bendigo. A brief inspection of this locality would be sufficient to convince even a casual observer of the existence in times past of the unequalled extent of surface diggings which used to be the boast of Bendigo. But the gullies which used to swarm with pick-and-shovel men are almost deserted, and "*Fuit*" is inscribed on most of them as plainly as the word "Welcome" on the arches beneath which the Prince passed to this part of the second great goldfield of the colony. It must be remembered, however, that shallow sinking has to a great extent been replaced by quartz-mining, which is carried on with all the scientific appliances known for the extraction of gold; and the tall chimney-stacks which come within view at almost every turn, attest the presence of valuable mining plants, consisting of the best and costliest machinery for the separation of the gold from its matrix. Here the preparations made for the reception of the Prince were of the customary kind. Several arches had been erected on the line of route, and the whole neighbourhood was prodigal in its display of bunting. Every large mine had its own demonstration of flags, and some of the houses were decorated with branches of trees and flowers. Opposite the Town Hall there was an arch, and in the body of the town the decorations were numerous. On his arrival, the Prince was conducted to the Town Hall, where the following address was presented to his Royal Highness by the mayor (Mr. Letheby), the town clerk (Mr. Tolhurst) reading the document:

May it please your Royal Highness—We, the Mayor and Council of the Borough of Eaglehawk, approach your Royal Highness with assurances of our devoted loyalty to the Throne and person of your august parent, Her Most Gracious Majesty Queen Victoria, and respectfully offer to your Royal Highness our warm congratulations upon your safe arrival in this portion of Her Majesty's dominions. We trust that your Royal Highness will deign to observe, not without interest, the evidences of that prosperous industry, love of law, and order and loyalty by which this great gold-mining district we represent has ever been distinguished. And in conclusion we beg your Royal Highness to believe that your visit to Eaglehawk will always be gratefully remembered, and to accept our earnest wishes for your health and happiness.

CHARLES LETHEBY, Mayor.
HENRY E. TOLHURST, Town Clerk.

REPLY.

Gentlemen,—I thank you warmly for your address welcoming me to Eaglehawk, and expressing your devoted loyalty to the person and Throne of Her Majesty. Even in my hurried journey through this portion of the country, I see much to indicate the future destiny which awaits a land to which so great energy and industry are devoted, and whose inhabitants are influenced by such attachment to the free institutions of the mother-country. Gentlemen, once more receive my warmest thanks.

ALFRED.

His Royal Highness subsequently partook of a lunch provided in the Town Hall, and then visited the Catherine Reef Company's mine. H.R.H. was received by the Board of Directors, consisting of Mr. D. C. Sterry (chairman), and Messrs. Burrowes, Latham, Cook, and Farnsworth, with Mr. Eyre, the mining manager. The Royal party having selected suitable dresses for the underground journey, descended the mine; and when at the bottom, his Royal Highness commenced operations on the hard face of the wall with a pick specially made for him, and obtained some specimens. After some light refreshments in the heart of the mine, the party returned to Sandhurst, where a ball was to take place in the Alfred Hall, an edifice of great size, specially erected for the purpose. About a quarter of an hour before the time for opening the ball the building took fire, and soon became a heap of ruins. When the excitement created by this unfortunate calamity had somewhat cooled down, the great question became—Would the Ball be held at all? This was soon set at rest, however, by the announcement that the supper, provided by Mr. Hourigan, would take place first, and then the hall set apart for that purpose would be cleared for dancing.

About eleven o'clock the supper was ready in the Town Hall; the company soon assembled, and the Prince arrived. The Mayor of Sandhurst presided, and on his right was the Prince, beside whom was Miss Agnes Grant, the Hon. Eliot Yorke, Lieutenant Ramsay, the Hon. Mr. Sullivan, M.P., Mr. Casey, M.P.; and on his left, Mr. Butters, Mayor of Melbourne, Mrs. L. M'Lachlan, Judge Skinner, Mrs. Skinner, and in their neighbourhood, Captain Burton, Colonel Ball, and Mr. M'Lachlan, P.M. The Mayor proposed the toast of "His Royal Highness the Duke of Edinburgh," which was drunk with most enthusiastic and long-continued cheering. His Royal Highness responded in a clear and distinct voice, and thanked the ladies and gentlemen for the hearty manner in which they had greeted the toast proposed in such eloquent terms by the Mayor, and expressed his great regret that circumstances had occurred tending to disturb the pleasure of the assembly.

The hall was then cleared, the company retiring to the council chamber and other rooms, and through the untiring energy of Mr. M'Intyre and Mr. Hourigan, the tables were speedily removed and a ball-room improvised. A quadrille was the first dance, and in H.R.H.'s set were—the Prince with Miss Agnes Grant, the Mayor of Sandhurst with Mrs. M'Lachlan as *vis-à-vis*, Lieutenant Ramsay and Miss Ball, Colonel Ball and Mrs. Stirling, Captain Burton and Mrs. Helm, the Hon. Eliot Yorke and Mrs. Watson. A waltz succeeded, and then a "foursome" reel, in which the Prince and Miss Boyd, and the Mayor of Sandhurst and Mrs. Sibley, formed a set. The Duke's piper played. The Prince then retired, and drove off to his hotel amidst the cheers of a crowd assembled at the door of the Town Hall. The dancing was continued until an early hour.

With the ball terminated the visit of his Royal Highness to Sandhurst, the Prince retiring at a comparatively early hour, as he intended leaving for Ballarat shortly after daylight the next morning.

Reception of the Consuls.

The Royal party left Sandhurst at six A.M. on Friday, *en route* for Ballarat, to attend the Races, arriving in Melbourne at twenty-five minutes past eight, and after partaking of an excellent breakfast, provided by Mr. Mallam, the Prince started for Geelong, where a short stoppage was made, and then proceeded to Ballarat. Having paid a brief visit to Craig's Hotel, his Royal Highness drove out to the course. After the first greetings, all formal ceremony was abandoned, and the Prince was for once permitted to enjoy himself on the course and stand without being bored. He left Ballarat at 6.35 P.M., and arrived in Melbourne in about two hours.

On the following day (Saturday, 21st November) his Royal Highness Prince Alfred accorded a reception to the Consular body, in the Picture Gallery of the Exhibition Building. The Prince was accompanied by his Excellency the Governor, the Hon. Mr. M'Culloch, Mr. O'Shanassy, and several other distinguished gentlemen. His Excellency the Governor introduced Mr. J. B. Were to his Royal Highness as the senior Consul, representing Denmark. Mr. Were then presented the other members of the Consular body, according to their respective rank and official position, as follows :—

NETHERLANDS.—Mr. Ploos Van Amstel, Consul-General ; Mr. Daniel Ploos Van Amstel, Vice-Consul.

FRANCE.—Count de Castelnau, Consul, represented by Mons. Follet, Vice-Consul (the Consul being precluded attending from the state of his health) ; Mons. Lissignol, Secretary.

ITALY.—Chevalier Biagi, Consul-General ; Mr. Cossu, Vice-Consul.

PORTUGAL.—Mr. Cooper, Consul.

BELGIUM.—An apology was made to the Prince for the absence of Mr. Beckx, Consul, arising from indisposition.

UNITED STATES OF AMERICA.—General Latham, Consul.

HAMBURG AND BREMEN.—Mr. Sali Cleve, Acting-Consul.

PRUSSIA.—Mr. Brahe, Acting-Consul.

RUSSIA.—Mr. Damyon, Vice-Consul.

This ceremonial having been concluded, Mr. Were proceeded to speak to the following effect :—We have to thank your Royal Highness for granting this interview. The Consular body now present represent the principal countries in Europe and America; and they considered it right that a Prince of blood of the reigning Monarch of England should not arrive here without the Consuls offering him their congratulations on his visit; for among their other functions it becomes their duty to act in such manner as may tend to the promotion of commercial relations, to bring about the settlement of foreign residents, and to protect their interests, to the material advantage of the countries they have the honour to represent in this important dependency of the British empire. Mr. Were concluded by again thanking the Prince for the interview, and stating that the Consuls desired to express a hope that his voyage, so auspiciously begun, would be as happily continued and concluded.

Prince Alfred bowed to the gentlemen of the consular body, and said he felt deeply obliged to them for their kind congratulations. He interpreted the presence of so important a body of foreign representatives as a mark of high respect to the Queen, as well as to himself personally, and he begged to thank them most heartily. His Royal Highness then again bowed, and the interview terminated.

The reception of the Consuls being concluded, the next duty of his Royal Highness was to preside at the ceremony of the first united Speech Day of the following Collegiate Schools:—The Church of England Grammar School, and St. Patrick's, Scotch, and Wesley Colleges. This interesting commemoration was held in the Exhibition Hall. The spectacle presented was brilliant in the extreme. The gallery, greatly enlarged, was filled with the boys, some seven hundred in number, while the body of the hall was occupied by a vast crowd, principally composed of ladies, whose light summer costumes gave colouring and animation to the scene. It was estimated that there were between four and five thousand persons present. At about twenty minutes past twelve the Duke of Edinburgh, accompanied by His Excellency the Governor, arrived at the Public Library entrance to the Exhibition, and was received by several gentlemen connected with the different schools. As soon as his Royal Highness entered the hall, three such clear and ringing cheers as boys alone can give rose from the gallery; and just as these died away the strains of the National Anthem pealed from the organ, and were taken up with heart and voice by the youthful assembly. The Prince, who was attended by his equerry, Mr. Haig, took his seat upon the dais, and around his Royal Highness were the following gentlemen:—His Excellency the Governor, the Hon. J. M'Culloch, the Hon. J. O'Shanassy, Sir James Palmer, Hon. J. Macpherson Grant, the Hon. C. Macmahon, Hon. J. G. Francis, the Hon. G. W. Cole, the Hon. D. Moore, the Hon. Archibald Michie, the Hon. T. T. A'Beckett, the Hon. C. G. Duffy, the Hon. A. Fraser, the Hon. J. Macrae, the Mayor of Melbourne, the Bishop of Melbourne, Dr. Cairns, the Rev. G. V. Barry, Rev. J. Lentaigne, Rev. J. S. Waugh, Lieutenant Rothwell, Mr. Manners-Sutton, Mr. Macbain, M.L.A.; Mr. O'Grady, M.L.A.; Mr. R. Ellery; the educational heads of the different schools, viz., Rev. Dr. Bromby, Church of England Grammar School; Mr. A. Morrison, of the Scotch College; Rev. J. Moore, of St. Patrick's College; and Dr. Corrigan, of Wesley College.

The programme of "speeches" was then begun. A small platform had been erected on the east side of the hall, near the centre, and on it the different performers were stationed. The first piece was an "Ode to the Duke of Edinburgh," which was delivered by Master Counsel, of St. Patrick's College, with excellent taste and expression. The "Boatman of the Downs" was then recited by Cooper, of Wesley College. The next piece on the programme was the song, "The flag that braved a thousand years," by King, of the Church of England Grammar School. The youthful vocalist possessed a voice of great clearness, power, and flexibility, and notwithstanding the enormous size of the hall, it came out full and clear in every part. A scene from *King John* was next given by four of the junior boys from the Scotch College, and was very well rendered; the most successful of the four probably being Dalrymple, the representative of Prince Arthur. Following this was an original Latin ode in Sapphics, delivered by Keogh, of St. Patrick's. A grand duo on the pianoforte was performed by Vaughan and Evans, of the Church of England Grammar School. The tent scene from *Julius Cæsar* was given by Little and Parnham, of Wesley College, with a good deal of spirit; and was followed by the recitation of the camp scene from *Henry V.*, by Smith, of the Church of England Grammar School. The masterpiece of the day, so far as elocution was concerned, was "Clarence's Dream," by Wright, of the Scotch College. A "Welcome to Prince Alfred," written by Mrs. T. P. Hill, was tastefully delivered by Hart, of Wesley College. The programme was finished at twenty minutes past one, and then commenced the distribution of the prizes. Owing to the excellent arrangements made by the masters, the ceremony was carried out with ease and rapidity, the precedence to be taken having been satisfactorily arranged by lot. The successful

Speech Day of the Collegiate Schools.

competitors walked in prescribed order up the centre passage, the head-masters of the different schools read out the names of the prize-takers, and handed the prizes to the Prince, who then presented them to the boys. First came the Church of England Grammar School, then the Wesley College, then the St. Patrick's College, and lastly, the Scotch College. The following are the Honor Lists of the several schools (the mark * representing a prizeman):—

Church of England Grammar School.

UNIVERSITY DISTINCTIONS GAINED DURING 1867.

Exhibition in classics at matriculation, by Frederick Pirani.
Exhibition in mathematics at matriculation, by Frederick Pirani.
Exhibition in mathematics at Christmas, by Frederick Pirani.
Proxime accessit to exhibition in classics at Christmas, by Frederick Pirani.
Exhibition in classics and logic at Christmas, by Charles Tynan.
Exhibition in medicine, by Walter Thomas.

UNIVERSITY HONOURS GAINED DURING 1867.

Two first class, by Frederick Pirani.
One first class, by Walter Thomas.
One second class, by Douglas Paterson.
One second class, by Charles Tynan.
One third class, by Samuel Summons.
One third class, by Frederick M'Coy.

SCHOOL DISTINCTIONS IN 1867.

School exhibition, awarded to William Henry Tuckett.
The Bishop's divinity prizes, awarded to James Holland and Frederick Jeremie Bromby.
Prize poem, gained by James Holland.
Special arithmetic prize, awarded to Newman Arnold.

PRIZEMEN OF THE YEAR 1867, AND THOSE ENTITLED TO HONOURABLE MENTION.

FIRST CLASS.—Classics: *Holland, *Towers, Bromby ma., Macnamara, Vaughan, Major ma., Lewellin. Latin only: Davidson mi., Harker ma., Barber, John Johnson. Natural Science: *John Johnson, Bromby ma., Harker ma. English: *Holland, *Harker ma., Towers, Bromby ma., John Johnson, Hebden ma., Barber, Cole, Vaughan, Davidson mi., Wynne. French: *Macnamara, *Bromby ma., Cole, John Johnson, Lewellin, Harker ma., Major ma., Wynne, Hebden ma., Shortt.

SECOND CLASS.—Latin: *Teague, *Skene ma., Sweeney, Bage ma., Major mi., Taylor max., Crewe. English: *Skene mi., *Sweeney, Bage ma. Teague, Clough ma., Goodman, Crewe, Major ma. French: *Teague, Teague ma., Crewe, Sweeney, Major mi., Evans ma., Goodman, W. Barker. Greek: *Harker ma., Davidson mi., Major mi., Shortt, W. Barker, John Johnson. Natural Science: *Clough ma., Teague, Bage ma. W. Johnson.

THIRD CLASS.—Latin: *Tuckett mi., *Green, Moule ma., Harris ma., Bromby mi., Taylor max., Fry ma., Farie, Skene mi., H. M'Pherson. English: *Taylor ma., *Skene mi., Smith mi., Bage mi., Fry ma., Harris ma. French Bage mi., Harris ma., H. M'Pherson, Fry ma., Bargmann, Farie, Tuckett mi., Menie mi., Bromby mi., Ford ma., Vieusseux, Skene mi., Mack ma., Stanford. Greek: *Moule ma., J. J. Smith, Tuckett mi. Natural Science: *Taylor max., Bage mi., Green.

SPECIAL ENGLISH CLASS.— English: *Davidson ma., *Middleton, *Mack. Natural Science: *Davidson ma.

FOURTH CLASS.—Latin: *Mack mi., *S. Miller, Smith min., Gatehouse, Hebden mi., Harker mi., Stephen ma., M'Pherson mi., Clough mi., Dixon. English:

*M'Pherson ma., *Dixon, Evans mi., Clough mi., Woolley, Harker mi., Mack mi., Mickelburgh, M'Pherson mi., Snowball ma., Riddell, Watson ma., Gatehouse. French: *M'Pherson mi., *Mickelburgh, M'Pherson ma., Gregory, Harker mi., *Watson ma., Gatehouse, Mack mi., Clough mi., Snowball ma., Stephen ma., Riddell, Dixon. Greek: *Sweeney, Moore, Riddell. Natural Science.—*M'Pherson ma., M'Pherson mi.

FIFTH CLASS.— Latin: *Tuckett ma., *G. Miller, Thomas, Deakin, Hearn mi., Moule min., Oliver, Henry Hearle. English:—*Deakin, *Thomas, H. King, Oliver, Campbell mi. French: *Tallerman, *Moule min., Mack min., Thomas, Hearn mi., Hearle, Deakin, Tuckett ma., G. Miller, Campbell mi., Raine, Oliver, Francis, Delias, Campbell ma. Natural Science: *Deakin. Greek : *Oliver, Thomas, Bear, Dixon, Turner ma., Deakin.

SIXTH CLASS.—Latin: *Schlicht, *Thomson mi., Campbell min., Willcatt, Bear, Stephen min., Whitton. English: *Willcatt, *Legyn, Schlicht, Thomson mi., Campbell min. French: *Schier, Moule mi., Arnold, Whitton, Ker, *Bear, Allen.

SEVENTH CLASS.— Latin: *Ford mi., *Mallett, Major min., Foot, Pike, Beggs, Galvin. English: *Foot, *Major min., Colyer, Galvin. French: *Mallett, Galvin, *Colyer, Foot, Major min., Crowl, Harper mi.

EIGHTH CLASS.— Latin (A): *Mullen, *Vance, Doyne and Snowball mi. equal, Ross min., Holt, Stander, Jukes ma. Eand. (B): *Horner, Byrne, Gresson, T. Taylor English (A): *Holt, *Ross min., Stander, Mullen, Snowball mi., Eand. (B): *T. Taylor, Horner, Gresson, Byrne. French: *Vance, Jukes mi., Snowball mi., Jukes ma., Stander, King Mus., Horner, Mullen, Murray mi., Ross min.

MATHEMATICS AND ARITHMETIC — I. (A): *Harker ma., Holland, Towers. (B): *Jno. Johnson, Bromby ma. II. (A): *Davidson mi., Shortt, Lewellin. (B): *W. Barker, Dixon, Moore, Skene ma., Sweeney, Taylor ma. III. (A): *Harris ma., Bage ma., Robinson, Crewe, Davidson ma., J. J. Smith, Allen, Major mi., Clough ma. (B): *H. M'Pherson, Tuckett mi., Moule ma., Bargmann, Goodman. IV. (A): *Arnold, *Mack min. and Middleton equal, Skene mi., Standford, Clough mi., M'Pherson ma., Bromby mi., Turner min., Hebden mi., Chase ma., Leddie, Ford mi., Mack mi. (B): *Bage mi., Fry ma., M'Pherson mi., Farie, Harker mi., Tuckett ma., Smith mi. V.: Vieusseux, Taylor mi. Arithmetic only: *Smith min., Babile and Schlicht equal, Fry mi., Armitage, Chase ma., S. Miller, Tallerman. VI.: Ker, Campbell ma. Arithmetic only: *G. Miller, Hearle, Deakin, Campbell min., Stephen ma., Hearn mi., Seward ma., Mack min. VII.: *Harper ma., *Foot, Pike, Balderson, Harper mi., Mallett. VIII. (A): *Ross min., T. Taylor. (B): *Vance, Gresson.

SURVEYING.— Crewe, Dixon, Sweeney, Taylor ma.

BOOKKEEPING.—(A): *Macnamara, Hodgson, Mickelburgh, Davidson ma., (B): *Thomson ma., M'Pherson ma., M'Pherson mi.

DRAWING.—In colours: *Looker ma. In sepia: *M'Pherson ma., Arnold. In chalk: *M'Pherson mi. In pencil: *Clough ma., Barker ma., *Macnamara, Gatehouse, Looker mi., Clough mi.

WRITING.—English Class: *Davidson ma., Tallerman, A. Miller. III.: *H M'Pherson, Farie, Moule ma. IV.: *Gregory, Dixon, Watson ma. V.: Tuckett ma., Thomas, Dallas. VI.: *Seward ma., Schlitch, Whatton. VII.: *Balderson, Galvin, Foot. VIII.: Vance, Stander, Jukes mi.

GERMAN.—*Bargmann, Jno. Johnson, Tallerman.

PRIZE POEM.—*Holland.
ELOCUTION.—*J. J. Smith, Macnamara, Tallerman.
GYMNASTICS.—*Ireland, *Macnamara, *Watson mi., *Schlicht, *Celyer, *Vance.
GENERAL RACE.—*Ireland, *Logan.
CONDUCT IN THE HOUSE.—*Holland, *Pike.

Wesley College.

Special prize given by Mrs. A. Fraser, Ablourie, St. Kilda, for first pupil matriculation with credit to the Melbourne University, books value £5 Grice.

Draper Scholarship, value £25— Amess max.

Special prize by S. Amess, Esq., for best classical scholar, exclusive of University class, books value £5—Hart ma.

Special prize by T. J. Sumner, Esq., for the best mathematical scholar, exclusive of University class, books value £5 Amess max. and Ralph, equal.

Special prize for best English poem, by H. M. Andrews, Esq. M.A., books value £2 2s—Atkins.

Special prize by A. F. Rennie, Esq., M.A. for best English Essay. Books, value £2 2s.— Archbold ma., Archbold ma., Anderson max.

GENERAL PROFICIENCY.—Class 1: Senior Division: *Dathie. Junior Division: *Robertson. Class 2: White ma. Class 3: Davies. Class 4: *Wright ma. and Harcourt equal.

BIBLE.—Class 1: *Poolman and *Sherrard, equal; Fowler, Cay, Robertson. Class 2: *Easton, Moffat, Jesse. Class 3: *Davies, Wright ma., Moss. Class 4: *Hart ma., Amess max. and Symons, equal; Minnett max.

CLASSICS.—Class 1: Senior Division: *Wearne mi., Booth, Jesse. Junior Division: Wright ma., *Amess mi., Duen, Lewis mi. Class 2: Stephens, *Hart mi., Easton, Webb, Walker, mi. Class 3: *Wigley, Davies, Wilson ma., Cook. Class 4: *Wright ma., Welshman mi., Newman, Harcourt, Daniel. Class 5: *Hart ma., *Atkins, Amess max.

MATHEMATICS.—Arithmetic. Class 1: *Dalrymple ma., Thomson, Dalrymple mi. Class 2: *Oakley ma., Towle mi., Jesse. Class 3: *Webb, Wigley, Easton. Class 4: *Davies, Wright ma., Laing. Class 5: *Amess max, Hart ma., Ralph, Little. Geometry.—Class 1: Stephens, *Rankin, Webb and Lupton ma., equal. Class 2: *Sides, Wright ma. and Jefferson equal, Moss. Class 3: *Ralph, Newman, Daniel. Class 4: *Little ma., Dredge, Amess max, Minnett max. Algebra.—Class 1: *Ralph, Newman, Dredge. Class 2: *Amess max, Hart ma., Little mi.

ENGLISH.—Grammar, Composition, and Dictation.—Class 1: Senior Division: *Hodgkinson mi., Wyatt, Hadley. Junior Division: *Hill mi., Jesse, Robertson. Class 2: Stephens, *Easton, Minnett ma., Wigley. Class 3: Welshman mi., Harcourt, Sherrard ma., Daniel. Class 4: *Amess max., Hart ma., Ralph, Dredge, Little ma. History.—Class 1: *Farquhar, Steane, Chambers mi. Class 2: *Straw ma., Hart mi., Robertson. Class 3: *Davies, Wyatt, White ma. Class 4: *Atkins, Anderson max., Minnett max., Moss. Geography.—Class 1: *Lewis mi., Hill mi., Amess mi. Class 2: *Little mi., Wigley, Stephens. Class 3: *Moss, Wright ma., Beauchamp. Class 4: *Sides, Amess max, Newman, Ralph.

MODERN LANGUAGES.—Class 1: Cay, Minnett ma., Class 2: *Booth, Wearne mi. Class 3: Stephens, *Veevers, Easton, Dunn, Brown. Class 4: *Wilson ma., and *Towle mi., equal; Little mi., Sherrard ma., Hart, mi. Class 5: *Sides, Row, Moss. Class 6: *Little ma., Amess max., Atkins.

WRITING AND BOOKKEEPING.—Class 1: Senior Division: *Wearne mi., Read, Wilson ma. Junior Division: *Bickford, Oakley mi., Dalrymple. Class 2: *Wright mi., Row mi., Easton. Class 3: Coles, Spottiswood, Boskin, and M'Vea, equal; Lewis ma., Watts ma. Class 4: *Wright ma., Wearne mi., Laing.

ELOCUTION.—Senior Class: *Little ma., Hart ma., Cooper ma. Junior Class: Robertson, Dothie, Mathews.

DRAWING AND PAINTING.—Senior Division: Painting in Water Colours: *Amess max. Figure Drawing in Crayon: *Wearne ma. Pencil Drawing: Senior Division: *Daniel. Junior Division: Read, Mi-canolds, Dalrymple ma. Map Drawing: *Welshman ma., Minnett max.

MUSIC.—Instrumental: Symons, Beauchamp. Vocal: *Wright ma., *Dredge. *Amess max.

GYMNASTICS.—Class 1: Little ma., Wearne mi., Poolman. Class 2.—*Wyatt, Row mi. Class 3. —*Wearne ma., Lupton mi., Little ma.

SPECIAL PRIZE for English Essay in Lower School.—*Anderson mi.

St. Patrick's College.

FIRST CLASS. Greek Prize: History, Chemistry, Ahearn; Latin, Bride; French, O'Shaugnessy; English, Keogh; physical geography, Carter; Algebra and Euclid, Fitzgerald.

SECOND CLASS.—Latin, Doyle; French, Croker; sacred history, Croker; Greek, Bride; English, Blair; do., second prize, Graham; history, M. Dalton; elocution, Counsel; writing, Bennehy; Euclid, Cody; arithmetic, M'Donnell.

THIRD CLASS.—Latin, Sheedy; French, Rahilly; sacred history, Bourke; elocution, Healy; writing, J. O'Grady; bookkeeping, English composition, Kelly; English composition (second prize) and history, Cormick; grammar and analysis, Chas. O'Grady; arithmetic, Crosby.

FOURTH CLASS.—Latin and history, W. Byrne; French, Macintosh; English composition, Croker; English composition, second prize, A. M'Donnell; sacred history, Davis; grammar and analysis, and writing, Fearon; elocution, Petty; arithmetic, W. Carter.

FIFTH CLASS.—English, first prize, Finn; second prize, Byrne; third prize, M'Cauley; arithmetic, Curtain; Christian doctrine, Ronson; Elocution, Wills; writing, Byrne.

SIXTH CLASS.—Christian doctrine, Dewey; English, Petty; arithmetic, Mouncy.

Speech Day of the Collegiate Schools.

Scotch College.

MELBOURNE UNIVERSITY MATRICULATION EXAMINATION, 1867.

Eight boys from the Scotch College presented themselves for examination in November, seven of whom passed as follows:— Number of subjects in which a boy must pass—six. Bennie passed in eight, with credit in four; Wilkie passed in eight, with credit in three; Inglis passed in eight, with credit in two; Orr passed in eight, with credit in one; Johnson passed in seven, with credit in two; M'Gregor passed in seven, with credit in none; Andrews passed in six, with credit in two; Shiels passed in February in eight, with credit in three.

SPECIAL PRIZES.—1. Dux of School: Knight's Pictorial Shakspeare (8 vols. super royal 8vo), the gift of Alexander Wilson, Esq., awarded to *1 Bennie. *2 Johnson. 2. Dux in Classics: Buckie's Homer and the Iliad (4 vols. demy 8vo), the gift of Andrew Scott, Esq., gained by *1 Bennie, awarded to *2 Wilkie. 3. Dux in Mathematics: Gibbon's Decline and Fall of the Roman Empire (8 vols. 8vo), the gift of Andrew Scott, Esq., awarded to *1 Swanson. *2 Bennie. 4. Dux in English: Staunton's Shakspeare (4 vols. demy 8vo) the gift of James M'Kain, Esq., M.L.A., gained by *1 Bennie, awarded to *2 Orr.

CLASSICS.— Latin and Greek: Class 1: Senior Division: *Taylor, Samson, Beer, R. M'Pherson, Bryant. Junior Division: *Jas. Macneilkan, A. Hill, C. Jacomb, Dalrymple, H. Smith. Class 2: *Davies, *T. Hadley, G. Barlow, Woods. Class 3: *A. F. Morrison and *L. Terry equal, F. G. White, J. B. Thomson, W. Carson. Class 4: Senior Division: *Purvis, *M'Farland, E. Wisewould, Adam, Elterman. Junior Division: *Lind, J. Hill, McCaw, Proctor, Heales, E. Hughes. Class 5: *Macdonald, Nathan, F. Haley, Lewis. Class 6: *G. Wise, *Henderson, Shields, Ad. Smith, M'Cracken, G. Haley. Class 7: Senior Division: *Bennie, Wilkie, A. Inglis, Johnson. Junior Division: *McKinley, Leonard, J. Inglis.

MATHEMATICS.— Arithmetic: Class 1: *R. M'Pherson, Ormond, Kennedy, Finlay, Graham. Class 2: *J. Macneilkan, Walker, J. Thompson, Moor, Samson, Taylor. Class 3: *Beer, J. R. Thompson, Turnbull and Dalrymple (equal), L. Terry. Class 4: Gardiner, Macgugan, Lind, Macdonald, A. Thompson. Class 5: *Nathan, Smith Purvis, Henderson, Ad. Smith, Hill. Class 6: Senior Division *Bennie, Swanson, M'Gregor, Fisher, Johnson. Junior Division: *J. Brady, J. Inglis.

ALGEBRA.— Class 1: Senior Division: *Macdonald, Lind, Hetherington, Gardiner. Junior Division: *Liddle, *D. Herald, A. Herald, Moor. Class 2: *Purvis, Ad. Smith, Coleman, Hill, F. Haley, Lewis. Class 3: *Moodie, Nathan, Wise, M'Cracken, Henderson. Class 4: Senior Division: *Swanson, *Fisher, Bennie, Johnson, M'Gregor. Junior Division: *Leonard, A. Inglis, J. Brady.

GEOMETRY.— *Guppy, Solomon, Lindsay, M'Farland, A. Thomson, M'Millan. Class 2: Macgugan, Rogers, Fenton, Lewis. Class 3: *Ad. Smith, Henderson, Gardiner, Nathan, G. Wise, M'Cracken. Class 4: Senior Division: *Swanson, *Bennie, Wilkie, A Inglis, M'Gregor, Andrews. Junior Division: *Stevens, J. Inglis.

ENGLISH (including Spelling, History, Geography, Grammar, and Composition).— Class 1, Senior Division: *Taylor, Samson, C. Jacomb, F. Wisewould, J. Hughes, J. Macneilkan. Junior Division: *Benjamin, A. Hill, Finlay, F. Tindale, Buzzard, Barry. Class 2: Senior Division: *Davies, R. M'Pherson and Cooke (equal), Cowan, Woods, T. Hadley. Junior Division: *Ormond, H. Smith, Harris, James Macneilkan, J. Thomson, G. White. Class 3, Senior Division: *Turnbull, J. R. Thomson, F. G. White, W. Carson, Ray, Dalrymple.

Junior Division: *G. Tindale, Moss, Garrett, J. Wise, Pattison. Class 4: M'Farland, Elterman, Odell, Guppy, W. Gibbs, Edwards. Class 5, Senior Division: *Macdonald, *Sathon, Lewis, Moodie. Junior Division: *Lind, Purvis, Macgugan, Gardiner. Class 6, Senior Division: *G. Wise and *Smith (equal), Henderson, Shiels, M'Cracken. Junior Division: *James Callaghan, Jacomb, Linacre, Rogers. Class 7, Senior Division: *Bennie, A. Inglis, Orr, Wilkie, Andrews. Junior Division: *M'Kinley, J. Inglis.

BIBLE.— Class 1: *A. Hill, C. Jacomb, Benjamin, Darcey, J. Hughes, F. Wisewould. Class 2: *G. Barlow, Davies, Cooke, T. Hadley, Cowan, Woods. Class 3: *W. Carson, Ray, Turnbull, J. R. Thompson, L. Terry, F. G. White. Class 4: *W. Gibbs, M'Farland, Simpson, D. Herald Elterman, Proctor. Class 5: Senior Division: *Macdonald, *Moodie. Junior Division: *J. Hill, Lind, Coleman, Macgugan. Class 6: *G. Wise, Henderson, Ad. Smith, Rogers, Jacomb, Shiels.

WRITING.— Class 1: *C. Stewart, Samson, Darcby. Class 2: *G. Stewart, Deacker, J. Thompson. Class 3: *Moss, G. Tindle, Dalrymple. Class 4.— *Elterman, Thompson, Gingerell. Class 5: *F. Haley, Lister, Wright, Fenton. Commercial Correspondence and Bookkeeping. Senior Division: *G. Wise, Shiels, Henderson, Ad. Smith. Junior Division: *Nathan, Macgugan, Moodie, Gardiner.

FRENCH. Class 1: Taylor, Benjamin. Class 2: A. M'Pherson, G. Stewart. Class 3: *J. R. Thomson, Turnbull, L. Terry, W. Carson, Ray. Class 4: *Hill, Lind and Little (equal). Class 5: *Shiels, G. Wise, Nathan. Class 6: *Bennie, Andrews, Wilkie, Orr.

NATURAL SCIENCE.— Class 1 and 2: Cooke, Beer, Davies. Class 3: *W. Carson, J. R. Thomson, Turnbull, Ray. Class 4: *Guppy, D. Herald, M'Farland Proctor. Class 5: *Coleman, Macgugan, Corcoran, Macdonald, Lind. Class 6: *G. Wise, *Henderson, Ad. Smith, Shiels, Rogers.

GYMNASTICS.— Class 1: *J. Morrison, A. Thomson. Class 2: *Rainey, Moss. Class 3: *Bostock, Lewis, Smith.

DRAWING.— Human Figures in Chalk: *F. Haley, G. Haley, Wright. Landscape: *Tozer, Lind, Oliver, Cattle, Johnson.

MUSIC.—Instrumental: *A. F. Morrison, *Moss, *Ad. Smith, Adam, Liddle.

ELOCUTION.— *Wright, *Dalrymple, Davies, J. R. Thomson, Turnbull, Taylor, Higginson.

SPECIAL PRIZES.— Third in Examination for Dux of School, Third for Dux in English, Third for Dux in Classics: *A. Inglis. First in Weekly Dictation Examinations: *Craig.

BOARDERS' SUNDAY LESSONS.—Class 1: *J. Thomson. Class 2: *Tozer, *A. Thomson. Class 3: *A. Inglis, *J. Inglis, Stevens. JUNIOR DEPARTMENT.

ENGLISH.—Class 1: *Smith, *Rutherford, Niven, J. Levy, Campbell. Class 2: *H. Terry, *A. Hadley, A. Stewart, Higginson. Class 3: *F. Barry, *A. Brady, N. Levy.

BIBLE. Class 1: *Niven, Rutherford, J. M'Mullen, J. Levy. Class 2: *A. Stewart, A. Hadley, Chapman, Higginson. Class 3: *N. Levy, A. Brady, F. Barry, Brodie.

ARITHMETIC.—Class 1: *J. Levy, Kidston. Class 2: *Higginson, Rutherford. Class 3: *J. M'Mullen, Chapman.

WRITING :—*Kidston, Campbell.
CONDUCT AND IMPROVEMENT.—*J. Stewart.

At the conclusion of the presentation of the Prizes, the Duke of Edinburgh said:—It has given me very great pleasure to preside at this meeting, and to distribute the prizes awarded to the successful competitors at the recent examinations. To commemorate this occasion, I wish to ask the principals of the different schools to grant an extra week's holiday.

Dr. Bromby, on behalf of the Heads of the several schools, expressed his gratitude to his Royal Highness for presiding on the occasion and distributing the prizes, and stated that they would have much pleasure in complying with his request.

Three cheers were then given successively for the Queen, the Duke of Edinburgh, and the Governor, and the proceedings of the day were concluded by the singing of "Rule Britannia," under the leadership of Mr. Thomas Ford. His Royal Highness took his departure amid the cheers of the assemblage.

THE CIVIC FANCY DRESS BALL,

Given by the Melbourne Corporation in honour of his Royal Highness the Duke of Edinburgh, took place in the Exhibition Building, on Monday, 23rd December, and was a most brilliant success. Nearly three thousand guests were present. His Royal Highness, his Excellency the Governor, the Hon. Lady Manners-Sutton, the Misses Manners-Sutton, Lord Newry, Mr. Yorke, Mr. Haig, Mr. Manners Sutton, Mr. Rothwell, and others of the suite, entered from the Public Library, the band playing "God save the Queen." The guests formed an avenue, down which the Royal party passed to the dais, and then the ball began. It was opened, as usual, by the Prince, whose partner in the quadrille was Mrs. Butters. Opposite were the Mayor and Miss Manners-Sutton, and on the same sides were Lord Newry and Miss Pitt, and the Hon. Eliot Yorke and Miss Mabel Manners-Sutton. The others in the same set were Alderman Cohen, Alderman J. T. Smith, Councillor Bayles, Mr. Fitzgibbon, and their partners. Neither his Excellency nor Lady Manners-Sutton danced. The Prince was in naval uniform, his Excellency wore his official costume, and the other ladies and gentlemen of the party were all in official or ordinary evening dress.

The dresses worn by the guests were in most instances superb and costly in the extreme. Although it is an invidious task to particularise any when nearly all were rich and beautiful, it is but fair to state that the costumes worn by the following ladies and gentlemen were especially admired:—

LADIES.

Aarons, Mrs.
Askance, Mrs. Robert
Allen, Mrs.
Amess, Mrs.
Amess, Miss
Amess, Miss J. M.
Anderson, Mrs. E. S.
Armitage, Mrs.
Armstrong, Mrs.
Arnold, Miss
Ashby, Mrs.
Attenborough, Mrs.
Blair, Mrs. John
Blaney, Mrs.
Benjamin, Miss E.
Bennett, Mrs.
Bigwood, Mrs.

Bowen, Mrs.
Bowman, Mrs.
Bright, Mrs. C.
Brush, Miss
Butters, Mrs. J. S.
Clark, Miss
Church, Mrs. J. H.
Cockburn, Miss
Craig, Miss
Craig, Miss J.
Crisp, Mrs.
Crook, Mrs. W.
Currie, Mrs.
Dawson, Miss
Dunedin, Madame
Ellis, Mrs. L.
Firth, Mrs.

Fitch, Mrs.
Flanagan, Miss
Flanagan, Miss Mary
Flockhart, Mrs.
Ford, Mrs.
Gillher, Miss
Garton, Mrs.
Green, Mrs. W. H.
Grey, Mrs.
Grice, Mrs.
Haig, Mrs. W.
Halley, Mrs. J.
Hanna, Mrs. P.
Hardie, Mrs. C.
Hart, Miss
Hazard, Miss
Henty, Mrs. Herbert

Hepburn, Miss
Highett, Miss
Hodgkinson, Mrs.
Hodgkinson, Miss
Hood, Mrs.
Hood, Miss
Hyland, Mrs.
Isaacs, Mrs. W.
Katzenstein, Mrs.
Knight, Mrs. J. G.
Lang, Mrs. J. S.
Langan, Mrs.
Lewis, Mrs.
Lewis, Mrs. L. L.
Lewis, Mrs. S.
Levy, Mrs. G.
Linacre, Mrs.

The Civic Fancy Dress Ball.

Littlewood, Mrs.
Lulman, Mrs.
Lydiard, Mrs.
Lyell, Mrs. A.
Macgregor, Mrs. John
Martin, Mrs.
Matheson, Miss Flora
Matheson, Miss
Meaney, Miss H.
Meaney, Miss M. A.
Meissner, Mrs. O.
Mellish, Mrs. B.
Middleton, Mrs.
Milton, Mrs. J. B.
Mitchell, Miss
Morton, Miss
Morton, Miss E.

Mount, Miss Jessie
Moolway, Mrs., Thomas
Murphy, Lady
M'Coy, Mrs.
M'Coy, Miss
M'Mullen, Miss
Ogg, Mrs. C.
O'Brien, Mrs.
Paley, Mrs.
Palmer, Mrs.
Parker, Mrs.
Parker, Miss
Picott, Mrs. H. C.
Pilley, Mrs.
Priestly, Mrs. P.
Rankin, Mrs.
Robertson, Mrs.

Rosenthal, Mrs.
Ross, Mrs. W. M.
Roy, Mrs. C.
Scott, Mrs. John
Sandilands, Mrs. R. N.
Sangster, Mrs.
Saunders, Mrs.
Scholes, Miss
Seddon, Mrs. Arthur
Snelling, Mrs.
Stevenson, Mrs. L.
Smonter, Mrs.
Sutherland, Mrs. C.
Sutton, Mrs. J. W.
Taylor, Mrs.
Taylor, Miss J.
Tulk, Mrs.

Talley, Miss
Turner, Mrs. H. G.
Twentyman, Mrs. H.
Wade, Miss
Waldock, Mrs. S.
Walton, Mrs.
Watson, Mrs. Edward
Weir, Mrs. J.
Welsh, Mrs.
Western, Miss
Whiteman, Mrs. J.
Wilson, Mrs. S.
Wither, Miss
Weadhouse, Miss
Zander, Miss
Zander, Miss F.

GENTLEMEN.

Allen, Mr. G. L.
Amstuck, Mr. E.
Anderson, Mr.
Appleton, Mr.
Barry, Mr.
Bevan, Mr.
Benjamin, Mr.
Braham, Mr.
Bright, Mr. R.
Bright, Mr. C. F.
Bright, Mr. S.
Capron, Mr. A. T.
Chew, Mr. S.
Currie, Mr.
Danone, Mr. C. Von
Davies, Mr. G. W.
Davies, Mr. J.
De Pass, Mr. J.

Fitch, Mr.
Foster, Mr. C.
Gatehouse, Mr.
Getudin, Mr.
Girdlestone, Dr.
Haddon, Mr. F. W.
Hanna, Mr. P.
Harvey, Mr. R.
Hogue, Mr.
Hughes, Mr. C. W.
Katzenstein, Mr.
Knight, Mr. J. G.
Kong Meng
Lazarus, Mr. S.
Levy, Mr. H.
Liston, Mr.
Littlewood, Mr.
Logan, Mr. C.

Lowe, Mr.
Lyall, Mr. A.
Mackenzie, Mr.
Malloson, Mr.
Martin, Dr.
Meissner, Mr.
Miller, Mr.
Mitchell, Mr.
Molesworth, Mr.
Montefiore, Mr.
Montgomery, Mr. Walter
Moore, Mr.
M'Ewen, Mr.
M'Farlane, Mr.
M'Pherson, Mr.
Nash, Mr.
Neild, Dr. J. E.
Newberry, Mr.

Ogg, Mr.
Palmer, Mr.
Porter, Mr.
Powell, Mr.
Remick, Mr.
Richardson, Mr.
Sewell, Mr.
Scott, Capt. J.
Sherwin, Mr.
Stark, Mr.
Starling, Mr.
Twentyman, Mr.
Westley, Mr. H.
Williams, Mr.
Wilson, Mr. S.
Woods, Mr. D.
Wyburn, Mr.

In the alphabetical list of the guests the characters in which these ladies and gentlemen appeared will be found catalogued. In the list will be found many grotesque titles, the one assumed by Mr. Thomas Carrington, the *Punch* artist, being particularly prominent.

AARON, Miss Deborah—Little Bopeep
Aaron, Mr. L.—Morning Star
Aarons, Mr. Joseph—Polish officer
Aarons, Mrs. Jos.—Night
Aarons, Miss—Swiss peasant
Aarons, Mr. L.—Garibaldian
Aarons, Mr. S.—Muleteer
Aaronson, Mr. G. P.—Tyrol, peasant
Abbott, Mr. B. M.—Father Calibear
Abbott, Mrs.—Night
Acting Consul for Prussia
Adam, Mr. John—Foxhunter
Adams, Mr. B.—Oliver Cromwell
Adams, Mrs. B.—Queen of Arragon
Adamson, Mr.—Hussar
Adet, Mr. E.—Cricketer
Adet, Mrs. E.—Cavaliere de la Seine
Adey, Mrs.—Azucena
Aitkin, Mrs. T.—Lady of Lyons
Aitkin, Mr. T.—Royal Arch Mason
Agnew, Mrs. G. F.—Spanish lady
Akhurst, Mr. A. C.—American soldier
Akhurst, Mrs. W. M.—Lady of the Court of Louis XIV
Aldwell, Mr. W. R.—Student of the nineteenth century
Alexander, Mr.—Maronite Gentleman of eleventh century
Alexander, Mr.—Duke of Naxara

Alexander, Mrs.—Spanish lady, national
Alexander, Mrs.—White Rose, in mourning
Alexander, Mrs.—Bone girl
Allan, Miss—Vivandière
Allan, Mrs.—Spanish lady
Allan, Miss H.—Greek shepherdess
Allan, Miss J.—French peasant
Allen, Mr. F.—Garibaldian officer
Allen, Mr. George F. Snow
Allen, Mr. G. L.—Spanish muleteer
Allen, Miss—Greek shepherdess
Allen, Mr. H.—Harlequin
Allen, Mr. S. J.—Briefless barrister
Allen, Mr. S.—Night
Allon, Miss—Jeanie Deans
Amery, Mr. S.—Eccentric gentleman
Amoss, Councillor—Official uniform
Amoss, Mrs.—Empress Alexandra Feodorovitna
Amoss, Miss—Spanish gitana
Amoss, Miss M. J.—Fairy queen
Amoss, Master—Captain, Cadet corps
Amoss, Mr. A.—Garibaldian volunteer
Amoss, Mrs. B.—Dolly Varden
Amoss, Mr.—Captain Shortcut, of the spitfire
Amstuck, Mr.—Don Basilio
Anderson, Mr. A.—Jean Pierre David

Anderson, Mr. A. M.—Monk
Anderson, Mr.—Student, Glasgow University
Anderson, Mrs.—Flora
Anderson, Mr.—Forester
Anderson, Mr. R. S.—Volunteer uniform
Anderson, Mrs.—Blanche La Magicienne
Anderson, Colonel W. A. D.—C'uniform
Anderson, Mrs. W. A. D.—Lady of the time of Edward VI.
Anderson, Mr. Wm.—Uniform of Volunteer Cavalry
Andrew, Mr. J.—Polish peasant
Angel, Mr. S.—Zouave
Angel, Mrs. S.—Daughter of the Regiment
Annan, Mr. J. C.—Elvino
Appleton, Mrs. L. F.—Queen of Spades
Appleton, Mr. L. F.—Indian rajah
Armit, Mrs.—Evening dress
Armit, Lieut. R. N.—Officer
Armstrong, Miss—Lady of the Lake
Armytage, Mr. G.—Court dress
Arraytage, Mrs. G.—Lady of the time of Henry IV.
Arnold, Mr. J. F.—Officer, Volunteer Force
Arnold, Miss—Catalonian girl

157

Arnold, Mrs. J. F.—Spanish lady
Arnold, Miss—Flower-girl
Arnold, Miss—Swiss peasant
Asche, Mr. T.—Norwegian peasant
Asche, Mrs. T.—Norwegian peasant woman
Ash, Miss J.—Maritana
Ashe, Miss Isabella—Maritana
Ashley, Mr. E.—Fancy dress
Ashley, Mrs. E.—Summer
Aspinall, Mrs. H. C.—Marguerite
Aspinall, Mr. H. C.—Don Montgomery Walltero
Atkens, Mrs.—Ricca (from "Oberon")
Atkin, Mr. C. A.—Nobleman of the fifteenth century
Atkin, Mrs. C. A.—Hop Queen
Atkins, Miss A.—Rose Bradwardine
Attenborough, Miss Phillis—A shepherdess
Attenborough, Mr. Thos.—Mr. Johnson (Christy's)
Attenborough, Mrs.—Madame de Maintenon
Attenborough, Mr. W.—A friar
Austin, Miss Anna—Nerissa
Austin, Mr. Albert—Yeoman officer
Austin, Mrs. Albert—Spanish lady
Austin, Miss—Florentine lady
Austin, Mr Thomas—Freemason
Austin, Mrs. Thos.—Athenian lady
Austin, Mr.—Hussar undress
Avent, Dr.—Monk
Ayliffe, Miss E.—Flower-girl

BACON, Mr. F. W.—Garibaldian
Bacon, Mr. T.—Forensic costume
Bailey, Mr. J.—Earl of Rochester
Bailey, Miss Annie—Undine
Bailey, Miss M.—Peasant of Picardy
Baillie, Mr. W. G.—Gentleman
Baillie, Mr. W. G.—Vivandiere
Baillie, Mr. Thomas—Omar Pacha
Baillie, Mrs. Thomas—Winter
Bailliere, Mr.—Mystical philosopher
Bailliere, Mrs.—À la Watteau
Bailey, Mr. J. B.—Albanian costume
Baker, Mr. John—Garibaldi escaped from prison
Baker, Miss—Vivandière
Baker, Major T. D.
Ballock, Mrs. C. G.—Thaddeus
Ballantyne, Mr. A.—Count Alberugo
Ballantyne, Mr. J. L.—Cassio
Banks, Mr J. H.—Ivanhoe
Barker, Mr. K.—Who I am
Barker, Mrs. E.—Russian lady
Barker, Mrs. J.—Official costume
Barker, Mr. A.—Neapolitan fisherman
Barker, Miss—Paperette
Barker, Miss—Aurora
Barnes, Mr. B.—Muleteer
Barnes, Mrs. B.
Barnes, Mr. F.—Garibaldi
Barnett, Mr. John—Don Sebastian
Barnett, Mr. J.—Polish gentleman
Barnett, Mr. J.—Polish lady
Barnett, Miss B.—Bride of Lammermoor
Barrett, Ensign W. K.
Barrow, Miss—Twilight
Barry, Mr. J., jun.—A New Zealand chief
Barry, Miss—Morning
Barry, Mr B.—Michael Cassio

Barry, Mrs.—Spanish lady
Barry, Mr. J. M.—Huntsman
Barry, Miss J.—French peasant girl
Barry, Mr Nicholas—Fra Diavolo
Bartlam, Mr. H.—Garibaldi
Barwise, Mrs. J.—Lady of the present century
Bassett, Mrs. W.—Queen of May
Bates, Mr. A. H.—Gentleman of the reign of George I.
Bath, Miss—Diana Vernon
Battersley, Mrs.—Faust
Bayles, Councillor—Official uniform
Bayles, Mrs.—Court costume time George II.
Bayles, Councillor William
Bayudam, Mrs.—Lady 19th century
Beaney, Mr. J. G.—Medical Officer, Volunteer Artillery
Benney, Mrs J. G.—Lady of Athens
Bear, the Hon. J. P.—Evening dress
Beattie, Mr. R.—B V. A. uniform
Beaver, Mr. A.—Mexican costume
Bell, Mr. W. M.—Sir Walter Raleigh
Bellman, Mr John—Cricketer
Bellman, Mrs. John—Gipsy queen
Benjamin, Mr. E.—Mon ha Minoa mot Bhuqqutz
Benjamin, Miss—Lady of the time of Henry III.
Benjamin, Mr. S.—Sailor
Benjamin, Mrs. S.—Court lady
Benjamin, Mr. Moss—A British ambassador
Benjamin, Mr. David—Don Adriano de Armado
Benjamin, Mr. B.—Garibaldi
Benjamin, Mrs. B.—Court Lady
Benjamin, Mr. H.—Swiss peasant
Benjamin, Mr. L.—Sir Henry Hudson
Benjamin, Mrs. L.—National colours
Bennett, Miss—Swiss peasant
Bennett, Miss—Bertha
Bennett, Miss M. S.—Annie Laurie
Bennett, Mr. H.—Lord Dundreary
Bennett, Mrs. T. K.—Indian princess
Bennett, Mr. T. K.—Hotspur
Bennett, Mrs. T. K.—Squire's daughter
Bennett, Miss G.—La Mexicana
Bennett, Mr.—Cricketer
Bennie, Mr.—A student of Padua
Berghoff, Mr. C.—Peasant of the Hartz Mountains
Berghoff, Mrs. C.—Peasant of the Hartz Mountains
Biddle, Mr. W. C.—Sir Maurice de Bracy
Biddle, Mrs. W. C.—Imagination
Bigwood, Miss—Fancy French hunting dress
Bigwood, Mrs.—Fancy dress
Binny, Mrs. B.—Margaret of Parma, Regent of Netherlands
Birkmyre, Miss—Christmas
Birtwistle, Mr.—Morris dancer
Black, Dr. J.—Uniform, staff surgeon volunteers
Black, Dr. Thos.
Blackwell, Mr.—"Fabian Franchi," Corsican Brothers"
Blair, Mr. J. W.—6th Hampshire Volunteer Rifles
Blackburn, Mr. J.—Zouave
Blackburn, Mrs.—Vivandière
Blackburn, Miss—Lady in 1814

Blackwood, Miss—Vivandière
Blackwood, Mr. J. H.—Montezuma
Blair, Mrs. J. W.—Summer
Blair, Mrs.—Bride of Lammermoor
Blair, Dr. J.—Roman citizen
Bland, Mr. J. J.—Zouave
Blamin, Mr. F.—Sir Walter Raleigh
Blamin, Mrs.—Hinda
Bloomfield, Mrs. M.—Patty Honeywood
Bloomington, Mr. G.—Chinese mandarin
Bloomington, Mrs. G.—Mexican lady
Blyth, Mr. John—Highlander
Bodington, Mr. B.—Morris dancer
Bogg, Mr J W.—Viceroy Mehemet Ali
Bogg, Mrs. J. W.—Madame de Sevigne (Louis XIII.)
Bogg, Miss—Queen of roses
Bonnleib, Mr. H. S.—Friar Tuck
Bonfield, Miss—Maritana
Bonkey, Mr.—Police uniform
Bonkey, Mrs.—Italian lady
Booty, Miss—Swiss peasant girl
Bowen, Mr. A.—Moldavian Hussar
Booth, Mr. John—Garibaldi uniform
Bowles, Mrs.—Lady of the reign of George III.
Bodetta, Mr.—Panaeolus
Bowen, Mr. Richard—P G M. of M.U.
Bowen, Mrs. Richard—Night
Bowen, Mr. W.—Russian peasant
Bowen, Mr. W.—Waiting-maid time Charles II.
Bowman, Mr. R.—Matador
Bowman, Mrs. R.—Hungarian peasant
Bradley, Captain J. D
Brally, Mr. C. F.—Spanish nobleman of the seventeenth century
Bradly, Mrs. C. F.—Night
Bradshaw, Mr. G. M.—Raoul
Bradshaw, Mrs. G. M.—Linda di Chamouni
Braham, Mr. B.—Muleteer
Brabe, Mr. H.
Brahe, Mrs.—Evening dress
Brett, Mrs. E.—Lady of the time of Louis XIV.
Brett, Miss—Mercedes
Brierly, Mr. J. P.—Morisco
Brettargh, Miss—Wild Irish Girl
Brierly, Mr. John—Morisco
Brind, Mr. G. F.—Swiss peasant
Bright, Mr. C.—La None, the Huguenot
Bright, Mrs. C.—Elizabeth, from Hyperion
Bright, Mr. C. E.—Courtier of the reign of George II.
Bright, Mr. J. S., jun.—Gentleman of the time of Louis XIV.
Brodribb, Mr. S. E.—German divinity student in Rome
Brodribb, Mrs. K. E.—Lady of King Arthur's court
Brodribb, Miss L.—Snow
Brodribb, Mr. L.—University student
Brodribb, Mr. W. K.—Neapolitan peasant
Brown, Mr. G S.—Roman noble of the Empire
Brown, Miss Sarah—Australia
Brown, Miss—Flower-girl
Brown, Miss—Greek shepherdess
Brown, Mr. B.—Victorian rifleman

Brown, Mr. C.—Abd-el-Kader
Brown, Mr. G.—Earl of Leicester
Brown, Mr. J. W.—A jolly tar
Bruce, Mr. M.—British tar
Bruce, Mrs.—Roman peasant
Brown, Miss A.—English peasant
Brown, Miss—Evening
Brown, Mr. C. F. E.—Sir Kenneth of Scotland
Brownless, Dr.—Doctor of Medicine of the University of Melbourne
Brownless, Mrs.—Spanish gipsy
Bruce, Mr. John V. A.—Boatman
Bruce, Miss Sarah B. A.—Zouave
Bruce, Miss—Daughter of Regiment
Bruce, Mr. James—Cannabar
Bruce, Miss—Fancy yachting costume
Brush, Mrs. S.—Preuscria, "L'Etoile du Nord"
Brush, Mr. S.—Admiral Fitz Toozle
Buchan, Mr. J. J.—Captain V.V.R.
Buchan, Miss—Iorline
Bucirolo, Miss—Calabrian peasant girl
Buckle, Mr.—Cricketer
Buckley, Mr.M.—Neapolitan fisherman
Buckley, Mrs. M.—Aquarium
Buckley, Miss—Greek shepherdess
Buckley, Miss—Night
Budd, Mr. H. H.—Ibrahim Ben Anon
Bunny, Mrs. B. F.—Margaret of Parma
Burke, Mrs. J. L.—Aurora
Burke, Mr. J. L.—French sailor
Burns, Mr. G. H.—Nobleman of the reign of Charles II
Burns, Mr.—Charles II.
Burns, Mrs.—Court dress seventeenth century
Burns, Miss S.—Swiss peasant
Burrell, Mr. J.—Mark, master mason
Burrell, Mrs. J.—Scotch shepherdess
Burt, Mr.—Volunteer uniform
Burt, Mrs.—Donna Isabella
Burt, Miss—Bohemian girl
Burton, Captain—Captain 1st Volunteer Cavalry, 1861
Butler, Mr. S.
Butters, Mr. J. Stewart—Mayor
Butters, Mrs.—The Mirror
Bushell, Mr.—Spanish lady
Byrne, Mr. W. G.—Sergeant-major
Byron, Mr. Matthew—Anglo-Saxon of tenth century

CADDY, Mr.—Australian stockrider
Cain, Mr. W.—Gentleman of 1780
Callaghan, Mrs. Jas.—Night
Campbell, Mrs. W.—Spanish lady
Campbell, Hon. W.—Eastern traveller
Campbell, Master W.—Cricketer
Campbell, Mr. Donald—Cricketer
Campbell, Mr. C. B.—Highland lassie
Campbell, Mrs. W.—Spanish lady
Campbell, Miss—Pythia
Campbell, Mr. A.—Official
Campbell, Miss A.—Oceania
Campbell, Mr. C. R.—Highland gentleman
Campbell, Mrs. D. S.—Lady of the seventeenth century
Campbell, Mr. D. S.—Cricketer of the M.C.C., aged
Cameron, Mr. A.—Highland gentleman, clan Cameron
Cameron, Miss—Spanish gitana
Cameron, Mr. D.—Masaniello

Candler, Dr. S. C.—Knight of Malta
Capron, Mr.—Incroyable, 1793
Capron, Mrs.—Undine
Carno, Mr.—A Garibaldian red-shirt
Carne, Mrs.—Peruvian lady
Carrington, Mr. Thomas—Baron Von Hugh Reldoole
Carroll, Mr. P.—Member of Prince of Wales Light Horse Cavalry
Carson, Mr. J.—Baillie Nicol Jarvie
Carson, Mrs John—Spanish lady
Carson, Miss E.—A Breton girl of the seventeenth century
Carter, Mrs.—Old English lady
Carter, Mr. W.—Court dress of George IV.
Carter, Mr. W.—Grey friar
Carter, Miss—Music (Enterpe)
Carter, Miss Millie—Court dress of Louis XIV.
Carson, Miss—A Polish lady
Carter, Mr. E.—Courtier of the time of Charles I.
Carter, Mrs. E.—Queen of Edward II.
Cartwright, Mr. H—Windsor Court costume
Case, Mr.—French officer of the Imperial Guard
Case, Mrs.—Sultana
Casey, Mr. J. J.—Rob Roy
Cashmore, Miss—Spanish peasant
Cattach, Miss A. S.—Cynthia
Caughey, Mrs. R.—Spring
Caughey, Mr. R.—Claude Melnotte
Cavell, Mr.—Volunteer
Cavell, Mrs.—Ivanhhoe
Chadwick, Mr. H.—Officer 11th Hussars
Chambers, Mr. D.—Officer of police
Chambers, Mr. W.—Volunteer officer
Chambers, Mrs. W.—Greek shepherdess
Chambers, Mr. R.—Patrick O'Toole
Champ, Colonel—Uniform
Champ, Mrs.—Evening costume
Champ, Mr. W.—Evening costume
Champ, Miss—Evening costume
Chapman, Mr.—A baker
Chapman, Mr.—Monk
Chapman, Mrs.—Gipsy
Charlwood, Mr. C.—Don Soluet an
Charlwood, Mrs.—Spanish lady
Cherry, Thomas—Maivoiso
Chevalier, Mr. N. Sir Peter Paul Rubens
Chevalier, Mrs. N.—Lady Rubens
Chew, Mr. Tom—Othello
Chippendale, Mr.—Rembrandt
Chomley, Mr.—Russian dress
Chomley, Mrs.
Christopherson, Mr. H. Gentleman of the eighteenth century
Christopherson, Mrs. H.—Russian court dress
Clarke, Mr. J. J.—1st Vict. Rifles
Clarke, Mrs J. J.—Donna Inca
Clarke, Mrs. T. F.—Boadicea
Clarke, Mr. T. F.—Lodorico Ariosto
Clarke, Mr. D. G.
Clarke, Mrs. D. G.
Clarke, Miss—Queen of the fairies
Clarke, Mr. W.,—pas—Russian peasant
Clarke, Mr. P. F.—Fancy dress
Clarke, Miss—Ogarita
Clarke, Mr. W.—Touchstone

Clarke, Dr. St. J.—Royal Arch mason
Clarke, Miss—Roman lady
Clarke, Miss J.—Russian lady
Clarson, Mrs. W.—Costume of 1760
Clarson, Mr. W.—Jungle hunter
Clarke, Mr. Hon—Captain Murphy Maguire
Clay, Mr. G.—Debardeur
Clay, Mr. P.—Debardeur
Clements, Mr.—Matador
Clements, Mrs.—Lady of the time of George III.
Clough, Mr. J. H.—Payson, Bretagne
Clough, Mrs. J. H—Lady Heron, reign of James IV. of Scotland
Cockburn, Mr. W.—Volunteer
Cockburn, Miss.—Marquise 13th cent.
Cockburn, Mr. L.—Knight of Malta
Cohen, Mrs. M. J.—Court lady
Cohen, Mr. D.—Elvira
Cohen, Mrs. D.—Queen of Navarre
Cohen, Mr. S. H.—Uniform, Royal Artillery
Cohen, Mrs S.—Eugenie de Laney
Cohen, Miss Rebecca—Castilian dancing-girl
Cohen, Mr. N. E.—Don Giovanni
Cohen, Alderman—Court dress
Cohen, Mrs. E.—Marie, Duchess of Burgundy
Cohen, Miss—Folly
Cohen, Mrs. S. H.—Lady of Arden
Cohen, Miss Rosa—Castilian dancing-girl
Cohen, Miss Sara—Castilian dancing-girl
Cohen, Alderman Edward
Cohen, Mr. A. A.—Carlo, Linda di Chamouni
Cohen, Mrs. A. A.—Court dress of time of Mary Queen of Scots
Cohen, Miss Fanny—Lorline
Cohen, Mrs. L.—Turkish lady
Cohen, Mrs. M. J.—Court lady
Cohen, Mr. M. J.—Dr. Hugh Chamberlain
Cohen, Mr. Isaac
Cohen, Mrs. Simeon—Marguerite
Cohen, Mr. Simeon—Benvenuto Cellini
Cohen, Mr. P.—Naval officer
Coker, Mr.—Dr Dulcamara
Coldnu, Mr. James—Muleteer
Collin, Mr. L. Figaro, Barber of Seville
Collin, Mr.—Spanish peasant
Collie, Mr. Jos.—Ivanhoe
Collie, Miss—Italian lady
Collier, Mr. H.—Shaun, the Post
Cohn, Miss Eliza—Zuleika, bride of Abydos
Considine, Mrs. J. W.—Night
Considine, Mr. J. W.—Louis XIII.
Consul for Denmark—Official dress
Consul for Italy—Official costume
Consul (Vice) of Italy—Official costume
Conway, Miss—Grecian shepherdess
Cook, Mr. W. M.—Garibaldi
Cooling, Mr. R. H.—Andreas Hofer
Cooper, Mr. B. A.—A body-guard of Henry XIII.
Cooper, Mr. Alfred—Charles II.
Corben, Mr. W. S.—Volunte. uniform
Corbett, Mr. L. A.—Zouare

Corcoran, Mrs. W. P.—Portia
Corcoran, Mr. W. P., Royal Arch Druid
Coreny, Miss A.—Huguenot
Couch, Mr. M. W.—Volunteer officer
Coulier, Mr.—Officer of the Guard, seventeenth century
Cowell, Mr. S. W.—Italian volunteer
Cowell, Miss—Oggerita
Cowley, Mr.—Nizam's entry, uniform
Cowley, Miss—Spring
Cowper, Miss—White Lady of Avenel
Cox, Mr. Ross—A monk
Cox, Mrs. Ross—Dew
Cox, Mr. W. S.—Henry Bertrand
Cox, Mrs. W. S.—Lady Teazle
Cox, Miss—Highland lady, 18th cent.
Craib, Mr. George—Masaniello
Craib, Miss—Spanish lady
Craib, Mr. James—Duckie fisherman
Craig, Mr. M.
Craig, Miss—La Fille du Regiment
Craig, Miss J.—The Spirit of Mischief
Cresswick, Mr. H.—Morning costume
Cresswell, Mr. H. C.—Romeo
Cresswell, Mrs. H. C.—Spanish Lady
Crisholm, Miss—Lusline
Crispy, Mr. T.—Gentleman of 1760
Crisp, Mrs. T.—La Siege
Crisp, Mr. Geo.—Royal Arch Mason
Crisp, Miss—Spanish lady
Crocker, Miss—Dress of the time of Francis I.
Croft, Mr.—An under-graduate
Croft, Mrs.—Sultana
Crook, Dr.—Masonic costume
Crook, Mrs.—Midnight
Crooke, J.W.—Evening costume
Crooke, Miss—Spanish lady
Crompton, Mr. T.—General Blucher
Cropper, Mr. E. B.—Glasgow student
Cropper, Mr. W. H.—Night
Cumming, Mr.—Prussian officer
Cumming, Mrs.—Autumn
Cunningham, Mr. F.—Mustapha Ali Khan
Cunningham, Mr. P.—Garibaldi
Cunningham, Miss—Gipsy girl
Currie, Mr. John—English nobleman, fourteenth century
Currie, Mrs. John—Queen of Hearts
Curtain, Mr., jun.—Selim
Curtain, Mr. M.—Evening costume
Curtain, Mrs. M.—Evening costume
Curtis, Miss—Soubrette of the time of Louis XV.

DA COSTA, Mr. H.—Spanish courtier, 1700
Daish, Mr. W.—Royal Arch Mason
Daish, Mrs. W.—Night
Daish, Mr. Joseph—Yachtsman
Dash, Mrs. Joseph—Christmas
Dalgleish, Mr. W.—Highland costume
Dalgleish, Mrs. W.—Scotch lassie
Dalrimore, Miss—Queen of May
D'Alembert, Mons. C. F.—Mayor of Paris
Dalziel, Mr. Robt—Fatima
Davey, Mr. John
Davidson, Mr. G.—Volunteer, Prince of Wales Light Horse
Davies, Mr.—Italian brigand
Davies, Mr. S.—Max, Der Freischutz
Davies, Mr. W.—Swiss peasant

Davies, Mr. B. G.—Sir Watkin W. Wynne
Davies, Mrs. W.—Spanish lady
Davies, Mrs.—Mexican girl
Davies, Mr. J. T.—Hungarian nobleman
Davies, Miss—Polish peasant
Davies, Mr. B. Neapolitan peasant, gala suit
Davies, Miss—Vivandière
Davies, Mr. J.—Victorian vigneron
Davies, Miss Mary—Highland Mary
Davies, Miss—Cuiba
Davies, Mr. P.—Court dress
Davies, Mr.—Courtier, reign of Queen Elizabeth
Davis, Miss—Lady of the time of Louis XV.
Davis, Mr. Thos.—Cavalry officer
Davis, Miss—Flower-girl
Davis, Mr. Alf.—Cavalry uniform
Davis, Mr. P. S.—Sons of Court Rifles
Davis, Mr. Ed., regimental costume of fourteenth century
Davis, Mr. W.—Uniform P.W.V.L.H.
Davis, Mr. G.—Biscayan
Davis, Mrs. P.—Autumn
Davis, Miss—Heath
Davis, Miss M.—Spring
Dawson, Mr. M.—Yachtsman
Dawson, Miss—Queen of Spades
Dawson, Mr. A. S.—One of the people
De Beer, Mr. B.—Dutch sailor
De Beer, Mrs. B.—Queen of Sheba
Defries, Mrs.—Mexican lady
Defries, Mr.—Mexican staff-officer
Degraves, Hon. W.—Napoleon Bonaparte
Degraves, Mrs. J. W.—Spanish dancer
De Grachy, Mr. H. G.—Galatea
De Grachy, Mr. H. G.—Paul Pry
Delaney, Mr. A.—Salim Aga
Demaine, Mrs. C. R.—Polish lady
Demaine, Mr. C. R.—Our American cousin
Denham, Miss—Queen of Spades
De Pass, Mr. John. Spaniard
Derrett, Mr.—Gentleman of the 17th century
Derrett, Mrs.—Spanish lady
Desailly, Mrs.—Aurora Australis
Devlin, Captain—A retired waterman
Devlin, Miss—Summer
Devlin, Miss J.—Swiss peasant
Dickson, Mr. H.—Young Australia
Dickson, Mr. Thos.—Robin Hood
Dickson, Mr. M. S.—Garibaldi
Dillon, Miss—Malaeska, huntress of the Mississippi
Dillon, Mr. W. H.—Pierrot
Disher, Master—Midshipman
Disney, Mr. R.—Uniform
Dixon, Mr. P. G.—Charles Surface
Dobbs, Mr.—Inquisition
Dobbs, Mrs.—English Gipsy
Dobson, Miss—Polly Varden
Don, Mr. J. W.—Earl of Rochester
Don, Mrs. J. W.—Roman lady
Donahoo, Miss—Ixion
Donaldson, Mr. C. A.—Fra Diavolo
Donaldson, Mrs. C. A.—Japanese lady
Donohoe, Mr.—Mr. Chas. Torrens
Dopping, Miss—Swiss peasant
Dougharty, Mr. J. J.—Victorian Yeomanry Cavalry

Dougharty, Mrs. S. G.—Spanish peasant
Dourdain, Madame—Greek lady
Dourdain, Mons.—Italian fisherman
Downie, Miss—Grecian princess
Downing, Mrs. H.—Spanish peasant
Draper, Mr.—Spanish gentleman
Drew, Miss—Sardinian peasant
Drew, Mrs.—Guess
Drury, Mr.
Drury, Mrs. W. S.—Marseilles
Drysdale, Mr. A.—Danish nobleman
Dudgeon, Mr. John—Ancient Druid
Dudgeon, Mrs. J.—Night
Duerdin, Mr., jun.—Matador
Duerdin, Miss Kate—Polish girl
Duerdin, Mrs. J.—Lady of the court of Louis XV
Duerdin, Miss—Watteau shepherdess
Duffin, Mr. R.—Cricketer
Duffy, Miss Gavin—Virginia
Dumas, Mr. A. G.—Assistant-clerk Legislative Assembly
Dumas, Miss—Tyrolese peasant
Dumas, Mr. George—Barrister
Dumas, Mrs. A. G.—Lady of the nineteenth century
Dunne, Miss—Swiss peasant
Dunkley, Mr.—Tyrolese peasant
Dyer, Mr. D.—Prince Paboban
Dyke, Miss, Young Lady, 1777
Dyson, Mrs. W. H.—A Venetian lady
Dyson, Mr. W. H.—Turk
Dyte, Mr. Chas.—Uniform of a Ballarat fireman

EASDOWN, Miss, Lady Marion Wallace
Eastwood, Miss—Lady of the eighteenth century
Eastwood, Mr.—Dr. Pangloss
Eaton, Mr. H. F.—An Asiatic Turk
Eaton, Miss—Rose Bradwardine
Eaton, Mrs. H. F.—Ayesha
Ecroyd, Mr. W. J.—Le Chevalier Palliser
Ecroyd, Mrs.—Donna Selina
Edonin, Mrs.—A romp
Edonin, Mrs. C.—Starlight Bess
Edonin, Mr. C.—The Kinchen
Edwards, Mr. William
Edwards, Mrs. William
Edwards, Mr. J., jun.—The Lord No Zoo, K.G.
Edwards, Mrs. John—Jeanne d'Arc
Edwards, Mr. A.—Victorian rifleman
Edwin, Mr. J.—Countryman
Egan, Mr. W.—French musketeer
Ehrmann, Mr.—Mexican gentleman
Elder, Mrs. H.—Swiss peasant
Elder, Mr. H.—Cavalry officer
Elliot, Mr. T. S.—Sergeant R.V.A.
Elliott, Mrs. J. S.—Swiss peasant girl
Ellis, Mr. J. E.—Paul Pry
Ellis, Mr. Joseph—Mortoco
Ellis, Mr.—Corsair
Ellis, Miss—Village coquette
Ellis, Miss—Irish gleaner
Ellis, Mrs. A.—A Lady of Lyons
Ellis, Mr. A.—A gentleman of Verona
Ellis, Mr. L.—Under-Sheriff
Ellis, Mrs. L.—Thetis
Ellis, Mr. M.—Puck of cards
Ellis, Mrs. M.—Starlight, Galatea

Binns, Mr.—Jockey
Eno, Mr. B.—Spanish nobleman of the fifteenth century
Enticing, Dr. W. H., Lieut. in army of Garibaldi, 1860
Emerson, Mr., Garibaldi
Emerson, Mrs., Spanish lady
Emanuel, Mrs.—Be Irose of Lancaster
Emerald Hill, Mayor of
Emmanuel, Mr. L.—John Bull
Emmerton, Mr. H.—Nemo
England, Mrs. E. Zuleika
England, Mr. R.—Captain volunteers Stuart period
Esott, Madame Lucy, Lady of the period of Marie Stuart
Eversed, Mr. J.—The Bearded Boy
Everard, Mrs. J.—Red, white and blue
Eville, Mr. James—Town Clerk of Emerald Hill
Evans, Mr. D. H.—Welsh bard
Evans, Mr.—Chinese mandarin
Evans, Mrs.—Flower-girl
Evan, Mr. G. B.—Druid

FAIRCHILD, Mrs. J. R.—Lady of seventeenth century
Farewell, Miss—Soubrette
Fario, Miss C. M.—La Liberté
Fario, Mr. Claud—Captain V.V. rifles
Farmer, Miss R.
Farquhar, Master
Farrell, Miss—Little Red Riding Hood
Faron, Mr W., Don Pedro
Father, Mr.—Volunteer officer
Fawcett, Mr. A., Cavalry officer
Fawcett, Mr. C., Royal Arch Mason
Fawcett, Mrs. C., Midnight
Fehon, Mr.—Senor Don Manuel
Fehon, Mrs.—Spanish girl
Fennessy, Miss, Zaidee
Fennessy, Miss K., Amina
Fenwick, Councillor—Official dress
Fenwick, Mrs. O.—Mme. Pompadour
Ferguson, Mr. J.—A man before the mast
Ferguson, Mrs. James—Lady of the sixteenth century
Fetherston, Dr.—Menotti
Fetherston, Mrs.—Maritana
Finlay, Mr. A.—Knight Templar
Finlay, Mr. W.—Moor of Granada
Finlay, Miss—Queen of May
Finlay, Miss Clara—Highland lassie
Firebrace, Mrs.—Egyptian girl
Firth, Mrs.—Autumn
Fisken, Mr., Yeomanry officer
Fisken, Miss
Fitch, Mr. R. A.—Turkish aga
Fitch, Mrs. R. A.—Duchess di Maffi
Fitts, Mr.—La Coscletier
Fitzgerald, Hon. N.—Graduate T.C.D.
Fitzgerald, Mrs. N.—Donna di Tivoli
Fitzgerald, G. C.—Don Pedro
Fitzgibbon, Mr. (Town Clerk)—Official costume
Fitzgibbon, Miss—Twilight
Flanigan, Miss—Portuguese gitana
Flannagan, Mr. J.—Knight Templar
Flannagan, Mrs. J.—Spanish lady, national costume
Flannigan, Miss Mary, Christina
Flatow, Mrs. H., Ayesha
Flaxman, Mr. John—Shakspeare

Flaxman, Miss—Turkish girl
Flaxman, Miss Alice—Peasant girl
Fletcher, Dr.—Royal Arch Druid
Fletcher, Mr. A. F.—Rob Roy
Fletcher, Mrs.—Night
Fletcher, Mr. J. M., Queen of Bavaria
Flemmore, Miss, Attendant Star of Night
Flemmore, Miss Lina—Flower-girl
Flockhart, Councillor—Corporation uniform
Flockhart, Mrs.—Marie Antoinette
Florence, Miss J.—Andalusian girl
Flower, Miss—Tyrolese lady
Flower, Miss E.—Zingara
Folk, Mr.—Venetian nobleman
Ford, Mr. F. T.—Past and present
Ford, Mr., Maurice
Ford, Mr. F., Frank Osbaldistone
Ford, Mrs. W., court dress, George III.
Forde, Mrs. J. M., Elly O'Connor
Forsyth, Mr. G.—Cardinal Wolsey
Forwood, Mr., Swedish gentleman of eighteenth century
Forwood, Mrs. C. R., Swedish lady of eighteenth century
Foobery, Mr. J.—Turkish merchant
Foskey, Mr. J.—Swiss peasant
Foster, Mr. C., Sicilian gentleman
Foster, Mrs. C., Spanish lady
Foster, Miss, Swiss peasant girl
Fox, Mr. W., Gustavus
Fox, Mrs. W., Elven
Francis, Mr. C.—Boating costume
Francis, Mr. H.—Peasant of Bretagne
Francis, Mr. J.—Boating costume
Francis, Mrs. J. G.—Fancy dress
Francis, the Hon. J. G.—Fancy dress
Francis, Mrs. H.—The Morning Star
Francis, Miss A.—Fancy dress
Francis, Miss M.—Fancy dress
Frankenberg, Mr.—German sailor
Frankenberg, Mrs.—Red, white, and blue
Franklyn, Mr. F. B., Yachtsman
Franklyn, Mrs. F. B., Russian peasant
Fraser, Mr. A. W., Neapolitan
Fraser, Mr. Simon—Iago
Fraser, Mr. W.—Sir John Falstaff
Fraser, Mr. W., Togodaboine, chief of the Druids
Fraser, Mrs. A. W., Fancy
Fraser, Mrs Simon—Sultina
Freeman, Miss, Night
Freeman, Mrs. G.—A monk
Fulton, Mr. G.—A monk
Fulton, Mrs. G.—A Polish lady
Furnell, Mr.—Uniform
Furnell, Mrs.—Christmas
Fykeman, Mr. H.—Spanish inquisitor

GALBRAITH, Mr D. S., Freemason
Galbraith, Mrs. D. S., Night
Ganson, Mr. David, the Cynic
Gane, Mr., a Spark from China
Gansce, Mr. B., Garibaldi
Gardner, Mr. A., Gustavus III.
Gardner, Mr. S., Mexican
Garrard, Mr. W., Monk
Garrett, Mr. R., Volunteer artilleryman
Garrett, Mrs. R., Highland lady
Garton, Mr. J., Duke of York
Garton, Mrs. J., Duchess of Orleans
Gatehouse, Mr. James, Roman consul

Gatehouse, Miss, lady of Finland
Gatehouse, Miss P., Flower-girl
Gault, Mr., member of the Spanish Inquisition
Gault, Mrs., Swiss lady
Gawson, Mr., Joe Brown
Geelong, Mayor of, Highland costume
Geoghegan, Miss, Odalisle
George, Mr. Hugh, courtier of the time of Queen Elizabeth
George, Mr. J., Volunteer drummer
George, Mrs. J., Swiss peasant
Gerschel, Mrs. Louis, Spanish gitana
Gerschel, Mr., German peasant
Gibbs, Mr., Mountford, gentleman of the reign of Charles I.
Gibbs, Mrs. Mountford, Mrs. Masham
Gibson, Mr. Arthur, Don Arturo
Gibson, Mrs., Spanish lady
Giderson, Mr., chalhopper
Gill, Mr. Jas., court dress, George III.
Gill, Mr., military officer
Gillbee, Surgeon-Major, uniform
Gillbee, Miss, Night
Gillbee, Mr. H., artillery officer
Gilbert, Mr. W. B., an attaché of the Court of Woolloomooloo
Gilbert, Mrs. W. B., La Vivandière
Gilbert, Mrs., red, white and blue
Gilchrist, Mr. A., boating costume
Gillies, Mr. E. F., Monk of the Screw
Gillies, Mrs. E. F., Swiss peasant
Gillies, Mr. D., gentleman of the next century
Gilloghby, Mr., a monk
Gilloghby, Mrs., black domino
Girdle-tone, Dr., Anglo-Saxon
Glansford, Mr. M., Italian noble
Glassford, Mrs. M., Havilah
Gleddon, Miss, Dolly Varden
Glen, Mr. W. H., Highland chief
Glen, Mrs. W. H., Highland lady
Glennon, Miss, Flora
Glynn, Mr., courtier of ye olden time
Goldberg, Mr. Abraham, King Charles II. of England
Goldberg, Mrs. A., Hedwig, wife of William Tell
Goldstein, Mr., Zerdishabel
Goldstein, Mrs., Paquerette
Gordon, Mr. G. H., cricketer of New South Wales eleven
Gordon, Miss, Dolly Mayflower
Gordon, Mr., Albert Cricket Club, Sydney
Gotch, Mr., Indian sirdar
Gotch, Mrs., Zuleika
Goulstone, Mr. J. P., corps diplomatique
Goyder, Mr. F. C., English huntsman
Goyder, Mrs. F. C., Annie Laurie
Graham, Miss, Night, or enchantress
Graham, Hon. J., Consul of Italy
Graham, Dr., doctor of Melbourne University
Graham, Mrs., court lady, time George II.
Graham, Miss, morning star
Graham, Miss K., Polish peasant
Graham, Mrs., Thisbe
Grahame, Mrs. E., December
Grahame, Mr. E., uniform, original V. R.
Grant, Mr. G. A., Asa Trenchard
Grant, Mr. D., a huntsman

Grant, Hon. J. M., evening dress
Grant, Mrs. J. M., evening dress
Grant, Miss, Matilda, heiress of Bohsby
Grant, Mr. James, Highland chief
Grant, Mrs. J., Scotch shepherdess
Grant, Miss, South Carolinian
Grassie, Mr. J. C., friar
Grasse, Mrs. J. C., Spanish lady
Gray, Mrs., Peruvian lady
Greene, Mr. R., foxhunter
Greene, Mrs., Spanish peasant
Greenwood, Mr., Louis XIII.
Greenwood, Miss, Spring
Gregson, Mrs. W., Heartsease
Greig, Mr. W. J., Turk
Gresson, Mrs., Castilian lady
Grey, Dr. de, Victorian volunteer
Grice, Mr. John, University student
Grice, Mr. J., Carlo Martini
Grice, Mrs., lady of fifteenth century
Grieve, Mr. R., smuggler
Griffin, Miss, Morning
Griffith, Mr. C., Egyptian
Grinwood, Mr. Thomas, Hungarian officer
Grinwood, Miss, flower-girl
Groves, Mr. G. E., court costume
Gunston, Mr. W. A., Polish gent.
Gunston, Mr., gentleman of the reign of George IV.
Gunston, Mrs., lady of the reign of George II.
Gurnet, Dr. J. W., meister mason
Gurnet, Mrs. J. W., Genoese lady
Gurner, Mr. H. F., Russian peasant
Gurner, Mrs. L. H., L'Africaine

HACKETT, Mr. C. P., evening costume
Hackett, Miss, Spanish lady
Hadden, Dr., Rob Roy
Hadden, Mr. F. W., a gentleman of the reign of George II.
Hadfield, Lieut. F. O., uniform
Hadley, Mr. T. H., sailor on shore
Hadley, Mr. T. H., Pomona
Haig, Dr., the sultan
Haig, Mrs., Undine
Haine, Mr. G. B., gentleman of the eighteenth century
Hailes, Mrs. G. B., lady of the seventeenth century
Haines, Mr. C., Zouave
Halfey, Mr. J., Circassian chief
Halfey, Mrs. J., Marie of Guise
Hafton, Mr. J., Garibaldi
Hall, Mr. A. G., huntsman
Hall, Miss, Britannia
Hall, Mr. J. L., capitaine aux Chasseurs d'Afrique
Hall, Mr. J. L., John Perrybingle
Hall, Mr. J. L., Springtime
Hall, Mr. ..., officer Royal Victorian Volunteer Cavalry
Halford, Prof., Doctor of Medicine, St. Andrew's University
Halford, Mrs., fancy dress
Hallenstein, Mr. Michael, German nobleman
Hallenstein, Mrs. Michael, French peasant girl
Hallenstein, Mrs. M., French peasant girl
Hancock, Miss, Neapolitan peasant

Handfield, Lieutenant F. O., officer
Handfield, Mrs., Spanish peasant
Hanna, Mr. P., Admiral Cochrane
Hanna, Mrs. P., Rose Bradwardine
Hanbury, Mr. O. L., a jockey
Hardy, Mrs., Polish lady
Hardy, Dr., dress of surgeon-major of the Dunedin Artillery
Harker, Mr. R., Sailor
Harker, Mr. Robert, court dress, time George IV.
Harker, Mr. George
Harker, Miss, Helena
Harnett, Miss A., French milkmaid
Harriman, Mrs. B. C., Rosa Devoniensis
Harriman, Mr. B. C., Devonshire Dumpling of 1860
Harrington, Lieutenant J. W., Lieutenant 14th Regiment
Harris, Mrs. A., court lady, time Louis XV.
Harris, Mr. A., Spanish muleteer
Harris, Mr. H. P., French peasant
Harris, Mrs. H. F., Spanish lady of rank
Harrison, Mrs., Portia
Harrison, Captain, naval officer
Hart, Mr. L. H., Greek nobleman
Hart, Miss, Maritana
Hart, Mr. I., Count of Monte Christo
Hart, Mrs. Isaac, lady of rank, reign Louis XV.
Hart, Mr. J. S., captain of Victorian Rifles
Hart, Miss, red, white, and blue
Hart, Miss, Donnadi Borabetto
Hart, Mrs. J., lady in black
Hart, Mr. H. J., Royal Victorian Yeomanry Cavalry
Hart, Mr. M. H., Mephistopheles
Hart, Mr. A., Gretiano
Hart, Miss Jane, Polish lady
Harvey, Mr. R., Knight Templar
Harvey, Mrs. R., a Flemish lady of rank
Harvey, Miss, Liberty
Harwood, Mr., Hubert de Burgh
Harwood, Mrs., Lady Percy
Hackett, Miss, Night
Hay, Mr. James, Baron Strathspey
Hay, Mrs. J., lady of the eighteenth century
Hayman, Mr., Tyrolese huntsman
Hayward, Mr., a cricketer
Hayward, Mrs., Mrs. Candour
Hazzard, Miss, French court dress, 1788
Heales, Mrs., Spanish lady
Healey, Mr. Thomas, Ulrico
Heath, Captain, officer of Victorian Volunteer Artillery
Heath, Miss, Red Riding Hood
Hein, Mr. Robert, military officer
Henderson, Mrs. M., Anne Chute, opera of Lily of Killarney
Henderson, Mr., Swiss peasant
Henningham, Mrs., Russian peasant
Henningham, Mr., Monk of the Screw
Henriques, Mr. C., Count Alvarez
Henry, Mr. J. S., minister of marine
Henry, Mr. J. S., Marquise de Lambelle
Henty, Hon. S. G.
Henty, Miss E., Asterope

Henty, Miss, Stella
Henty, Mr. T., swell stockman
Henty, Mr. H., gentleman of the time of Charles I.
Henty, Mrs. H., Twilight
Hepburn, Mr. T., Count Rodolphe
Hepburn, Mrs., the mother of the Gracchi
Hepburn, Miss J., Juliet
Hepburn, Miss, Lucrezia Borgia
Hepburn, Miss A., Rebecca
Herald, Mr. D., Antipholus of Syracuse
Herald, Miss, Ceres
Herald, Miss L., Spanish lady
Herring, Mr., Friar Lawrence
Herne, Miss A., Summer
Hetherington, Mr. James, Israfel
Hewett, Mr., N.S.W. cricketer
Heymanson, Miss, Princess Battigani
Heymanson, Mr. W., courtier time of Charles I.
Henty, Mr. L., English gentleman
Henty, Mrs. E., Night
Hick, Mr. Wm., monk
Hick, Mrs. Wm., gipsy
Hickey, Mr., Pierrot
Hickey, Mrs., Spanish lady
Hickey, Mr. James, St. Bris
Hickinbotham, Mr. W., Knight of Ava
Hicks, Mr., Greek costume
Hicks, Mrs., Polish lady
Highett, the Hon. Wm., fancy dress
Highett, Miss, Empress Maria Theresa, 1747
Hildreth, Mr. J. H., sailor
Hildreth, Mrs. J. L., Christmas
Hill, Mr. W., Sir John Falstaff
Hill, Mr., Algerian soldier
Hill, Mrs. W., Victorian flower-girl
Hill, Mrs. W. E., La Katarina
Hinds, Mr., Garibaldi
Hinds, Miss, Greek shepherdess
Hotson, Mrs., walking dress George III.
Hockin, jun., Mr., Kokoloeum
Hockin, Miss, Gipsy (Spanish)
Hodgkinson, Mr. C., French boatman
Hodgkinson, Mrs. C., court lady time of Queen Anne
Hodgkinson, Miss, Polish maiden
Hodgkinson, Mr. Percy, Steeplechaser
Hodgson, Mr. A. G., Russian peasant
Hodilnett, Miss E., Ceres
Hodilnett, Miss B., Red Riding Hood
Hood, Mr. J. H., Matelot Français
Hood, Mr. J. W., Doctor Bartleus
Hood, Mrs., Mercedes
Hood, Mr., Robin Hood
Hood, Mrs., lady, court of Henry IV.
Hood, Mr. W. H., Turkish noble
Hood, Miss, lady of the reign of Charles le Chauve
Hopkins, Mr., militia officer
Hopkins, Miss, Night
Hoppe, Mrs., The Enchantress
Horne, Deputy-Com.-Gen., uniform
Horne, Mr., lieutenant of the Waikato Regiment
Horne, Miss, White Rose of York
Horne, Miss Edith, Red Rose of Lancaster
Howe, Miss, Flora M'Donald

The Civic Fancy Dress Ball.

Hosie, Mr James, Russian officer
Hosworth, Mr., Turkish nobleman
Howarth, Mrs., Spanish gipsy
Howse, Mr. S., Mexican noble
Howse, Mrs. S., Zuleika
Hughes, Mr., gentleman of rank, fifteenth century
Hughes, Alderman, official costume
Hughes, Mrs., Catherine of Arragon
Hughes, Mr. C., uniform
Hughes, Mr. W., Blazer
Hughes, Mrs. W., Night
Hughes, Sir C. J., military costume
Hughes, Mrs. C. J., Pierrette
Hunter, Miss, Aurora
Humphrey, Mr. F., his grandfather
Humphrey, Mrs. F., Zingara
Humphries, Mr. W. B., a student of the Druidical law
Hunt, Dr., uniform, volunteer officer
Hurst, Mr. W., Andrastrom
Hurst, Miss, Starlight
Husband, Mr. W. H., student
Husband, Mrs. W. H., Sardinian peasant girl
Hutchison, Mr. D., Lord Townshedy
Hyams, Mr., Will Watch
Hyams, Miss, Zauberflöte, Queen of Night
Hyland, Mr. C., Chinese prince
Hyland, Mrs. F., Lady of the Court of George III.
Hyland, Miss, Bavaria peasant
Hyman, Mr. M., Prussian officer
Hyman, Mrs. M., Sardinian peasant
Hyndman, Mr. W., sergeant V.V. Engineers
Hyndman, Mrs., Spanish lady

IEVERS, Mr. William, Vincentio
Iffla, Miss, a-wee-girl
Iffla, Mrs F., Spanish lady
Inglis, Mr. T. A. F., gentleman, time George III.
Ireland, Mr. T. C., Old Virginia
Ireland, Mr. De Courcy, Matador
Ireland, Miss S., May
Ireland, Mr. R., Circassian prince
Ireland, Hon. R. D., United Irishman
Ireland, Mr. R. D., Spanish lady
Ireland, Miss, June
Ireland, Mr. J., Yeomanry Cavalry officer
Irvine, Mr., uniform
Irvine, Mr. W F., Knight Templar
Irvine, Mrs. E. A., Zuleika
Isaacs, Mr. H., madress, Prince of Wales Cavalry
Isaacs, Mrs. W. B., Catherine, Empress of Russia
Isaacs, Mr. W. B., Garibaldian uniform
Isaacs, Mr. A. M., Earl of Leicester
Isaacs, Mrs., Mason Lescault

JACK, Mr., Italian brigand
Jack, Mrs., Finland lady
James, Dr. E. M., Dr. Pangloss
James, Mrs. F., Swiss peasant
James, Mr. W. Wilbrake
James, Mr. J. B.
James, Mr. T. B., gentleman of reign of Charles II.
Jarvis, Miss, Clarissa Harlowe
Jeffray, Mr. R. J., Russian effendi

Jeffray, Mrs. R. J., Norwegn. villager
Jennings, Mr., volunteer of the nineteenth century
Jeremy, Mr., Turk
Jeremy, Mrs., English gipsy
Jeremy, Miss, Ophelia
Jervis, Mr. W., Attorney-General of Timbuctoo
Jervis, Miss, Portuguese peasant
Jervis, Mr., captain Hon. Artillery Corps, London
Johnstone, Mr. R de H., Highland costume
Johnstone, Miss, Greek shepherdess
Johnston, jun., Mr., Sultan Scudder
Johnston, Mr. W., Aroun al-Raschid
Johnston, Mr. W., Monk of the Screw
Johnston, Mrs. W., lady of time of Commonwealth
Johnson, Miss, Polish girl
Johnson, Mr. J., Summer
Johnson, Mr. G. R., Knight Templar
Jones, Mr. C. E., Sergeant Buzfuz
Jones, Mrs. C. E., Night
Jones, Mr. John, Garibaldi
Jones, Mrs. John, Esther Gruzebrook
Jones, Miss, Parquerette
Jones, Mr. W. B., David, high priest, court of Prince Alfred
Jones, Mrs. W. B., Summer
Jones, Mr. C. G., Don Carlos
Jordan, Miss, Folly
Jordan, Miss Lizzie, Rosalind
Jordan, Mrs., Madame de la Vallière
Joseph, Miss J., Norma
Joseph, Mr Walter, the Sultan
Joseph, Mr Alfred, Richmond
Joshua, Mr J. M., cordelier
Joske, Mr. Paul, Don Pablo
Joske, Mr. A., Friar Tuck
Jude, Mr. A., Polish gentleman
Jude, Mrs A., Polish lady

KATZENSTEIN, Mr. I., court dress
Katzenstein, Mr. J., Friar Joseph
Katzenstein, Mrs. J., Maid of Saragossa
Kavanagh, Mrs., Bassigrappo
Kavanagh, Mr., Je ne was quoi
Kearney, Mrs., Moorish gipsy
Kelleher, Mr., Lazarillo, Marchese
Kelleher, Miss, La Figlia del Reggimento
Kelson, Mr., Hubert
Kennon, Mr. B., Cassio
Kennon, Mrs. B., Polish lady
Kennedy, Mr. C., Dick Turpin
Kennedy, Mrs., Hungarian dress
Kennedy, Miss Marian, Adine, Elixir of Love
Keogh, Mr. E., a cricketer
Keogh, Master, a cricketer
Keogh, Mr. S.
Keogh, Mr. T., Venetian, 16th cent.
Keogh, Mrs. E., Lady Nithsdale
Keon, Miss, flower-girl
Keon, Miss M., Forget-me-not
Kerr, Miss, Lady Isabel Vane
Keys, Miss, Swiss peasant
Killey, Mr., Metropolitan Artillery
Kirby, Miss, Night
King, Miss M. J., Spanish lady
King, Mr. W. C., Arab merchant
King, Mr. M. L., Royal Arch Mason
King, Miss, Chinese lady

King, Mr. Stephen, captain of the Dublin City Militia
King, Mr. James, page, 10th century
King, Mr. C., Cornstalk
King, Mr. A. S., Indian costume
King, Mr. T. J., officer of artillery
King, Mr. John, gentleman time of George III.
King, Miss, souleste
King, Mr. J. C., an antiquated cootume
Kinnimont, Mr. D. S., French nobleman, sixteenth century
Kinnimont, Miss J., Swiss lady
Kirkpatrick, Mr. W. M., Foxhunter
Kirkpatrick, Mrs. W. M., Galiyanni
Kirkby, Miss, Linda di Chamouni
Kirby, Miss, village coquette
Klemin, Mr., Hamlet
Klemm, Mrs., Spanish lady
Knight, Mr. J. G., Sir Thos. Clifford
Knight, Mrs. J. G., Miss. Ro—aster
Knight, Miss, Night
Knox, Miss Gerke, peasant girl
Koch, Mr. J. A. B., Swiss peasant
Koch, Miss B., Swiss girl
Kong Meng, Mr., Mandarin
Kong Meng, Mrs., Grecian lady

LABERTOUCHE, Mr., Duc de Nevers
Labertouche, Mrs., Marguerite
Lacy, Mr., Hans Skeldt
Langaud, Mr. W. B., volunteer rifleman, 1863
Lamond, Mr. W. B., Daily Varden
Lansdale, Mr. A., medical student
Lane, Mrs. W., Countess de Grignon
Lane, Miss, Undine
Lane, Mr G., Queen's Own
Lane, Mrs. G., Titania
Lang, Mr. Gideon
Lang, Mrs. Gideon, Esmeralda
Lang, Mr. W., Armenna
Lang, Mr. Matthew, Lockelsy
Langan, Mr. P. J., Medus
Langan, Mr. P. J., Hulon
Langford, Miss, Columbia
Langhorne, Mr. A., Mr. Brietless
Langridge, Mr. G. D., P.O. Manchester Unity
Langridge, Mrs. G. D., French grisette
Langton, Mr. E., gentleman of the nineteenth century
Langton, Mrs. E., morris-dancer
Langtree, Mr H., Oliver Goldsmith
Langtree, Mr. C. W., Turkish cavalry officer
Langtree, Mr. O., General Fairfax
Laurence, Mr., N.S.W. volunteer
Laurens, Mrs. J., lady of Normandy
Laurens, Mr. J., Hungarian
Law, Mrs. J. M., lady of rank, time fifteenth century
Law, Mr. Robert, yachtsman
Law, Mr. W., a Lowland farmer, 1660
Lawes, Mr., King of Clubs
Lawes, Mrs., Twilight
Lawes, Miss, Bernese peasant
Lawrence, Mr. O. V., Spanish lady
Lawrence, Miss, lady of Finland
Lawrence, Mr. W. French mariner, sixteenth century
Laurence, Capt. J., Admiral Duncan

Lawrence, Mrs. James, Christmas
Lawrence, Mr. G. V., Bachelor of Medicine, Melbourne University
Lawrence, Mr. J. B., the Grand Turk
Latham, Miss, peasant, 17th century
Lazarus, Mr. Isaac, Garibaldian
Lazarus, Mrs. Isaac, Marie de Bolos, period of 1500
Lazarus, Mr. L. H., Tyrolese peasant
Lazarus, Mrs. Samuel, court lady of the seventeenth century
Lazarus, Mr., Elvino
Leslie, Mr., a guardian of the peace
Learmonth, Major, staff officer
Learmonth, Mr. A., uniform
Lecky, Mr. G., Neapolitan fisherman
Lee, Mr. David, Robin Hood
Lee, Mr. Harcourt, uniform of the Victorian Volunteer Light Horse
Lees, Mr., brigand
Legge, Lieut., officer R. A.
Lempriere, Mrs., Turkish costume
Lempriere, Dr., Bedouin Arab
Lempriere, Miss, evening star
Leopold, Mr. G. Slim Jim
Lepelletier, Ensign, 14th Regiment
Leplastrier, Mr. W. H., Edgar, *King Lear*
Leplastrier, Mr., Claudio, *Measure for Measure*
Leplastrier, Mrs. L. H., Neapolitan lady
Levey, Mr. G. C., Captain Crosstree
Levey, Mrs. G. C., Proserpine
Levi, Mr. N., an abbot
Levi, Mr., Don Alvara
Levy, Mr. A., postilion
Levy, Mr. H., Mameluke
Levy, Mrs. Goodman, Octavia
Levy, Mr. Goodman, a page
Lewis, Mr., Uniform
Lewis, Mr. L. L., Spanish matador
Lewis, Mr. L. L., Mrs. Page, reign of Henry IV.
Lewis, Mrs. C. J., Neapolit. peasant
Lewis, Mr. E., Neapolitan peasant
Lewis, Mr. J. P., Spanish muleteer
Lewis, Mrs. J. P., Spanish gitana
Lewis, Miss, Turkish lady
Lewis, Mr. G., hermit
Lewis, Mr. G., volunteer artilleryman
Lewis, Mr. W., improved volunteer
Lewis, Mrs. S., Neapolitan peasant
Liddle, Mr., Masaniello
Liddle, Mrs., Spanish lady
Lightfoot, Miss, Bohemian gipsy
Lightfoot, Mr. E., Dalmatian chief
Lilienfeld, Dr., academic dress, W.D.
Linacre, Councillor, city councillor
Linacre, Mrs., Athenian lady
Lindsay, Mrs., lady in winter
Lindsay, Mr., Franciscan monk
Lingham, Miss, evening star
Lipscombe, Mrs., fancy dress
Lissignol, Mr., French uniform
Lister, Mr. Charles, the debardeur
Lister, Mrs. Charles, Night
Liston, Mr. John, Turkish officer
Littlewood, Mrs. H. T., Neapolitan lady
Littlewood, Mr. H. T., Neapolitan noble
Livingstone, Mrs., vivandière
Llewelyn, Mr. E., Navarain
Lloyd, Mr., Waverley

Logan, Mr. T. G., Garibaldian
Logan, Mrs. T. G., fancy dress
Loier, Mr. A. E., yachtsman
Lone, Mr. J. E., Ellen of Mar
Long, Mr. F., medical student of University of Moscow
Long, Mr., gentleman, Queen Elizabeth's time
Long, Mr. H. J., Bow Bowline
Long, Mrs. H. J., Veroine Embusschee
Lord, Miss, Polly
Lord, Mr. S. P., nestador
Lord, Mrs S. P., lady of Georgia
Lorimer, Mr. J., yachting costume
Love, Mr. A., one of the Light Brigade
Lowe, Miss, Spring
Lowe, Mr. R., Garibaldian officer
Lowe, Mrs R., lady of last century
Lucas, Mrs. C. J., Bertha, from "Le Prophete"
Lucas, Mr. C. J., student of Glasgow University
Lucas, Capt. W., field-marshal
Ludwick, Mr., official costume
Ludwick, Miss, May Queen
Luhaan, Mr., Turkish civilian
Luhaan, Mrs., Lady of Medeah Algiers
Lydiard, Mr., monk
Lydiard, Mrs., lady of honour, time of Queen Mary
Lyell, Miss, Annot Lyle
Lyell, Mrs. A., Night
Lyell, Mr. A., Highland costume, clan Stuart
Lynch, Miss, Lurline
Lynch, Mr. W., Serjeant Buzfuz
Lyons, Mr. Isaac, Punch
Lyons, Mrs. Isaac, Queen of Diamonds
Lyons, Master H., officer
Lyons, Mr. David, gentleman in black
Lyons, Miss, Euterpe
Lyons, Mr. S., Ophelia
Lyons, Mr. S., Peter Spyke
Lyttleton, Mr. T. H., Victorian police uniform
Lyttleton, Mrs. T. H., Morning

MACDONALD, Miss, gipsy
Macgregor, Mr. S., Highlander
Macgregor, Miss, Night
Mackenzie, Mr. Jno., Russian citizen
Mackie, Miss, Tyrolese lady
Mackinnon, Mr. John M. M., Highland fancy dress
Macklin, Mr., Charles Surface
Macpherson, —
Macpherson, Mrs. J. M., Jeannie Deans
Macquarrie, Mr., sailor
MacRae, Miss K., Greek girl
Madden, Mr., Melshiquam
Madden, Mr. D., uniform of the Ballarat Light Horse
Madden, Miss, Dinorah
Madden, Mr. F., Hachem Assem
Madden, Mr. W., Elvino
Madden, Mr. J., Court d'Artois
Madden, Mr. J., sen., member of the V.R.C.
Madden, Mr. James, volunteer
Maguire, Mr. J. F., Darnley
Maguire, Mrs. J. F., Katarina
Maister, Mr. W. I., man-of-war's man
Mallam, Mr. W. B., M. Davis, Esq.

Malleson, Mr. A. B., Corsican chief
Malleson, Mrs. A. B., lady of the reign of Louis XIV.
Mann, Miss Rosa, gitana
Mann, Miss, Turkish lady
Mannens, Miss T. F., Marie Antoinette
Manton, Mr. A. B., Louis XIII.
Marks, Mrs. Henry, Queen Elinor
Manton, Miss M., Punch
Manton, Miss Jessie, Dolly Varden
Manton, Miss Lucy, a peasant girl
Maplestone, Mr. H., English officer
Maplestone, Mrs. H., lady of the court of Charles I.
Marden, Mr. G.
Marie, Mr. I., French sailor
Marks, Mr. H., Bugler in Scotch regiment
Marks, Miss, Ann Hathaway (Shakspeare's wife)
Marks, Mr. C., Ancient Druid
Marks, Mr. C., Lady of rank, reign of Charles I.
Marks, Miss, Maritana
Marks, Mr. Lionel, a Garibaldian
Marks, Mr. Henry, Spanish cavalier
Marks, Mr. B., Doge of Venice
Marks, Mrs. E., Phrosine
Marks, Mr. J., Count Almaviva
Marks, Mr. Jos., sergt. of volunteers
Marks, Mr. A., an Oxonian
Marks, Mrs. A., Cleopatra
Marks, Mr. Jos., Prince Chas. Stuart
Marks, Miss, La Katarina, *Crown Diamonds*
Marks, Miss, village girl
Marks, Mrs. Mark, naval officer
Marks, Mrs. Mark, lady of the court
Martin, Mr. John, volunteer rifleman
Martin, Mr., Trin. Hall B.C.
Martin, Mrs., Fanchonnette
Martin, Miss, La Papillon
Martin, Miss, dame, sixteenth century
Martin, Mr. C. B., Earl of Warwick
Martin, Mr. P. J., Major Vol. Artillery (undress uniform)
Martin, Mrs., Oddity
Martin, Mr. T. J., muleteer
Martin, Mr. L. J., Fra Diavolo
Martin, Mrs. L. J., lady of the time of George III.
Martin, Mr. S., major of V.V. force
Martin, Mrs. S., lady of the seventeenth century
Martin, Mr. A., naval uniform
Martin, Mrs. A., Swiss costume
Marwood, Mr. Matt., Master Thomas Randall
Marwood, Mrs. M., lady of seventeenth century
Masters, Mr. S., uniform
Masters, Mrs. S., fancy dress
Matheson, Mr. John, court dress, in reign of George III.
Matheson, Mrs. John, court dress in reign of George III.
Matheson, Miss, shepherdess, after Watteau
Matthews, Miss Mary, Summer
Mathewson, Miss Flora, French dress in reign of Louis XV.
Matthews, Mr. B., French officer in reign of Louis XV.
Matthews, Mrs. B., lady fm. antipodes
Matthews, Mr. G., Dr. Malatesta

Matthews, Mr. J., officer of Victorian Volunteers
May, Mr. Thomas, Turk
Mayor of East Collingwood, P.G.M., M.U.I.O.O.F.
Mayor of Hotham, gentleman of the present century
Mayor of St. Kilda, artillery officer
Mayor of Prahran, gentleman of the seventeenth century
Mayor of Belfast, a cricketer
Mayor of Adelaide, medical student
Meanham, Mr. A. D., officer in the United States army
Meaney, Mrs., lady of the eighteenth century
Meaney, Miss, Polish lady
Meaney, Miss M. A., Virginia
Meaney, Miss H., Greek shepherdess
Mearns, Mr. Geo., a debardeur
Mearns, Mrs Geo., Spring
Mearns, Mr. R. S., cavalier of the sixteenth century
Mearns, Mrs. R. S., Morning Dew
Medlicott, Mrs., Cassio
Medlicott, Mrs., Evening
Meissner, Mr. O., Fra Diavolo
Mellish, Mr. Richard, courtier of Charles II.'s reign
Mellish, Mrs., court lady of Charles II.'s reign
Menzies, Mr. A., Highland gentleman
Merrett, Mrs. S. T., Night
Merrifield, Mrs. O., Morning
Messiner, Mrs. O., Zerlina, from Fra Diavolo
Messiter, Miss, a gleaner
Michael, Miss, Red Riding Hood
Michie, Mrs., fancy dress
Michie, Miss Janet, a Prussian peasant of the Bismarck era
Middleton, Mr. T. M., Ruy Gomez
Middleton, Mrs., Polish lady
Mier, Mr. F., Sandhurst V.F.B. full dress
Mier, Mr. B., councellor of ancient date
Mier, Miss, Australian damsel
Millar, Mr. D. H., gentleman of the time of Queen Elizabeth
Millar, Mr. B. C., court gentleman of the reign of George III.
Millar, Mrs. B. C., Queen of Spades
Miller, Mr. W., fireman
Miller, Mrs. Wm., Snowstorm
Miller, Mr. Albert, Czarovitz Alexis
Miller, Miss, Flora
Miller, Mr. K. L., Psycho
Miller, Mr. N. M., Knight of the East and West
Miller, Mr. Jas., Garibaldian
Miller, Mr., naval officer
Miller, Mr., Sir Walter Raleigh
Miller, Mr., fancy volunteer uniform
Miller, Mr., English gipsy girl
Miller, Mr. Edward, Comte di Luna
Millish, Mr. and Mrs.
Mills, Mr. Thomas, Master Mason
Mills, Mrs. Thomas, Amphitrite
Mills, Mr. Thomas, jun., smuggler
Milne, Mr. G. M., Macduff
Milne, Mrs. George M., Urania
Milton, Mr. J. R., William Tell
Milton, Mrs. J. R., Dame Marion Milton, 1530

Mitchell, Mr. M. A., gent. in black
Mitchell, Miss, Swiss girl
Mitchell, Mr. M., Fra Diavolo
Molesworth, Mr.
Moncrieff, Mrs., an Arcadian peasant girl
Montefiore, Mr. E. L., Abd-el-Kader
Montefiore, Mrs. E. L., lady of the thirteenth century
Montefiore, Mr. A., Menotti Garibaldi
Montgomery, Mr. W., Lavater
Moodie, Miss M. S. Robertson, lady time 1614
Moody, Major L. A., officer
Moody, Miss, Zorlina, Fra Diavolo
Mooney, Miss, evening costume
Morley, Mrs. W., La Papillon
Moore, Dr., capt.-surgeon R.V.V.A.
Moore, Mr. H. Byron, Vondhiri de Madagascar
Moore, Mr. F. F., Peter the Hermit
Moorly, Mr. F. A., Massaniello
Moore, Mr. Geo., Croatian costume
Morrah, Mr., Court dress
Morrah, Mrs. Colleen Bawn
Morrah, Mrs. A., Spanish lady
Morris, Mr. Thomas, morris-dancer
Morris, Mrs. Thomas, Mistress Page
Mortley, Mr., Jose
Morton, Mr. W., monk
Morton, Miss, Lurline
Morton, Mrs. A. H., cavalier of time of Charles II.
Morton, Miss F., Galatea
Morton, Miss H., Maid of Athens
Moselly, Mr. H., Gobb
Moselly, Mrs. H., Lisette
Moses, Mr. Hyam, military officer
Moses, Mrs. Hyam, court lady of the eighteenth century
Moss, Mr. Mark, Turkish nobleman
Moss, Mrs. Mark, Spanish gitana
Moss, Mr. Moton, Captain of the St. Josef
Moss, Mrs. Moton, a Spanish lady
Moss, Mr., Diana
Moss, Miss, Morning
Motherwell, Miss E., English peasant
Motherwell, Miss, Spanish lady
Motherwell, Dr., a Kabyle chief
Moual, Miss, Lady of the Lake
Mowbray, Councillor
Moule, Mr., cavalier of time of Charles II.
Moule, Mrs., Roman costume
Moyle, Mr. T. H., Mercutio
Mueller, Dr. F., U.S., German cavalier
Muir, Mr. W.P., Turkish ambassador
Mullaly, Mr., Spanish gentleman
Mullaly, Mrs., Arabella Stuart
Munday, Mr. John, artillery officer
Munday, Mrs. J., Lady Jane Seymour
Munro, Mr. David, Duke of Aranza
Munro, Mr. Lawrence, muleteer
Murray, Mr. J. G., oriental prince
Murray, Mr. A., hornpipe
Murray, Mrs. A., court dress of time of Henry IV. of France
Murray, Mrs. W. G., Autumn
Murray, Mr. W. G., student of the University of Glasgow
Murray, Miss, Roman lady
Murphy, Hon. Sir F., mayor, 2nd Volunteers

Murphy, Lady, lady of court of Francis I., 1521
Murphy, Miss, Starlight
Murphy, Mrs., Donna Ingracia
Murphy, Miss, Spanish lady
Murphy, Hon. H. M., collegian
Murphy, Mrs. H. M., flower-girl
Murphy, Mr. E., Zouave
Murphy, Mr. E. J., Turkish officer
Myers, Mr., Hussar officer
Myring, Mrs., Harvest
M'Bean, Councillor, official costume
M'Carthy, Dr. C., University costume, doctor of medicine
M'Combie, Miss, La Fille du Regiment
M'Combie, Mr. A. G., Turkish noble
M'Coy, Professor, a foreigner, age uncertain
M'Coy, Mrs., court dress of the time of Chas. II.
M'Coy, Miss, Christabelle
M'Coy, Mr. F. H., Lord Chief Justice of the Common Pleas in his younger days
M'Crea, Dr. W., Royal Arch Mason
M'Crea, Mrs. W., Night
M'Crea, Miss, gipsy
M'Cullagh, Miss, Night
M'Donald, Mr. Jas., Count Rodolpho
M'Donald, Mrs. Jas., Australian lady
M'Donald, Miss, Colleen Bawn
M'Donald, Mr. W., Hungarian peasant
M'Donald, Miss, gipsy
M'Donald, Mr. E., Charles II.
M'Donald, Mr. gentleman, 1750
M'Donald, Mr. F., Pantaloon
M'Donald, Mr. A., Old Marcel
M'Donald, Miss, Polish lady
M'Donald, Mr. A., General, U.S. army
M'Donnell, Mrs. A., Spanish gipsy
M'Donnell, Mr. T. M., gentleman of the time of Charles II.
M'Donnell, Miss, May Queen
M'Dougall, Mr. C. F., Swiss peasant
M'Dougall, Mr. A., Sir L. O'Trigger
M'Dougal, Mr. D., Hungarian costume
M'Ewan, Mr. J. T. H., King Edward VI.
M'Ewan, Mr. James, Victorian rifleman
M'Farlane, Mr. A., Council
M'Gee, Mr. John, member of Royal Yacht Club
M'Gee, Mrs. John, red, white, and blue
M'Gill, Mr., infantry officer in mess uniform
M'Grath, Mr., Kentucky farmer
M'Grath, Mrs., Rebecca
M'Gregor, Mrs. John., Summer
M'Guire, Mr. R., Marquis of Waterford
M'Hugh, Mr. P. H., Boatswain Pipes
M'Kay, Mr., Captain Heath
M'Kay, Mr. J., Chief of the M'Kays
M'Kay, Mr. John, modern lady of Russia
M'Kean, Mr. Jas., a Garibaldian officer
M'Kean, Mrs. Jas., Spanish lady
M'Kee, Miss, Polish dancing-girl
M'Kenzie, Mr. Robert, V. Artillery

M'Kenzie, Dr., officer of Warrnambool Artillery
M'Kenzie, Mr. James, Capt. Murphy Maguire
M'Kinley, Mr.
M'Lachlan, Lieutenant D.
M'Lean, Mr. Jas., cavalier time of Henry VIII.
M'Lean, Mrs., Folly
M'LeIean, Mr. W., Highland chieftain
M'Leod, Miss K., fancy dress, nineteenth century
M'Mechan, Mr H., Parsee merchant
M'Mekon, Mrs. H., Madame Whitcoasky
M'Millan, Mr. W., Sydney Volunteer Artillery
M'Millan, Mrs. A., Night
M'Mullen, Mr. J. F., Armenian merchant
M'Mullen, Mrs., lady of olden times
M'Mullen, Miss, Leo Giocoml
M'Namara, Mr. John
M'Neil, Miss, English peasant
M'Pherson, Mr., court dress
M'Pherson, Mr. J., Cluny M'Pherson
M'Pherson, Mrs. W., Winter
M'Pherson, Miss, Scotch shepherdess
M'Pherson, Mr., Mustapha Pacha
M'Pherson, Miss, gitana
M'Pherson, Councillor
M'Pherson, Miss P., the Lily of the Valley

NAGLE, Mr., Highlander
Nagle, Mrs., Modera
Nalder, Mr., Member of Cambridge Boating Club
Nash, Mr., German Court hunting suit
Nasmyth, Capt., Egyptian gentleman
Nathan, Mr., jun., Chinese mandarin
Nathan, Mrs., fancy dress
Nathanson, Mr. G., Corsair
Neill, Mrs. colonel, Turkish bride
Neild, Dr., Calderon de la Barca
Netherlands, Consul-General
Nettleton, Mrs. C., La Vivandière
Nettleton, Mr. C., Swiss gentleman
Newton, Miss, Holly
Newbery, Mr. J. C., the Corsair
Newell, Mr. A., Spanish peasant
Nichols, Mrs., costume, time Louis XIV.
Nichols, Mr., Our American Cousin
Nicholls, Mr. T. W., Spanish gentleman
Nicholls, Mrs., Castilian peasant
Nicholls, Mr. G. M., Elvino
Nicholls, Mrs. G. M., Christmas in England
Nicholls, Mr. A., Thackleton
Nicholson, Mr. C. H.
Nicholson, Mrs. C. H.
Nicholson, Sir Arthur, Bart., court dress of the time of George III.
Nicholson, Miss, a Vivel lady
Nicholson, Mr. Germain, maître de arrondissement du Parks
Nicholson, Mrs. Germain
Nicholson, Miss, Daughter of the Regiment
Noble, Mr. J. W., midshipman
Noel, Mr. W. B., a monk
Nordt, Miss, Rutanella

Norman, Captain, Commander Victorian Navy
Norman, Mrs., lady of nineteenth century
Norman, W. G., Prince of Wales Light Horse
Norman, Mrs. W. G., court lady, reign Charles II.
Norman, Miss, Bavarian peasant
Norris, Mr J. F., Spanish muleteer
Norris, Mr. R., Sir R. Walpole
Norton, Mr. H. F., Count Egnert
Sperr Astowski
Norton, Mrs. H. F., Grecian lady
Norton, Miss A. W., red, white, and blue
Noyes, Lieutenant R. W., officer of the nineteenth century

O'BRIEN, Mr., Mickey Free
O'Brien, Mr. P., Polish refugee
O'Brien, Miss S., Helen M'Gregor
O'Brien, Miss, Cordelia
Occleston, Mr. T. J., Charles II.
O'Connell, Mr. M., Claude Melnotte
O'Dell, Mr., student of the nineteenth century
Officers H.M.S. Victoria, naval officers
O'Grady, Mr. Thomas, courtier time Charles I.
O'Grady, Mrs. T., Neapolitan peasant
Ogg, Mrs., Harvest
Ogg, Mr., muleteer of Toledo
O'Hara, Miss H., Dawn
O'Hara, Miss G., Amina
O'Hara, Miss Harriet, Undine
O'Hara, Miss, Spanish girl
Oldham, Mr., Danish nobleman of the fifteenth century
Oldham, Mrs., Winter
O'Mullane, Miss, early morning
O'Neil, Mr., Victorian Yeomanry Cavalry
Ormond, Mrs., Infanta Isabella
Orrock, Mr. W., Courtier, time of Charles I.
Orr, Miss, flowergirl
O'Shanassy, Hon. John
O'Shanassy, Mrs. John, lady of the fifteenth century
O'Shanassy, Mr. John, jun., a gentleman rider
O'Shanassy, Mr. E., Pythagorean philosopher
Osmond, Miss, Virginius
O'Sullivan, Miss, young lady of the nineteenth century
Oswey, Mr., 13th Hussars
Outridge, Mr. J. B., Lieut. R.N.R.
Oxley, Mrs. A. W., Dolly Varden
Oxley, Mr. A. W., Duke of Buckingham
Oxtoby, Mr. C. C., Rumsemy

PAGE, Mr., Hamlet
Page, Miss, America
Page, Colonel G. H., Deputy Quartermaster-General
Paley, Dr., an Oxford graduate
Paley, Mrs., lady of honour to Marie Antoinette
Paling, Mr. R. J., Spanish nobleman
Paling, Mrs. R. J., May Queen
Palmer, Miss, Night

Palmer, Mr. H. P., court costume of seventeenth century
Palmer, Mrs., court costume of seventeenth century
Palmer, Miss E., Spanish lady
Palmer, Mrs., Modern
Pardon, Mr., Harry Nalseel
Pastoe, Mrs., Highland lass
Payton, Mr. W. H., Don Jose
Parcy, Mr. J., Melbourne volunteer
Parker, Mr. D. M., Spanish nobleman
Parker, Mr. T. S., Tomahawas
Parker, Mrs. H., Katharine of Brangmen
Parker, Mr. A., a Magyar
Parker, Mrs. A., Scotch lassie
Parker, Mr. H., Garibaldi
Parker, Miss, Greek shepherdess
Parr, Mr. E., Ferdinand of Spain
Parr, Mrs. E., Spanish lady
Pascoe, Miss, outre nymph
Passmore, Miss, Juliana
Passmore, Miss E., Grecian shepherdess
Paton, Miss, Lady Teazle
Patterson, Staff Surgeon, uniform
Patterson, Mr. W., yachtsman
Patterson, Mr., Polish peasant
Patterson, Miss, Rose Bradwardine
Patterson, Mr. Thos., morris-dancer
Patterson, Mr. Henry, Victorian Yeomanry Cavalry
Pavey, Mr Thomas, Lord Alkenah
Payne, Mr. T. B., cavalier of reign of Charles II.
Payne, Mrs. T. B., Christmas
Payne, Mrs. John, Polish dress
Payne, Mr., Fortio
Payne, Mr. John, Irish gentleman
Peake, Miss, Maid of Caledonia
Pear, Mr. J., Spanish hidalgo
Pear, Mr J., German peasant girl
Pearson, Mr. A., Hungarian peasant
Pender, Mr. W., French officer of the nineteenth century
Pender, Mrs. W., Spanish lady
Pender, Mrs., Louline
Pender, Mr. M. L., huntsman
Pennington, Mrs., Spanish dress
Peppin, Mr. G., Capuchin friar
Peppin, Mrs G., autumn leaves
Perraud, Mr. E., graduate of University
Perragalli, Mr., Sadi
Perragalli, Mrs., French griselte
Perrin, Mr. B., Mephistopheles
Perry, Miss, evening dress, time of Louis XV
Perry, Miss, evening costume
Perry, Mr. W., evening costume
Perry, Mr. George, evening costume
Pettett, Mrs. W. H., French peasant
Phair, Mrs. John, a nun
Phair, Mr. John, Garibaldi
Phillips, Mr. S. D., Prince Arthur
Phillips, Mr. J. W., academic costume
Phillips, Mr. James, evening dress of the eighteenth century
Phillips, Mr. James, French lady of the sixteenth century
Phillips, Mrs. P. R., Midnight
Phipps, Mr. H. F., Anemoscobe
Phipps, Mrs., Dolly Varden
Pickersgill, Mrs. F. R., Juanita
Pickersgill, Mr. Jos., Paul Pry

Picot, Mr., Spanish court dress in the reign of Charles II.
Picot, Mrs., Polish lady
Pierce, Mr., a collegian
Pierce, Mrs., Night
Pigott, Mr. I. J., East India merchant
Pigott, Mrs. I. J., Zingara
Pigott, Mr. H. C., Antonio
Pigott, Mrs. H. C., Athenian lady
Pilkington, Miss, Polish peasant
Pilley, Mr. George, Turk
Pilley, Mrs. George, Countess Gyonow
Pinnock, Mr. C. B., gentleman of the reign of Queen Elizabeth
Pinnock, Mr. J. D., citizen of Hermannstadt
Pinnock, Miss, Turkish lady
Pinnock, Mr. H. S., Mr. Augustus Doodle/onfleek
Pirani, Mrs. J. C., court lady of the eighteenth century
Pirani, Miss, Cinderella
Pirani, Mr. Fred., academic dress
Pitt, Mrs., Night
Pitt, Colonel, C.B., staff uniform
Pitt, Miss L., Winter
Pitt, Miss, Ondine
Pittnam, Mr. E. D., Turkish officer
Plummer, Mrs. W., Snow
Plummer, Mr. W., Master Mason
Plunkett, Mrs., lady of the nineteenth century
Plunkett, Mr. J. H., First Attorney-Gen. of Port Phillip and Melbourne
Plunkett, Mr. C. T., Don Cæsar de Bazan
Plunkett, Mrs. C. T., Madame Elizabeth of France
Pollard, Mr., Spanish muleteer
Pope, Mr., an Arab chief
Pope, Mrs., Polish lady
Porter, Mr. W., Oliver Cromwell
Porter, Mrs. W., Court lady, 1650
Porter, Mr. G. W., Turk
Porter, Mrs. G. W., Italian lady
Powell, Mr. C., D'Artagnan
Powell, Mrs. John, Spanish lady
Powell, Mr John, Banedick
Powell, Mr., Conrad the Corsair
Prance, Mr., Incorrupable, 1795
Prendercoat, Mr., yachtsman
Prendergast, Mr., Colleen Dawn
Price, Mr. B. S., officer of Cape Mounted Rifles
Price, Mrs. E. S., May Morning
Price, Miss A., Lorraine
Priestly, Mrs. A., Hungarian baroness
Priestly, Mr. A., Arch Druid
Prince, Mr. A. G., officer of Austrian Hussars
Prince, Miss, French lady
Pritchard, Miss, Night
Pryde, Captain, naval officer
Pryde, Mrs., Lady Teazle
Pryse, Master A., Midshipman Easy
Pryde, Miss, Highland lassie
Purves, Mr. J. L., barrister
Purves, Mrs., Maria Theresa
Purves, Miss, Astarte
Purves, Miss M., Marguerite

QUINLAN, Mr. F., Lord Dundreary
Quinlan, Mrs. F., Norma

RADCLIFFE, Major, major of volunteers
Radcliffe, Mrs., English lady, reign of George III.
Ranaldes, Mr. G., muleteer of Toledo
Randell, Mr. G. W., William Tell
Rankin, Mr., Schamyl
Rankin, Mrs. J. D., lady of Finland
Ramsom, Mrs., Queen of Spain
Rawlings, Mr. T. H., Guicciardini, historian of Italy
Ray, Mrs. B. N., Circe
Raymond, Mr., ensign of 12th Foot
Rea, Miss, gleaner
Rede, Colonel, brigade major local staff
Reed, Councillor Thomas
Reid, Dr., uniform
Reid, Mr. J., Samovine
Reid, Mrs., Christmas
Reilly, Miss, the Bohemian girl
Reilly, Miss, Lady Ashton
Reilly, Miss, vivandière (Napoleon's)
Reilly, Miss E., Maritana
Reilly, Mr. P., Jockey Featherweight
Reilly, Mr. John, Sir Thomas Clifford
Renwick, Mr., Neapolitan
Renwick, Mrs., Flora M'Ivor
Reynolds, Mr. J. N., Ching-no-fat-too-icum, Chinese merchant
Reynolds, Mrs. J. N., Victorian garden of flowers
Rhind, Mr., Conrad the Corsair
Rhind, Mr., François, Richelieu's page
Rhind, Mrs., Dennis Beatrice
Rich, Mrs. Edward, Summer
Richardson, Mr. B., Italian brigand
Richardson, Mr. W. C., Weather Jock
Riddell, Miss, Ariel
Riddell, Mr. J. C., uniform
Riddell, Mr. Thos., Hindoo
Rigby, Miss, Annie Laurie
Rigby, Mr., graduate of Melbourne University
Rigby, Mr. G., Turkish costume
Roberts, Officer, evening costume
Roberts, Miss J. A., modern Galatea
Roberts, Mrs. W. G., Bohemian queen
Robertson, Dr., Turkish officer
Robertson, Miss, Neapolitan queen
Robertson, Mr. A. W., Marquis del Merji
Robertson, Mr. E. B., Count Rodolph
Robertson, Mr. G. P., bandit
Robertson, Mr. J. R., morris-dancer
Robertson, Mr. Jas., Highland chief
Robertson, Mr. John
Robertson, Mr. T. O. W., Highland chief
Robertson, Mr. W., uniform
Robertson, Mrs., Scotia Fifa
Robertson, Mrs. A. W., Hinda
Robertson, Mr. T. J. D. W., Lowland lassie
Robinson, Dr., Egyptian officer
Robinson, Mr. G. D., midshipman
Robinson, Mrs. J. H., Spanish lady
Robison, Miss, Ivy
Robison, Mr. T., a student
Rookridge, Miss, Red Riding Hood
Rooklidge, Mr. Thos., officer of Prince of Wales Light Horse
Rolls, Mr. Benj., Friar Tuck
Rosenthal, Mr. D., Windsor uniform
Rosenthal, Mrs. D., Portia
Rosenthal, Mrs., Catalonian peasant
Ross, Mr. A., Hassan
Ross, Mr. C. S., yachting costume
Ross, Mr. Fred., Bob Acres
Ross, Mr. J. B., Chief of the Ross
Ross, Mr. W. M., military monk, order of St. John
Ross, Mrs. A., lady of 1760
Ross, Mrs. C. S., Roxerabla
Ross, Mrs. W. M.
Row, Mrs. Fred., Greek lady
Rowe, Miss
Rowe, Mr.
Roy, Miss C., court lady of the reign of George III.
Roy, Mr. C., Serjeant Bufus
Roycroft, Mrs., Night
Royse, Mr., a Greek
Rudall, Mr. J., Faust
Rudall, Mrs. J. T., Autumn
Ruchn, Mr. G. W., Yittaclairu, Australian chief
Rushworth, Mr., Robin Hood
Russell, Mr. J., ride uniform
Russell, Mr. Thomas, a Greek

SABELBERG, Miss J., Polish lady
Sabelberg, Mr. J., Charles Surface
Salway, Mr. W., B.A. Melbourne University
Salway, Mrs. B., Empress Josephine (1804)
Salway, Mr. B., officer 3rd Light Dragoons
Samuel, Mr. E., yeomanry officer
Samuel, Mrs. E., Saxon lady
Sanders, Councillor
Sanderson, Mrs., court lady, time of Charles II.
Sanderson, Mr., Peter Spyke, from The Loan of a Lover
Sandhurst, Mayor of, Thane of Fife
Sandilands, Mr. B. N., Royal Artillery
Sandilands, Mrs. B. N., Hedwig (Tell's wife)
Sandridge, Mayor of, official costume
Sanders, Councillor, official costume
Sanders, Mrs., Night
Sangster, Mr., Polish general
Sangster, Mrs., court dress, time of Louis XIV.
Saunders, Captain, cavalry
Saunders, Mrs., Spanish lady
Saunders, Mr. L., Mexican gentleman
Savouri, Mr. J. G., French page, 1614
Say, Mr. W. B., Mortezo
Say, Mrs. W. B., gipsy
Sayce, Mr., French gentleman, time of Revolution
Sayce, Miss, Scotch lady
Sayce, Mrs. Jones, Waitress
Sayce, Mr. James, volunteer band uniform
Scales, Miss, Anne of Bretagne
Scrobs, Miss, Athenian lady
Scott, Mr. J., captain of marines
Scott, Mrs., Sound
Scott, Miss, Forget-me-not
Scurry, Mr. F., Gonzaro
Scurry, Mrs. F., Inch di Lora
Scddon, Mr. J., Reat. Voluntr. Artilry.
Seddon, Mrs. Night
Seddon, Mr. Elvus
Serrell, Mr. T., Pueblos
Serrell, Mr. C., a debardeur

Serrell, Miss
Serrell, Mr. W., French royal postilion
Serrell, Dr., Orozco
Shackell, Mrs., Sylvia
Sharp, Mr. J. H., Metropolitan Volunteer Artillery
Sharp, Mrs. J. H., Swiss peasant girl
Sharp, Mr. T. C., Garibaldian
Sharp, Mrs. T. C., Bride of Lammermoor
Shaw, Mr., Spring
Shaw, Mr., Garibaldi
Shaw, Mr. S. H., Student of Salamanca
Shaw, Mrs. S. H., Spanish lady
Sherwin, Hon. J., Count Charles Sobieski
Sheahan, Miss, a Portuguese peasant girl
Sheahan, Mr., Merchant of Venice
Sheahan, Mrs., court lady of the sixteenth century
Sherwin, Mrs. J., Countess Von Nordlen, Finland
Shier, Mr. John, Mephistopheles (burlesque)
Shier, Mr. Patrick, harlequin
Shier, Miss, Dolly Varden
Shillinglaw, Mr. J. J., Warpaint
Shillinglaw, Mrs. J. J., the bonnie fishwife
Short, Mr. A., Grand Turk
Short, Mrs., Turkish lady
Short, Miss, Spring
Sichel, Mr., grey friar
Sichel, Mrs., Marquissette Carabas
Siddeley, Mrs. W., Milanaise
Siddeley, Mr. W., gentleman of the time of Charles II.
Simeon, Mr. J., Lord Mockmergrose
Simeon, Miss, Coquette, court of Louis XV.
Simons, Mr. W. P., Sir Peter Teazle
Simons, Mrs. W. P., Lady Teazle
Simpson, Mr., Pierrot
Simpson, Mrs., Madame Pompadour
Simpson, Miss, a wood nymph
Simpson, Mr., a Turk
Simpson, Mr. G., Highland gent.
Simson, Mr., shepherd
Simson, Mrs., Spanish lady
Sinclair, Mr., N. S. W. Cricketer
Skene, Mr. J., Haroun-al-Raschid
Skinner, Mr., king's jester
Skinner, Mrs., Cleopatra
Skinner, Miss H., red, white, and blue
Sleight, Mrs. J. A., Paysanne
Sleight, Mr. E., court gentleman time of George II.
Sloman, Miss, Sardinian peasant
Smith, Miss, French waitress, 18th century
Smith, Colonel C. H., uniform
Smith, Miss F. J., sweet-brier
Smith, Mr. J., Henry II. of Germany
Smith, Mrs. J., Kunigunda, wife of Henry II. of Germany
Smith, Mr. James, debarteur
Smith, Miss Fanny, Snow
Smith, Mr. W. H., casuist
Smith, Councillor A. K., civic costume
Smith, Mr. T. T., head of N.Z. Rifles
Smith, Mr. Wm., merchant of 16th century

Smith, Alderman, and party
Smith, Mr., monk
Smith, Mrs. John, jun., Spanish lady
Smith, Mr. J., jun., Knight Templar
Smith, Miss J.
Smith, Mr. W. H., courtier of the seventeenth century
Smith, Mrs. H. J., snow-drift
Smith, Mr. H. J., Mr. Mantilini
Smith, Mrs. W. H., Mirabla
Smith, Mr. W. H., Turkish dress
Smith, Mrs. W. H., huntress
Smith, Dr L. L., Melancholy Jacques
Smith, Mrs. L. L., May Queen
Smithett, Lieut. A. L., Royal Artily.
Smyth, Mr. J. K., Louis di Franchi, from Corsican Brothers
Smyth, Mrs. Geo., lady of the time of Geo. I.
Smyth, Mr. Geo., Monk of the Screw
Smyth, Mr. W. F. F., cavalier, seventeenth century
Smyth, Mr. F. L., Sir Pierx Shovelle
Snee, Major, uniform staff officer of local force
Snellgrove, Mr. C., nobleman of the time of Queen Elizabeth
Snellgrove, Mrs. C., Night
Snelling, Mrs., Polish lady
Snelling, Mr., Manoel
Snelling, Mrs., lady of sixteenth century
Snowden, Mr. A., Florizel
Snowden, Mrs. A., Perdita
Snowden, Mr. E. G., Inigo Jones
Snowden, Mrs. E. G., Hungarian peasant
Solomon, Mr. L., French peasant
Solomon, Mrs. L., waitingmaid, 14th century
Solomon, Mr. R., French peasant
Solomon, Miss, Columbine
Solomon, Miss A., Larline
Solomon, Mr. S., Rydolph
Solomons, Miss, Bohemian girl
Solomons, Miss Adelaide, cottage girl
Spankie, Mr. D., Fra Diavolo
Spooner, Mr. James
Spoors, Mr. J., Snowstorm
Spain, Acting Vice-Consul for, consular uniform
Spensely, Mr. Howard, Sir Marmaduke Howard, period 1645
Sparrow, Mrs. G., court lady time of Louis XIX.
Squires, Mr., gentleman of the fourteenth century
Stafford, Mrs., Princess of Hungary
Staley, Mr., volunteer officer
Staley, Mrs., lady, time Charles II.
Standish, Captain
Stanley, Mr. H. J., uniform Royal Navy
Stanley, Mr. John, jun., Blinker
Stanley, Mrs. John, jun., court lady, time George III
Stark, Miss Annie, the colony of Victoria
Stark, Miss Susanna, Le Nozze di Figaro
Stark, Mr., ancient Druid
Stark, Mrs., German peasant holiday costume
Stearns, Mr., Lemuel
Stebbing, Mrs., the Village Queen

Steel, Mr. W., uniform, 1st V. E.
Stephen, Miss M., priestess of the sun
Stephen, Mr. F., volunteer officer
Stephen, Mr. W., boatman
Stephen, Mrs. F., court dress
Stephens, Colonel, uniform of H.M. Bengal European Cavalry
Stephenson, Miss, evening star
Stephenson, Miss C., morning star
Stevens, Miss, Sunrise
Stevenson, Mr. Geo., court dress of reign of Geo. II.
Stevenson, Mrs. G., Queen Catherine
Stewart, Dr., Mayor of Richmond
Stewart, Miss D., Lotty Hyde
Stewart, Miss M., Ravina the Bohemian
Stewart, Mr. H. P., gentleman of the nineteenth century
Stewart, Mr. James, Henry IV.
Stewart, Mr. R., Duke of Queensberry
Stewart, Mr. W., stockrider
Stewart, Mrs., Edith of Lorn
Story, Councillor, official costume
Story, Mr. W., Spanish Don
Story, Mrs., Night
St. Pinnock, Mr. R. D., student time of Edward IV.
Strachan, Hon J. F., Windsr. uniform
Strachan, Mrs. John, Morgiana
Strachan, Mr. J., Ali Baba
Strachan, Mr. W., captain F.V.V.A.
Stranges, Major, uniform
Stratford, Mr. B., Spanish nobleman
Strettle, Mr. S., Long Tom Coffin
Strettle, Mr. A., French officer
Strettle, Miss, Maritana
Strudwick, Mr., captain of artillery
Stuart, Mr. F. G., V. V. Rifles
Strutt, Mrs., Duchess of Milan
Stubbs, Mr. E. F., Selim, from Bride of Abydos
Stubbs, Mr. Thomas, Servian officer
Stubbs, Mr., jun., chasseur
Stubbs, Miss, soubrette, time of Louis XV.
Styles, Captain, Windsor uniform
Sullivan, Mr. P., volunteer of the Light Horse
Summerfield, Mr. J. W., gentleman of the reign of James I.
Summerfield, Mrs. J. W., Spring
Sumner, Mr. T. J., gentleman of sixteenth century
Sumner, Mrs. T. J., Christmas
Sutherland, Mr. C., Russian nobleman in reign of Peter the Great
Sutherland, Mrs. C., French duchess in reign of Francis I.
Sutherland, Mr. J., captain of volunteers
Sutton, Mr. J. W., Garibaldian
Sutton, Mrs. J. W., Bergere de Watteau
Swanson, Lieut. H.
Swanston, Mr. J., Highland gentleman
Swanston, Miss, Queen of May
Sydenham, Mr., Garibaldian
Sydenham, Mrs., Spring
Symonds, Lieut. P. H.

TAIT, Mr. John, L'Abbe de la Tour
Tallerman, Mr. D., Austrian cadet
Tallerman, Mrs. D., Cornelia Knight

Tully, Miss, Vivandière
Tankard, Mrs., English gipsy
Tannock, Miss, French milkmaid
Tarrant, Mr., a black friar
Tarrant, Mrs., née tile Sidney
Taylor, Mr., Lloyd, Czarowitch Alexis
Taylor, Mrs. Lloyd, Moorish lady
Taylor, Miss, Christmas
Taylor, Miss Isabella, Spring
Taylor, Miss Mary, Turkish girl
Taylor, Mr., Saney Gamp
Taylor, Mr. W., George II.
Taylor, Mr. C., Earl of Leicester
Taylor, Mr. J., member of Corps Diplomatique
Taylor, Mr. J., Vernon
Taylor, Mr. M., Monk
Taylor, Mrs. M., Night
Taylor, Mr. W., Snow
Templeton, Mr., crown prosecutor of New South Wales
Templeton, Mr. E., volunteer officer
Templeton, Mrs., Bride of Lammermoor
Tetley, Mr., Spanish inquisitor
Tetley, Mrs., Christmas in England
Thomas, Miss M., Spanish girl
Thomas, Miss, lady of time Louis XV.
Thomas, Mrs. D. J., lady, sixteenth century
Thoms, Lieut., 11th Regiment
Thompson, Miss, La Fille du Regiment
Thompson, Mr., Garibaldian volunteer
Thompson, Mr. W. F., Hector Fermosty
Thompson, Mr. W. F., a Mexican
Thompson, Mr. H., grey friar
Thompson, Mrs. Jas. W., Spring
Thompson, Mrs. W. F., lady of the sixteenth century
Thomson, Miss, Annie Laurie
Thomson, Mrs. James, Chieftain's Daughter
Thomson, Mr. W. K., Charles I.
Thomson, Mrs. W. K., Rose Bradwardine
Thouenon, Mr. E., Comte di Luna
Thouenon, Mrs. E., German peasant girl in national colours
Thorne, Miss, Last Rose of Summer
Thorne, Mr. G., Autumn
Thorogood, Mr., student
Thorogood, Mrs., modern Russian lady
Tickell, Captain, friar
Tierney, Mrs., Madame Esmond
Tipou, Miss, Russian peasant
Tipon, Miss Annie, young lady, time of George III.
Tipper, Mr. G. H., Paul Clifford
Tipper, Mrs., Distaffina
Todd, Mr. A. C., Chief of the Cameron clan
Todd, Mrs. A. C., Lady of the Cameron clan
Tolhurst, Mr. G. E., Louis XV.
Topp, Miss, Swiss girl
Topp, Mr. S., Bachelor of Arts
Topping, Mr. H., Iago
Topping, Mr. T., Dubevloire
Topping, Mrs., Spring
Topping, Mrs. H., Swiss peasant
Towers, Mr. H. St. John, Greek noble
Tracy, Mr. B. T., French court dress, time Louis XV.

Trevor, Mr., gentleman of the period of George IV.
Trenmery, Mr. G., P.W.V.V. Light Horse
Trevor, Colonel, uniform
Tuckett, Miss, Spanish lady
Tuckett, Mr. W. H., Yeomanry Cavalry corps
Tuckett, Mr. J. R., Sam, a downeaster gamecocker
Tuckett, Mr. J. R., Scotch lady of eighteenth century
Tulk, Miss A., Klymeno, Nymph of the Ocean
Tulk, Miss, Eurydice, the Nymph of Flowers and Wood
Tulk, Mr., gentleman of the nineteenth century
Tulk, Mrs., Lady Fanshaw—portrait of an ancestor
Tulley, Mr. J. L., Sailor
Turnbull, Miss, Summer
Turner, Mr. H. G., Bluebeard
Turner, Mr. W., Rashi Bazouk
Turner, Mrs. H. G., Beatrix, Duchess of Burgundy, thirteenth century
Tweedie, Captain, officer of the nineteenth century
Tweedie, Miss, Araby's daughter
Twendyman, Mr. L., Sir T. More
Twentyman, Mrs. R., Dame Margaret Roper
Twomey, Mr. D. J., Charles II.

UMPHELBY, Mr. C. W., cornet of R.V.V. Cavalry
Uther, Miss, Flora M'Donald

VALENTINE, Mr. D. H., Highland costume
Vaughan, Mrs. S. B., lady of the nineteenth century
Vaughan, Mr. Bradford, university student
Van Damme, Mr. C., His Majesty the King of Fiji
Van Damme, Mrs. C., Night
Vaughan, Mr. S. B., gentleman of the time of George II.
Vaughan Miss, une Babylière
Vickers, Mr. R. E., lieutenant of Leeds Volunteer Artillery
Vienseau, Mr. L., gentleman, sixteenth century
Vienseau, Madana L., Marguerite d'Alençon
Vincent, Mr. Charles, M. de Frontienac, eighteenth century
Vincent Mrs. Charles, Cleopatra
Vine, Mr. H., Elvino

WADE, Miss, Roman peasant
Wade, Mr. James, Sultan
Wade, Mrs., Sultana
Wadsworth, Mrs., Spanish lady
Wadsworth, Mr., Knight
Wainwright, Mr. H. P.
Wakley, Mr. J., German professor
Wakley, Mrs. Spanish peasant
Waldock, Mr. S., huntsman
Waldock, Mrs. S., huntress
Waldock, Mr. W. B., M.V.R.
Walford, Mr. F. A., a Turk
Walford, Mr., the Sable Brother
Walker, Councillor

Walker, Miss Helen, Spring
Walker, Miss P., Catalonian girl
Walker, Miss, Scotch girl
Walker, Mr. Michael, Scotch farmer of the seventeenth century
Walker, Mr. P., English Garibaldi
Walker, Mrs. Robert, Parthenia
Wall, Miss, Swiss girl
Wallace, Miss, Neapolitan peasant
Wallace Mr. J. C., Royal Eastern Yacht Club
Wallace, Mr. J. C., Snowstorm
Wallace, Mr. H., Charles II.
Wallace, Miss M., Child of the Regiment
Wallen, Mr. Robert, fisherman of Sorento
Walpo, Mr. Jno., Bravo of Venice
Walpole, Mr. H., uniform
Walsh, Mr. H. S., M.C.
Walsh, Mrs., vivandière
Walsh, Mr. A. W., volunteer officer
Walsh, Mrs. F. A., Palestine costume
Walsh, Mr. F. A., Lombard merchant of the sixteenth century
Walsh, Mrs. H., Twilight
Walsh, Mrs F., Fenella
Walsh, Mr. F., Oliver Cromwell
Walters, Mr. Thos., naval officer
Wardell, Miss, Neapolitan peasant
Wardill, Mr. R. W., Tom Bowling
Ware, Mr. J., Roderigo
Ware, Mrs., court dress of Louis XIV.
Ware, Mr., Pierrot Lousdel
Ware, Mr. J., huntsman
Ware Mrs. Joseph, lady of the reign of Francis I.
Warner, Mr. A., Arch Druid, priest of Norma
Warner, Mrs. A., Norma
Warner, Mr. C., John Buttercup
Warner, Mr. C., Helen Mar
Waterman, Mrs., court dress of time of George III.
Waterman, Mr., officer of V.A.R. 1858
Waterfield, Mr., Spanish hidalgo
Watheys, Mr., Charles II of Spain
Watkins, Mr. W., M L.A., gentleman of the eighteenth century
Watmough, Mr. G. G., Turk
Watmough, Mrs G G., Spanish lady of rank
Watson, Mr. R. T., captain Royal Victorian Volunteer Artillery
Watson, Mrs. R. T., Grecian lady
Watson, Mr. George, Garibaldi
Watson, Misses, Vivandières
Watson, Mr., Bachelor of Arts, Trinity College, Dublin
Watson, Mr. D., Swiss peasant
Watson, Mrs. D., evening dress, 1814
Watson, Mr. Robt., Tyrolese gentleman
Watson, Mrs. R., lady time of Queen Anne
Watson, Mrs. E. G., lady of the court of Marie Antoinette
Watson, Mr. E. G., Prince Rupert
Watt, Miss Lizzie, Donna Lisa
Watt, Mr. Alex., Free Gardener
Watt, Mrs. Alex., Spanish lady
Watt, Mrs., lady of the eighteenth century
Watt, Miss, the Maid of Nasni

Watt, Mrs., court lady of eighteenth century
Watt, Miss, Mariana
Watt, Miss Jessie, the White Lady of Avenel
Watt, Miss Bessy, a gipsy girl
Watts, Miss, Indian lady
Waxman, Mr. A., captain of militia
Waxman, Mrs., Swiss peasant
Webb, Mr. J. H., Gil Blas
Webb, Mr. J. H., Donna Mencia, of Mosquera
Webb, Mrs F., Aetiva (a sea nymph), one of the Nereides
Webb, Miss, Galatea (a sea nymph), one of the Nereides
Weedon, Mr. James, gentleman of seventeenth century
Weedon, Mrs. James, lady of the seventeenth century
Weeker, Mr. W. C., Lord No Zoo
Welsh, Mrs. S., Queen of the Roses
Were, Miss E., Greek girl
Westley, Mr., Cambridge graduate
Westly, Mr. H., Spanish nobleman
Weston, Miss A., Marie Antoinette
Whatnuff, Mr., military engineer
Whatnuff, Miss, the Colleen Bawn
Wharton, Mr. Geo., Royal Victorian Yeomanry Cavalry
Wharton, Mrs. Geo., Italian peasant
Wheeler, Mr. D. D., Ben Bowline
White, Mrs. James Hugh, lady of court of George II.
White, Mr. J. H., Druid
White, Mr. F. M., monk
White, Mr. F. D., Lieut. Treguose
White, Mr. A. B., a monk
White, Mrs. A. B., Swiss dress
White, Mr. W., Victorian Volunteer Cavalry
White, Mrs. W., Swiss girl of Berne
Whiteman, Mr. P., Turk
Whiteman, Mr. J., Hyscop
Whiteman, Mrs. J., Ophelia
Whitty, Mr. G. W., Huguenot officer
Whitty, Miss, Adina
Whitworth, Mr. R. P., Don Torreno Cabral, a Mexican randeero
Whitworth, Mrs. R. P., Marie Antoinette
Wildicomb, Mr., Greek corsair
Wildicomb, Mrs., Persian lady

Wilkins, Miss, Spanish lady
Wilkins, Mr. Alfred, matador
Wilkins, Mrs. Alfred, peasant
Wilkins, Mr. Jno., uniform, Staff-surgeon Victorian Volunteer Force
Wilkinson, Mr. J. R., Arcturo
Wilkinson, Mrs. J. R., Polish peasant
Wilkinson, Mr., cricketer
Wilkinson, Miss, Tirilla
Wilkinson, Mr. S. M., Gould Mahomet
Willan, Mr. Robert, Italian volunteer
Williams, Councillor, court suit
Williams, Mrs. W., Tricolour
Williams, Mr. J. H., Zouave
Williams, Hon. Ben.
Williams, Lieutenant
Williams, C. P., English court dress
Williams, Miss, Grecian lady
Williams, Mrs. C. P., fancy dress
William, Mr., court dress of time of Charles II.
Williams, Mr., Court dress of the nineteenth century
Williams, Mrs., court dress time of George IV.
Willis, Mr., Don Cesar de Bazan
Willis, Mrs., enchantress
Willoughby, Mr. A. H., Roderic Mauprat
Willoughby, Miss, Juanita
Wills, Mrs. John, lady of the time of Louis XV.
Wilson, Professor, Zero
Wilson, Mr. W., Dromio of Syracuse
Wilson, Mrs. Samuel, Morning
Wilson, Mr. Samuel, Brigand chief
Wilson, Mr. D., Highland gentleman
Wilson, Mrs. D., Jessica
Wiltshire, Mr. C. R., Charles I.
Wiseman, Miss A., Madora
Wiseman, Mr. A., Sir Rupert, of the "Ingoldsby Legends"
Wiseman, Mrs. A., court dress of the reign of George III.
Wiseman, Mr. W., cavalier of the reign of Charles II.
Wiseman, Mrs. W., court dress of the reign of Louis XV.
Withers, Miss, Madame Esmond, reign of George II.
Wolsely, Mr. F. Y., Mustapha Pacha
Wolstenholme, Mrs. J., French peasant girl

Wolstenholme, Mr. J., Victorian engineer
Wood, Mrs., Night
Wood Mr., Turk
Wood, Miss, Morning
Woodhouse, Mr., Bavarian
Woodland, Ensign H. L.
Woods, Miss F. C., Forget-me-not
Woods, Miss, soubrette
Woods, Mrs. A. T., Spanish lady
Woolf, Mr., barrister
Wooll, Mrs., Leonora from opera of Il Trovatore
Woodley, Mr. H. K., Leicester
Woodley, Miss, lady of Queen Elizabeth's reign
Woodley, Miss M. J., Winter
Wootton, Miss, Oriental girl
Wragge, Alderman, city alderman
Wragge, Mrs., Night
Wragge, Mr. J. P., Quebec cavalry
Wragge, Mr. H., veterinary surgeon P.V.V.V.L.H.
Wright, Mr., Knight Templar
Wyborn, Mr. T. J., Claude Duval

YELLAND, Mrs. Geo., Duchess of Berkenfeld
Yelland, Mr. George, jockey
Young, Mrs. G., lady of sixteenth century
Young, Miss, Annie Laurie
Young, Mrs. John, morning star
Young, Mr. James, chansing
Young, Mr. James, military officer
Young, Mr. James, Circassian chief
Young, Mr. James, nautical mariner
Young, Mrs. Jas., flower girl
Young, Mrs. Geo., Fides, from Le Prophète
Young, Mrs. Wm., lady of the Lake
Young, Mr Geo., Francesco the Pirate
Young, Mr., a Garibaldian
Young, Mr. Wm., officer of 42nd Highlanders
Younghusband, Mrs., snowflake

ZANDER, Miss F., flower-girl
Zander, Miss, Spanish gitana
Zevenboom, Mr. Geo., morris-dancer
Zevenboom, Mrs. Jas., Spanish lady
Zox, Mr. E., Figaro
Zunstein, Mr. H., troubadour

The decorations by Mr. J. G. Knight were, as usual, varied from those adopted by him on the previous occasion of the building being used. Notwithstanding the vast crowd, so excellent were the arrangements that the dancers were rarely incommoded, and though the arrivals were continued to a late hour, still the waltzes, quadrilles, and galops proceeded without interruption in the main hall, with Chapman's band in the gallery, and a smaller band in the rotunda. At eleven o'clock the signal was given for supper, to which H.R.H. led the the way with Mrs. Butters, accompanied by his Excellency the Governor, the Mayor and the members of the Prince's suite with their partners, and the supper-room was soon filled with guests. The supper was provided by Mr. R. U. Miller, of Collins-street; the wines were provided by Mr. E. G. Smythers, of Elizabeth-street, and could not be improved upon. Such a profusion of the first qualities of champagne—Mumm, Roederer, and Cliquot—has rarely been witnessed in Melbourne. The supper-room was decorated as at the Governor's ball, and presented a very pleasant spectacle, the epergnes and other table ornaments, the coloured lamps, and the gay dresses making up a pretty kaleidoscopic picture. Supper over, the Mayor gave one toast "The Queen," which was responded to with the usual cheering. After supper the Prince danced a "foursome" reel with Miss Grant, and soon afterwards retired, with a view to subsequently appearing *incognito*. It was known to a few of the Duke's party that H.R.H. reappeared in the disguise of a Monk, and so perfect was his make-up effected, that he was enabled to mingle freely with the general company without being recognised. His Royal Highness danced with Mrs. J. G. Knight, and thoroughly enjoyed his brief immunity from State ceremony. The dancing was kept up until some time after daybreak, and the sun was shining on the revellers as they sought their respective homes.

On Tuesday, the 24th, the Prince honoured the Haymarket Theatre with his presence, to witness the farewell performance of Madame Celeste.

Wednesday was Christmas day.

On Thursday, the 26th December, the Volunteer Review took place on the racecourse, before his Royal Highness the Duke of Edinburgh, the Governor, and five or six thousand spectators. His Royal Highness wore the uniform of a general officer of Saxe-Coburg and Gotha, to which duchy the Prince is next heir. He was accompanied by the Governor, Lord Newry, Sir Redmond Barry, Major Venlon, Mr. Yorke, Mr. Haig, Lieutenant Colonel Page, Lieutenant-Colonel Pitt, Major Baker, Mr. Rothwell, &c. In the course of the morning, they came up to the grand stand, where they were received by Captain Standish, Mr. Creswick, and Mr. Dougharty. The field officers in command were as follows:—

STAFF.—Colonel W. A. D. Anderson, colonel commandant; Lieutenant-Colonel Rede, brigade-major; Captain Stubbs and Captain Burton, staff captains; and Major Spread, Major Learmonth, and Captain Bowling.

CAVALRY.—Major Bell, Major Anderson, and Captain Sherard.

NAVAL BRIGADE.—Captains Fullerton and Elder, and Lieutenant Handfield.

FIELD ARTILLERY.—Major Krone, and Captains Sargood, Strachan, and Steel.

ENGINEERS.—Captain Parnell. (The torpedo firing party was under Sergeant Phelon.)

FIRST BATTALION (GARRISON ARTILLERY).—Majors Stewart and Raven.

SECOND BATTALION (METROPOLITAN RIFLES).—Lieut.-Colonel Champ and Major Martin.

THIRD BATTALION (METROP. RIFLES).—Major Irving.

FOURTH BATTALION (BALLARAT RIFLES).—Captain W. C. Smith.

FIFTH BATTALION (CASTLEMAINE RIFLES).—LA.-Cl. Bull.

His Royal Highness attended the Haymarket Theatre in the evening to witness a performance in aid of the formation of a Theatrical fund, in which some of the Royal party took part. The *Area Belle* was the first piece given, Lord Newry playing "Tosser," and Mr. Fitzgeorge "Pitcher." Mr. Eliot Yorke took the part of Henri Desant in the *Isle of St. Tropez*. *Box and Cox* concluded the entertainments, in which Lord Newry played "Box." There was a brilliant audience, and a large sum was raised for the benefit of the charity.

On Friday, the 27th, the foundation stone of the Mechanics' Institute and Free Library, East Collingwood, was laid by his Royal Highness. Great preparations were made for the event, and accommodation was provided for ladies to witness it from a platform erected within the area upon which the buildings were to be erected. The weather was unfortunately exceedingly unpropitious, and sadly marred the ceremony. His Royal Highness arrived at two p.m., and was received by the Mayor of East Collingwood and the members of the Borough

Council, the Chief Secretary, the Attorney General, the Minister of Justice, and the members for the district in the Assembly. The following address was presented on the occasion:—

May it please your Royal Highness—We, the Mayor, Councillors, and Inhabitants of the Borough of East Collingwood, the premier municipality of Victoria, avail ourselves of the earliest opportunity after the arrival of your Royal Highness of offering to you a most cordial welcome, and of expressing our heartfelt loyalty to the Throne, and devoted attachment to the person and family of Her Most Gracious Majesty your Royal mother. On the present occasion we desire briefly but heartily to thank your Royal Highness for the distinguished honour you have been pleased to confer upon us, and through us on the working classes generally, in laying the foundation stone of a building which, as a public library, reading-room, and lecture hall, and intended as it is to encourage the diffusion of useful knowledge, the practical union of science with industry, and the intellectual, moral, and social improvement of the people generally, may be justly considered a working man's Institute. With your Royal Highness's permission, we would desire to have this building named the Royal Albert Institute, as an humble but sincere tribute of respect and reverence for the memory of the good and great Prince Albert, who was pre-eminently the friend of the working man, and the most illustrious patron of industrial pursuits, and who led men to compete, not in arms, but in science and industry, bringing the inventions, the discoveries, and improvements of each to contribute to the benefit of all; thus teaching the nations of the earth, not the art of war, but the God-like art of universal peace, harmony, and good-will among men. We sincerely pray that your Royal Highness may, in a prolonged, happy, and prosperous voyage through the ocean of life, enjoy Heaven's choicest blessings.

SAUNDERS BAYNHAM, Mayor.
GEORGE BENNETT, Town Clerk.

REPLY.

Gentlemen—You are fully justified in believing that in assenting to your request that I should lay the foundation-stone of a Mechanics' Institute in your borough, I desired to testify my high appreciation of these institutions in general, and the interest which I feel in the success of your endeavours to promote the intellectual, moral, and social improvement of the people. It will afford me pleasure, when I have left this colony, to remember that my name will be associated with a building devoted to these high and benevolent objects. I thank you for the good wishes which you have expressed for my personal welfare.
ALFRED.

After the presentation of the address, a prayer was offered up by his Lordship Bishop Perry; and at the conclusion of the ceremony an adjournment took place to a marquee, where a cold collation was served, and after the toasts of "The Queen," "The Prince," and "The Governor" had been proposed by the Mayor, his Royal Highness left the ground.

In the evening a dinner-party took place at Toorak, after which a concert was held, and Mr. Summers played his odaic cantata "Galatea Secunda," by command of his Royal Highness. There were present his Royal Highness and suite, His Excellency, Lady Manners-Sutton, and suite, and Sir John and Lady Young. At the conclusion of the performance of the cantata, his Royal Highness requested that the poet, Mr. R. H. Horne, and Mr. J. Summers, should be presented to him, and to them he expressed his great pleasure at hearing the work. The principal performers were Mrs. Fox, Miss Bassett, Mr. Donaldson, and Mr. Amery. Mr. King led the orchestra.

On Saturday Sir John Young, late Governor of New South Wales, accompanied by Lady Young, left Australia for England. His Royal Highness the Duke of Edinburgh and the Hon. Eliot Yorke, accompanied Sir John Young and family, to see them off. His Excellency Sir Henry Manners-Sutton took leave of Sir John Young at Sandridge. The Duke also bade farewell, and wished a pleasant voyage to Madame Celeste, who was also a passenger by the same vessel.

On Monday, 30th December, the Duke paid a visit to the Richmond Police Barracks, and witnessed the mode of training adopted in the Riding School.

The Caledonian Games, after being discontinued for a long time in this colony, were resumed this year, the Scottish people and the Highland Society having determined to give a demonstration in honour of the Duke of their metropolis and the son of her Majesty, who has during her lifetime peculiarly identified herself with the northern portion of her dominions. Accordingly, measures were determined upon, and a programme arranged on a grand scale, to be carried out in the Zoological Gardens on the 30th and 31st December. The games commenced about 12 o'clock on the 30th, and soon afterwards the committee of management received an intimation from H.R.H. the Duke of Edinburgh, who had previously been requested to attend, that he would visit the ground during the day. The Prince came about four o'clock, in the Governor's private carriage. His Royal Highness was received by Mr. Panton, Dr. Hadden, and other Highland gentlemen, and was immediately conducted to a reserved covered compartment in the middle of the grand stand, where he remained nearly half an hour. Having read over the programme, he requested that the race in Highland costume should be run; and whilst the preliminaries of that were being proceeded with, Mr. W. Harcourt, J.P., of Taradale, by request, executed the sword dance in a very skilful manner. A handsome youth, about twelve years of age, dressed in very pretty Highland costume, also danced the Highland fling before his Royal Highness, and was loudly cheered. During the time the Prince stayed rain came on, and he departed before the sports had concluded, but an intimation was left with Dr. Hadden, requesting him to inform the promoters that he would visit the ground on the following day; his numerous engagements, however, prevented the fulfilment of his promise.

Next day, at the Melbourne Club, the Prince received the following address from the Borough Council of Echuca :—

May it please your Royal Highness We, the Mayor, Councillors, and Burgesses of the Borough of Echuca, respectfully tender to your Royal Highness our sincere congratulations on your arrival among us, and take occasion to assure your Royal Highness of our devoted loyalty and warm attachment to the Throne and person of our beloved Queen, a fresh instance of whose considerate regard for these colonies we cannot fail to recognise in thus having an opportunity of welcoming you to this continent. We wish your Royal Highness a safe and happy return to your native land, and hope your visit to Victoria may be one of very many pleasant memories which your Royal Highness will hereafter associate with your Australian voyage.

EDMUND ELLIGET, Mayor.
CHARLES E. PASCOE, Town Clerk.

REPLY.

Gentlemen—In tendering to you my very warm acknowledgments for the address which you have presented to me, and for the assurance of your loyalty to Her Majesty, I wish to express to you my regret that I was unable to fulfil my intention of personally visiting your borough. I am not the less sensible of your kind wishes for my personal welfare and happiness.
ALFRED.

THE SAILORS' HOME BALL.

Not the least enjoyable of the entertainments provided in honour of the Royal visit was the Ball which took place in the Exhibition Building on 31st December, in aid of the Sailors' Home, and at which some 1500 persons were present. The ball-room presented a most elegant appearance. A large number of flags had been kindly lent by the captains of H.M.S. *Galatea*, the steam-sloop *Victoria*, Messrs. Bright Brothers, Messrs. W. P. White and Co., and the Marine Department. Under the supervision of Mr. J. G. Knight, the great collection of bunting was displayed to the best advantage. A flagstaff was erected in the centre of the hall, and from its summit lines of flags radiated to all points of the room, forming altogether a sort of flag canopy to the hall. Along the side-aisles some of the splendid large national flags from the *Galatea* were displayed to advantage. Festoons of flowers were suspended from the apex of the roof, intertwined with the ensigns, and upon the whole, with the numerous sunlights and starlights, a highly picturesque and novel effect was produced. The band was placed in the organ gallery. The rotunda was not used for dancing, but set apart as a refreshment-room and lounge.

His Royal Highness the Duke of Edinburgh, attired in half-dress naval uniform, wore the star and ribbon of the Order of the Garter, and arrived shortly after nine o'clock, accompanied by his Excellency the Governor, Lady and the Misses Manners-Sutton, Lord Newry, Mr. Manners-Sutton, the Hon. Eliot Yorke, Lieut. Haig, R.N., Mr. Brierly, and Lieut. Rothwell. Dancing was shortly afterwards commenced. His Royal Highness joined in the first set of quadrilles with Miss Manners-Sutton, and during the evening engaged in several other dances. A large number of the officers of H.M.S. *Galatea* were present, and the handsome blue and gold uniform of the Royal Navy was relieved by the regimental scarlet of the military officers of the garrison. About twelve o'clock the company proceeded to the supper-room, his Royal Highness conducting in Lady Manners-Sutton. There was only one toast, that of "Her Majesty the Queen," proposed by the Hon. J. G. Francis, and which was right loyally responded to. The supper, which was supplied by Mr. Miller, of Collins-street, was exceedingly well served. The wines, supplied by Mr. E. Smythers, were all of the best quality, and served as plentifully as on the occasion of the Civic Fancy Dress Ball.

On New Year's Day a race meeting took place on the Flemington Course, at which his Royal Highness and the vice-regal party were present. The portion of the grand stand set apart for the accommodation of his Royal Highness, the Governor, and their suites, was tastefully decorated with ferns and flowers, supplied principally by the courtesy of Mr. Hugh Glass; and a private room was also provided for Lady Manners-Sutton and the ladies accompanying her. His Royal Highness the Duke of Edinburgh arrived on the course at the time advertised for the first race, in a carriage and four, with postilions and outriders, accompanied by his Excellency the Governor, Lieut. Haig, and Lord Newry. Lady Manners-Sutton, with the Misses Sutton, drove up soon after in a close conveyance; and Major Baker drove a four-in-hand drag, in which were the Hon. Eliot Yorke, Mr. Manners-Sutton, Lieut. Rothwell, and several officers of the *Galatea*. His Royal Highness was received by Captain Standish and other members of the committee, and conducted to the stand; after which he was, as before, able to stroll about as he pleased, without being obtrusively noticed, and witnessed the greater part of the running from the top of the stewards' stand. An excellent luncheon, provided by Mr. Scott, was laid out in a handsomely-fitted tent, as on the last occasion of the Duke's visit to the races. To this tent at about two o'clock his Royal Highness adjourned, escorting Lady Manners-Sutton; and here the members of the committee entertained the Duke, the Governor, and a select party of ladies and gentlemen. As soon as the last race was over, his Royal Highness drove away in one of the Governor's close carriages, attended by Captain Standish, and shortly after the Governor and Lady Manners-Sutton followed in a carriage and four.

On the same evening his Royal Highness dined with the officers of the Royal Artillery and H.M. 14th Regiment, a party of about twenty guests being invited to meet him.

On Wednesday, 2nd January, his Royal Highness paid a visit to the St. Kilda Bowling Club, close to the railway terminus. H.R.H. arrived on the ground at about one o'clock, in an open barouche, drawn by four greys. He was accompanied by Lieutenant Haig, and was received at the entrance to the green by Mr. William Nimmo, president of the club,

Address of the Old Colonists 175

and the Hon. Alexander Fraser, M.L.C. On entering he was loudly cheered; he then retired to the pavilion, and after remaining there for a few minutes, he came on to the ground and tried a few bowls, but did not take part in any of the rinks that were playing. He was accompanied over the ground by the Mayor of St. Kilda (Dr. Patterson), the Mayor of Melbourne, Mr. Lord, and several other gentlemen, and there were also present Messrs. Knight and Gilbert, of the Royal Reception Commission. Between three and four hundred persons, principally ladies, were within the enclosure. After the Prince had viewed the green, he proceeded to plant a Wellingtonia Gigantea, in honour and commemoration of his visit, in a highly workmanlike manner, a cross with the following inscription being placed beside it:— " Wellingtonia Gigantea, mammoth pine, a native of California, planted 2nd January, 1868, by his Royal Highness the Duke of Edinburgh." His Royal Highness again retired to the pavilion, where he had some refreshment, and in a few minutes left, driving round by the esplanade, and then back to Toorak. In the course of the day his Royal Highness visited the establishment of Messrs. Johnstone and O'Shannessy, the photographers, and sat for his likeness; the artists succeeded in taking some excellent portraits of their distinguished patron, one of which forms the frontispiece to this work. His Royal Highness also visited the establishment of Mrs. Gardner, in Collins-street west, and purchased a large number of furs for presentation to members of his family. In the evening the Prince paid another visit to the Theatre Royal, where Mr. W. H. Akhurst's deservedly popular pantomime, *Tom, Tom, the Piper's Son*, was performed, with great success, to a crowded house. The Prince, accompanied by the Hon. Eliot Yorke, Lord Newry, and Captain Standish, arrived shortly before nine o'clock, and occupied the right-hand proscenium box. The audience was a most enthusiastic one, and when the band played the National Anthem—upon the appearance of the *petit* representative of the reigning Sovereign—the vast concourse of people in boxes, pit, and stalls rose *en masse*, and gave three hearty cheers.

A ceremony of a most interesting nature took place at the Public Library on Friday, 3rd January; a large number of gentlemen who had been resident in the colony over twenty-five years, having assembled to present an address to his Royal Highness the Duke of Edinburgh. About sixty-five of the fathers of the colony were present altogether, including the Hon. J. O'Shanassy, the Hon. J. P. Fawkner, Hon. W. Degraves, Messrs. D. M'Arthur, A. Woolley, J. King, M'Kenzie, J. B. Were, F. and E. Henty, O'Brien, Rutherford, &c., &c. At about 12 o'clock, his Royal Highness drove up to the Swanston-street entrance of the Library, accompanied by the Governor, Lord Newry, and Lieutenant Haig, and followed by Mr. Manners-Sutton, Lieutenant Rothwell, and Mr. Brierly. His Royal Highness was received on alighting by Sir Redmond Barry, Sir James Palmer, and Sir Francis Murphy, as trustees, and by Mr. Augustus Tulk, the Librarian; the Prince was conducted to the library, where Mr. E. Henty, after stating in a few words that those gentlemen who had the honour of waiting on his Royal Highness were the first colonists of Port Phillip, read the address as follows:—

Address of the Old Colonists.

May it please your Royal Highness—We, the undersigned, being colonists of Victoria for a period of a quarter of a century and upward, venture to approach your Royal Highness with expressions of unaltered loyalty to Her Majesty's Throne and person, and our very sincere and hearty congratulations to your Royal Highness on your auspicious visit to this distant dependency of the British empire.

We can confidently assure your Royal Highness that, however attractive republican institutions may be to young communities generally, Victoria is in the main free from the taint of any such predilection. The loyalty and attachment to monarchical government of those numbered amongst her older colonists have been strengthened by their enlarged experience, and by the deep conviction, ever increasing with their ripening years, that their material interests will be best protected by the perpetuation of an intimate connection with the great empire over which Her Majesty rules—an empire the language, laws, customs, and institutions of which it is their privilege to inherit.

We may be allowed to esteem the visit of your Royal Highness to these shores as of the utmost importance, regarded from an Imperial as well as from a colonial point of view. Your Royal Highness has now had an opportunity of satisfying yourself, and may bear testimony, on your return to Europe, that the colonists of Victoria, though they have left their mother-country, have not lost the spirit of enterprise, the energy, the self-reliance, the love of law and order, which distinguish the British race; and that, in common with their fellow-countrymen at home, they possess qualities the possession of which by her people has made England great and glorious amongst the nations; while your presence here proves to the colony at large, but especially to our colonial-born youth, that Her Majesty's solicitude for our welfare is unabated.

With a sincere hope that the visit of your Royal Highness to the other colonies of the Australian group may be gratifying to you, and your ultimate return to the Royal circle safe, and attended with every happiness,

We beg leave to remain, with the greatest respect, your Royal Highness's most humble and most obedient servants,

[*The names which follow have been arranged in alphabetical order, and according to date.*]

1831.
Wall, James Eagan, first visit, 1831; second, 1833

1834.
Cannon, Alfred John
Henty, Edward
Henty, Francis

1835.
Broomfield, James
Carter, William
Faukner, John Pascoe
Pender, William
Roberts, Joseph
Scarborough, George
Solomon, Joseph

1836.
Brock, Alexander
Campbell, Alexander
Carr, Patrick
Falkiner, F. Edward
Fowler, Henry
Henty, S. G.
Hill, James
Langhorne, Alfred
Matson, J. M.
Maxwell, John
M'Meekan, —
Osbourne, Richard
Boothright, Thomas
Roach, John
Russell, Robert
Sutherland, J.
Taylor, Fred.
Tregurtha, J. W. H.

1837.
Alexander, Thomas Barry
Austin, Thomas
Barnett, James
Caulfield, John
Champion, Fred.
Crooke, Edward
Cumming, William
Ewart, John
Faker, Alfred
Fattall, William

Fleming, John Wood(born in Melbourne 2nd June)
Henson, Daniel
Henty, Richmond (born in colony 3rd August)
Hind, Isaac
Hoddle, Robert
Jennings, Thomas
Learmonth, Thomas
Mawley, Henry
Mossman, Charles S.
Murray, A. J.
Nash, W. H.
Neafor, James
Oliver, William
Pettett, W. H.
Pinkerton, William
Scott, John
Sharp, William
Spoil, William, jnr.
Sutherland, John
Turner, William
Urquhart, George
Wallace, John

1838.
Allee, John
Barnett, —
Bowden, John Searle
Brown, John
Cameron, G. H.
Campbell, Robert
Coghill, David
Coleman, Solomon
Conroy, Patrick
Cosgrave, John
Cropper, W. H.
Dods, William
Dougharty, John George
Draper, Ambrose
Fitzsimons, Edward
Frost, Robert
Hayes, Robert
Heffernan, —
Highett, William
Hughes, Charles W.
Kember, James
Laidles, James
Macarthur, Don Gordon
Moffat, Robert

Murchison, John
M'Arthur, D. C.
M'Culloch, Thomas W.
Osbourne, James
Rankin, John
Robins, W. A. (born in Melbourne 13th Sept.)
Sadler, James
Stuse, G. M.
Strode, Thomas
Sugden, W. J.
Trotteman, Thomas
Tulloch, John
Vinge, George
Wistle, C. J.

1839.
Addison, Henry
Anderson, Adam
Anderson, C. G.
Armstrong, Robert G.
Arnold, Thomas
Bartlie, Thomas
Barry, James
Belcher, —
Broadfoot, Alex. A.
Burke, Robert Bartlett
Butler, Alexander E.
Butler, Spilsbury
Butler, W. M.
Cameron, Alexander
Campbell, D. S.
Capper, Richard
Carmichael, Geo.
Cavenagh, G.
Clark, R. S.
Cockburn, Owen
Craig, G. N.
Cuske, Thomas
Dall, Richard
Davies, B.
Davis, Peter Stevenson
Davis, Peter
Desailly, George P.
Dredge, Theophilus
Emory, William
Empson, William
Felstead, John
Fisken, Archibald
Fraser, Alexander

Fraser, George
Gray, James
Gray, William
Grice, Richard
Haley, C. S.
Hall, Henry
Hamilton, Thomas T.
Herring, Muston William
Hervey, Matthew
Hitchins, Frederick
Hobson, Francis
Hogan, John
Hope, George
Hope, James
Howard, Fred. William
Hurst, William
Jamieson, Alex.
Johnson, William
Joyce, William
Lambert, John S.
Lang, Thomas
Lang, William
Locke, Charles
Lynn, Colin
Lyons, David
Main, M. Isabella
Martin, Robert
Milter, Henry
Montgomery, James
Morgan, Alexander
Moss, Meton
Mount, T. A.
Mowat, William
Murphy, James
Murray, Andrew
Murray, H. D. F.
M'Bean, William
M'Clelland, W.
M'Connell, James
M'Illaffee, J. D.
M'Kinnon, John
M'Lachlan, Ronald
M'Millan, Godfrey
M'Mutrie, David
M'Waiters, Sampson
O'Culk, Richard
O'Donovan, Barth John
Orr, Frederick, M.D.
Orr, John
O'Shanassy, John
Palmer, Thomas L.

Address of the Old Colonists.

Payne, Thomas B.
Pohler, Michael
Pinkerton, James
Porter, Geo. W.
Porter, John A.
Riddell, J. Carre
Riley, James
Rohn, Arthur
Ryan, Charles
Scott, Robert
Scott, Thomas King
Sievwright, Marcus
Simson, H. Newman
Shaw, Henry S.
Sterny, Robert
Stewart, Thos. W.
Swanson, Geo.
Symonds, Charles H.
Thomas, D. T.
Tolson, Joseph
Walker, Hugh
Walker, R. V.
Watson, James
Waugh, John
Waugh, Robert W.
Webb, James
Were, J. B.
White, Geo.
Wilkie, David
Williamson, Charles
Wills, Thomas W.
Wilson, Charles
Wilson, James
Woolley, Alfred

1840.

Anderson, James
Andrews, Robert
Aplin, C. D'Oyly H.
Ballingall, W.
Barker, Edw.
Barry, James
Beaver, F. E.
Blair, James
Booth, Henry
Born, James Ford
Bourke, Henry
Bowater, John
Brand, William
Brodribb, P. C.
Brown, James
Campbell, Archibald
Carr, James
Carter, Joseph
Cashmore, Michael
Cleland, John
Colgin, John
Costello, Patrick
Crawley, Jeremiah
Creswick, H.
Curtain, Michael
Dall, W. M.
Dollimore, F. W.
Davidson, George
Dawson, James
Dawson, Michael
Dodd, George
Douglas, William
Evans, W. B.
Everest, Thomas James
Farie, Claud
Franckle, John
Frencham, Henry
Geraghty, Patrick
Gillet, Edward

Groves, Augustus T. H.
Gregory, Samuel
Hailes, C. B.
Hall, William
Hammond, R.
Harris, John
Hart, Isaac
Henderson, Thomas
Hervey, William
Higginbotham, Thomas
Higginbotham, William
Himsley, Fredk. Gowan
Hood, John
Howitt, W. G.
Howitt, Godfrey, M.D.
Hunter, J. P.
Jamieson, Neil
Johnston, J. A.
Jukes, John Montague
Kelcher, J. B.
Kennedy, Donald
Ker, E. Charles
Kilburn, Douglas T.
King, William Oliver
Kirwan, Patrick Thomas
Kyte, Ambrose
Le Souef, Albert A. C.
Lewis, Richard
Lindsey, Algernon
Long, Daniel Butter
Long, Thomas
Longman, H. N.
Lynch, Michael
Main, James M'Nab
Marden, Charles
Marris, John B.
Mayne, James
Michel, H E.(B.A. Oxon.)
Michel, Louis J.
Monkton, John M.
Moore, James
Mouritz, G. H.
Murray, Robert
Macpherson, Dugald
M'Gregor, John
M'Grath, Patrick
M'Laurin, Archibald
M'Laurin, James
M'Lean, Angus
Nicholson, W. H.
O'Brien, Patrick
Ogilvy, David
Oliver, Thomas
Palmer, J.
Passmore, J. C.
Pohlman, Robert William
Ransom, Thomas
Roberts, George
Roberts, R.
Robertson, A. G.
Rutherford, John
Scott, Peter
Selby, G. W.
Sheppard, Thomas
Smith, Sydney
Stevenson, John
Stevenson, William
Sturt, E. P. S.
Taylor, William
Tulnie, E.
Umphelby, Thomas L.
Wallace, James C.
Wheatley, Alfred E.
Wills, John
Wills, Thomas F.

Winter, Alfred
Winter, James

1841.

Allan, Robert
Anderson, Anthony
Auketell, John
Armstrong, J.
Barker, James
Barwick, James
Baynton, Thomas
Bell, B.
Bingley, Thomas Peacock
Bignell, Henry
Boadle, J. F.
Bond, Thomas
Brooks, James
Brown, Charles
Brown, J. Hatchell
Brown, Robert
Campbell, W. H.
Cherry, Robert
Cherry, William
Clarke, William
Cochrane, James
Cole, Thomas C., M.A.
Coleman, William
Conroy, W. Corcoran
Crook, James E.
Currie, John Lang
Curtis, Ambrose
Dalton, Jeremiah Patrick
Dalton, W. H.
Dangon, James
Davidson, Henry Mullaly
Davis, Alexander
Dendy, Henry
Drew, Francis L.
Drew, G. B.
Dunn, Thomas
Edwards, George Thomas
Elliget, Edmund
Finn, William, M.R.C.P.
Firebrace, E. B.
Firebrace, J. B.
Fisher, Owen
Fitzgerald, John
Flanagan, James Jos.
Foxton, J. G.
Gahagher, Robert
Gibney, Michael
Glass, James P.
Gleeson, P. J. P.
Goode, Samuel
Gregory, Robert K.
Groom, Wm. Alfred
Guener, Henry Field
Harding, Silas
Hart, Henri J.
Harwood, William
Heffernan, John
Heelan, Richard
Hinds, William
Hinkins, John Thomas
Hobbs, Alexander
Hoffman, William
Howell, Richard
Johnston, Archibald
Johnston, Robert
Johnston, Robert
Johnston, William
Kestevan, William
Kidd, William
King, Alexander Henry
King, F. W.

King, John C.
King, Robert
King, Robt. Henry
Long, Gideon L.
Leyes, Samuel
Lingham, H.
Lovelock, E.
Macfarlane, Walter
Mackintosh, Daniel
Macnamara, John
Marr, Adam
Martin, E. W. K
Marwken, Joseph Ankers
Mason, Thomas
Matthews, Stewart
Mathewson, H. W.
Melougan, Robert
Monahan, John
Monahan, Thomas
Moggan, Charles
Morrison, Hugh
Morton, William
Murphy, Matthew
Mulally, John
M'Cae, M.
M'Combie, Thos.
M'Cracken, P.
M'Cracken, Robert
M'Crae, A.
M'Crae, George Gordon
M'Donough, Patrick
M'Dougall, H. C.
M'Laurin, Robert
Ninano, William
O'Brien, Hugh
O'Felan, Henry
Orr, Edward
Peoble, Cornelius
Pinnock, James Denham
Plummer, Wm., M.L.A.
Pollack, John
Punch, James
Purvis, Henry
Raven, William George
Raven, William
Robertson, Francis
Robertson, James
Rooney, Philip
Russell, Thomas
Ryan, William
Seward, James M.
Sinclair, John
Sleight, John
Shacklock, John
Shearer, John
Sheppard, Sherbourne
Short, Hugh
Smith, Ebenezer
Smith, Robert
Stanbridge, W. E.
Stanaway, William
Stevenson, R. B.
Summers, Isaac
Sutcliffe, Richard
Treacy, E. M.
Tuckett, W. H.
Usher, Robert
Usher, William
Walker, Alexander
Watt, Ross
Welsh, George A.
Welsh, William
Westby, Edmund Wright
White, James E.
White, John J.

177

178   *Visit of H.R.H. Prince Alfred.*

Wright, Edward Byam	Evans, Evan	Martin, Septimus	Sumner, John
Wilkinson, John	Ewart, John	Messiter, Thomas	Taylor, Alfred
Wilson, John	Fairchild, Jesse	Miles, Frederick G.	Thompson, Patrick
Wilson, William	Panefie, Joseph P. (Victorian)	Moody, R. S. ii.	Thwaites, George
Winter, W. J.		Moston, Wm. Lockhart	Thwaites, John
Wright, Thomas Walne	Freer, Henry William	Murray, Thomas	Thwaites, Thomas H.
	Gillman, John Francis	Murray, Thomas	Turner, George N.
1842.	Guthrie, William	M'Donnell, John	Umphelby, C. P.
	Ham, Cornelius T.	M'Laine, John Campbell	Urquhart, W. S.
Aiken, F.	Ham, Theophilus J.	M'Lean, N.	Webb, Fredk. Thomas
Aplin, Dyson	Hammond, William	Nicholson, Germain	Were, W. D.
Ball, William	Hawthorn, Reilby	Nixon, James	White, Isaac
Battye, L.	Heales, R.	Nolan, David	Whitehead, Joseph
Bear, J. P.	Houston, John	Norton, Charles	Whitelaw, W. S.
Bennett, William	Hucldart, Peter	Officer, R., junr.	Wintle, Edwin (born in Melbourne)
Bignell, William	Hull, William	Park, James	
Birkett, Joseph	Hull, W. H.	Pascoe, J. B.	
Birchall, Arthur	Hutton C. B.	Perlavel, David Louis	**1843.**
Burns, Joseph R.	James, Joseph	Pinnock, James Denham	
Campbell, A. M.	Jones, William B.	Pittman, Joseph	Clarke, William
Carson, John	Kerr, Robert	Raphael, Henry	Coats, Thomas S.
Croll, Andrew	Knight, William	Richardson, Joseph	
Cumming, Thomas	Leahy, William	Riddle, Thomas Casby	**1846.**
Cunningham, R.	Leahy, W. H.	Ross, Mired	
Dennys, Charles John	Learmonth, William	Rostron, Lawrence	Willis, Charles
Dow, James Foot	Linacre, James	Sayce, Edward	
Dougharty, John George	Lloyd, Henry	Smith, William	No date given.
Downing, Robert	Lock, W. H.	Sproul, A.	
Ebler, Thomas	Mackenzie, John	Stroke, Henry	Anderson, Joseph, Lieut.-Colonel, C.B., K.H.

The address was very handsomely emblazoned on vellum in variegated colours, bound in red morocco and gold, and signed by more than six hundred gentlemen who had been resident in the colony over twenty-five years. His Royal Highness listened to the reading of the document with marked attention, and at its conclusion read the following reply :—

TO THE OLD COLONISTS OF VICTORIA.

Gentlemen—Though one of the last of the many addresses which I have received since my arrival in Victoria, yours is, I assure you, very far from being the least interesting to me; and I thank you sincerely, in the name of the Queen, for the expressions of loyalty to Her Majesty's Throne and person contained in it.

I can well understand that you, who have watched the wonderfully rapid rise and progress of this colony from its infancy to the present day, must often have felt anxious lest the natural feeling of pride in the great success and prosperity to which Victoria has attained, should weaken the loyalty of its people, and cause them to underrate the advantages of being so closely connected with the mother-country ; but now, when you have witnessed the unbounded enthusiasm with which your fellow-colonists have received me, the son of their Queen ; when you have observed that their chief aim has been to impress upon me that their loyalty and devotion to Her Majesty are unaltered, and that they cling with affection to England and English institutions—you may well rest assured, as I confidently do, that this colony is second to none in loyalty and attachment to their Sovereign.

The present prosperity and wealth of this colony, of which I have had the privilege and pleasure of judging for myself, could, indeed, never have been attained without those great characteristics of the British race to which you allude ; and while I feel convinced that the youth of this colony inherit these virtues, I also hope that my stay among you may help to convince them, born so many thousand miles from England, of the love and solicitude which Her Majesty feels for all her subjects.

In thanking you for your kind wishes for my welfare and happiness, I cannot conclude without assuring you that I shall leave your hospitable shores with deep regret, and that I shall always regard with the sincerest attachment and interest the colonists, old and young, of Victoria.

The Hon. J. P. Fawkner then made a short speech, to the effect that he was the earliest settler who had landed in Victoria. After which, Mr. E. Henty expressed thanks for the Prince's kindness in receiving the address, and the ceremony concluded.

His Royal Highness was then conducted by Mr. Tulk over the library, picture gallery, and museum, in each of which he spent some time in carefully examining the different specimens of art and science. An adjournment was next made to the committee-room, where the trustees presented his Royal Highness with a very handsome work, bound in morocco gilt by Mr. John Ferres, the Government Printer, consisting of *Biographical Charts of Italian Painters of the Old Schools of Naples, Bologna, Florence, and Venice*, compiled under the direction of the trustees, and containing more than fifty effectively executed photographs, taken by Mr. Noone, from the best line and steel engravings of the productions of the above schools now extant. In addition to the above, presentations of handsomely bound copies of the catalogue of the Melbourne Public Library were made to Her Majesty the Queen, Her Royal Highness the Princess of Wales, and Her Royal Highness the Princess of Prussia. The copy intended for Her Majesty was bound in scarlet morocco, that for the Princess of Wales in purple, and that for the Princess of Prussia in maroon. The several presentations were received by the Duke with a few words of acknowledgment, and after briefly expressing his satisfaction with all he had seen, his Royal Highness and suite retired.

After leaving the Public Library, his Royal Highness the Duke of Edinburgh proceeded to the Melbourne University, where due preparations had been made to receive him. As the Royal carriage drove up the avenue, the members of the University present, to the number of about one hundred, in full academic dress, formed on each side of the central path of the quadrangle, members of the senate to the south, the bachelors next, and then the undergraduates. On alighting from his carriage the Prince was received by the Chancellor (Sir Redmond Barry), the Vice-Chancellor (Dr. Brownless), the warden, and the members of the council, by whom he was conducted to the library. Nearly all the members of the senate were present, including the Bishop of Melbourne, Sir James Palmer, Sir Francis Murphy, and others; and among the professors and lecturers were Messrs. Wilson, M'Coy, Hearn, Halford, Drs. Tracy and Neild, Mr. J. G. Knight, &c. As the procession passed through the lines, his Royal Highness was saluted by the removal of the "trenchers," and he raised his hat in return; the senate, bachelors, and undergraduates then fell into line, and followed. On reaching the library, in which chairs and a dais had been prepared, his Royal Highness and the Governor took their places, and Sir Redmond Barry, as Chancellor, read the following address:—

We, the University of Melbourne, beg to assure your Royal Highness of our unswerving loyalty to the Queen, and of our dutiful and respectful affection for her Majesty and the members of the Royal Family. We desire to be allowed to greet your Royal Highness with a hearty welcome. We pray be permitted to express a hope that, in the survey of the institutions of this country, you will feel satisfaction in recognising the wisdom and liberality of the Government and Legislature which, in the earliest years of its history, founded and endowed this University for promoting sound learning in Victoria, the importance of which object has already caused the University to be honoured by the marked distinction of Her Majesty's gracious favour. We trust that, having achieved the high purpose which prompted the voyage you have undertaken, and having witnessed in many lands the true attachment of the inhabitants of numerous dependencies of the empire to British institutions and British government, your Royal Highness may, by the blessing of Divine Providence, return in safety to our mother-country, bearing with you the sincere good wishes of all communities for your success in the honourable profession you have adopted, and for your continued prosperity and welfare.

The address (of which a photograph was taken by Mr. E. Meyers, of Little Collins-street) was handsomely engraved on parchment, and framed in crimson velvet and gold bullion fringe. Appropriate heraldic bearings encircled the body of the address, and to it were affixed the seal of the University and the signatures of the Chancellor, the Vice-Chancellor, and the Registrar. Copies of the University Calendar were also presented to his Royal Highness, after which he was ushered, accompanied by his suite, to the council-chamber, off the library, where he took the requisite declaration, signed the rolls, and robed himself. In the interval the Chancellor and Vice-Chancellor took their places on the dais, and shortly afterwards his Royal Highness was led in by Professor Wilson, who, after conducting the royal visitor to the front of the dais, said: " I present unto you his Royal Highness the Duke of Edinburgh, Doctor of Laws of the University of Edinburgh, as a fit and proper person to be admitted to that degree in the University of Melbourne."

The Chancellor then replied:—" In virtue of the power I am invested with, I receive your Royal Highness, Alfred Ernest Albert, K.G., K.T., Duke of Edinburgh, Earl of Kent and Earl of Ulster, Prince of Saxony and Duke of Saxe Coburg Gotha, Captain in the Royal Navy, Doctor of Laws of the Edinburgh University, and invest you with the rank and privileges of the same degree in the University of Melbourne." The Chancellor then shook hands, and conducted the Prince to the dais, after which

Professor Wilson presented Francis Charles Needham, commonly known as Viscount Newry and Morne, B.A. of the University of Oxford, as a fit and proper person to be admitted to the rank and privileges of the same degree in the University of Melbourne; and the Chancellor received his Lordship accordingly. The two new graduates having been thus received,

Sir Redmond Barry, in a few words, said that he was certain all the members of the University, from the senate to the undergraduates, were of one accord in their estimation of the honour conferred upon the University by the admission into her ranks of his Royal Highness. Her Majesty had already granted to the University the distinction and privilege of placing her degrees on a par with those of the English colleges, and if anything could add a stimulus to the exertions of the University, it would be the enrolment of his Royal Highness as a member.

The conferring of the degree upon his Royal Highness was greeted with loud applause; after which, at the call of the Chancellor, three hearty cheers were given for the Queen, and three more for the Royal graduate. His Royal Highness then left the Library, and proceeded to inspect the different lecture-rooms, the medical hall, and the museums, where the different objects of interest were presented to his notice by Professors Wilson, Halford, and M'Coy.

On the evening of the same day his Royal Highness visited the Princess's Theatre to witness the performances of the Japanese troupe of acrobats and jugglers.

THE DEPARTURE FROM WILLIAMSTOWN.

Saturday, the 4th day of January, 1868, was fixed as the date of the departure of his Royal Highness from the colony of Victoria. It having been decided that the embarkation should take place at Williamstown, the loyal residents of this marine borough had testified their appreciation of the honour by a general illumination of a really brilliant character, and great credit is due to the Mayor, councillors, and burgesses of Williamstown for the effective display made. As at Emerald Hill, the Council had been assisted by a local Reception Committee, owing to which, no doubt, is attributable the success attending the demonstration.

It had been arranged that the last item in the programme of the Prince's visit should be the laying of the memorial stone of the Williamstown Graving Dock—the dock from that day forth to bear the Prince's name.

The journey from Melbourne to Williamstown on Saturday morning was quickly made, and as the train drew up at its destination the royal occupant was welcomed with enthusiastic cheers. The group about him was a distinguished one. Besides military officers and the Governor, there were Lord Newry, the Hon. Eliot Yorke, Mr. Haig, R.N., Mr. Brierly, Mr. Manners-Sutton, Lieutenant Rothwell, R.A.; the Hon. J. M'Culloch, the Hon. G. F. Verdon, C.B., the Hon. Captain MacMahon, the Hon. J. G. Francis, the Hon. J. M. Grant, the Hon. J. F. Sullivan, the Hon. W. M. K. Vale, the Hon. S. H. Bindon, the Hon. Captain Cole; Commander Norman, of H.M.C.S. *Victoria*; Captain Fullarton, of the *Pharos*; Mr. J. S. Butters (the Mayor of Melbourne); Mr. M'Intyre, Mayor of Sandhurst, Mr. Myring, Mayor of Castlemaine, Mr. T. Mason, Mayor of Williamstown, Mr. Morley, Mayor of Sandridge, Mr. Thistlethwaite, Mayor of Emerald Hill, and other municipal notabilities. In front was a guard of honour of the Williamstown Volunteer Artillery Corps, under Major T. Stewart; the school children, appropriately attired, waiting to sing the National Anthem; and beyond, the general public, numbering perhaps some two or three thousand; and the police, under Inspectors Hare, Kabat, B. Smith, and Disney, kept the whole in order. The first business was the local address, which was handed in. It was as follows :—

May it please your Royal Highness—We, the inhabitants of the borough of Williamstown, approach your Royal Highness with the assurance of our devoted attachment to Her Majesty's Throne and person. We, in common with our fellow-colonists, rejoice that your Royal Highness has visited this portion of Her Majesty's empire, and in so doing has had opportunities of judging for yourself of the resources of this young and prosperous colony; and we trust that you have enjoyed your sojourn amongst us. As your Royal Highness is about to leave Victoria, we pray that Providence may watch over you on your voyages. Signed on behalf of the inhabitants,

THOMAS MASON, CHAIRMAN.
J. E. RUSSEL, HON. SEC. RECEPTION COMMITTEE.

REPLY.

Gentlemen—I am sincerely gratified by the warm expression of your kind feeling towards me contained in the address I have received from you, and thank you most heartily for your congratulations upon my safe arrival in this portion of Her Majesty's dominions. I am proud to belong to the profession which enables me to visit the Australian colonies in a vessel under my own command, and in which so many besides myself have the opportunity of seeing the loyalty, energy, and prosperity which characterise the people of this colony of the British empire, and of sharing in the welcome you have given me. ALFRED.

Then the school children sang two verses of the National Anthem, under the leadership of Mr. G. F. Smith. Three cheers for the Prince having been called for by the Mayor, and given with considerable heartiness, the whole party proceeded to their carriages for the procession round town.

Williamstown had put on a fair holiday appearance for its welcome to the Prince. In Nelson-place there was an arch somewhat after the model of the one in Collins-street, and inscribed on one side with "Welcome, Alfred," and on the other "Farewell, Alfred." Armorial devices were painted on either side, and the Royal arms were displayed on small shields surmounted by little flags. On the side first presented to the Prince's view were brackets in the middle of the piers, and on these stood a number of the Naval Training ship boys, waving flags. Williamstown, being a nautical place, seemed to determine to revel in flags, of which it displayed a prodigious number. It was not enough that in the Bay every ship was dressed fore and aft in coloured bunting, but in the town every house showed its flagstaff—at least one, and frequently half-a-dozen—while lines of flags were drawn from house to house, from chimney to chimney, across and along the street, and from whatever other points they could be stretched.

Something had been done to render the unfinished appearance of the Graving Dock less unsightly than usual. From the different workshops on the ground streamers of all kinds and sizes were floating, and over the dock itself were lines of ropes, which were covered with bunting and the heraldic banners of the various suburban boroughs. On the west side of the dock had been erected a large platform, which was carpeted, and was also covered with a canopy of blue velvet, and beside this was the memorial-stone which his Royal Highness was to lay. The dock was crowded with persons who had assembled to view the ceremony, two thousand five hundred invitations having been issued, and there were fully that number of persons present.

A guard of honour, consisting of the Williamstown Naval Brigade, under the command of Captain Elder, was drawn up in the centre of the dock, and the Williamstown Artillery were also present, under Major Stewart. A detachment of police was also in attendance, under Superintendents Lyttleton and Hare, and Inspector Kabat.

On the Royal party arriving at the gates of the dockyard, they were received by Mr. Vale (the Commissioner of Public Works), the Chief Secretary, the Minister of Mines, the Minister of Justice, and other members of the Ministry, who conducted the Prince to the dais, on which were grouped his Excellency the Governor, Lord Newry, Mr. Yorke, Mr. H. C. Manners-Sutton, most of the members of the Legislative Council and Legislative Assembly. Sir Redmond Barry, Mr. Wardell (Inspector of Public Works), Mr. A. C. Todd, of the Public Works Department, &c.

Mr. Vale, addressing his Royal Highness, said—It will be a source of satisfaction to the people of this colony in time to come to have your name associated with one of their great public works. I have, therefore, on their behalf, to ask that your Royal Highness will allow this dock to bear your name; and I have further great pleasure in asking that you will this day lay the memorial stone of it.

His Royal Highness having bowed assent to Mr. Vale's request, the latter introduced to him Mr. W. W. Wardell (Inspector-General of Public Works), the engineer of the dock, who, having ordered the upper stone to be raised, placed in the cavity prepared for the purpose a glass-case containing copies of *The Argus*, *Age*, and *Herald*, the current coins of the realm, and a parchment scroll containing the following inscription:—

ALFRED GRAVING DOCK, WILLIAMSTOWN.

The stone covering this scroll was laid by His Royal Highness Prince Alfred, K.G., &c., as a memorial of his visit, 4th January, A.D. 1868, in the thirty-first year of the reign of Her Most Gracious Majesty Queen Victoria—Sir T. H. Manners-Sutton, K.C.B., Governor of the Colony of Victoria.

MEMBERS OF THE CABINET.—Chief Secretary, Hon. J. M'Culloch; Attorney-General, Hon. G. Higinbotham; Minister of Justice, Hon. S. H. Bindon; Treasurer, Hon. G. F. Verdon, C.B.; President Board of Land and Works, Hon. J. M. Grant; Commissioner of Trade and Customs, Hon. J. G. Francis; Commissioner of Roads and Railways, Hon. J. F. Sullivan; Minister of Mines, Hon. J. Macgregor; Commissioner of Public Works, Hon. William M. K. Vale; the Hon. G. W. Cole, R.N., M.L.C., without office.

ENGINEER.—W. W. Wardell, Inspector-General of Public Works; assisted by W. H. Steel and A. C. Todd.
CONTRACTOR FOR THE WORKS NOW IN PROGRESS.—James Leggatt.
RESIDENT INSPECTOR.—H. Woods.

Mr. Vale then handed to the Prince a gold trowel, which had been made for this occasion; and the surface of the lower stone having been spread with mortar by the workmen, some mortar was handed to the Prince, which his Royal Highness spread on the memorial stone, which was then lowered to its place, and his Royal Highness applied the level and plumb-line to it, and, having received a mallet from Mr. Wardell, gave the stone two taps, and declared it well and truly laid. The band of the Naval Brigade played the National Anthem, and at the invitation of Mr. Vale, the assembly gave three cheers for the Queen, three for the Prince, and three for the Governor. This concluded the ceremony, which did not last more than five minutes. The Royal party then withdrew.

The following document was handed by Mr. Vale to the Prince :—

VICTORIA, AUSTRALIA.

GOVERNOR.—Sir J. H. T. Manners-Sutton, K.C.B., &c.

MEMBERS OF THE CABINET —Chief Secretary, Hon. J. McCulloch ; Attorney-General, Hon. G. Higinbotham ; Minister of Justice, Hon. S. H. Bindon ; Treasurer, Hon. G. F. Verdon, C.B. ; President of the Board of Land and Works, Hon. J. M. Grant ; Commissioner of Trade and Customs, Hon. J. G. Francis ; Commissioner of Roads and Railways, Hon. J. F. Sullivan ; Minister of Mines, Hon. J. Macgregor ; Commissioner of Public Works, Hon. William M. K. Vale ; Hon. G. W. Cole, R.N., M.L.C., without office.

ALFRED GRAVING DOCK, WILLIAMSTOWN.

Memorial Stone laid by H.R.H. Prince Alfred, 4th January, 1868.

This dock now in course of construction will, when completed, be 126 feet in length over all, and 100 feet long on the floor within the entrance. It will be 97 feet in width on the top, and the entrance will be 80 feet wide in the clear. At ordinary spring tides there will be a depth of water of 24 feet 6 inches on the sill at low water, and 27 feet at high water. The entrance will be closed by an iron caisson. The dock is built of the basaltic stone of the neighbourhood, known as bluestone, and is estimated to cost when complete, with pumping machines, &c , £185,000.

The dockyard comprises an area of fifteen acres, and includes the present Patent Slip, which is capable of raising vessels of 2000 tons, and within this dockyard workshops for the several trades connected with the building will be erected.

The works of the dock were commenced in November, 1864, and its completion is expected by the end of 1869.

ENGINEER.—W. W. Wardell, inspector-general of public works ; assisted by W. H. Steel and A. C. Todd.

CONTRACTOR FOR WORKS NOW IN PROGRESS.—J. Leggatt.

RESIDENT INSPECTOR. H. Woods.

The following description of the trowel which was used at the ceremony is taken from the *Argus* :—Its weight is nearly fifty ounces. The blade had as its principal ornament the Victorian arms, standing in demi-relief, beautifully enamelled in crimson and light and dark blue, surrounded by a white enamel border. Around this are four of the Australian flora, the *Asplenium flabellifolium, Correa speciosa, Gleichenia dicarpa,* and *Geranium dissectum*. Rising from the blade, and forming an admirable and graceful connection with the handle, is a cluster of fern fronds. The handle itself was a remarkable as well as an excellent result of the goldsmith's art. Its pattern, including tridents and anchors in bold relief, surrounded by rope borders, and between them enamelled laurels, was clasped by the *Galatea's* pennant, which twines gracefully from top to bottom. On either side, and pinned on to the laurel, was the letter "A," and the handle terminated with dolphins, surmounted by the coronet of a Royal Duke. *Fleur de lis* and Maltese crosses showed well against the crimson enamel of the cap, and the ermine enamel in its turn assists the circle of diamonds and rubies which surrounded the coronet, and gave an admirable finish to the design. The blade had on its obverse side the following inscription :—" This trowel was used by his Royal Highness Prince Alfred, when laying the memorial-stone of the Alfred Graving Dock, Williamstown. Victoria, January 4, 1868." On its reverse is a plan of the dock, with the names of the Governor, the Ministry, the Inspector-General of Public Works, and his assistants.

The Prince, on leaving the dock, immediately proceeded to the Breakwater Pier in order to embark, and, accompanied by the Governor and Captain Norman, stepped into the barge of H.M.C.S.S. *Victoria*. While the people were cheering, the oarsmen had got clear, and were steadily pulling for the *Galatea*. As his Royal Highness passed the end of the pier he turned back to look, and not till then did the spectators seem to feel that he was gone, and set up another cheer louder than ever. It was the last real Victorian cheer the Prince heard ; and as its echoes died away, the cannon took them up again. The Royal Artillery fired a royal salute from the Williamstown battery, which the *Galatea*, by this time carrying the ensign at her fore, the royal standard at her main, and the white ensign at her mizen, replied to, after the customary form, with yards manned. As the barge passed H.M.C.S.S. *Victoria*, she fired her salute too, and with admirable rapidity and regularity. The scene in Hobson's Bay had now become a very effective one.

The Prince got on board his vessel at about one p.m., and following were an immense number of boats the *Pharos* included—conveying the Prince's guests, invited to his farewell luncheon. These invitations only included members of the Legislature and their wives, but a considerable number of other persons managed to thrust their way in on various pretexts. The luncheon finished, the *Galatea's* anchor was weighed, and she slowly steamed away. The time for departure had been fixed for three o'clock p.m., and the Prince was punctual to the second. Following in the wake of the *Galatea* was a fleet of smaller steamers, their decks crowded with passengers. There were H.M.C.S.S. *Victoria*, the *Pharos*, the *Resolute*, the *Warhawk*, the *Bendigo*, the *Sophia*, the *Titan*, the *Hercules*, and the *Prince Alfred*. None, however, could keep up with the great steamer long after the first mile, when she went at full speed, under a tremendous head of steam. The *Hercules* and the *Prince Alfred* were the first to turn back, and the *Pharos* followed; but the others kept on as hard as they could till opposite Point Cook, when it was time to part company. The *Victoria* then fired another royal salute, and turned away. The *Resolute* and the *Warhawk* still kept up gallantly, but at a quarter to four o'clock the *Galatea* was fading in the distance, clouded in her smoke, and then the last of the escort reluctantly turned their prows homeward. In a few minutes the royal vessel was lost to sight, and Prince Alfred—last seen on the bridge looking at the fading prospect—had left Victoria.

CHILDREN'S AND OTHER FESTIVITIES.

One of the most significant phases of the visit of his Royal Highness the Duke of Edinburgh to the colony of Victoria, was the general anxiety shown by the adult population on behalf of the children. In no instance where there were any public rejoicings were the children omitted from participating therein; and if any one had been previously disposed to question the loyal training of the rising generation of Victoria, the demonstrations made at the numerous juvenile fêtes must have dispelled all misgivings on that head. A yearning to see a son of our beloved Queen pervaded all classes, but in the case of the children the desire was intensified, and became almost a mania. There was something higher and better than mere curiosity at the bottom of all this. The tens of thousands of children of the industrial classes who greeted the presence of his Royal Highness with such ringing applause, and who were specially attired in honour of our illustrious visitor, were but the exponents of the feelings of their parents, and it may with safety be prophesied that the Australian children of 1867-8 will not in future years be less loyal than their progenitors. The limits to which the present work is restricted render it impossible to do anything approaching justice to the various children's fêtes held in honour of the Prince. Those which follow are but little more than mentioned, and many of the juvenile treats which were afforded by patriotic persons, not being reported in the newspapers, are altogether omitted. Enough, however, is probably given to show that the youth of the colony played a prominent as well as a highly interesting part in the reception of his Royal Highness.

Industrial Schools, Geelong.

On the 2nd December, the children of the Industrial Schools, Geelong, had an extra treat in commemoration of the visit of the Duke of Edinburgh, provided for out of the funds placed at the disposal of the Mayor by the Reception Committee. Among the things supplied for the enjoyment of the children were twenty-eight pounds of lollies, two cases of cherries, one hundred pounds of cake, and a quantity of oranges. Some fireworks were also supplied and let off for the amusement of the children, who enjoyed themselves thoroughly.

Brunswick.

The children's *fête* and free banquet at Brunswick, on the 3rd December, was one of the most successful of the suburban demonstrations which took place in honour of the Prince. The affair came off in the Royal Park, and was attended by some fifteen hundred to two thousand persons. Money and goods to the amount of over £100 had been collected. Proceedings were commenced at eleven o'clock in the morning by the assembling of the children, some seven hundred in number, in the Retreat Paddock, from whence, after singing the National Anthem, they marched in procession to the ground, headed by the juvenile band of the hulk *Deborah*, who had been brought from town in gaily decorated waggons, lent for the occasion by the superintendent of the Pentridge Stockade. All sorts of athletic sports, such as running, jumping, racing in sacks, &c., were provided, and refreshments were served in three marquees. The utmost good order was observed throughout the day, and the occasion was one of general enjoyment.

Essendon and Flemington.

The *fête* given to the children by the Council of the borough took place on Saturday, 7th December, in a paddock belonging to Mr. John Connell, at Moonee Ponds. The children, numbering about five hundred, were assembled at noon in front of the Post Office, under the direction of Mr. Hinkins, who directed the arrangements, and where the National Anthem was sung. Two bands of music were provided. As soon as the youngsters had marched to the paddock, refreshments were served, and then commenced the round of amusements. The Mayor and other members of the Council were present, and the day was altogether one of unalloyed success. The car-drivers of the district conveyed the children home free of expense.

Donnybrook and Wallan Wallan.

The picnic given to the children of the Donnybrook and Wallan district, in honour of the Royal visit, came off on Saturday, 7th December. The site chosen for it was Mount Fraser, which is well adapted for such a purpose, the bottom of the crater being like a bowling-green, the banks round it forming an amphitheatre, and covered here and there with groves of the shady wattle. There were upwards of two hundred children present, chiefly from the schools of Beveridge, Donnybrook, Meikleham, and Wallan Wallan, who, with their friends, made up a goodly assemblage of about five hundred. Ample provision was made for supplying their wants, there being upwards of five hundred pounds of beef and mutton, one hundred pounds of ham, three hundred pounds of plain bread, three hundred and fifty pounds of cake, one hogshead of beer, several scores of gallons of gingerbeer, and tea and coffee *ad libitum*. The feasting being over, the little ones took to swinging, foot-racing, &c., &c., whilst their elders indulged in "kiss-in-the-ring," dancing, throwing the stone, foot-races on flat and over timber, cricket, &c. In the afternoon, Mr. Godfrey, J.P., having converted a dray into a platform, addressed a few appropriate remarks to those present, and asked for three cheers for the Queen, the Royal family, and Prince Alfred severally, which were most enthusiastically given. Three cheers more were warmly accorded to Mr. Fraser, the owner of the ground.

Dunolly.

A local demonstration in honour of his Royal Highness's visit to Victoria was held in the Borough of Dunolly on Thursday, the 12th December. The principal features of the day's rejoicings were a grand procession, in which the Borough Council, the Council of the Shire of Bet Bet, and other corporate bodies, the Prince Alfred Lodge of Oddfellows, M.U., the Rescue Tent of Rechabites, the clergy, local magistracy, about seven hundred and fifty school children, &c., &c., joined—a substantial feast for the children—a free banquet for adults, of whom about one thousand or twelve hundred sat down—old English sports in the Recreation Reserve—and in the evening illuminations, a grand display of fireworks, and monster bonfire. The affair was an unqualified success, and was thoroughly enjoyed by all who took part in it.

Richmond.

This gathering took place on Saturday, 14th December, in the Yarra Park. The number of children who assembled could not have been short of five thousand. Dr. Stewart, the mayor, on horseback, acted as marshal, and was ably assisted by the members of committee in carrying out the arrangements. Among the good things provided were two hogsheads of ale, a pipe of wine from the vineyard of the Hon. J. G. Francis, at Sunbury, presented by that gentleman; one hundred gallons of gingerbeer in casks, a liberal supply of milk, a proper provision for water, four thousand buns, the same number of rolls, one thousand pounds of cherries in bags, seven hundred pounds of plum pudding, six hundred pounds of cake, two hundred pounds of lollies in bags, and fifty pounds' worth of toys to be distributed as prizes for races, &c. On the ground was a large marquee lent by Captain Parnell, for commissariat purposes, and twenty-eight tents lent by the military authorities for the use of the children. The band of the naval training-ship was in attendance, as well as a band hired by the committee. Swings, and many other appliances suitable for the occasion, were scattered over the ground. Dancing, singing, racing, swinging, and games were carried on with zest, and were kept up till nearly seven o'clock in the evening.

St. Kilda.

The Borough Council and inhabitants of St. Kilda fêted the children of the locality in the local park, on Saturday, 14th December, and the event passed off with the greatest possible satisfaction to all parties interested. A short time before the Corporation voted a sum of £120, to be appropriated in making a display of fireworks on the night of the arrival of the *Galatea* in Hobson's Bay, and contributing to a fête to be given to all the children of the borough, without distinction. The inhabitants of the district subscribed towards the latter event about £150, and a committee, composed of the borough councillors and several private residents of St. Kilda, was formed to carry out the arrangements in connection with it. At a quarter to twelve the army of youngsters was mustered at the gates of the park, and, marshalled in admirable order by the teachers of the respective schools, marched to the scene of the day's amusements, which lay about a quarter of a mile from the gate in Fitzroy-street, and a little north of the main road through the park. Here tents were erected to the number of twenty-nine, one being made to represent each school, with its flag flying from the summit, and three devoted respectively to the storage of provisions, the entertainment of the committee and teachers, and the band of the St. Kilda Volunteers. At the height of the day's recreation there were on the ground about 3000 children and 1000 adults, including 500 day and Sunday-school teachers, the friends of children, and visitors. An object of much amusement to adults and amazement to juveniles was the Brobdignagian teapot, which was placed on a stand in the centre of the animated throng, and formed an object of prominence from every point of view. This machine was composed of galvanised corrugated iron, and had three taps connected with it. There was ample provision made for the children to amuse themselves, and the merry-go-rounds, swings, &c., found numerous votaries, and races for boys and girls. A little lady named Alice Woolcott, aged seven, proved herself a capital runner, having come in first in five races, and second in two or three; and Miss Alice Cook also signalised herself in a marked degree. Masters Seacamp, Farrell, and Bell were some of the best of the boys at running and jumping. Races in sacks found numbers of adherents, and were a fruitful source of amusement. The sports were kept up with great spirit until seven o'clock, when the children were conducted to their homes.

City of Melbourne.

The fête given by the Corporation of Melbourne to the children attending the different Common and Sabbath Schools within the metropolitan district, took place on Monday, 16th December, in the Zoological Gardens reserve, and passed off in the most satisfactory manner. His Royal Highness the Duke of Edinburgh, attended by the Hon. Eliot Yorke, drove down to the gardens in his four-horse drag, and having alighted at the gates, walked through the crowd of little children, by whom he was most enthusiastically cheered. His Royal Highness appeared to be much pleased with the juvenile demonstration, and to be interested in the proceedings. After remaining in one of the marquees for a few minutes, the Prince was obliged to leave, in order to be present at the funeral of Captain Wilkinson, R.N. Although no absolute record of the number of children present was kept, it is estimated that there could not have been less than 10,000 on the ground, including those from the Immigrants' Home and the Blind Asylum. They began to arrive before noon, and when all were present, a plentiful supply of provisions of the best kind and description was distributed, after which toys and sweetmeats were given to the children. Suitable games and amusements were resorted to in different parts of the reserve. The Mayor, aldermen, and councillors all exerted themselves most strenuously in providing for the children's entertainment, and their efforts were attended with the greatest possible success. Mr. Grimwood, the caterer, provided for 15,000, so that there was more than sufficient, and some to spare. There were 2000 loaves of bread, 1000 lbs. of biscuit, 20,000 buns, 15,000 bags of lollies, meat by the ton, and everything else in proportion. Altogether, the Corporation fête to the children was a decided success, and the members of the Council must be congratulated upon the manner in which everything was conducted.

Collingwood.

The children of Collingwood were invited to a fête, given at Dight's Paddock on Monday 16th December. They thoroughly enjoyed themselves, and had reason to be grateful to the Mayor (Mr. Baynham), the council, and the members of the committee, for the excellent manner in which the arrangements were carried out. Swings, games, and dancing were amongst the amusements provided. Several races, of 250 yards each, were run; the prizes being cricketing materials. The first one, for boys under fourteen years, was won by Hughes; the second, for boys under twelve years, by Seward. O'Meara was the winner in the next race, which was for boys under ten years. The teachers' race, for which a copy of Macaulay's *History of England* was given, fell to Charles Crook, the blindfold race to Turnbull, and the hurdle race to Beard. Each of the children was presented with a medal. The amusements did not terminate until sunset. It was estimated that during the day nearly 8000 persons, mostly children, were on the ground.

Pentridge.

The fête in commemoration of the visit of Prince Alfred, which had been postponed in consequence of wet weather, was resumed on Monday, 16th December. The locality selected was a vacant piece of ground in the centre of the district, used principally for parade purposes by the local volunteers. Some four hundred children attended, and were well cared for, and regaled with cakes, buns, fruit, &c.

On the 19th the Pentridge Schools fête took place in Mr. Thorp's paddock, on the banks of the Merri Creek. The children were mustered on the vacant ground in front of the Stockade, and after singing the National Anthem, under the leadership of Mr. Stranger, were marched through the village *en route* to the ground, where, by the kindness of Colonel Champ, tents were provided. The amusements consisted, amongst other things, of merry-go-round, football, cricket for the boys, and swings and skipping-ropes for the girls. The number on the ground could not have been less than one thousand.

Moorabbin.

The children's festival at Moorabbin came off on 19th December, when, notwithstanding the excessive heat of the day, it proved a success. The locality chosen for it was the drill-ground at South Brighton, where a large marquee had been erected, as well as two smaller tents, for the accommodation of the children and visitors, of whom there were in all about two thousand present. Various amusements were provided. The St. Kilda brass band was in attendance, and there was a plenteous supply of provisions.

Brighton.

The children's fête at Brighton, on Thursday, 19th December, was a most gratifying success. The committee, consisting of the Mayor and members of the Borough Council, the ministers of the several congregations, and teachers of the various schools, had invited their young *protégés* at ten a.m., when a very numerous gathering was on the ground. The National Anthem was sung by over eight hundred children, comprising three hundred and twenty-six boys and five hundred and fifty-four girls, besides one hundred and fifty more not attached to schools, and was delivered with very pleasing effect. The only address given was by the Mayor (Mr. James Webb), after which grace was sung, and a liberal distribution of refreshments was made, including buns, cake, pudding, gingerbeer, lemonade, &c. Medals were also given to all children who had not previously been furnished with them. Sports of all kinds were provided, including revolving boats, football, and racing and jumping for prizes of useful books. After the distribution of prizes, tea and coffee, &c., were again served out, and the young folks resumed their play. A splendid marquee sheltered the guests from the heat of the sun, and formed not the least pleasing feature of the day's arrangements.

Prahran and South Yarra.

The juvenile treat given to the children of Prahran and South Yarra on December 19th was attended by upwards of two thousand five hundred children. The various schools represented, thirty in number, marched from the Town Hall at noon, under their respective banners; and soon after their arrival on the picnic ground, were in full enjoyment of the various means of amusement provided for their entertainment. Refreshments were provided in two large tents, and each school had also a tent of its own as a rallying point. Seven pounds ten shillings was distributed in toy prizes to the winners of the flat and hurdle races, feats of jumping, &c. The arrangements of the managing committee were very good, and excellent order was maintained. The proposal to provide this treat for the children of the district originated with the Borough Council of Prahran, and the funds were raised by public subscription, assisted by a donation of one hundred pounds from the Council, with one hundred pounds from the Reception Commission, and twenty-five pounds from the City Corporation, given in consideration of the erection by the Council of two triumphal arches. The affair was under the management of the following committee:— Mr. E. L. Vail (chairman), Dr. Fetherstone, and Messrs. Hole, Wilson, Girdler, Widdicombe, Presswell, T. C. Wright, and Ceruty, and these gentlemen deserve to be complimented on the success of their undertaking.

Hotham.

The school children's fete at Hotham, on Saturday, the 21st December, was not one whit behind any of the others, so far as regarded the success attending it. About five thousand children assembled at the Town Hall at ten o'clock, and, marshalled by Mr. Carroll, the ex-Mayor, went in procession to the Royal Park. Each school carried its distinguishing flag, and the little ones marched well to the strains of a leading band. Mr. Barwise, the mayor, although suffering from the effects of a severe accident, was present. Councillor Lancashire and Mr. Gillam attended as caterers, and performed the onerous duties attached to that office with credit to themselves and satisfaction to those who required their services. Councillors Marks and Flanagan took charge of the sports, and the other members of committee were busy attending to the necessary details. The band of the training-ship *Deborah* was in attendance, and there were also a string band and a company of Ethiopian minstrels. A box of toys, the gift of Mr. Atkin, was reserved as prizes for those taking part in the races, &c.; and toys were also distributed to the younger of the children, who could not participate in these diversions. Tents, kindly lent by Captain Irving, were erected in various parts of the ground for the children's use. The butchers and bakers of Hotham to a man supplied largely the various comestibles in their line. The ladies on the ground were invited to lunch with the committee, and over two hundred accepted the invitation. The Borough Council had voted a sum of money, which was supplemented by Messrs. Reddish, Fry, Gillam, Sullivan, and others. Swings, see-saws, merry-go-rounds, &c., were scattered over the ground. What was originally intended for a picnic swelled during the day into the proportions of a large banquet, and at the end of the proceedings a distribution of provisions, &c., took place amongst those who applied for them.

Footscray.

On 26th December the children's entertainment was given at Footscray, and proved in every way successful. Games of all kinds were provided, and seemed to be thoroughly enjoyed. At intervals, refreshments, consisting of buns, cakes, fruit, gingerbeer, milk, and other good things, were supplied in abundance. The amusements were kept up to a late hour. The arrangements of the committee having been perfect in every respect, a most delightful day was spent.

Fitzroy.

On Friday, 3rd January, a children's pic-nic was held at Fitzroy, in honour of the visit of Prince Alfred; this entertainment was one of the last that was given on the occasion of these rejoicings, but was one of the most successful. The Borough Council had voted one hundred pounds in aid, and this sum was supplemented by subscriptions from the inhabitants to the amount of eighty pounds, and by donations of goods to the value of forty pounds. The management of the affair was under the direction of a committee, which included the Borough Council and about forty of the principal inhabitants, Mr. W. J. Gilchrist acting as secretary. Soon after ten o'clock in the morning the children began to muster at the court-house, in Napier-street, and by eleven o'clock a procession was formed, marshalled by Messrs. Eastwood and Raven. Headed by the Mayor, Councillors Grant and Rushall, and Mr. Ewing, and accompanied by a brass band, the procession marched along Napier street to Gertrude street, and thence by Brunswick-street to the Cricket Reserve at North Fitzroy. The number of children was about three thousand. Arrived on the ground, the little ones dispersed in search of amusement, as their different tastes inclined—some to football, others to cricket, whilst still larger numbers betook themselves to "kiss-in-the-ring," and those of maturer years to dancing. The band provided was that of the Naval Training-ship, and the young musicians certainly did credit to their training. A couple of merry-go-rounds were in great request, and the horses and carriages never wanted riders and occupants. For the more active of the lads a number of races were improvised, in which knives, tops, and cricketing materials were the prizes; and for the girls, skipping races were also got up, for skipping-ropes, dolls, and ladies' companions. The catering arrangements were under the control of Mr. Grinwood, who provided for his guests in his accustomed satisfactory manner.

Warrnambool.

It will not be out of place here to notice the rejoicings at Warrnambool in honour of the Royal visit, which took place on Tuesday, 26th November. The town was decorated with flags, and wore a gay and holiday appearance; the public bodies assembled, the children under their various teachers gathered together, and, as eleven o'clock drew near, the streets became crowded. Residents from the country round about had also come to share in the festivities. A procession of local bodies and friendly societies was arranged in good order in Merri-street by the committee, who were mounted, and acted as marshals. On arriving at the ground reserved for the pic-nic, a centre was formed by the volunteer corps and the children, the latter of whom must have numbered upwards of fifteen hundred, and the estimate of the whole was from five to six thousand. The free supply of provisions, including five hogsheads of beer, was a very popular part of the entertainment, and, in spite of the inconvenient crowding, the utmost good humour prevailed. The amusements occupied the greater part of the afternoon. The volunteer corps were employed for some time in manoeuvring and in firing volleys. The Aunt Sallies were an attraction, and footballs were kicked about with indomitable energy and perseverance for hours. A game at cricket was going on in one part of the field. Swings were in active exercise. Several round games were started on various principles, and participated in by many. In other parts of the reserve races were run by boys and girls, the prizes being medals which have been struck to commemorate the Prince's visit. As night fell, numbers assembled near the battery to witness the fireworks; and the bonfire, which was subsequently lit, as well as the illuminations, became each in their turn centres of attraction. The fireworks were discharged under the superintendence of Captain Helpman. The bonfire, which was under the charge of Mr. J. A. Smith, and which was lit upon the hill above Tattersall's Hotel, was a great success. Among the illuminations, the most striking and original was that of Mr. Cramer. The windows were decorated with flags and drapery. In one was a cannon, mounted on its carriage, with rifles stacked beside it. In the background was a transparency of the *Galatea*, while the scroll bore the words, "Volunteers' Welcome—Royal Salute." In the other window was a silver bugle, with swords crossed, the Duke of Edinburgh's Arms, and an inscription, "Sound a loud welcome." The idea of the whole was excellent, and well carried out. Above the Post Office there was a centre transparency of the *Galatea*, with the words, "Victoria's Welcome to Britannia's Pride," with a side transparency of a star, and another of an anchor. The Royal Hotel was illuminated with the Oddfellows' arms, a crown, and other decorations in the window. Messrs. Cramond and Dickson had a coronet above the door of their premises, and also an effective representation of a vessel. Mr. Jamieson and Mr. Hider showed the ducal arms, well executed. The illumination over the stores of Mr. Coleston and Mr. Thomas, bearing the words, "Welcome to Prince Alfred," in bold letters, shone out well. Mr. Edwards exhibited a bust of the Prince, and a full length figure was above Mr. Breckon's premises. The Irish harp and motto was shown in one of Mr. Dooley's windows, and a crown and "V.R." on the store of Messrs. F. P. Stevens and Co. In one of Mr. Bromfield's windows was the pharmaceutical coat of arms. Mr. Brady, Messrs. Dodds and Burnett, Mr. Scott, and others also showed illuminations more or less meritorious.

Fête to the Boys of the Galatea.

The boys of the *Galatea* had a great day's amusement, and one which doubtless will invest their visit to Hobson's Bay with pleasant reminiscences. Through the kindness of the Royal Commission, they were driven to some of the principal sights in the city, and then to the grounds of the Acclimatisation Society at the Royal Park, which they reached about half-past one o'clock. They were accompanied by five petty officers and by the fife-and-drum band of the naval training-ship. The youthful visitors were under the charge of Mr. W. C. Rees, Secretary to the Steam Navigation Board. They were received by Dr. Black, the president of the Acclimatisation Society, and the secretary, Mr. G. Sprigg. A marquee had been erected in the grounds, and here the boys were served with an excellent and substantial dinner, to which they did ample justice. The chair was occupied by Dr. Black, and after the toasts of "The Queen," and "Captain the Duke of Edinburgh," one of the petty officers proposed the health of Mr. Rees, who replied, and stated that for the fête they were indebted to the kindness of the Government and the Royal Commission. The health of the chairman, Dr. Black, having been given and duly honoured, the boys adjourned to the lawn outside, where cricket, Aunt Sally, and other games were entered into with spirit. In the evening the boys returned to town, and partook of an excellent tea at Grimwood's Hotel. Afterwards, through the generosity of Mr. Coppin, they visited the Haymarket Theatre, and returned by the last train to Williamstown, after spending an agreeable and memorable day.

Sandhurst.

After taking part in the reception of the Prince, the school children of Sandhurst were indulged with a picnic, and to secure an equal division of spoils, each child was presented with a bag containing two buns, two tarts, an apple, and a packet of lollies, tea being supplied in abundance. Various amusements were afterwards organised, and the treat fully realised its name. In addition to this a "monster picnic" was given on the following day at Harcourt, under the management of Messrs. Newcombe, Stead, Crow, and Grover. The gathering embraced two thousand children and one thousand adults. There was a prodigal supply of provisions, plenty of amusements, and the whole affair proved a great success.

Eaglehawk.

The school children of this borough marched with banners and flags to the California Gully Cricket Ground, where they were amply supplied with refreshments, after which they indulged in the usual festivities, the only drawback to the enjoyments of the day being the excessive heat.

Echuca.

The Borough Council of Echuca gave an entertainment to the children of the district, which was also largely patronised by the adult population. The usual round of amusements was gone through, and commemorative medals given to the children. A display of fireworks and a bonfire concluded the festival, which was altogether highly successful.

Northcote.

The inhabitants of this suburb subscribed most liberally for the purpose of giving a children's feast in honour of the Royal visit, and their efforts were completely successful. All the children of the district were welcome to attend, and an immense number availed themselves of the general invitation. One hundred prizes, varying from a doll to a copy of *Longfellow*, were given away, and a profusion of good viands was freely distributed.

Malvern Hill and Gardiner.

A holiday, with village sports, including a feast to the children of the district, constituted the loyal demonstrations of the above district. A large sum of money was subscribed by the local residents, and barrels of ale, hams, fruit, and pastry were presented without solicitation. A large number of persons joined in the rejoicings, and everything passed off admirably. The Rev. Mr. Cole, pastor of the district, and Mr. J. Henry, aided materially in promoting the success of the fête.

MISCELLANEOUS ITEMS.

His Royal Highness the Duke of Edinburgh honoured the Melbourne Botanic Gardens with a visit, and planted two young trees in commemoration of the day. The trees selected were *Saxons-Gothea conspicua*, from Patagonia, and *Abies Albertii*, from California. Both these pines were named in honour of Prince Albert.

Mr. John Murchison—an old "overlander" and pioneer of the colony—was specially presented by his Excellency the Governor to his Royal Highness the Duke of Edinburgh, who

Miscellaneous Items.

received him most graciously. The grandfather of Prince Alfred—the Duke of Kent—gave Mr. Murchison his first commission in 1813. After twenty years' service he retired from the army, and emigrated to these colonies, where he has since resided as a squatter.

The hunting party, got up under the auspices of the Royal Reception Commission for the officers of the *Galatea*, enjoyed some excellent sport in the neighbourhood of Schnapper Point, and were sumptuously entertained at the station of Mr. Sumner, of Coolart.

The sergeants of Her Majesty's second battalion of the 14th Regiment entertained in their mess-room the sergeants of the Royal Marines, and the chief and first-class petty officers of H.M.S. *Galatea*, to a supper. The chair was occupied by Quartermaster-Sergeant W. Hopkins, and the vice-chair by Colour-Sergeant Drill. About seventy in all sat down to an excellent and well-served repast. After supper had concluded, the "Health of Her Majesty" was given by the chairman, and warmly responded to. The vice-chairman then gave "The Prince of Wales and all other Members of the Royal Family," which was followed in succession by the usual loyal toasts. "Our Guests of the *Galatea*" was next given; after which song and mirth abounded, intermixed with other toasts, including "The Garrison," "The Ladies, on sea and land, and of every clime," which was received with loud cheers, as was also "Sweethearts and Wives." The evening was spent very pleasantly. The Galateans, after the "Guests of the Evening" had been ably responded to by the Master-at-Arms of the *Galatea*, proposed the health of the sergeants of H.M. 14th Regiment, who had so kindly entertained them, and expressed a wish that they might all meet again. Every one present enjoyed the night to the fullest extent. Previous to parting, the National Anthem was sung.

Mr. Walter Montgomery had the honour of giving one of his Royal recitals before his Royal Highness at St. George's Hall. The building was crowded with a most select and appreciative audience. The gallery was considerately set apart by Mr. Montgomery for the accommodation of two hundred of the men and boys of the *Galatea*. Mr. Montgomery read with his usual refinement and ability, and was enthusiastically applauded.

His Royal Highness was highly pleased with the proficiency of the Victorian Volunteers, and his testimony to that effect was made the subject of a brigade order, expressing the Prince's gratification in observing the thorough discipline and efficiency of the "local forces" at the late review, and his warm acknowledgments of the efficient manner in which the Volunteers performed their duties during his stay, whether as escorts or guards of honour.

The manner in which the police force of the colony discharged its onerous labours throughout the stay of the Prince was heartily recognised and acknowledged by his Royal Highness, who presented some of the principal officers with souvenirs of his visit.

The Melbourne Philharmonic Society (the oldest musical association in Victoria) employed its well-organised strength in giving a high-class concert, at which his Royal Highness and suite, his Excellency the Governor and family, and all the leading members of the community were present. Mendelssohn's "Athalie" was the principal work on the programme, and this was rendered in the most effective manner by a band and chorus of four hundred and fifty performers. The great hall of the Exhibition Building was crowded, and his Royal Highness, who is himself an accomplished musician, expressed his gratification at finding classical music so highly appreciated in Victoria.

The Victorian Musical Association gave a special farewell concert in the great hall of the Exhibition Building, in honour of his Royal Highness, and at which an original work, an Odaic Cantata, written by Mr. R. H. Horne, the music by Mr. Summers, and entitled "Galatea Secunda," was performed with great success. Selections from Mr. C. E. Horsley's "South Sea Sisters," the words of which are also by Mr. R. H. Horne, and an overture by Mr. Siede, constituted the local contributions to the programme; Mendelssohn's "Hymn of Praise," and other classical subjects, completing the entertainment.

The frontispiece to this work is a reduced copy of a portrait taken by Messrs. Johnstone and O'Shannessy of his Royal Highness, who consented to sit for it at the desire of the Trustees of the Melbourne Public Library, and also of the members of the Melbourne Club. At the same time Messrs. Johnstone and O'Shannessy took excellent photographic likenesses of Lord Newry, the Hon. Eliot Yorke, Lieut. Haig, and of several officers of the *Galatea*. The appointment of photographers to his Royal Highness was conferred upon Messrs. Johnstone and O'Shannessy by the Prince.

Presents to his Royal Highness.

Most of the presents made to his Royal Highness have been described in proper order in the course of the preceding narrative, but many other interesting offerings were made to the Royal visitor, of which no formal record has been made. A few of the items which were made public are here given:—

The very handsome carriage built by Messrs. M'Cartney and Aldred, of Ballarat, for the use of his Royal Highness during his visit to that city, was presented to the Prince by the joint Councils of Ballarat and Ballarat East. His Royal Highness expressed his intention of having it shipped to London for his private use.

Mr. Green, of Swanston-street, presented to his Royal Highness the skin of a very fine kangaroo, the animal having been shot by the Prince himself. The skin was well tanned, and lined with scarlet cloth, the head and claws of the animal were added in a most ingenious manner. There was also a handsome fire-screen, made from the wings of a pelican, prepared and mounted with great taste and skill.

Mr. H. U. Alcock presented his Royal Highness with a very handsome set of billiard cues.

Mr. Thomas Chuck, of Collins-street east, presented an album containing an extensive series of photographic views of Melbourne streets and Victorian scenery.

Mr. Charles Nettleton, of Madeline-street, presented a fine collection of large-sized photographic pictures, including public buildings and views of Melbourne.

Mr. N. Chevalier, who was honoured with a special invitation to accompany his Royal Highness to Tasmania and New South Wales, presented his Royal Highness with a great number of admirably executed and highly artistic sketches, most of them being illustrative of the Royal tour.

The Monster Clothing Company forwarded to his Royal Highness a fine silk coat, which was pronounced to be a very excellent specimen of colonial workmanship.

The mining equipment of his Royal Highness was made up by Mr. Miller, of Armstrong-street, Ballarat, who presented mining boots; Mrs. Warren, of Lal-Lal-street, who furnished beautifully knitted socks; and Mr. Kiddie, who prepared a complete suit of flannel. The personal comfort of his Royal Highness was thus studied by the people of Ballarat.

Messrs. L. Giraud and Co., of Collins-street, manufacturers of bon-bons and crystalline fruits, made a handsome presentation of their productions to his Royal Highness, who expressed himself as highly pleased with their quality.

Mr. E. Whitehead, engraver and stationer, of Collins-street east, presented an appropriate assortment of stationery to his Royal Highness. The arms and monogram of the Prince were so artistically worked as to call forth a handsome acknowledgment.

A very beautiful present was made to his Royal Highness by Mrs. Gray, of Nareeb Nareeb. It consisted of a pair of vases, the bowls of which were black swans' eggs, elegantly mounted in silver. On the surface of the bowls were exquisite little etchings, executed by Mrs. Gray, who is known to possess a very fine taste as well as great skill in this branch of art. The Prince expressed himself as being highly pleased with these unique offerings.

Royal Appointments.

The following persons have been honoured with formal authority to hold trade offices on the Household Staff of his Royal Highness:—

H. U. Alcock, of Russell-street, billiard-table maker to his Royal Highness.

Charles Anderson, of St. Kilda, baker to his Royal Highness.

T. K. Bennett, of Bourke-street east, purveyor to his Royal Highness.

G. Chapman, Swanston-street, music publisher to his Royal Highness.

F. Gardner, 84 Collins-street west, furrier to his Royal Highness.

Johnstone and O'Shannessy, Bourke-street, photographers to his Royal Highness.

M. E. Meyers, 81 Little Collins-street, caligrapher and illuminator to his Royal Highness.

R. U. Miller, of Collins-street, cook and confectioner to his Royal Highness.

Moubray, Lush and Co., of Collins-street, silkmercers, drapers, and upholsterers to] his Royal Highness.

M'Cartney and Aldred, of Ballarat, carriage-builders to his Royal Highness.

McFadzean and Lambert, Collins-street east, hairdressers and perfumers to his Royal Highness.

E. J. Prévôt, 120 Queen-street, manufacturer of aërated waters and cordials to his Royal Highness.

Roberts Brothers, of Ballarat, photographers to his Royal Highness.

E. Smythers, Elizabeth-street, wine and spirit merchant to his Royal Highness.

J. Stanley, Collins-street east, tailor to his Royal Highness.

Paul Thomas, 3 Collins street east, bootmaker to his Royal Highness.

George H. Tipper, Haymarket Hotel, Bourke-street east.

Henry Watts, 71 Bourke-street east, perfumer to his Royal Highness.

Visit of H.R.H. Prince Alfred.

ADDITIONAL ADDRESSES.

The following addresses to his Royal Highness the Duke of Edinburgh, and the replies thereto, were not received in time to be placed in their proper order:—

From the Borough of Richmond.

May it please your Royal Highness—We, the Mayor and Councillors of the Borough of Richmond, representing more than 12,000 inhabitants, in approaching your Royal Highness, would humbly, and with cordial feelings, express our deep, strong, and embracing attachment to your Royal mother, our gracious Queen, and our unfeigned dependence on, and unflinching support of, the British Constitution. That we would wish to present to your Royal Highness, in the simpleness of sincerity, our heartfelt congratulations on this auspicious occasion, when the majesty of royalty is amongst us, so distant from the mighty centre of the British empire. That the visit of your Royal Highness shall confer great and permanent benefit on our infant colony, " in distant ages sire to son shall tell;" we would desire to testify and to record the magnitude of the obligation. That it is our earnest prayer that the God of the universe will protect and bless, as I on the desert wastes of waters be the unerring guide of our Sailor Prince.

CORNELIUS STEWART, Mayor.
THOMAS GARDNER, Town Clerk.

REPLY.

Gentlemen—I have received your address with much pleasure, observing, as I can, that the spirit which animates it is one of deep and devoted loyalty to the Queen, and of attachment to the Constitution of Great Britain. I thank you for your hearty congratulations, as well as for your prayers on my behalf; and I assure you that it will ever be a source of great gratification to me, to think that my visit has assisted in any degree in benefiting this great colony.
ALFRED.

From the Borough of Brunswick.

May it please your Royal Highness—We, Her Majesty's most dutiful subjects, the Mayor, Councillors, and Burgesses of the Borough of Brunswick, beg to approach your Royal Highness with the expression of our devoted loyalty to Her Most Gracious Majesty's Throne and person. We hail with the highest satisfaction the visit of your Royal Highness to this portion of Her Majesty's dominions, and trust that your Royal Highness will be assured, from personal observation, that in no part of Her Majesty's empire is there a more ardent attachment to Her Majesty's beneficent rule than in this colony, which is honoured by bearing Her Majesty's name. We trust that your Royal Highness will allow us to offer our warmest and most sincere wishes for your Royal Highness's personal safety and happiness, and for the bestowment of every gift of the Divine Providence requisite to sustain your Royal Highness in the exalted position which you occupy.

W. JNO. LOBB, Mayor.
G. W. FREDK. GRYLLS, Town Clerk.

REPLY.

Gentlemen—It is a very great satisfaction to me to find that the chief aim of every address which I have received here, is to impress upon me the devotion and loyalty to the Queen which actuate all Her Majesty's subjects in Victoria. I assure you that it will be very gratifying to Her Majesty to learn from me that distance has not weakened the love for their Queen in the hearts of her Australian subjects. Pray accept my thanks for your kind wishes and prayers on my behalf.
ALFRED.

From the Shire of Stawell.

May it please your Royal Highness—We, the President and Councillors of the Shire of Stawell, on behalf of the general body of residents, beg to tender to your Royal Highness our warmest congratulations on your safe arrival in this colony, and to record our appreciation of the honour conferred by this visit. We most heartily embrace the opportunity thus afforded us of expressing to your Royal Highness our assurance that there exists amongst us a deep and earnest loyalty and devotion to the Throne and person of our beloved Queen, which, although neither time nor distance can efface, we are certain will be intensified by your Royal Highness's visit to our shores; and we sincerely hope that your stay amongst us will yield you pleasurable reminiscences in the future, when memory shall call up the golden land at the antipodes.

JOHN CHILDE, J.P., President.
GEORGE JENNINGS, Councillor.
DANIEL McALLAN, J.P., Councillor.

REPLY.

Gentlemen—I accept with the greatest pleasure your address, conveying to me the expression of your loyalty to the Throne and person of Her Majesty the Queen, and I thank you heartily for your welcome.
ALFRED.

Additional Addresses.

From the Borough of Tarnagulla.

May it please your Royal Highness—We, the Mayor and Councillors of the Borough of Tarnagulla, beg to approach your Royal Highness, the son of our beloved Queen, with an assurance of our loyalty and attachment to the Throne and person of Her Most Gracious Majesty, and to give to your Royal Highness on behalf of our fellow-townspeople, a warm and cordial welcome to the colony of Victoria. We fondly believe that your visit here will very materially strengthen the bonds of union and friendship that already happily exist between the Australian colonies and the parent state. We pray that your stay with us may prove instructive and interesting, that your subsequent voyage may be pleasant and prosperous, and that by the blessing of Almighty God you may long be spared to a career of usefulness and honour. We beg to subscribe ourselves your Royal Highness's most humble and devoted servants,

JOHN BEYNON, Mayor.
CHAS. E. RANDALL, Town Clerk.

REPLY.

Gentlemen—Accept my best thanks for this hearty welcome to Victoria. It has afforded me the greatest pleasure to visit this colony, where the cordiality of the reception I have received, and the spirit of loyalty and devotion displayed towards Her Majesty and Throne, will cause me ever to remember with affection and pleasure the stay I made amongst the people of Victoria.
ALFRED.

From the Shire of Mount Rouse.

May it please your Royal Highness—We, the President and Councillors of the Shire of Mount Rouse, in the colony of Victoria, beg to approach your Royal Highness with expressions of congratulation upon your safe arrival in this distant portion of the British empire. We esteem it a privilege to be afforded this opportunity of expressing our loyalty to the Throne and attachment to the Royal Family of England, and trust that your Royal Highness may receive ample proof during your stay in this colony that in no part of her dominions does Her Most Gracious Majesty the Queen, your illustrious mother (whom may God long preserve), possess more dutiful and loyal subjects than in her colony of Victoria—a name it bears with pride. We feel much gratified by the prospect of your visit to the western district, which has always been regarded as the fairest and most fertile portion of Australia Felix; and while no doubt your Royal Highness will be gratified by the inspection of the vast mineral resources of the colony, as displayed at the goldfields, we venture to express a hope that the more stable assurance of a country's prosperity exhibited in its adaptability and capacity for the development of the pastoral and agricultural interests, will not fail to impress you with a sense of the magnificent future in store for Victoria. We trust that your Royal Highness may be preserved in the enjoyment of perfect health during the continuance of your tour in these sunny lands of the south, and that when your most gracious and welcome visit has terminated, you may accomplish your return voyage to dear old England in peace and safety, carrying with you, as you will, the loyal sympathies of the Australians, and their fervent prayers for the happiness and welfare of yourself and your illustrious family.

JAMES ALEXANDER, President.
T. M. KNIGHT, Secretary.

REPLY.

Gentlemen—I have received with satisfaction the expression conveyed to me in your address, of your devotion to the Throne, and I am fully assured of the loyalty of the people of Victoria. I thank you for your congratulations on my arrival, and for your good wishes; and I assure you I very gladly availed myself of the opportunity which my tour in the western district afforded me, of observing its great and valuable resources.
ALFRED.

From the Borough of Clunes.

May it please your Royal Highness—We, the residents and burgesses of the district and borough of Clunes, desire to approach your Royal Highness with sentiments of affection and respect, and to congratulate your Royal Highness on your arrival at this great colony, named after our Most Sovereign Lady Queen Victoria. We most humbly beg to assure your Royal Highness of the deep feelings of devoted loyalty and love we bear towards the Throne and person of our illustrious Queen, and pray Almighty God that He may be pleased long to spare her to be her people's guide and ruler. We also beg to congratulate your Royal Highness on your arrival at this the metropolitan goldfield, and beg to express the hope that your Royal Highness may be induced to pay a visit to Clunes, where are carried on the most extensive quartz-mining operations in these colonies. With every sentiment of esteem and respect, we humbly beg to subscribe ourselves your Royal Highness's most devoted humble servants.

REPLY.

Gentlemen—I thank you for your congratulations on my arrival in Victoria, and I am fully sensible of the devoted loyalty you bear towards her Majesty the Queen. I am aware of the great importance and extent of the quartz-mining operations which are carried on at Clunes, and I sincerely regret that it is not in my power to visit the scene of these operations.
ALFRED.

From the Mining Board of the Mining District of Ballarat.

May it please your Royal Highness,—We, the Chairman and Members of the Mining Board for the Mining District of Ballarat, as the representatives of the miners in this district, respectfully congratulate your Royal Highness on your safe arrival, and heartily welcome your Royal Highness to this land, which has the honour to bear the name of our beloved and Most Gracious Queen. We beg leave to approach your Royal Highness with assurances of our dutiful affection and loyal attachment to Her Most Gracious Majesty, and to all the members of the Royal Family, and to assure your Royal Highness that in loyalty to the Throne and person of our most gracious Sovereign, and in veneration for the laws and institutions of Great Britain, the miners of this district are equal to the most loyal subjects of the British Crown. We trust that your Royal Highness may be graciously pleased to visit some of the mines in this district, and we believe that your Royal Highness will (considering gold mining is so new a branch of industry) be gratified at the progress made. In conclusion, we crave permission to express our earnest wish that your Royal Highness may long enjoy the blessings of health and happiness, and that at some future period the pleasing duty of welcoming your Royal Highness once again to this colony may be permitted to us.

J. M. DICKETT, CHAIRMAN.

Messrs. LAMB   Messrs. SYLVESTER
WHEELDON   CROKER
JONES   M'DONELL
NETTELL   EDDY

REPLY.

Gentlemen,—I accept with peculiar pleasure this address, as it comes from men who have by the sweat of their brow, and the skilled labour of many a hard day's toil, made the mining district of Ballarat what it now is. The impressions made upon me by the warm and splendid reception I have just received from your hands in this city, can never during my life be eradicated from my mind. It is a sterling proof of your attachment to the Throne, and of your affectionate devotion to Her Majesty and Family. I hope to be able to visit many of the mines in this district, and I rejoice at the opportunity which has been afforded me of so doing. This town offers a striking example of what may be effected by energy and enterprise under the influence of free institutions. That its success may be still further enlarged is the hope of one who wishes you every happiness and increased prosperity. Allow me once more to thank you for your congratulations, and for your earnest prayers for my present and future happiness.

The list of addresses to his Royal Highness would be incomplete without the following from *Melbourne Punch*, written, it may now be confessed, by Mr. Charles Bright. It is scarcely necessary to explain that the document was published, and not presented in the customary way.

TO CAPTAIN H.R.H. THE DUKE OF EDINBURGH, R.N., K.G., &c., &c., &c.—The voice of eulogy is no novelty to you, and with flattery you must long ere this have been sufficiently nauseated. Let it be permitted to Punch, dear Prince, as a chartered libertine, to address you in homely phrases of outspoken affection. Welcome, thrice welcome, then, to Victoria. The name of the colony will commend itself to your warmest filial sympathies. Before you leave it you may be bound by a closer tie, arising out of the personal knowledge you will have acquired of the loyalty of its people, and the earnest regard they entertain for the institutions of the old land and the Throne towards which they converge. We were prepared to like you before you came for the sake of her who holds

> A nobler office upon earth
> Than arms, or power of brain, or birth,
> Could give the warrior-kings of old.

We like you better now we have seen your honest sailor-like face, and read there, as in a book, that the son of Albert the Good is not unworthy of his father. The country you are now visiting is young as yourself. You and it were in the cradle together. Both are growing to lusty manhood; both showing fair promise of future greatness. Young yourself, you will the more readily forgive the follies of youth. If we are a trifle exuberant in our display of loyalty, and fail to perform our parts closely "by the card," you will see no evil in our boisterous ovations, but, perhaps, relish our welcome the more for the lack of ceremony accompanying it. We believe in ourselves and our adopted country, and would fain appear before you at our best. If, in the attempts to accomplish this, the design be sometimes made too roughly apparent, we will ask you to look upon our efforts not with the cold eyes of European court etiquette, but rather with the generous instincts of the sailor who can forgive much which comes commended by the spirit of true hospitality. Nations, like men, may be hypocrites—" Look like the innocent flower, but be the serpent under it." It may safely be said of this people, however, that with whatever other faults they may be charged, they cannot fairly be accused of cant and lip-service. They are not prone to hero-worship. You may rate their welcome, therefore, to be genuinely what it appears—a cordial outburst of gratification at your coming amongst them. You bear a name honoured in the history of the great nation of which we form a part, and the branch of the service to which you belong is endeared to all our hearts. In that service you are believed to be no holiday official, but a true and ardent son of Neptune, ready, should occasion need, to do your duty as the noblest and bravest of your predecessors have done it in days gone by. This, as well as the more generalities of loyalty, is the meaning of our cheers. In honour of your profession and of you, Punch, on your arrival, sent forth to the world one number of his immortal publication clad in "true blue;" and now repeats his vehement "three times three" for the British navy and its Royal Captain, and once more bids you heartily welcome to the Australian land which proudly bears your honoured mother's name. We have the honour to be your Royal Highness's obedient humble servant,

Melbourne, 28th November, 1867.   MELBOURNE PUNCH.

To the above address his Royal Highness forwarded a very complimentary answer under cover to the Editor.

Reply to the Borough Council of Queenscliff.

Gentlemen— I have received with pleasure the expression of your loyal attachment to the Throne and person of Her Majesty, and thank you cordially for your welcome. I congratulate you on the prosperity which prevails throughout the colony, of which Queenscliff afforded me the first sight.   ALFRED.

Reply to the Royal Society of Victoria.

[NOTE.—The address will be found on page 64.]

Gentlemen—I have received the address of the Royal Society of Victoria with much satisfaction, and I thank you for the expressions of gratification at my arrival in this colony. The description you give me of the objects and scope of your society, including, as it does, the very important branch of scientific study to which you refer, convinces me of the beneficial nature of your institution; and I sincerely trust you may always share with the mother-country the benefit that will follow from her energy in the pursuit of science, and from the general spread of the knowledge of all those studies which your society fosters. I cordially concur with you in hoping that my visit to this port of the empire may conduce to the increased unity and solidity of our national position; and I also trust that a concentration of all interests connected with science, literature, and art may be promoted by the increased acquaintance with this flourishing country which may result from my presence among you.

Reply to the Grand United Order of Oddfellows.

[NOTE.—The address will be found on page 64.]

Gentlemen—I thank you for your congratulations upon my safe arrival in Victoria. It will give me much pleasure to make known to the Queen the devotion to Her Majesty's Throne and person with which the industrial classes of Victoria are animated. The success of the Friendly Societies in Australia affords most gratifying evidence of the prosperity, the providence, and the fellowship of the people. My visit to Victoria has given me much pleasure, to which the heartiness of the reception accorded to me everywhere by all classes of the community has greatly contributed.

Reply to the Shire Council of Strathfieldsaye.

[NOTE.—The address will be found on page 143.]

Gentlemen—I thank you heartily for the welcome with which you greeted me at Strathfieldsaye, and in the name of the Queen for the expressions of loyalty and devotion to her throne and person contained in your address. If, as you kindly assure me, you are grateful to Her Majesty for permitting me to visit this country, I may also say for my part with truth, that it has been a very great pleasure to me to have received so hearty a welcome among you, and to have had this opportunity of learning the great resources of this colony, and of judging of their rapid development.   ALFRED.

The following names should have been included in the account of the Royal Levee:—

Ellery, R. L. J., President Royal Society   Sturt, E. P. S.
Rawlings, T. H., Hon. Sec. Royal Society   Foord, George

Under "special entrée":—

Clove, Ball, Acting-Consul for Hamburgh.

The undermentioned names were omitted in the general account of the Fancy Dress Ball:—

Cairns, Mrs. John, Peruvian lady, wearing the Saya y Manto   Cairns, Mr., a Garibaldian
Shelley, Mrs. W. W., Undine   Shelley, Mr., Cardinal Richelieu
Wallen, Mrs. Robert, Parthenia

TASMANIA.

As the present volume pretends to be but little more than a narrative of the Prince's visit to Victoria, it is not attempted to give anything beyond a very brief outline of the proceedings of his Royal Highness outside of Victorian boundaries. The following summary of events which took place in Tasmania in honour of the illustrious Captain of the *Galatea* is mainly compiled from the *Hobart Town Mercury* and the *Tasmanian Times*.

ARRIVAL OF H.M.S.S. GALATEA.

Shortly after nine o'clock on the morning of January the 6th, H.M.S.S. *Galatea* was telegraphed off Eaglehawk Neck, and the telegraph subsequently announced her position at various times during the day. As soon as it became known at Hobart Town that the vessel was in sight, great excitement prevailed, and business was almost entirely suspended. The public offices were gaily decked with flags, and from the tower of St. David's Cathedral the colours of various nations were displayed; most of the citizens followed the example, and towards noon the city was gay with bunting. At noon three guns were fired from the Queen's Battery in the Domain, as a signal to the artillerymen to muster, and the gun detachments were soon at their posts at the Albert Battery. At 2.30 p.m. three guns from the Albert Battery announced that the *Galatea* was off the Iron Pot, and crowds of persons at once made for the wharves, the battery, the hill at the back of Franklin-square, and every other point from which a good view of the approaching vessel could be obtained. In the city most of the shops were closed for a brief period, and the excitement ran high. The Hampden-road, from the Ordnance Stores to the crown of the hill, and the whole bank of the river, were lined by eager spectators, while the hill at the signal-station was also the resort of several hundreds of persons. At length, at a few minutes before three o'clock, dense volumes of black smoke rising over the hill at Crayfish Point announced the approach of the steamer; a few minutes more and the tall masts hove in sight over the land, the jack at the flagstaff was dipped, and the *Galatea* rounded the point and came in full view. It was twenty minutes before the vessel arrived off the battery, and then the volunteers opened their welcoming salute, and on the first gun being fired the *Galatea's* ensign was dipped twice. On the salute being fired, the bells of Trinity Church, under the amateur bell-ringers, rang out a merry peal of welcome. As soon as the *Galatea* anchored, his Excellency's private secretary, Captain Steward, accompanied by Lieutenant Lloyd, R.E., acting aide-de-camp, and Mr. Sheriff Forster, proceeded on board the vessel to ascertain his Royal Highness's pleasure. After remaining a short time on board, these gentlemen returned, and his Excellency the Governor, accompanied by the Hon. Sir Richard Dry and the members of his Excellency's staff, proceeded to the *Galatea*, his Royal Highness receiving his Excellency and friends at the gangway. The party remained but a short time on board, and on leaving the vessel his Excellency was saluted from the ship's guns in the customary manner. Shortly before seven o'clock two boats left the *Galatea*, conveying the Prince and a small party of the officers and friends to Government House, where his Royal Highness had accepted an invitation to dine. Accompanying the Prince were the Hon. Eliot Yorke, Lord Newry, Mr. Brierly, Mr. Haig, and Commander Campbell. The party landed at the bathing-house, and were met by two of his Excellency's carriages, in which they were conveyed to Government House. The dinner party included Her

Majesty's Ministers. The Duke and suite went on board again at night, as the State Reception was to take place on the following day.

THE LANDING AND FESTIVITIES.

Tuesday, the 7th of January, will be marked as a red-letter day in the history of Tasmania, that being the day upon which the first scion of English royalty set foot upon her shores. The importance attached by a loyal populace to the event was most unmistakeable, and if the demonstration of affectionate greeting which was made on the occasion was in any degree less imposing than that shown in richer colonies, it was on account of the smaller proportions of the city, and from no want of genuine liberality and loyal feeling on the part of the citizens. Suffice it to say, that from the moment of his Royal Highness's landing until his arrival at Government House, the welcome which greeted him was spontaneous, heartfelt, and sincere. By nine o'clock in the morning the streets were crowded with people who had turned out to view the general decorations, and to make sure of their positions for obtaining a good sight of the procession. From the river and wharves, wherever a clear view of the town could be obtained, the sight was most imposing, and seen from the top of the hill behind Franklin-square, the marshalling of the procession was a most magnificent sight. The dense mass of heads moving about in the plateau below, the waving of the flags and banners borne by the friendly societies, the red shirts of the firemen, and the emblematic arch with its two whaleboats manned by crews of native youths in red shirts and sailor hats, and beyond all the long clear space, with the dais for the accommodation of the Mayor and Corporation standing out in bold relief, dotted here and there by groups of officials in uniform, and the clergy in their robes of office, besides little knots of private citizens: the whole scene enlivened by the regular lines of scarlet coats, white belts, and glittering bayonets, distinguishing the guard of honour, combined to form a scene of great brilliancy.

A large portion of the lower end of the New Wharf had been strongly fenced off for the accommodation of the officials and gentlemen holding cards of *entrée* from the Royal Reception Commission. This position was flanked by lines of flagstaffs bearing various flags, and alongside the wharf at the same point lay the s.s. *Southern Cross*, crowded with spectators. In the centre was a raised dais for the accommodation of the Mayor, Aldermen, and Officers of the Corporation. From this point the wharf was covered with coir matting to the landing stage. The company holding invitations began to arrive shortly after eleven o'clock, and at the time the Duke left his vessel there were present on the wharf their Honours the Judges in their robes; the Lord Bishop of Tasmania, wearing a purple cassock, and the scarlet gown and black velvet collegiate cap of a doctor of divinity. His Lordship was attended by his chaplain, the Rev. Mr. Bromby; the Venerable the Archdeacon in his robes, attended by his chaplain, the Rev. Mr. Wilson; the Rev. Dr. Nicolson, Free Church of Scotland, and the Rev. J. Service, Moderator of the Scottish Presbyterian Church, both wearing Geneva gowns; the Right Rev. Dr. Murphy, Bishop of the Church of Rome, attended by his chaplain the Rev. M. J. Beechinor. The Bishop wore his green soutan, trimmed with scarlet, a purple feriola, and the Roman episcopal hat, with a green band and tassel. Round his neck was a massive gold chain, pendant from which was a pectoral cross of gold. Besides his chaplain he was accompanied by the Right Rev. the Vicar-General, W. J. Dunne, and the Ven. and Rev. Archdeacon Hunter, both in full canonicals. The Hon. the President of the Legislative Council, and the Hon. the Speaker of the House of Assembly, in their robes; the Usher of the Black Rod, E. Abbott, Esq., and the Clerk of the

House of Assembly, and Secretary to the Reception Commission, Hugh M. Hull, Esq.; the Hon. Sir R. Dry, Knt., Premier; the Hon. W. L. Dobson, Attorney-General, and the Hon. Thos. D. Chapman, Colonial Treasurer; the Hon. Captain Langdon, M.L.C.; the Hon. J. A. Dunn, Esq., M.L.C.; the Hon. P. O. Fysh, Esq., M.L.C.; the Hon. T. Y. Lowes, Esq., M.L.C.; the Hon. A. Kennerley, Esq., M.L.C.; the Hon. Jas. Whyte, Esq., M.L.C.; John Meredith, Esq., M.H.A.; R. Walker, Esq., M.H.A.; David Lewis, Esq., M.H.A.; John Davies, Esq., M.H.A.; Chas. Meredith, Esq., M.H.A.; W. Sibley, Esq., M.H.A.; Dr. Butler, M.H.A.; J. R. Scott, Esq., M.H.A.; J. Swan, Esq., M.H.A.; G. Salier, Esq., M.H.A.; J. Pratt, Esq., M.H.A.; the Hon. Mr. Isaacs, Solicitor-General of New South Wales; T. T. Watt, Esq., Collector of Customs; J. E. Calder, Esq., Surveyor-General; F. J. Manley, Esq., Auditor-General; James Barnard, Esq., Government Printer; Mr. Commissary Bartlett; Lieut.-Colonel Crawford; Lieut. Lloyd, R.E., acting A.D.C.; Capt. Warren, R.E.; Major Maycock, 2-14th Regt.; Mr. J. T. Robertson; Mr. Thomas Horne; Mr. T. Stephens; Captain Ogilvy; Dr. Agnew; Mr. R. W. Nutt; Mr. Sheriff Forster, with the Under-sheriff, Mr. Crouch; Mr. Falconer, Director of Public Works; the Rev. Mr. Wright, of Hamilton, and Dr. F. S. Hall. The Right Worshipful the Mayor arrived about a quarter to twelve o'clock, accompanied by his chaplain, the Rev. J. H. Buckland, B.A., and the Town Clerk, Mr. Wilkinson. His Worship was in an open carriage, drawn by four bay horses, driven by Mr. Joshua Moore, the attendants wearing a handsome livery of blue and silver. His Worship was in his robes of office and full court suit. His chaplain wore his college robes, and the Town Clerk was also habited in his robes of office. At twelve o'clock the state carriage and outriders arrived conveying his Excellency the Governor, Captain Steward, and Major Vivian, 2-14th Regt. A guard of honour composed of one hundred men of the same Regiment, under command of Captain Fairtlough, with Lieutenants Daly and Whidburn as subalterns, were on duty on the wharf.

At twelve o'clock his Royal Highness disembarked, the men lying out on the yards as the Duke entered the state barge, which was manned by twelve men under the command of Sub-Lieutenant Guy Mainwaring, and Mr. P. A. C. De Crespigny, the officers of the ship attending his Royal Highness. In attendance upon his Royal Highness were also Lieutenant Haig, R.E., equerry-in-waiting, the Hon. Eliot Yorke, Lord Newry, and Mr. Brierly. When about midway between the ship and the landing stairs a Royal salute was fired from the ship's guns, and at the conclusion of the firing the ship's band played the National Anthem. All the vessels in harbour were dressed in honour of the occasion, and the several lines of wharf frontage presented a very gay and handsome appearance.

It was about five minutes past twelve o'clock when the barge conveying his Royal Highness the Duke of Edinburgh arrived at the landing stairs at the end of the New Wharf. On the barge approaching the steps, his Excellency the Governor, attended by his Honour the Chief Justice, his Honour Sir F. Smith, the Hon. Sir R. Dry, Lieutenant Lloyd, R.E., Captain Steward, Private Secretary, and Major Vivian, commander of the forces, descended the steps to the lower stage, and as soon as his Royal Highness placed his foot on the stage he welcomed him in a few words to the colony of Tasmania. The carriage then drove up to the dais, where his Worship the Mayor and Corporation were in waiting to receive the Prince. His Worship, advancing to the front of the dais, addressed his Royal Highness in the following words:—
"Permit me, Sir, to welcome your Royal Highness to the capital of Tasmania, on behalf of the loyal citizens of Hobart Town. I assure you, Sir, that we are deeply grateful to Her Majesty for this gracious visit, and we are proud to see a son of our beloved Sovereign come amongst us

as a guest. The City Council has endeavoured to embody our sentiments on this auspicious occasion in an address, which your Royal Highness has graciously consented to receive. With your Royal Highness's permission, the Town Clerk will now read the address."

The Town Clerk advanced and read the address as follows :—

May it please your Royal Highness—We, Her Majesty's most loyal and most dutiful subjects, the Mayor, Aldermen, and citizens of the city of Hobart Town, humbly beg leave to assure your Royal Highness of our attachment to the Throne and person of our beloved Queen. We heartily welcome your Royal Highness to the capital of Tasmania, and pray your Royal Highness to accept, on behalf of our Most Gracious Majesty, our grateful acknowledgments for this opportunity of expressing our loyal affection for the Royal Family in the personal presence of one of its most honoured and eminent members. We trust your Royal Highness may find much to admire and enjoy in the many natural beauties of scenery and climate of Tasmania, and that amidst your recollections of this brief visit your Royal Highness may cherish a kindly memory of the cordial welcome and loyal enthusiasm of its capital. We heartily pray the Almighty Disposer of events that the remainder of your Royal Highness's voyage may be accomplished in safety and comfort, and that on your return to our common country this auspicious visit to the Australian colonies may be found to have supplied another illustration of the close identity which happily unites Her Majesty's dominions in all parts of the globe in sentiment, interests, and institutions, in loyal and harmonious dependence upon the Imperial Crown and Government.
JAMES MILNE WILSON, MAYOR.
HENRY WILKINSON, TOWN CLERK.

Having read the address, the Town Clerk handed it to the equerry-in-waiting, Mr. Haig, together with a handsome octagonal casket of polished Tasmanian light wood, ornamented with forget-me-nots in silver, and the lid surmounted by a ducal coronet and plate bearing the Prince's arms. His Royal Highness in a clear tone read the following :—

REPLY.

Gentlemen—I accept with sincere gratification the address you have just read, in which you bid me welcome to your shores; and on behalf of the Queen I thank you for the expressions of loyalty to Her Majesty contained in it. The beauty of the scenery in the neighbourhood of your town, as well as the hearty reception with which you have greeted me, will long remain in my memory; and while I thank you for the prayers you offer up on my behalf, I wish to assure you that nothing has gratified me during my visit to Australia more than the unanimous desire of the people of each colony to impress upon me their loyalty for the Queen, and their love for England.

The ceremony of presenting the address over, a procession was formed along the principal streets of the city. The procession terminated as soon as the Prince reached the Club Hotel, which had been engaged for the Duke and suite. A most agreeable feature in the day's proceedings was the children's demonstration, four thousand of whom, standing on a platform, sang the National Anthem, with admirable effect, as the procession paused for the purpose, and showered countless bouquets upon those below.

Triumphal arches were erected in various parts of the city, and one, worthy of note from its elegance and beauty, was the structure erected by the citizens, designed by Mr. C. Walch. The decorations of the public buildings and private dwellings were profuse in the extreme, and at night the city was brilliantly illuminated. A pleasing novelty, in the shape of a torchlight aquatic procession, also took place. The ladies and gentlemen who were to take part began to assemble on board the *Twins* steamer about half-past seven o'clock. The sea breeze, which had been blowing briskly all day, died away, and gave place to a westerly wind. The moon shone beautifully, and rode through an almost cloudless sky. The temperature was sufficiently cool to render shawls and wrappers a comfortable addition to the ordinary dress. There were on board altogether about six hundred ladies and gentlemen, including many of the leading inhabitants of the city. The formation and maintenance of the line, a task of no small difficulty, was conducted by Mr. James Johnston, the marshal elect of the regatta flotilla; and considering the necessarily haphazard manner in which the crews of the various boats were got together to carry out so novel and difficult an undertaking, all parties acquitted themselves in very creditable style. The arrangements to give effect to the demonstration were as perfect as they possibly could be. The whole of the living freight being on board, the steamer got slowly under way, and proceeded towards the *Galatea*, amid cheers from the shore. A little delay was caused in arranging the flotilla, during which the rockets and red and green fires were occasionally burnt, and the band on board the steamer played some most inspiring strains. The steamer went slowly round the *Galatea*, the company singing "Rule Britannia" with precision and effect. The scene at this time was brilliant and beautiful in the extreme. The long line of boats, with lighted torches undulating with the waves, and slowly advancing, was one of the prettiest sights ever witnessed on the banks of the Derwent. Three hearty cheers were given as the steamer passed the *Galatea*, which were returned by the men on board the frigate, the band at the same time striking up a lively air. Green fires were now burnt and several rockets thrown up, the band playing a march, and then the company sang "O'er the calm and sparkling waters," which sounded very beautifully, the voices blending well. As soon as this ended, the *Galatea* exhibited a blue fire at each port-hole, and one from the jibboom end. The effect was magnificent, and there was but one feeling of delight at this brilliant exhibition. The flotilla, on reaching its appointed place off Government House, dropped anchor, rockets were fired, the orchestra went through the programme again, and, amidst the cheers of the assembled populace, the proceedings terminated.

LAYING THE FOUNDATION-STONE OF THE NEW CATHEDRAL.

The foundation-stone of the church designed to be the Cathedral Church of the Diocese of Tasmania was laid at eleven o'clock on the forenoon of Wednesday, 8th January, by the Duke of Edinburgh. Long before the hour appointed for the commencement of the ceremony, the streets leading to the cathedral were thronged by many hundreds of spectators, while every available window was filled by eager occupants. The large stand was crowded to excess at the hour appointed for the ceremony to commence, the majority of its occupants being ladies. The square space in front of the stand was kept clear for the accommodation of the clergy and others connected with the proceedings of the day. At half-past ten o'clock the clergy assembled in the church, habited in their surplices, and a procession was arranged to march to the stone on the arrival of the state carriage. Shortly after half-past ten o'clock a guard of honour, composed of one hundred men of the 2-14th Regiment, arrived in front of the cathedral to receive his Royal Highness. In attendance were the churchwardens, Messrs. H. Cook, T. Giblin, and H. Roberts, the local architect (Mr. Henry Hunter), and the contractor (Mr. Robert Wiggins). The silver trowel used, and afterwards presented to the Duke, was manufactured by Mr. Charles Gaylor, and engraved by Mr. W. R. Bock, and also a beautifully-designed level of Tasmanian lightwood, in the form of a triangle, having a lion *couchant* at either end of the base, a ducal coronet at the top surmounting a cross, and a plummet of silver. This implement was designed by Mr. H. Hunter, and executed by Messrs. Hamilton and Sons. There was also a mallet of she-oak wood, highly polished, turned by Mr. Powell, of Collins street. Let into the front of the stone was a plate of brass, bearing a suitable inscription. The plate was a beautiful piece of engraving, executed by Mr. Jarman, of Murray street. The churchwardens also deposited on the stone the box to be lodged in the cavity, containing copies of the Tasmanian newspapers and current coins of the realm. The following inscription was also placed in the box:—

This church, designed to be the cathedral church of the diocese of Tasmania, and also the parish church of Saint David (replacing an earlier structure, founded in the year of our Lord 1817), was solemnly founded on the 8th day of January, in the year of our Lord 1868, by his Royal Highness Alfred Ernest Albert, Duke of Edinburgh, Duke of Saxony, Prince of Coburg-Gotha, K.G., K.T. His Excellency Colonel Thomas Gore Browne, C.B., being Governor of Tasmania; the Right Reverend Charles Henry Bromby, D.D., the Lord Bishop of Tasmania; the Venerable Rowland Robert Davies, B.A., Archdeacon of Hobart Town; the Venerable Thomas Reibey, M.A., Archdeacon of Launceston; Sir Valentine Fleming, Chancellor of the Diocese; William Lambert Dobson, Esquire, Church Advocate; John Harrison, Esquire, Registrar; the Reverend Frederick Holdship Cox, B.A., Incumbent of St. David's Church; the Reverend Henry Boiley Bromby, B.A., Assistant-Curate of the same, and chaplain to the Bishop; Henry Cook, Thomas Giblin, and Henry L. Roberts, Esquires, Churchwardens; George Frederick Reibey, architect; Henry Hunter, local architect and superintendent of the works.

The following were the clergymen present: The Bishop, Archdeacon Davies, Revs. F. H. Cox, H. B. Bromby, A. Davenport, T. Gellibrand, Dr. Parsons, G. B. Smith, J. R. Buckland, F. Hudspeth, New Town; E. C. Williams, Glenorchy; T. Stansfield, Huon; S. Wayn, Green Ponds; G. Wright, Hamilton; E. Freeman, Brown's River; W. W. F. Murray, New Norfolk; G. Eastman, Port Arthur; D. Galer, Richmond; R. Wilson, Clarence Plains; R. D. Harris, E. P. Adams, Deloraine; H. W. Adams, Jericho; G. M. Wilson, Campbell Town; E. Symonds, D'Entrecasteaux Channel; C. J. Brammall, J. H. Smales, St. John's; — Dunning, Queensland.

The Duke of Edinburgh, accompanied by his Excellency the Governor, having arrived, the opening prayers and versicles and the 8th Psalm, were chanted. The prayers were said by the incumbent, the Rev. F. H. Cox. On the recitation of that portion of the service commencing "Behold, I lay in Zion a chief corner-stone," &c., the box containing the coins, inscription, newspapers, &c., was deposited in the cavity, the mortar was spread, and the stone lowered. The Bishop then advanced towards the Prince, and said, "In the name of the committee charged with this work, I now beg your Royal Highness to lay the foundation-stone of this building." His Royal Highness then in a clear voice said, "In the faith of Jesus Christ, we place this foundation-stone in the name of God the Father, God the Son, and God the Holy Ghost.—Amen." His Royal Highness then tested the stone with the plummet, and, giving three taps with the mallet, declared it to be well and truly laid.

THE LEVEE.

A Levee held in Tasmania by a member of the Royal Family was, of course, an event of sufficient importance to attract a larger attendance than had been collected on any previous occasion.

The road to Government House was kept by a body of special and regular constables. In front of the portico of the viceregal building was drawn up the military guard of honour, consisting of one hundred men of the 2-14th Regiment, under the command of Captain Saunders, and Lieutenants Daly and Churchward.

Previous to the ceremony, addresses were presented by the Legislative Council and Legislative Assembly of Tasmania, and were replied to by his Royal Highness.

The following gentlemen, having the entrée, were presented by the Private Secretary: The Officer Commanding the Troops, Major Vivian, H.M. 2-14th Regiment; the Chief Justice, Sir V. Fleming; the Puisne Judge, Sir F. Smith; the members of the Ministry—the Hon. Sir R. Dry, Premier; the Hon. T. D. Chapman, Treasurer; and the Hon. W. L. Dobson,

Attorney-General; the Bishop of Tasmania, the Right Rev. Charles Henry Bromby, D.D., attended by his chaplain, the Rev. H. Bromby; the Bishop of the Church of Rome, the Right Rev. Daniel Murphy, D.D., attended by his chaplain, the Rev. Mr. Beechinor; the President of the Wesleyan Conference, Rev. W. A. Quick; the President of the Legislative Council, the Hon. W. E. Nairn; the Usher of the Black Rod, E. Abbott, Esq.; the Hons. J. Whyte, C. Meredith; the Speaker of the House of Assembly, the Hon. R. Officer; Captain Fenton; Major Maycock, 14th Regiment; Captain Warren, Royal Engineers; Archdeacon the Venerable G. Hunter; Vicar-General the Very Rev. W. J. Dunne; Captain Tarleton, A. C. G. Bartlett, Esq., R. P. Adams, Esq., E. J. Manley, Esq., J. E. Calder, Esq., T. T. Watt, Esq., H. J. Buckland, Esq., the Hon. J. M. Wilson, J. Forster, Esq.; T. Stephens, Esq., M.A.; Major Lloyd, W. S. Sharland, Esq., J. Dunn, Esq., J. Barnard, Esq., Colonel Crawford, the Hon. M. Isaacs, Solicitor-General New South Wales; and T. Horne, Esq.

After the levee, addresses were presented to his Royal Highness as follows:—By the Bishop and Clergy of Tasmania, the Ministers of the Church of Scotland, the Bishop and Catholic Clergy of Hobart Town, the Ministers of the Wesleyan Methodist Church, the Congregational Union, Hebrew Synagogue; also the Masonic Body, Ancient and Independent Order of Oddfellows, Manchester Unity do., Rechabites of Hobart Town, the Warden and Councillors of Glenorchy, Independent Order of Rechabites of the Northern Division of the Island, Independent Order of Oddfellows of the Cornwall District, and from the Working Men's Club of Hobart Town.

To all the above, gracious and appropriate replies were made by his Royal Highness.

THE GOVERNOR'S BALL.

The fine assembly room of the Town Hall had been specially decorated for the occasion, and presented a very brilliant appearance, on the evening of the 9th January, when filled with the gay company assembled to do honour to the Royal visitor. His Royal Highness the Duke of Edinburgh arrived with the Governor soon after ten o'clock. He was received at the entrance by a guard of honour of the 2-14th Regiment, and on his arrival in the ballroom by the general company standing, the band playing the National Anthem.

The ball was attended by between seven hundred and eight hundred persons, including the officers of the *Galatea* and of the garrison, in full uniform.

The Prince led off the first set with Mrs. Gore Browne, the Governor and Lady Fleming *vis-à-vis*. Other dances followed, and his Royal Highness retired about twelve o'clock.

At the supper the Governor proposed the health of Her Majesty, which was responded to in the usual manner. His Excellency then proposed the health of his Royal Highness the Duke of Edinburgh. The toast, which was received with great applause, was drunk with all the usual honours.

VISIT TO NEW NORFOLK.

On Friday, 10th January, the Duke paid a visit to New Norfolk. Along the route were erected a number of triumphal arches. On the arrival of the royal party, the Warden and Councillors of the district presented a loyal address, to which his Royal Highness was graciously pleased to accord a reply. After this ceremony, a little fellow about five years old (Master James L. A. Moore), dressed in sailor's costume, was held up to the carriage, and presented the Prince with a beautiful nosegay enclosed in a very handsome bouquet-holder, on which was engraved the Duke's arms on a gold shield, and an inscription to the effect that it was presented to his Royal Highness by one hundred and sixty native-born residents of the district. From the state of the weather it was found quite impossible to extend the trip to the Salmon Ponds ; and, after lunching with the Hon. Robert Officer, Esq., the Speaker of the House of Assembly, and a short stay in the township, the party returned to town.

CITIZENS' BANQUET TO THE CREW OF THE "GALATEA."

At half-past one p.m. on Saturday, January 11th, two hundred and thirty of the seamen under command of Lieutenant Fitz-George, and thirty marines under Sergeant-major Thacker, accompanied by his Royal Highness's band, were brought ashore in the launch *Acis*, and landed at the Duke's stairs, when they were received by several members of the Banquet Committee, with whom and the Artillery Volunteers they proceeded to the Town Hall, at which place the band halted, the citizens drew aside, and the men marched in and took their places at the tables, where there were above one thousand dishes, and wines and ale were provided in profusion, and the sailor guests to all appearance did ample justice to the good cheer set before them. Charles Colvin, Esq., Chairman of the Banquet Committee, was in the chair, with A. Rheuben, Esq., as vice-chairman. In the course of the afternoon, the Premier (Sir R. Dry), the Colonial Treasurer, and the Mayor of Hobart Town, entered the room, and took their seats by the chairman.

After a number of toasts had been proposed and responded to, the ship's company gave three cheers for the Mayor, citizens, and ladies of Hobart Town, and the proceedings terminated.

REGATTA.

The same day the Annual Regatta took place, and amongst the events was the "*Galatea* Match Race," between a crew from H.M.S. *Galatea* and one picked from the crews of boats entered for other races. The Tasmanians came in easy winners, and the steerer of the winning craft, Mr. Hopwood, was presented with the prize, a purse of twenty sovereigns, by his Royal Highness.

JOURNEY TO LAUNCESTON.

The Duke left Government House at nine o'clock a.m. on Monday, 13th January, for Launceston, accompanied by his Excellency the Governor, Sir R. Dry, Lieutenant Haig, and Mr. Brierly. At New Town were two arches spanning the main road, and opposite the Queen's Orphan School the children from that institution, to the number of about four hundred, were drawn up, and sang "God save the Queen" as the carriage approached. On reaching O'Brien's Bridge, his Royal Highness was met by a large number of the inhabitants, including the members of the Municipal Council of Glenorchy, and was most enthusiastically received, the Warden, Dr. Butler, presenting a loyal address, to which His Royal Highness gave a reply. At Pontville an arch of welcome had been erected and a dais constructed close to the bridge, where were congregated the Warden and councillors, and many of the neighbouring gentry. A. Finlay, Esq., warden, presented an address of welcome and congratulation on the part of the inhabitants, to which his Royal Highness replied. Passing through Bagdad, the next township arrived at was Green Ponds, where a very fine arch had been erected with evergreens and flowers, having the words "Welcome, Royal Duke." Here the royal party stopped a short time, and the Warden, G. A. Kemp, Esq., read an address. At half-past one Melton Mowbray was reached, where a lunch was provided by Mr. Blackwell. This pretty little township was decked out with flowers and flags, the inhabitants all turning out in their holiday attire to greet the Prince with their mite of welcome. At Spring Hill there was an arch embellished with floral decorations. At the township of Oatlands the preparations were most elaborate. A large triple arch was thrown across the road opposite the principal hotel, and a dais erected for the accommodation of the members of the municipal body. The address was read by the Warden, J. R. Roe, Esq., to which a reply was given. The little village of Tunbridge had done its best to give evidence of its loyalty, floral decorations of all kinds being displayed. It had been arranged that his Royal Highness should dine and pass the night at Mona Vale, the estate of the Hon. R. Q. Kermode, M.L.C. Along the avenue leading from the main road to the house and grounds reception arches had been erected, decorated in the most tasteful manner, with banners, floral devices, and appropriate mottos. The interior of the noble mansion had been most elegantly fitted up by Messrs. Hamilton and Son. The whole arrangements had been completed under the personal superintendence of the proprietor, whose princely fortune and large establishment enabled him to entertain his Royal Highness in such a manner as probably no other private gentleman in Tasmania could pretend to.

Soon after eleven o'clock the following morning his Royal Highness left Mona Vale house. At Ross, his Royal Highness was received by the Warden and councillors, who were in waiting at the principal arch, which had been erected about the centre of the township. The address was presented by P. T. Smith, Esq., warden. Campbell Town was the next stage reached, and here also were signs of great rejoicing. The Prince arrived at the picturesque township of Perth, situate on the banks of the Esk, the inhabitants of which had constructed an immense triple arch. At Franklin Village the Duke took his seat in the carriage and four that awaited him, accompanied by the Governor, Sir D. Dry, and Mr. Haig. About one hundred horsemen escorted the Prince to the foot of the Sandhill, where a more ceremonious reception awaited him.

RECEPTION AT LAUNCESTON.

The volunteers, fire brigades, and other public bodies marched out from their different places of meeting to the great muster-ground, the triumphal arch on the Wellington Road, and waited until the Royal cortège hove in sight, and the salute soon announced the fact for miles around. His Royal Highness was escorted by a detachment of the First Light Cavalry, and about a hundred gentlemen, well mounted. The carriage was the property of T. C. Archer, Esq., who drove it, accompanied on the box by Joseph Archer, Esq., M.L.C. In the carriage with the Prince were his Excellency the Governor, Sir Richard Dry (Premier), and Mr. Haig.

The Artillery Corps was drawn up as a guard of honour at the triumphal arch, and presented arms. The band played the National Anthem. On a platform were seated his Worship the Mayor, Aldermen, and Town Clerk, and officers of the Corporation, members of the Royal Reception Committee, wardens, and councillors of the northern rural municipalities, &c.

The carriage drew up opposite the Mayor and aldermen, amidst enthusiastic cheering, and his Worship the Mayor read and presented an address from the Council and Burgesses of Launceston, to which the following reply was handed in :—

Gentlemen : I have received your address with much satisfaction, and in thanking you for the cordial manner in which you have welcomed me to Launceston, and for your kind wishes for my well-being and happiness, I also gratefully acknowledge on behalf of the Queen your expression of devotion and loyalty for her Majesty's Throne and person. I assure you that it has added, in no small degree, to the happiness of my stay among you, to find that you are all so eager to assure me that nowhere has Her Majesty more devotedly loyal subjects than in Tasmania.

The procession passed along Wellington to Frederick-street; up Frederick-street to St. John-street, at the junction of which, beside St. John's Church, about three thousand Sunday-School children, with their teachers, were assembled on an immense platform specially erected for the purpose. On the approach of the procession the children sang the National Anthem. Three cheers were then given for the Queen, three for the Duke of Edinburgh, three for the Governor, and three for the Mayor of Launceston. The streets were strewed with bouquets of beautiful flowers, and, taken altogether, the scene at Prince's-square was one peculiarly interesting.

The procession passed on down St. John-street to Cimitiere-street, thence to Charles-street, and through Brisbane street to the Town Hall, where a guard of honour of the Launceston Artillery, under the command of Captain Harrap, received the Prince.

His Royal Highness stepped lightly from the carriage and up the steps in front of the house, acknowledging the presentation of arms by the guard of honour as he passed.

His Royal Highness Prince Alfred held a levee in the hall of the Mechanics' Institute, and the following gentlemen had the private entrée:—The Hon. the Treasurer; the Mayor of Launceston; the Ven. Archdeacon Reiby; the Recorder, John Whiteford, Esq.; the Collector of Customs, the Hon. F. M. Innis, Esq., M.L.C.; Lieutenant-Colonel Horne; the Sheriff, John Foster, Esq.; the Deputy-Recorder of Titles, R. C. Gunn, Esq.; the Police Magistrate, W. Gunn, Esq.; the Under-Sheriff, George Smith, Esq.; H. E. Lette, Esq., M.L.A.; and W. Archer, Esq., M.L.C. The general presentations were comparatively numerous, and included the principal residents in the northern side of the island.

At night the Town Hall and public buildings were splendidly illuminated, and the fronts of the houses in most of the streets were decorated with brilliantly and tastefully executed designs in gas and transparencies.

On the 15th the Duke planted two oaks in Prince's-square, and on the same day turned the first sod of the Launceston and Deloraine Railway, after which his Royal Highness inspected the General Hospital. His Royal Highness visited the Cataract gorge in the evening, accompanied by the Governor, Mrs. Browne, Sir R. Dry, Lady Dry, Mr. Brierly, Miss Boyd, Lieut. Haig, and R. Green, Esq. His Royal Highness expressed great admiration of the magnificent scenery of the Cataract and Falls, and sketches of the same were taken by Mr. Brierly.

The aquatic procession took place at half-past eight o'clock, but his Royal Highness was not present.

The ball took place in the evening at the Mechanics' Institute. The ball was opened with a quadrille, Prince Alfred dancing with Mrs. Gore Browne, with the Governor and Lady Dry as *vis-à-vis*; Lieut. Haig with Miss Walker, and Mr. Brierly with Miss Boyd. At twelve o'clock supper was announced, after which the health of the Royal guest was drunk with the usual honours, and responded to.

RETURN TO HOBART TOWN, AND DEPARTURE.

The Duke returned the following day to Hobart Town, where, on the evening of the 17th, a grand ball was held in his honour. Her Majesty's Ministers, the Bishop, the Judges, the members of the late Ministry, the Mayor of Hobart Town, Mr. Tarleton, and Mr. John Forster, had the honour of meeting the Prince at dinner at Government House during the Royal visit.

His Royal Highness the Duke of Edinburgh had issued special invitations for twelve o'clock on Saturday, 18th January (the day fixed for his departure), on board the *Galatea*, to his Excellency the Governor, Mrs. Gore Browne, and Miss Gore Browne, Her Majesty's Ministers, the Chairman of the Reception Committee (the Hon. J. M. Wilson, M.L.C.), and Mr. Tarleton; and advantage was taken of this farewell interview to place in the Prince's hands the album of photographs of Tasmanian scenery which had been prepared under the direction of the Reception Committee for presentation to him from the colonists as a memorial of his visit. The album contained eighty-three photographs illustrative of the scenery of Tasmania, forty-eight portraits of children born in the colony, and nine plates immediately connected with the Prince's visit. The title page was drawn by Mr. Alfred Randall, and illustrated by Mr. W. C. Piguenit. His Royal Highness was pleased to request that the Reception Committee would furnish him with duplicate copies of all the pictures, for the illustration of a work which his Royal Highness is preparing in connection with his visit to the Australasian Colonies. After the presentation, the guests sat down to luncheon with his Royal Highness in the state reception saloon of the *Galatea*. Lord Newry and the Prince's suite were also present. The Prince's guests bade their Royal host farewell about half-past two p.m., when steam was got up and the anchors were weighed. At three o'clock the noble vessel steamed slowly down the estuary of the Derwent, and the Prince, bidding adieu to Tasmania, proceeded on his voyage to Sydney.

From the detailed accounts which have been published, as well as from other authentic sources of information, it is well known that the people of Tasmania welcomed his Royal Highness with the greatest fervour and enthusiasm. It was not to be imagined that his reception would be otherwise, as the Tasmanian community has always shown the highest public spirit on all occasions of importance. At the Great Exhibition in London in 1851 and 1862, and recently at the Intercolonial Exhibition at Melbourne of 1866-7, Tasmania displayed more taste, skill, and liberality than any other colonial contributor, and it was therefore but natural that she should accord to a son of Queen Victoria a brilliant and generous reception.

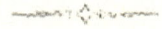

NEW SOUTH WALES.

FROM the time when the first intimation arrived of the projected visit of the Prince to the Australian colonies, the citizens of Sydney had determined that the welcome given in New South Wales should not be less enthusiastic and demonstrative than proposed to be vouchsafed to the Royal traveller in each of the other dependencies. Arrangements were at once made for the reception, and when it was definitely known that the Duke might be expected during the month of January, preparations were pushed forward, and public attention was absorbed in the eager expectation of his arrival. The Legislative Assembly, when appealed to by Government, voted in the first instance £5000, and subsequently another £5000, for the purpose of entertaining the Duke in a becoming manner, and spontaneously assured the Government that if more were required it should be forthcoming. Party strife was laid aside, and notwithstanding that it was a period of great political excitement, an adjournment of Parliament until the 25th February was unanimously agreed to.

Arrival at Sydney.

On Monday, 20th January, a telegram arrived that the *Galatea* had touched at Twofold Bay, some two hundred miles south of Sydney, and that the Royal ship would probably be off Port Jackson Heads some time during the 21st. Early on the forenoon of the latter date, the steam fleet, which had been prepared to escort the Duke, was got ready for putting to sea, and the following particulars of the naval reception, landing, and subsequent events up to the date of the publication of this work, have been condensed from the Sydney *Empire*, *Morning Herald*, and *Mail*:—

The Naval Commission, to whom the management of the reception was entrusted, consisted of Captain Hixson, Commodore; Captain Trouton, Vice-Commodore; Mr. H. C. Dangar, Commodore of the yacht squadron; Captain Smith, Captain Watson, and Captain Williams. Under the direction of this commission the following twenty-one steamers moved out from their respective wharves into the stream at twelve o'clock:—The *Auckland* (Captain Harris), the *City of Adelaide* (Captain Walker), the *Morpeth* (Captain Budd), the *Coonanbara* (Captain Thomas), the *Lady Bowen* (Captain Lake), the *City of Melbourne* (Captain Paddle), the *Balclutha* (Captain Hill), the *Wonga Wonga* (Captain Fitzsimmons), the *Kembla* (Captain Mailler), the *Florence Irving*, the *Agnes Irving*, the *City of Newcastle*, the *Hunter*, the *Collaroy*, the *Ballina*, the *Grafton*, the *James Paterson*, the *Womora*, the *Fire King*, the *Helen Macgregor*, and the *Sir John Burgoyne*. These steamers moved very slowly down the harbour, until they had all taken up their proper relative position in two lines; the *Auckland* (which conveyed the Ministry and their friends), and the *City of Adelaide* (on which were most of the members of the two Houses of Parliament and their friends), respectively heading the starboard and port lines. A large number of passengers occupied the remaining vessels. After these came another fleet of smaller steamers—the *Prince Alfred*, the *Breadalbane*, the *Adelaide*, the *Phantom*, the *Emu*, the *Culloden*, the *Atalanta*, the *Courier*, the *Waratah*, the *Ysabel*, the *Peri*, the *Brothers*, the *Gipsy Queen*, the *Vesta*, the *Transit*, the *Pelican*, the *Black Swan*, the *Herald*, the *Gemes*, the *Boomerang*, the *Sir John Young*, the *Kirribilli*, the *Perseverance*, and the *Fairy Queen*. These last-named steamers went to Watson's Bay only, and there awaited the entrance of the *Galatea*. The first fleet passed out through the heads into the ocean. The morning was wet and cheerless, and a stiff north-easterly wind was blowing. But as soon as the fleet was outside the heads, about half-past one, through rain and sleet they saw to the southward, within ten miles, the expected Royal steamer; and the whole fleet moved steadily onward in two lines to meet her as she approached. On coming near the *Galatea*, the steamers wheeled off, one line headed by the *Auckland* to the westward, the other headed by the *City of Adelaide* to the eastward; every one of them unfurling the signal "welcome," and dipping the ensign to the *Galatea*, which returned the salute. On rounding the South Head the *Galatea* came in view of the second fleet of steamers lying in Watson's Bay, which all saluted in turn. When the next point was turned, there lay the flotilla of yachts waiting to join in the general welcome, and a swarm of small boats with adventurous passengers, eager to witness the arrival of the *Galatea*. Lying at anchor were the P. and O. Company's large steam-ships, the *Avoca* and the *Bombay*, and the *Tinara* and *Kaikoura*, the *Globe*, and the *Napoleon III*. The sailors of the *Bombay* and *Kaikoura* manned their yards, and the boys on the *Vernon* training-ship followed their example. As soon as the *Galatea* came in sight of Commodore Lambert's flag, she fired a salute of eleven guns; which was answered by the Commodore with a salute of seven. At 4 o'clock, the *Galatea* came to anchor, and shortly afterwards the Duke went in his boat to the private steps leading to Government House, and there landed.

THE PUBLIC LANDING.

On Wednesday, 22nd January, his Royal Highness made his public entry into Sydney. For an hour or two before the time appointed for his landing, a number of members of Parliament, ministers of religion, and other citizens, were assembled under a triumphal arch erected at the Circular Quay for the reception of the Prince. At half-past eleven the Mayor and aldermen came up; and, almost immediately after, the Premier, the Treasurer, the Minister for Lands, the Postmaster-General, the Minister of Works, and others connected with the Government arrived at the arch, nearly all being dressed in court costume. The Hon. E. Deas Thomson was present, accompanied by Professors Badham and Pell, and other members of the University. As the time drew near for the Prince's landing, the rain held off, and the aspect of the clouds almost promised a return of fine weather. Shortly before eleven his Excellency the Earl of Belmore arrived, and was loudly cheered. Some ten minutes before, twelve guns from the ships announced that his Royal Highness had left the *Galatea*, and in a short time the white boat bearing the Royal standard came into view, and a Royal salute was fired from Fort Macquarie. His Excellency the Earl of Belmore then went forward to the steps to meet the Prince, and was followed by the members of the Government present, namely, the Hon. James Martin, the Hon. Henry Parkes, the Hon. J. B. Wilson, the Hon. G. Eagar, the Hon. James Byrnes, and the Hon. J. Docker, the members of the Reception Committee, and a number of the clergy. His Royal Highness upon landing shook hands with Lord Belmore, who introduced him to the Premier and his Ministerial colleagues. An address of welcome was read by the Mayor of Sydney, in the name of the Corporation, after which the Prince and the Earl of Belmore walked forward to the carriage, which stood in waiting a few paces from the arch. A procession of great length was formed in the following order :—

Volunteer Fire Companies, with their Engines.
Manchester Unity Lodges of Oddfellows.
Grand United Order Lodges of Oddfellows.
Royal Foresters.
Ancient Order of Foresters.
Sons of Temperance.
Protestant Friendly Alliance.
Mayors and Members of Suburban Municipalities.
Graduates and Students of the University.
H.R.H. THE DUKE OF EDINBURGH.
His Excellency the Governor.
Officers in command of H.M. Naval and Military Forces.
Members of the Executive Council.
Members of the Reception Commission.
Members of the Suite of his Royal Highness.
Members of the Suite of his Excellency the Governor.
The Consular Body.
Judges of the Supreme Court.
Members of the Legislative Council.
Members of the Legislative Assembly.
The Mayor and Aldermen of the City of Sydney.
The Chancellor, Vice-Chancellor, Senate, Professors, and Officers of the University.
Warden of St. Paul's College and Rector of St. John's College.
District Court Judges and the Bar.

The procession moved by Bridge-street to George-street, along George-street as far as the Cathedral of St. Andrew, then up Bathurst-street, round the southern end of Hyde Park by

Lyons'-terrace, and then along College-street and Macquarie-street to Government House, a little more than two miles. There were four triumphal arches—one at the landing place, one at the corner of Hyde Park and the South Head road, one opposite the statue of Prince Albert, in Macquarie-street, and one at the entrance to Government House. Spectators were gathered in thousands all along the line, and greeted the Prince with a most hearty and unanimous welcome. As the long line of march passed on, reaching from Prince Albert's statue to Lyons'-terrace, the variety of costume, the bands of music, the many-coloured symbolic flags, and the myriads of human faces, made up a scene of lively interest. As his Royal Highness turned from St. Mary's-road, and arrived at the statue of his lamented father, he was received by a guard of honour formed by the Volunteer forces; but no stoppage was made, as the rain at this time came down in torrents. The procession then proceeded through the triumphal arch at the end of Macquarie-street, and passed the Mint, the Infirmary, and the Houses of Parliament, to Government House. On the Prince's carriage turning into Government House gates, through the triumphal arch there erected, the procession halted until the school children of Sydney, under the conductorship of Mr. Fisher, sang the National Anthem. The procession then proceeded to Government House, where the Prince alighted.

ILLUMINATIONS.

In the evening of 21st January an illumination and display of fireworks took place in the harbour. Blue lights and coloured fires were burnt on many of the vessels. Others were plentifully adorned with lanterns slung in the rigging. The most remarkable sight of all was a great sea dragon, formed by the decoration of the A.S.N. Company's steamer *Yaamba*. This vessel was so set out with transparencies and lights as to resemble a gigantic dragon one hundred and two feet in length, with a tail composed of twenty-two boats hung with lanterns. It was towed about by the *Atalanta*, which was invisible in the darkness, and the effect was very striking.

In the evening of the 22nd the city was brilliantly illuminated. The public buildings were adorned with appropriate transparencies; some, however, put up by private parties, vied in splendour with those on the public buildings. Fireworks added to the attractions of the exhibition. Sydney was crowded by tens of thousands of visitors from various parts of the country, but the streets were free from disorder.

THE LEVEE.

On Thursday, the 23rd, the Duke of Edinburgh received at Government House loyal addresses from the two Houses of Parliament, to which he replied, thanking them for the expression of their loyalty to Her Majesty the Queen, and for their good wishes towards himself. Shortly after one o'clock, carriages began to arrive at Government House, and by two, the hour fixed for the commencement of the levee, there was a continuous and eager stream of visitors. The British standard floated over the tower of Government House, proclaiming the presence of royalty. On the right of the entrance (to persons approaching) the Duke's body guard of mounted police was drawn up; opposite to the door was a guard of honour of the 50th; and on the left a detachment of the regular police.

The levee was very numerously attended. His Royal Highness—in full uniform as a Captain in the Royal Navy—wore the blue ribbon and other splendid insignia of the Order of the Garter, with the stars and crosses of the other orders of knighthood which have already been conferred upon him. At his right hand stood his Excellency the Earl of Belmore, behind whom were the Hon. Eliot Yorke and Lieutenant Haig, equerries to the Duke. In the immediate suite of his Royal Highness were Lord Newry, Lord Bertram Gordon, and Mr. O. W. Brierly. The Earl of Belmore wore the uniform of a Privy Councillor ; and the members of the Executive Government of this colony—all of whom, except the Solicitor-General, were present—wore the uniform prescribed for members of colonial ministries by the revised regulations of July, 1867, which place the civil servants of the colonies on a footing with the civil servants of the Crown in England.

Addresses were presented from the Presbyterian Churches of New South Wales, the Congregational Union, the Wesleyan Churches, the Sons of Temperance, the Freemasons, and the Sydney University.

FIREWORKS IN THE DOMAIN.

There was a most extensive exhibition of pyrotechny in the domain, in honour of his Royal Highness Prince Alfred, arranged by Messrs. Scott and Korff, and carried out at the expense of the Government; the display attracted an immense number of spectators. The gem of the whole was the finale, which surpassed anything of the kind ever before seen in New South Wales. The design was most beautiful, and consisted of three large arches formed of laurel leaves, adorned with numerous devices. On the summit of the centre arch was a trophy of flags surmounting an Imperial crown, the words " Alfred, Welcome," being defined in large and brilliant letters below. On each of the small arches was a ship, and in the panels were anchors with cables twisted round them.

TREAT TO THE AGED AND INFIRM.

The visit of his Royal Highness the Duke of Edinburgh was very thoughtfully, and with proper feeling on behalf of the Reception Committee, made an occasion of rejoicing even among the inmates of institutions for the destitute and aged poor. At the recommendation of the committee, certain sums of the funds placed at their disposal by the Government were set apart for special festivities at the following institutions:—The Hyde Park Asylum, the Benevolent Asylum, the Ragged School, the Soup Kitchen, the Liverpool Asylum, the Asylum at Randwick, and in addition provision was made for feasting five hundred families receiving out-door relief. The entertainment of the inmates at Hyde Park Asylum, under the care of Mr. and Mrs. Applethwaite and Mr. F. King, took place on Thursday. During the dinner the institution was visited by a number of ladies and gentlemen of distinction. The inmates evidently enjoyed the occasion heartily, and drank the healths of the Prince and Royal Family with much enthusiasm. They also paid a similar compliment to the master, matron, and the members of the Reception Committee.

REVIEW OF THE TROOPS AND VOLUNTEERS.

On Friday, the 24th, his Royal Highness, accompanied by the Earl of Belmore, the Bishop of Sydney, Lord Newry, Lieutenant Haig, the Hon. Eliot Yorke, and others, inspected the troops and the volunteers of each force—the Artillery, the Rifles, and the Naval Brigade—in the Outer Domain. There were two hundred and eighteen troops and one thousand three hundred and sixty nine volunteers, all under the direction of Colonel Waddy. Their evolutions and order elicited the approval of his Royal Highness.

DRAMATIC PERFORMANCE AT THE UNIVERSITY.

The same evening his Royal Highness attended the University of Sydney, to witness the performance of the *Phormio* of Terence and the *Pourceaugnac* of Moliere, by some of the students. The performance was highly creditable, the company was large and brilliant, and the Duke testified his appreciation of the result.

THE RACES.

On Saturday, the 25th, the Duke's visit was celebrated at the Randwick Racecourse, and the meet was esteemed by sporting men to be the grandest ovation yet got up in honour of the Prince's advent in New South Wales. At eleven in the morning the course was thronged with almost as large a number of spectators as proportionately could be found at Epsom or Ascot. The committee of Tattersall's Club and their indefatigable secretary very worthily discharged their duty. The Governor's box was tastefully and elaborately fitted up for the convenience of the Royal visitor. His Royal Highness arrived on the course about one o'clock, and was received with vociferous cheering as he alighted from his carriage. His Excellency the Governor's carriage followed the Royal Duke's, immediately succeeded by a splendid turn-out of Sir George Bowen's. His Royal Highness the Duke of Edinburgh and his suite, with Lord and Lady Belmore, were present throughout the whole of the sports.

THE ANNIVERSARY REGATTA.

The eightieth anniversary of the foundation of the colony of New South Wales was welcomed on Monday, the 27th January, with enthusiastic and holiday festivity by a people proud of the position they hold as a colony, and the race from which they spring. On the 26th of January, eighty years ago, a few scattered native camps stood where flourishing cities and towns now raise their heads. To celebrate the anniversary by the good old English sport of boat-racing had long been the custom of the port, and on this birthday of the colony it was determined to carry out the time-honoured custom with all the glory which the prestige of the Royal visit could lend to it.

The principal feature in the day's performance was the yacht race, for boats of the Royal Sydney Yacht Squadron; and there was a good deal of speculation as to the result. After a beautiful race, the first prize, valued at £100, was carried off by Messrs. Fairfax and Lasselter's *Norvid*, and the second prize by Mr. Wilshire's *Haidee*.

The committee had the good fortune to be able to secure the fine ship *Sobraon* as flagship for this occasion, and on board of this vessel were his Royal Highness and suite. The *Sobraon* was gaily decorated in rainbow fashion, with bunting from stem to stern, every flag fluttering in the wind. Nor was her decoration confined to her exterior. The immense saloon was gaily adorned with wreaths and festoons of flowers, real and artificial, the whole of the latter being the work of Mrs. Lethely. The saloon table was loaded with every delicacy of the season, the display and arrangement of which were in excellent taste. The chair was occupied by Mr. Dangar, and his Royal Highness sat upon his right, the Earl of Belmore on his left hand. Next his Royal Highness sat Mrs. Lambert, her *vis-à-vis* being Mrs. Parbury. Near the distinguished guests were seated Lord Newry, Colonel Waddy, Sir George and Lady Bowen, Mr. Lempriere, Mr. Parkes, Mr. Dalley, Captain Williams (of the *Parramatta*), Captain Elmslie (of the *Sobraon*), Mr. E. Vickery, and many other of the leading members of society of Sydney. The vice-chair was occupied by Mr. George Thornton. The usual loyal and gallant toasts were well sustained, and the day was one of great enjoyment to the citizens and those who joined them in the celebration of the anniversary.

VISIT TO ST. ANDREW'S CATHEDRAL.

On Tuesday Prince Alfred visited the Cathedral of St. Andrew, when he was presented by the Bishop of Sydney with a Bible and Prayer Book, in a casket of myall wood, richly ornamented, the gift of the children of the Church of England Sunday-Schools of the dioceses of Sydney and Goulburn. There was a large concourse of children, clergy, and ladies and gentlemen on the occasion.

ANNUAL FLOWER SHOW.

On Wednesday his Royal Highness opened the Annual Flower Show, one of unexampled variety and beauty, in the Botanic Gardens.

VISIT TO THE WATERFALLS.

On Friday, 31st January, his Royal Highness the Duke of Edinburgh and a select party visited the Waterfalls at the Weatherboard, on the Blue Mountains, a distance of sixty-two miles from Sydney. The route thither was by the Western Railway. The locality of the Waterfalls is one of the most interesting in New South Wales. The party consisted of the Bishop of Sydney, the Bishop of Goulburn, the Earl of Belmore, the Hon. James Martin, Q.C. (Premier); the Hon. Henry Parkes, Colonial Secretary; the Hon. J. Bowie Wilson, Secretary for Lands; the Hon. James Byrnes, Minister for Works; the Hon. J. Docker, Postmaster-General; the Hon. T. A. Murray, President of the Legislative Council; Dr. Badham, professor of classics, Sydney University; Commodore Lambert, Colonel Waddy, C.B.; Lord Newry, the Hon. Eliot Yorke, Mr. Brierly, the Hon. George Allen, M.L.C.; Sir William Macarthur, M.L.C.; the Hon. W. Byrnes, M.L.C.; Captain Beresford, Mr. Piddington, M.P.; Mr. Lord, M.P.; Mr. Windeyer, M.P.; Mr. Barnet, colonial architect; the Countess of Belmore, and about twelve other ladies. The party left the Sydney station at half-past nine o'clock, Prince Alfred, the Earl of Belmore, the Bishops of Sydney and Goulburn, the Countess of Belmore, and three other ladies occupying the royal carriage, designed by J. H. Thomas. The train travelled at a rapid pace until it reached Penrith, which town had arrayed itself in holiday costume and a display of bunting. The railway station was very handsomely decorated. The Parramatta Volunteer Band was in attendance, and about seven hundred school-children formed into a semicircle. When the train stopped, the children sang the National Anthem.

The train was then put in motion, and passed over the Nepean Bridge. A fine semicircular curve brought the party to the foot of Lapstone Hill, where the Zigzag commences, by means of which an altitude of upwards of two thousand feet above the sea-level is gained, and the Blue Mountains rendered as passable as the plains. From this elevation the Emu Plains below appear like a panorama, and the surrounding country for thirty miles can be seen. A more lovely sight could not be desired. The corn fast filling, the orange groves, and orchards, with nicely cultivated paddocks, contributed to give a pleasing variety to the picture. But these soon disappeared. The carriages were now flying along the ridge of a mountain, and gradually getting into the fog which hangs upon its summit. Ravines on both sides, with the Blue Mountains still in front. Onward speeds the iron horse, puffing and panting, for his labour is hard; nor will he cease till he has risen fully two thousand feet. On the summit of one of the highest mountains the traveller can overlook the dense foliage of other mountains, can glance at the deep ravines on either side, and catch occasional glimpses of gaps and chasms as wonderful as they are grand.

On arriving at the Weatherboard, sixty-one miles from Sydney, the Prince alighted on a platform specially constructed. The Prince stood alone on the platform for several minutes when he got into his private carriage, which had preceded him, and drove away to the Waterfalls with the Earl of Belmore and his suite. Six other large carriages conveyed the remainder of the party to the tents near the waterfall, where a substantial luncheon had been provided. It was raining and misty, and the spectacle could not be seen to great advantage. The party spent about three hours at this place, after which they returned to Sydney, where they arrived at half-past six o'clock. The Duke's carriage was in waiting at the Sydney terminus, whence he drove with Earl Belmore, the Countess of Belmore, and suite, to Government House.

BALL AT GOVERNMENT HOUSE.

In the evening a grand ball took place at Government House, at which his Royal Highness the Duke of Edinburgh, the naval and military commanders, members of the Ministry, and members of Parliament, were present.

VISITS TO THE THEATRE.

On Saturday evening his Royal Highness the Duke of Edinburgh visited the Prince of Wales Opera House, accompanied by the Earl and Countess of Belmore, Commodore and Mrs. Lambert, Lord Newry, the Hon. F. Yorke, Mr. Brierly, and several officers of the *Galatea*. The pieces selected for the occasion were *Paul Pry* and Craven's *Milky White*, and an interlude from the Christmas pantomime known as the *Middies of the Galatea*.

His Royal Highness again visited the Prince of Wales Opera House on Monday, 3rd February, and witnessed Mr. Walter Montgomery's first appearance in that theatre. The pieces chosen for representation was the tragedy of *Hamlet*, the entertainment concluding with the farce entitled *A Thumping Legacy*. The house was crowded to excess.

PRESENTATION OF A BIBLE AND CASKET TO PRINCE ALFRED.

On Tuesday, 4th February, the children of the Church of England Sunday Schools presented a Bible and Casket to his Royal Highness. The presentation took place in the Domain, and the attendant circumstances were of a most gratifying nature. The binding of the sacred volume, which was a splendid specimen of workmanship, was by Mr. John Sands, of George-street; the casket was the production of Mr. Dean, the goldsmiths' work being by Messrs. Hardy Brothers, of Hunter-street. In every respect the present was a thoroughly artistic production.

There were not less than twelve or thirteen thousand children present, and there were upwards of five thousand visitors, who lined the carriage drive on both sides, from the gates of the Inner Domain to Government House. The management of the children was undertaken by a sub-committee. Through the judicious exertions of the police, under the personal direction of Captain M'Lerie, the Inspector-General, a clear course was kept open for the little ones, and the utmost good order prevailed.

On arriving at the ground, his Royal Highness was received by the superintendents and secretaries of the various schools, by two of whom (Mr. Reeve and Mr. Mailer) the Bible and Casket were presented, together with the following address:—

May it please your Royal Highness,—We, the undersigned, in name of the teachers and scholars of Sabbath schools belonging to the various Protestant denominations in New South Wales, approach your Royal Highness with the profound respect due to your exalted station, and bid you a hearty welcome to our shores. We rejoice in the opportunity thus afforded us of assuring your Royal Highness of the sentiments of loyalty and attachment universally entertained by the young, no less than the old, throughout the colony, towards the person and Government of her Most Gracious Majesty, your illustrious mother, together with the affectionate veneration in which all unite to cherish the memory of your late illustrious father, whose name as "Albert the Good" has become among us a "household word." We beg most humbly to request your Royal Highness to accept, as a small but sincere tribute from the Sabbath Schools represented by us, the accompanying copy of the Holy Bible, enclosed in a casket of New South Wales materials and workmanship.

We feel persuaded that your Royal Highness will regard it as a pleasing indication of the spirit which pervades the rising generation of the colony, that the children of our Sabbath Schools, in selecting their humble offering, should have instinctively turned to that book of books which has "God for its Author, Salvation for its end, and Truth without any mixture of error for its matter." That God may fulfil, in the experience of your Royal Highness, the "exceeding great and precious promises" of His Holy Word; that He may abundantly replenish you with His heavenly grace here below, and at length crown you with life and glory everlasting, through our Lord and Saviour Jesus Christ, is the sincere desire and prayer of, may it please your Royal Highness, your Royal Highness's most dutiful and most obedient servants.

The above address was signed by Messrs. Mailer, Rowe, Medcalf, Goold, Reeve, Wearne, Miller, and Catley.

His Royal Highness the Duke of Edinburgh replied as follows:—"I accept the gift which has to-day been presented to me with feelings of heartfelt gratitude, and I sincerely appreciate and thank you for the sentiments contained in the address that accompanies it. I receive this present not only as a token of goodwill to myself and affectionate loyalty to Her Majesty, but I also recognise in it the assurance that these young children are being brought up in the fear of God and in reverence for their Queen. The allusion which you have made to my dear father should remind us that it behoves us all—young and old—to endeavour to be guided by the lofty principles of self-denial and love of duty which were manifested in his life, which won for him the hearts of the English nation, and which, above all, are inculcated in that Book of Truth, which I have had so much pleasure in receiving this morning."

The children then sang very heartily another verse of the National Anthem, and the Prince returned to Government House.

THE CITIZENS' BALL.

The next event of interest was the Citizens' Ball, given on the evening of the following day. The guests began to arrive about nine o'clock, and probably not fewer than three thousand persons must have been present. The Duke of Edinburgh and suite, and his Excellency and Lady Belmore were received by his Worship the Mayor and the Mayoress. Her ladyship the Countess was accompanied by Miss Gladstone, Mrs. Beresford, and Mrs. Toulmin. His Royal Highness was accompanied by Lord Newry, the Hon. Eliot Yorke, and Lieutenant Haig. Captain Beresford and Mr. Toulmin (the Governor's Aide-de-Camp and Private Secretary) were in attendance upon his Excellency. All the members of the Ministry were present, with the lady members of their respective families. Amongst the company were also Sir Alfred Stephen (Chief-Justice) and Lady Stephen, Sir William and Lady Manning, the Hon. John Hubert Plunkett, and, indeed, most of the representatives of the leading families of the colony, Colonel Waddy and all the military officers stationed in Sydney, and Commodore Lambert and the naval officers in the harbour, were amongst the more distinguished guests. His Royal Highness opened the ball with the Mayoress (Mrs. Charles Moore), his Worship the Mayor leading out the Countess of Belmore; His Excellency also joined in the dance.

The ball commenced shortly after the arrival of the Royal guest and the Vice-regal party. Mr. John Clark, of the Colonnade, Elizabeth-street North, acted as master of the ceremonies, and Mr. D. Callan was conductor of the volunteer band.

In the supper-room everything provided was of the most *recherché* description, and the decorations were of the most gorgeous character. After supper the usual loyal toasts, including that of the Royal guest, were given and responded to, the toast of the Countess of Belmore and the ladies of the colony, being replied to by Lord Newry.

MISCELLANEOUS ITEMS.

During his stay in Sydney, up to the period of our going to press, his Royal Highness occupied his time in visiting the environs of the city. On the 10th he went up the river to Parramatta, and was received at the wharf by the Corporation and a large number of people. An address was presented by the Mayor, to which the Prince replied. A procession took place to the Domain, where the school-children sang the National Anthem. The Prince planted a tree, lunched in the pavilion, and drove out to the orangeries, and then back to Sydney.

Another day he visited the Orphan Asylum at Randwick; and his Royal Highness also took the opportunity of inspecting the Training Schools, Infirmary, and other institutions of Sydney. The time of the Duke was likewise taken up in making arrangements for the docking of his ship for some necessary repairs, and these works were carried out under his personal superintendence.

On Friday evening, 14th February, his Royal Highness and his Excellency Earl Belmore attended the theatre on the occasion of Mr. Walter Montgomery's benefit.

A grand Picnic was the next item on the programme of festivities in honour of the Royal visitor. When this narrative was sent to press it was understood that his Royal Highness would shortly proceed to Queensland, returning to Sydney to complete his engagements there, and afterwards continuing his tour to the several Provinces of New Zealand.

ADDENDA.

ADDRESS FROM THE ROMAN CATHOLIC BODY OF THE COLONY OF VICTORIA.

To His Royal Highness Prince Alfred, K.G., Duke of Edinburgh.

The respectful address of the Roman Catholic Clergy and Laity of Victoria.

On behalf of the Roman Catholic Body, numbering as it does one-fourth of the Christian population of Victoria, we cordially welcome your Royal Highness on your arrival in this colony.

We respectfully assure you that the circumstances of our living, as we do, under a perfectly free constitution, and in the enjoyment of complete civil and religious liberty and equality, have strengthened our feelings of attachment to the mother country and loyalty to the Throne.

In conclusion, we wish your Royal Highness health, happiness, prosperity, and a safe and pleasant return to your native land. On behalf of the Roman Catholic Body,

JOHN FITZPATRICK, D.D.,
Vicar-General administering the Diocese in the absence of his Lordship the Bishop.

REPLY.

Gentlemen—I thank you for your congratulations, and the welcome you offer me upon my arrival in Victoria. I am glad to know that, under the free Constitution of Victoria, all classes of the community enjoy complete civil and religious liberty, and that your regard for the mother country, and your attachment to the Throne, are strengthened by the justice and equality of the laws under which you are governed. I thank you for the wishes you express for my prosperity and happiness, and for my safe return.
ALFRED.

The Secretary to the Geelong Vinegrowers Association has received the following reply to the address presented to his Royal Highness the Duke of Edinburgh by that body.

[NOTE.—The Address will be found on page 120.]

Gentlemen—The welcome which you accorded to me in passing through your district was very gratifying to me. You have my hearty good wishes for the success of your industry.
ALFRED.

ADDRESS OF THE OLD COLONISTS.

At the moment of going to press (February 20) the following additional names to the Address of the Old Colonists have just been received from the Western Districts:—

1833.
Must, Thomas

1836.
Henty, John

1837.
Campbell, L. H.
Fawthrop, James
M'Leod, J. N.
Williams, Lew.

1838.
Anderson, Henry Wood
Comstock, James

Crouch, George Godwin
Dubledee, William
Scott, Thomas P.

1839.
Cobham, John
Kerr, John Hunter, by the Midlothian, first ship from Great Britain.
Morris, Richard
Savage, Robert
Wilson, James Yelverton

1840.
Corney, William
Macgregor, Samuel

M'Carthy, Dennis
M'Kinley, Andrew
Neate, James
Ritchie, John
Vine, Richard

1841.
Ardlie, John Martin
Barber, George
Chisholm, G.
Craig, John H.
Finn, Edmund
Foggas, James
Irvine, James H.
Jackson, Thomas

Johnstone, J.
M'Knight, Charles H.
Murray, Adam

1842.
Claridge, G. G. P.
Finn, Thomas
Phillips, Henry
Richardson, J. F.
Rutledge, Richard
Stevens, H.
Traugmar, James
Tulloh, William
Tuxer, Francis
Urquhart, Roderick
Woodward, F. H.

The vignette of the *Galatea*, on the title-page, is taken from a photograph by Messrs. Gaul and Dunn, of Collins-street East.

MASON, FIRTH AND CO., PRINTERS, MELBOURNE.

JOHNSTONE, O'SHANNESSY & CO.,

ARTIST

PHOTOGRAPHERS

BY APPOINTMENT

TO H.R.H. THE DUKE OF EDINBURGH, K.G., AND HIS EXCELLENCY THE GOVERNOR.

3 BOURKE STREET EAST.

Next to the Post Office.

MELBOURNE.

WHITNEY, CHAMBERS & CO.,

Have on view at their Show Rooms, Corner of Collins and Swanston Streets, a large variety of Cut Crystal and Bronze

GAS CHANDELIERS,

From 2 to 8 Light.

ELECTRO-PLATED WARE, From Dixon and Sons and Elkington.	**PARAGON KITCHENERS,** 3 to 7 feet.
	REGISTER STOVES.
CUTLERY, From Rogers, Fenton, and Others.	**FENDERS AND FIREIRONS.**
	IRONING STOVES.
TEA TRAYS, In Iron and Papier Maché.	**HALL TABLES AND STANDS,** With Marble Tops.
DISH COVERS, In Block-tin and G. Metal.	**HAT AND COAT HOOKS AND RAILS.**
IRON AND BRASS BEDSTEADS.	**CHILDREN'S COTS AND BEDSTEADS.**

W., C. & Co. have also a Splendid Assortment of

EXHIBITION LAMPS,

In China, Cut Glass, Bronze, &c., suitable for Public Buildings, Halls, Dining and Drawing Rooms, Kitchens, Shops, &c. These comprise Novelties from England, France, and America.

FURNISHING IRONMONGERY IN ALL ITS DEPARTMENTS.

WHITNEY, CHAMBERS & CO., GENERAL IRONMONGERS.
60 Collins Street E.; 7, 47, 49, 51 Swanston Street; and 103 Flinders Street, Melbourne.

By Appointment  in Victoria

TO H.R.H. THE DUKE OF EDINBURGH.

E. SMYTHERS,
WINE AND SPIRIT MERCHANT,

A Choice Stock of Australian Red and White Wines, in Bulk and Bottle.

Stores 41 ELIZABETH STREET, and BLIGH PLACE, FLINDERS LANE WEST.

19 COLLINS STREET WEST.

R. U. MILLER
(LATE COCKBURN),

Purveyor to His Excellency Sir J. H. T. Manners-Sutton,

AND

H.R.H. Prince Alfred, Duke of Edinburgh,

WHOLESALE & RETAIL PASTRYCOOK & CONFECTIONER, &c.

Balls, Suppers, Picnics, and all other Private and Public Parties supplied in the most recherché and reasonable manner.

19 *COLLINS STREET WEST.*

BRIGHTON PARK SCHOOL.
ESTABLISHED FIFTEEN YEARS.

Young Gentlemen are carefully prepared by experienced Teachers for Commercial Pursuits, Civil Service, and the University. Extensive Playground. Convenient for Sea Bathing. The Quarter begins with the Pupil's entrance.

Terms Thirteen and Fifteen Guineas per Quarter.

JOHN A. MACFARLANE.

WESLEY COLLEGE.

President—Rev. J. S. WAUGH.   Head Master—J. CORRIGAN, LL.D.
Assisted by a highly efficient staff of Professors and Masters.

Terms per Quarter—Day Pupils, under twelve years, Three Guineas; do., over twelve years, Four Guineas;
Day Boarders, Five and Six Guineas. Resident do., Fifteen and Twenty Guineas.
Pupils of all religious denominations admitted.
Prospectus and last year's Report forwarded on application to the Rev. J. S. WAUGH.

W. LOVELL

(INTERCOLONIAL EXHIBITION, 1866-7—AWARDED HONORABLE MENTION FOR CABINET WORK),

CABINET MAKER
AND
UPHOLSTERER,
93 & 95
Bourke Street West,

Spring Mattresses and all kinds of Window Blinds Made to Order.
COUNTRY ORDERS PUNCTUALLY ATTENDED TO.

WOOD ENGRAVING.

E. WINTER ENGRAVER,

Formerly pupil to Messrs. Edmund Evans, J. Cooper, J. Knight, Leighton,—Thomas, Ebbet Foster, Harrison Weir, &c., &c.

Has recently arrived in this colony, and is prepared to give Estimates for the proper execution of any and every description of Wood Engraving in Figure, Landscape, Ornamental, Mechanical, and Microscopical, either from Photograph or Sketch, &c., &c.

His extensive experience as Engraver for the "Illustrated London News," "Ladies' Newspaper," "London Society," "Cornhill," "Mechanics' Magazine," "Engineer," and many other first-class periodicals, will enable him to perform a class of work hitherto unattempted in the colonies.

COLOUR PRINTING.

This peculiar class of work, depending as it does so much for its effect on a thorough knowledge of the artistic manipulation required in its production, will meet with Mr. WINTER'S special attention, his knowledge of this branch of it having been derived from six years' practical experience in one of the leading foreign establishments.
N.B.—Any Proofs of Blocks ordered from E. W. will be carefully examined by him before delivery.

104 COLLINS STREET EAST, MELBOURNE.

PRINCIPAL ESTABLISHMENTS OF THE GROVER & BAKER SEWING MACHINE COMPANY.—

HEAD OFFICE FOR THE AUSTRALIAN COLONIES 80 COLLINS STREET EAST. MELBOURNE.

H. G. DE GRUCHY & CO.,
ENGRAVERS & LITHOGRAPHERS,

PRINTERS AND STATIONERS.

BY SPECIAL APPOINTMENT TO H.R.H. THE DUKE OF EDINBURGH, K.G.

CHARLES ANDERSON,

BREAD AND BISCUIT BAKER,

AWARDED PRIZE MEDAL, INTERCOLONIAL EXHIBITION, 1866-7.

J. JONES,
Surgical Instrument and Truss Maker,
106 LONSDALE STREET EAST

Messrs. Artificial Legs, Hands, Arms, Spinal Supports, Leg Instruments, Lace Stockings, Knee Caps, Belts, Crutches, Splints, and all kinds of Instruments for the cure of Deformities. Surgical, Dental, and Veterinary Instruments, Cutlery, &c., Made and Repaired.
MRS. JONES WILL ATTEND LADIES.

MR. A. M. TOWNSEND,

SUCCESSOR TO

MR. J. BAMFORD,

STATIONER, &c.,

109 SWANSTON STREET

Corner of Flinders Lane, five doors from Bourke Street.

 ## WILLIAM DETMOLD,

Manufacturer of

ACCOUNT BOOKS,

Bookbinder and Paper Ruler,

IMPORTER OF PAPER AND STATIONERY.

PRIZE MEDAL AWARDED AT THE INTERNATIONAL EXHIBITION, LONDON, 1862.

LADIES' COLLEGE.

SELECT EDUCATIONAL ESTABLISHMENT FOR YOUNG LADIES.

WILSON STREET, BRIGHTON

Near the North Brighton Station.

Established in St. Kilda 1857; Removed to Brighton 1868.

Circulars can always be obtained at Robertson's Circulating Library, 18 Collins Street West, Melbourne, or on application to the Principals.

ESTABLISHED 1850.

WILKIE, WEBSTER & CO.,
15 COLLINS STREET EAST, MELBOURNE.

IMPORTERS OF

PIANOFORTES,
BY BROADWOOD, COLLARD, ERARD, &c.,

HARMONIUMS by Alexandre, and **MUSICAL INSTRUMENTS** of every description.

COLONIAL PIANOFORTES
Prepared expressly for extreme climates, possessing an excellent quality of tone, and warranted to stand admirably in tune.

Vocal and Instrumental Music, including all the Standard and Popular Works of the Day.
MUSIC FORWARDED FREE BY POST TO ANY PART OF THE COLONY.

www.ingramcontent.com/pod-product-compliance
Lightning Source LLC
Chambersburg PA
CBHW021829230426
43669CB00008B/914